A·N·N·U·A·L E·D·I·T·I·O·N·S

Social Psychology 00/01

Fourth Edition

EDITOR

Mark H. Davis
Eckerd College

Mark H. Davis received a doctorate in psychology from the University of Texas at Austin and is currently an associate professor at Eckerd College in St. Petersburg, Florida. He is a member of the American Psychological Association and serves as a consulting editor for the *Journal of Personality and Social Psychology*. His primary research interest is the study of empathy. He is the author of a number of articles on this topic, as well as the book, *Empathy: A Social Psychological Approach* (Westview Press, 1996).

Dushkin/McGraw-Hill
Sluice Dock, Guilford, Connecticut 06437

Visit us on the Internet
http://www.dushkin.com/annualeditions/

Credits

1. The Self
Unit photo—© 1999 by Cleo Freelance Photography.
2. Social Cognition and Social Perception
Unit photo—© 1999 by Cleo Freelance Photography.
3. Attitudes
Unit photo—Courtesy of Rebecca Holland.
4. Social Influence
Unit photo—© 1999 by Cleo Freelance Photography.
5. Social Relationships
Unit photo—Courtesy of Louis P. Raucci Jr.
6. Prejudice, Discrimination, and Stereotyping
Unit photo—Courtesy New York Convention and Visitors Bureau
7. Aggression
Unit photo—© 1999 by PhotoDisc, Inc.
8. Helping
Unit photo—© 1999 by Cleo Freelance Photography.
9. Group Processes
Unit photo—© 1999 by PhotoDisc, Inc.

Copyright

Cataloging in Publication Data
Main entry under title: Annual Editions: Social Psychology. 2000/2001.
1. Psychology—Periodicals. I. Davis, Mark, *comp.* II. Title: Social psychology.
302'.05   ISBN 0–07–236583–8   ISSN 0730–6962

© 2000 by Dushkin/McGraw-Hill, Guilford, CT 06437, A Division of The McGraw-Hill Companies.

Fourth Edition

Cover image © 2000 PhotoDisc, Inc.

Printed in the United States of America   234567890BAHBAH543210   Printed on Recycled Paper

Members of the Advisory Board are instrumental in the final selection of articles for each edition of ANNUAL EDITIONS. Their review of articles for content, level, currentness, and appropriateness provides critical direction to the editor and staff. We think that you will find their careful consideration well reflected in this volume.

EDITOR

Mark H. Davis
Eckerd College

ADVISORY BOARD

Anita P. Barbee
University of Louisville

Thomas Blass
University of Maryland Baltimore County

Bernardo J. Carducci
Indiana University Southeast

Marilyn N. Carroll
Rockhurst College

Susan E. Cross
Iowa State University

Stephen L. Franzoi
Marquette University

Karen L. Freiberg
University of Maryland Baltimore County

Malcolm J. Grant
Memorial University of Newfoundland

Curtis Haugtvedt
Ohio State University

Martin Heesacker
University of Florida Gainesville

Robert J. Pellegrini
San Jose State University

Ronald E. Riggio
Claremont McKenna College

Mark Schaller
University of British Columbia

Ross A. Seligman
Clatsop Community College

Jonathan Springer
Kean University

Charles G. Stangor
University of Maryland College Park

Abraham Tesser
University of Georgia

Shelley A. Theno
University of Alaska–Southeast

Fred W. Whitford
Montana State University

EDITORIAL STAFF

Ian A. Nielsen, Publisher
Roberta Monaco, Senior Developmental Editor
Dorothy Fink, Associate Developmental Editor
Addie Raucci, Senior Administrative Editor
Cheryl Greenleaf, Permissions Editor
Joseph Offredi, Permissions/Editorial Assistant
Diane Barker, Proofreader
Lisa Holmes-Doebrick, Program Coordinator

PRODUCTION STAFF

Brenda S. Filley, Production Manager
Charles Vitelli, Designer
Lara M. Johnson, Design/Advertising Coordinator
Laura Levine, Graphics
Mike Campbell, Graphics
Tom Goddard, Graphics
Eldis Lima, Graphics
Juliana Arbo, Typesetting Supervisor
Marie Lazauskas, Typesetter
Kathleen D'Amico, Typesetter
Karen Roberts, Typesetter
Larry Killian, Copier Coordinator

Editors/Advisory Board

Staff

To the Reader

In publishing ANNUAL EDITIONS we recognize the enormous role played by the magazines, newspapers, and journals of the public press in providing current, first-rate educational information in a broad spectrum of interest areas. Many of these articles are appropriate for students, researchers, and professionals seeking accurate, current material to help bridge the gap between principles and theories and the real world. These articles, however, become more useful for study when those of lasting value are carefully collected, organized, indexed, and reproduced in a low-cost format, which provides easy and permanent access when the material is needed. That is the role played by ANNUAL EDITIONS.

New to ANNUAL EDITIONS is the inclusion of related World Wide Web sites. These sites have been selected by our editorial staff to represent some of the best resources found on the World Wide Web today. Through our carefully developed topic guide, we have linked these Web resources to the articles covered in this ANNUAL EDITIONS reader. We think that you will find this volume useful, and we hope that you will take a moment to visit us on the Web at *http://www.dushkin.com* to tell us what you think.

The field of contemporary social psychology is a little difficult to define. Historically, of course, it was easier. Initially, social psychology was the study of groups (or crowds, or mobs), and, in particular, the effect that groups had on individual behavior. As the years have gone by, however, social psychology has steadily expanded its focus to encompass phenomena that are less clearly "social" in nature. Social psychologists today now study a wide variety of topics, some of which necessarily involve groups (even if the group is only two people), but many of which deal with internal cognitive processes that can occur when a person is completely alone.

In fact, one way to define contemporary social psychology is this: It scientifically examines the thoughts, feelings, and actions of normal humans. As you may notice, this is an incredibly broad definition. While it eliminates persons with psychological disorders, it keeps for itself the study of virtually anything that the average person might think, feel, or do. The good news, for those about to read this book, is that many of the most interesting kinds of human activity will be represented here.

The form in which social psychological research is usually summarized and communicated is the research article, written by scientists for scientists. The goal in such writing is precision and, although it is sometimes hard to believe, clarity. Unfortunately, such writing is often impossible for a nonprofessional audience to understand or enjoy. The purpose of this volume is to provide interesting, highly readable examples of some of the ideas and insights that social psychology can offer about the human experience. The selections come primarily from magazines and newspapers in the popular press, a medium that sacrifices some detail and precision in exchange for a much livelier style of writing. My hope is that by reading these articles in conjunction with your textbook, you can have greater appreciation for just how fascinating and important the topics of social psychology can be.

This volume is divided into nine units, each of which deals with issues falling into one of contemporary social psychology's areas of concern. Although social psychology textbooks differ somewhat in how they "carve up" these topics, you will probably find that each of the units in this volume corresponds, at least roughly, to one of the chapters in your text. The articles generally fall into one of two categories. Some of them describe, in an interesting and readable way, social psychological research in a particular topic area. Other selections take a different approach, and explicitly try to apply social psychological findings to real-world problems and events. Some articles, of course, do both.

Although the units are organized to mirror the content usually found in social psychology textbook chapters, you might also find it useful to consult the *topic guide* that appears after the *table of contents*. This guide indicates how each article in the volume is related to a number of different topics that have traditionally been of concern to social psychology. Thus, no matter how your own textbook is organized, it should be possible to find articles in this volume that are relevant to any subject.

Also in this edition of *Annual Editions: Social Psychology 00/01* are *World Wide Web sites* that can be used to further explore the topics. These sites are cross-referenced by number in the *topic guide*.

Finally, I hope that you will take the time to provide some feedback to guide the annual revision of this anthology. You can do this by completing and returning the article rating form in the back of the book; by doing so you will help us understand which articles are effective and which are not. Your help in this revision process would be very much appreciated. Thank you.

Mark H. Davis
Editor

Contents

UNIT 1

The Self

Five articles in this section examine
the evolution of an individual's
personality and sense of self.

UNIT 2

Social Cognition
and Social
Perception

Seven articles in this section discuss
how an individual gains a sense of
reality and social understanding.

The concepts in bold italics are developed in the article. For further expansion please refer to the Topic Guide and the Index.

The concepts in bold italics are developed in the article. For further expansion please refer to the Topic Guide and the Index.

UNIT 3

Attitudes

Three section articles discuss how individuals' attitudes can be influenced by memory, other people's opinion of them, and propaganda.

UNIT 4

Social Influence

Four selections in this section look at how social dynamics influence an individual.

UNIT 5

Social Relationships

Five articles in this section consider how social affiliation and love establish personal relationships.

UNIT 6

Prejudice, Discrimination, and Stereotyping

Six articles in this section look at what influences an individual's sense of prejudice, discrimination, and stereotyping.

The concepts in bold italics are developed in the article. For further expansion please refer to the Topic Guide and the Index.

UNIT 7

Aggression

Six selections in this section consider how biology, early social experiences, and the mass media impact on the level of an individual's aggression.

The concepts in bold italics are developed in the article. For further expansion please refer to the Topic Guide and the Index.

ix

UNIT 8

Helping

Four articles in this section examine how an individual develops a sense of social support and personal commitment.

The concepts in bold italics are developed in the article. For further expansion please refer to the Topic Guide and the Index.

UNIT 9

Group Processes

Five selections in this section
discuss how an individual gains a
sense of the social community.

The concepts in bold italics are developed in the article. For further expansion please refer to the Topic Guide and the Index.

This topic guide suggests how the selections and World Wide Web sites found in the next section of this book relate to topics of traditional concern to social psychology students and professionals. It is useful for locating interrelated articles and Web sites for reading and research. The guide is arranged alphabetically according to topic.

The relevant Web sites, which are numbered and annotated on pages 4 and 5, are easily identified by the Web icon (◎) under the topic articles. By linking the articles and the Web sites by topic, this ANNUAL EDITIONS reader becomes a powerful learning and research tool.

TOPIC AREA	TREATED IN	TOPIC AREA	TREATED IN
Accuracy	5. Forecasting Their Emotions 10. Face It! ◎ **7**	**Conflict**	24. Marriage Styles 32. Violence and Honor 36. Anatomy of a Violent Relationship 43. Group Processes in the Resolution of International Conflicts 44. Psychology's Own Peace Corps ◎ **10, 14, 15, 18, 27**
Aggression	30. Huck Finn vs. the "Superpredators" 31. Gunslinging in America 32. Violence and Honor 33. America Way of Blame 34. Aggression and Self-Esteem 35. Low Self-Esteem Does Not Cause Aggression 36. Anatomy of a Violent Relationship 44. Psychology's Own Peace Corps ◎ **25, 26, 27**	**Conformity**	16. Heavy Burden of Black Conformity 41. Collective Delusions ◎ **10, 21, 22**
		Cooperation	43. Group Processes in the Resolution of International Conflicts ◎ **25, 26, 27, 33**
Attitudes	5. Forecasting Their Emotions 15. Social Psychological Perspective ◎ **8, 9, 12**	**Credibility of the Source**	14. How to Sell Pseudoscience
Attribution	9. Inferential Hopscotch 12. Culture, Idealogy, and Construal ◎ **7**	**Culture**	1. Nature of the Self 10. Face It! 12. Culture, Idealogy, and Construal 32. Violence and Honor 44. Psychology's Own Peace Corps ◎ **5, 6, 7, 10, 13, 33**
Automatic and Controlled Processes	7. Seed of Our Undoing 9. Inferential Hopscotch 25. Where Bias Begins 26. Breaking the Prejudice Habit ◎ **7, 21, 22, 23, 24**	**Decision Making**	27. Sex, Schemas, and Success 42. Group Decision Fiascoes Continue ◎ **10, 33**
Biology	22. Biology of Beauty ◎ **1, 2, 3, 4, 20**	**Discrimination**	27. Sex, Schemas, and Success 28. Is Feedback to Minorities Positively Biased? ◎ **21, 22, 23, 24**
Bystander Intervention Model	39. Cause of Death ◎ **10, 33, 34**		
Childhood and Adolescence	2. Race and the Schooling of Black Americans 33. American Way of Blame 34. Aggression and Self-Esteem 35. Low Self-Esteem Does Not Cause Aggression ◎ **3, 5, 6, 7**	**Education**	2. Race and the Schooling of Black Americans ◎ **21, 22**
		Elaboration Likelihood Model	13. Mindless Propaganda, Thoughtful Persuasion 15. Social Psychological Perspective ◎ **8, 9, 12**
Cognitive Biases	6. Like Goes with Like 8. Something Out of Nothing 27. Sex, Schemas, and Success 42. Group Decision Fiascoes Continue ◎ **6, 10, 33, 34**	**Emotions**	3. Science of Happiness 5. Forecasting Their Emotions 7. Seed of Our Undoing 23. Infidelity and the Science of Cheating 24. Marriage Styles 28. Is Feedback to Minorities Positively Biased? 36. Anatomy of Violent Relationship ◎ **6, 15, 18, 21**
Cognitive Dissonance	15. Social Psychological Perspective		
Community	20. Isolation Increases with Internet Use 38. Cities with Heart ◎ **10, 25, 26, 27, 33, 34**		
Compliance	18. Reciprocation 19. Suspect Confessions ◎ **6, 7, 10, 27, 33**	**Evolutionary Psychology**	4. Making Sense of Self-Esteem 10. Face It! 22. Biology of Beauty

● AE: Social Psychology

The following World Wide Web sites have been carefully researched and selected to support the articles found in this reader. If you are interested in learning more about specific topics found in this book, these Web sites are a good place to start. The sites are cross-referenced by number and appear in the topic guide on the previous two pages. Also, you can link to these Web sites through our DUSHKIN ONLINE support site at *http://www.dushkin.com/online/*.

The following sites were available at the time of publication. Visit our Web site—we update DUSHKIN ONLINE regularly to reflect any changes.

General Sources

1. Journals Related to Social Psychology
http://www.socialpsychology.org/journals.htm
Maintained by Wesleyan University, this site is a link to journals related to the study of psychology, social psychology, and sociology.

2. Psychology Web Archive
http://swix.ch/clan/ks/CPSP1.htm
The links listed at this public noncommercial site mostly focus on social psychology issues. This archive is an excellent jumping-off place for students of social psychology.

3. Social Psychology Network
http://www.socialpsychology.org
The Social Psychology Network is the most comprehensive source of social psychology information on the Internet, including resources, programs, and research.

4. Society of Experimental Social Psychology
http://www.sesp.org
SESP is a scientific organization dedicated to the advancement of social psychology.

The Self

5. FreudNet
http://plaza.interport.net/nypsan
FreudNet is part of the Abraham A. Brill Library of the New York Psychoanalytic Institute. This site provides information on mental health, Sigmund Freud, and psychoanalysis.

Social Cognition and Social Perception

6. Cognitive and Psychological Sciences on the Internet
http://matia.stanford.edu/cogsci/
This site, maintained by Ruediger Oehlmann, is a detailed listing of cognitive psychology Web sites. Information on programs, organizations, journals, and groups is at this site.

7. Nonverbal Behavior and Nonverbal Communication
http://zen.sunderland.ac.uk/~hb5jma/1stbersn.htm
This fascinating site has a detailed listing of nonverbal behavior and nonverbal communication sites on the Web, including the work of historical and current researchers.

Attitudes

8. Propaganda and Psychological Warfare Research Resource
http://www.lafayette.edu/mcglonem/prop.html
This Web site provides links to sites that use propaganda to influence and change attitudes. At this site, you can link to contemporary fascist, political, religious, and Holocaust revisionist propaganda.

9. The Psychology of Cyberspace
http://www.rider.edu/users/suler/psycyber/psycyber.html
This site studies the psychological dimensions of environments created by computers and online networks.

Social Influence

10. AFF Cult Group Information
http://www.csj.org
AFF's mission is to study psychological manipulation and cult groups, to assist those who have been adversely affected by a cult experience, and to educate.

11. Center for Leadership Studies
http://www.situational.com
The Center for Leadership Studies (CLS) is organized for the research and development of the full range of leadership in individuals, teams, organizations, and communities.

12. Social Influence Website
http://www.influenceatwork.com/intro.html
This Web site is devoted to social influence—the modern scientific study of persuasion, compliance, and propaganda.

Social Relationships

13. American Association of University Women
http://www.aauw.org
The AAUW is a national organization that promotes education and equity for all women and girls.

14. American Men's Studies Association
http://www.vix.com/pub/men/orgs/writeups/amsa.html
The American Men's Studies Association is an organization of scholars, therapists, and others interested in the exploration of masculinity in modern society. Click on Men's Issues.

15. Coalition for Marriage, Family, and Couples Education
http://www.smartmarriages.com
CMFCE is dedicated to bringing information about and directories of skill-based marriage education courses to the public. It hopes to lower the rate of family breakdown through couple-empowering preventive education.

16. GLAAD: Gay and Lesbian Alliance Against Defamation
http://www.glaad.org
GLAAD was formed in New York in 1985. Its mission is to improve the public's attitudes toward homosexuality and put an end to discrimination against lesbians and gay men.

17. The Kinsey Institute for Reasearch in Sex, Gender, and Reproduction
http://www.indiana.edu/~kinsey/
The purpose of the Kinsey Institute's Web site is to support interdisciplinary research and the study of human sexuality. The institute was founded by Dr. Alfred Kinsey, 1894–1956.

18. Marriage and Family Therapy on the Web
http://www.nova.edu/ssss/FT/web.html
This site is maintained by the School of Social and Systemic Studies at Nova University. It is a link to numerous marriage and family therapy resources on the Web.

19. The National Organization for Women (NOW) Home Page
http://www.now.org
NOW is the largest organization of feminist activists in the United States. It has 250,000 members and 600 chapters in all 50 states and the District of Columbia. NOW's goal has been "to take action" to bring about equality for all women.

20. The Society for the Scientific Study of Sexuality
http://www.ssc.wisc.edu/ssss
The Society for the Scientific Study of Sexuality is an international organization dedicated to the advancement of knowledge about sexuality.

Prejudice, Discrimination, and Stereotyping

21. NAACP Online: National Association for the Advancement of Colored People
http://www.naacp.org
The principal objective of the NAACP is to ensure the political, educational, social, and economic equality of minority group citizens in the United States.

22. National Civil Rights Museum
http://www.civilrightsmuseum.org
The National Civil Rights Museum, located at the Lorraine Motel, where Dr. Martin Luther King Jr. was assassinated April 4, 1968, is the world's first and only comprehensive overview of the civil rights movement in exhibit form.

23. United States Holocaust Memorial Museum
http://www.ushmm.org
The United States Holocaust Memorial Museum is America's national institution for the documentation, study, and interpretation of Holocaust history, and serves as this country's memorial to the millions of people murdered during the Holocaust.

24. Yahoo—Social Psychology
http://www.yahoo.com/Social_Science/Psychology/ disciplines/social_psychology/
This link takes you to Yahoo!'s social psychology Web sites. Explore prejudice, discrimination, and stereotyping from this site.

Aggression

25. Contemporary Conflicts
http://www.cfcsc.dnd.ca/links/wars/index.html
This site, maintained by the Canadian Forces College/ Department of National Defence, has an interactive map listing all current world conflicts. Detailed information regarding each conflict can be accessed through this site.

26. MINCAVA: Minnesota Center Against Violence and Abuse
http://www.mincava.umn.edu
The Minnesota Center Against Violence and Abuse operates an electronic clearinghouse via the World Wide Web with access to thousands of Gopher servers, interactive discussion groups, newsgroups, and Web sites around the world. Its goal is to provide quick, user-friendly access to the extensive electronic resources on the topic of violence and abuse.

27. National Consortium on Violence Research
http://www.ncovr.heinz.cmu.edu/docs/data_mission.htm
The National Consortium on Violence Research is a newly established research and training institute that is dedicated to the scientific and advanced study of the factors contributing to interpersonal violence.

Helping

28. Americans with Disabilities Act Document Center
http://janweb.icdi.wvu.edu/kinder/
This Web site contains copies of the Americans with Disabilities Act of 1990 (ADA) and ADA regulations. This Web site also provides you with links to other Internet sources of information concerning disability issues.

29. Give Five
http://www.indepsec.org/give5/give5_1.html
The Give Five Web site is a project of Independent Sector, a national coalition of foundations, voluntary organizations, and corporate giving programs working to encourage giving, volunteering, not-for-profit initiatives, and citizen action.

30. HungerWeb
http://www.brown.edu/Departments/World_Hunger_Program
The aim of this site is to help prevent and eradicate hunger by facilitating the free exchange of ideas and information regarding the causes of and solutions to hunger. It contains primary information made available by the World Hunger Program as well as links to other sites.

31. Mandel Center for Nonprofit Organuizations
http://www.cwru.edu/msass/mandelcenter
The mission of the Mandel Center is to foster effective management, leadership, and governance of nonprofit organizations in human services, the arts, education, community development, religion, and other areas.

32. University of Maryland Diversity Database
http://www.inform.umd.edu/EdRes/Topic/Diversity
The University of Maryland's Diversity Database is sponsored by the Diversity Initiative Program. It contains campus, local, national, and international academic material relating to age, class, disability, ethnicity, gender, national origin, race, religion, and sexual orientation.

Group Processes

33. Center for the Study of Group Processes
http://www.uiowa.edu/~grpproc/
The mission of the Center for the Study of Group Processes includes promoting basic research in the field of group processes and enhancing the professional development of faculty and students in the field of group processes.

34. Center for the Study of Work Teams
http://www.workteams.unt.edu
The Center for the Study of Work Teams is a nonprofit organization whose vision is to become the premier center for research on collaborative work systems to create learning partnerships that support the design, implementation, and development of collaborative work systems.

We highly recommend that you review our Web site for expanded information and our other product lines. We are continually updating and adding links to our Web site in order to offer you the most usable and useful information that will support and expand the value of your Annual Editions. You can reach us at:
http://www.dushkin.com/annualeditions/.

www.dushkin.com/online/

Unit Selections

Key Points to Consider

❖ Think about those aspects of your life that you believe most clearly define who you are. How would they fit into James's theory? Would they be aspects of the material self? The social? The spiritual?

❖ Of what does a person's self-concept consist? Which characteristics are the most important in determining how a person views the self? Why would people differ in the kind of characteristics they use to define the self? In particular, what differences in self-concept would you expect to find between men and women? People of different ethnic groups? People of different socioeconomic status?

❖ Is there such a thing as a "true self," or are we all social chameleons, changing our behaviors to fit whatever situation we are in? How could you tell what your "true" self is? What would make it the "true" one?

 **Links**   **www.dushkin.com/online/**

These sites are annotated on pages 4 and 5.

What are you *really* like? Are you extraverted or introverted? Are you optimistic or pessimistic? The kind of person who is spontaneous and impulsive, or the kind who is organized and orderly?

How do you define yourself? That is, if called upon to describe yourself to others, which characteristics would you mention first? Would it be personality characteristics, such as extraversion, shyness, impulsivity, and so on? Would it be physical characteristics such as your height, weight, speed, strength, or physical attractiveness? Would you mention social categories such as your sex, race, religion, or nationality? Finally, no matter which of these characteristics you focus on, what is your overall evaluation of yourself—that is, do you generally see yourself in a positive or negative light?

As you can see from these questions, there are many ways in which people can define themselves, and an issue of considerable interest to contemporary social psychologists is where these different views of the self come from and what implications they have for how we act. This interest in the individual self, however, is of relatively recent vintage; traditionally the field of social psychology placed more emphasis on the ways in which individuals are influenced by situations. That is, the traditional approach was to manipulate features of the situation and see what effect it had on behavior. Essentially, in this approach people were thought to be similar and interchangeable; the focus was on the role of environmental factors.

More recently, contemporary social psychology has recognized the important role played by stable characteristics of the individual. That is, not only do certain situations tend to make all people act alike, but some people act in consistent ways no matter what the situation. Thus, one feature of modern social psychology is the realization that personality variables—shyness, self-esteem, and many more—can be important influences on human behavior. This growing emphasis on the self has also coincided with modern social psychology devoting considerable attention to understanding the notion of self-concept: that is, how people go about acquiring self-knowledge, organizing and integrating such knowledge, and how self-information then influences our thoughts, feelings, and actions.

In the first selection in this unit, "The Nature of the Self," Jonathan Brown describes one of the more influential models for conceptualizing how the self is organized: the self-theory of William James. According to James, there are three fundamental components to the self—the material, social, and spiritual. The second selection, "Race and the Schooling of Black Americans," argues that the components of self-concept frequently differ between white Americans and African Americans. Author Claude Steele contends that while performance in school is typically a significant influence on the

self-esteem of white children, it frequently is not for African American children. In essence, Steele believes, these children learn that there are few rewards for them in educational settings, and so they come to define their self-worth in nonacademic ways. The next selection in this section, "The Science of Happiness," takes a different approach to the issue of self-concept and examines the factors that contribute to a generally happy and satisfied outlook on the world. In "Making Sense of Self-Esteem," Mark Leary offers an interesting new explanation for the purpose of self-esteem. In essence, Leary argues that our levels of self-esteem are signals to us that indicate our relative social standing. When others value us, our self-esteem rises; when others reject us, our self-esteem falls. Self-esteem is important, Leary asserts, because it is such a good gauge of our social standing, and social standing is extremely important to human beings, who are such a social species. Finally, in the article "In Forecasting Their Emotions, Most People Flunk Out," Philip Hilts describes some interesting work that indicates how often people are unable to predict their own emotions and attitudes; it appears that we do not have as accurate a knowledge of ourselves as we often think we do.

The Nature of the Self

THE NATURE OF THE ME[*]

Jonathan D. Brown

We will begin by considering the nature of *Me* . . . [W]e use this term to refer to people's ideas about who they are and what they are like. Before reading further, take a moment to reflect on how you think about yourself by completing the questionnaire shown in Table 1.

TABLE 1. Self-Exercise #1

Imagine you want someone to know what you are really like. You can tell this person 20 things about yourself. These can include aspects of your personality, background, physical characteristics, hobbies, things you own, people you are close to, and so forth—in short, anything that helps the person know what you are really like. What would you tell them?

1._____
2._____
3._____
4._____
5._____
6._____
7._____
8._____
9._____
10._____
11._____
12._____
13._____
14._____
15._____
16._____
17._____
18._____
19._____
20._____

Three Components of the Empirical Self

William James used the term "the empirical self" to refer to all of the various ways people think about themselves. His analysis is very broad.[1]

> The Empirical Self of each of us is all that he is tempted to call by the name of *me*. But it is clear that between what a man calls *me* and what he simply calls *mine* the line is difficult to draw. We feel and act about certain things that are ours very much as we feel and act about ourselves. Our fame, our children, the work of our hands, may be as dear to us as our bodies are, and arouse the same feelings and the same acts of reprisal if attacked. And our bodies themselves, are they simply ours, or are they *us*? (p. 291)

James went on to group the various components of the empirical self into three subcategories: (1) the material self, (2) the social self, and (3) the spiritual self.

Material Self

The material self refers to tangible objects, people, or places that carry the designation *my or mine*. Two subclasses of the material self can be distinguished. These are the bodily self and the extracorporeal (beyond the body) self. Rosenberg (1979) has referred to the extracorporeal self as the extended self, and we will adopt this terminology throughout the book.

The bodily component of the material self requires little explanation. A person speaks of *my arms* or *my legs*. These entities are clearly an intimate part of who we are. But our sense of self is not limited to our bodies. It extends to include other people (my children), pets (my dog), possessions (my car), places (my hometown), and the products of our labors (my painting).

It is not the physical entities themselves, however, that comprise the material self. Rather, it is our psychological ownership of them (Scheibe, 1985). For example, a person may have a favorite chair she likes to sit in. The chair itself is not part of the self. Instead, it is the sense of appropriation represented by the phrase "my favorite chair." This is what we mean when we talk about the extended self. It includes all of the people, places, and things that are *psychologically* part of who we are.

It is interesting to consider why James argued for such a sweeping definition of self. Prior to the time he wrote his book, psychological research on self was restricted to the physical self. Recall from Chapter 1 that the introspectionists had people report what they were thinking and feeling when exposed to various stimuli. Some of these reports concerned an awareness of one's bodily states. For example, a person might report that "my arms

feel heavy" or "my skin feels warm." These are aspects of self. But James wanted to expand the study of self to include nonphysical aspects of the person. He believed that the self was fluid and encompassed more than our physical bodies.

Given this fluidity, how can we tell whether an entity is part of the self? James believed we could make this determination by examining our emotional investment in the entity. If we respond in an emotional way when the entity is praised or attacked, the entity is likely to be part of the self.

> *In its widest possible sense, . . . a man's Self is the sum total of all the he CAN call his,* not only his body and his psychic powers, but his clothes and his house, his wife and children, his ancestors and friends, his reputation and works, his lands and horses, and yacht and bank-account. All these things give him the same emotions. If they wax and prosper, he feels triumphant; if they dwindle and die away, he feels cast down—not necessarily in the same degree for each thing, but in much the same way for all. (pp. 291–292)

Another way to determine whether something is part of the extended self is to see how we act toward it. If we lavish attention on the entity and labor to enhance or maintain it, we can infer that the entity is part of the self.

> [All of the components of the material self] are the objects of instinctive preferences coupled with the most important practical interests of life. We all have a blind impulse to watch over our body, to deck it with clothing of an ornamental sort, to cherish parents, wife and babes, and to find for ourselves a home of our own which we may live in and "improve."
>
> An equally instinctive impulse drives us to collect property; and the collections thus made become, with different degrees of intimacy, parts of our empirical selves. The parts of our wealth most intimately ours are those which are saturated with our labor . . . and although it is true that a part of our depression at the loss of possessions is due to our feeling that we must now go without certain goods that we expected the possessions to bring in their train, yet in every case there remains, over and above this, a sense of the shrinkage of our personality, a partial conversion of ourselves to nothingness, which is a psychological phenomenon by itself. (p. 293)

In addition to underscoring the important role motivation plays in identifying what is self from what is not, James also made an interesting point here about the nature of things that become part of the self. These possessions, James argued, are not simply valued for what they provide; they are also prized because they become part of us. "Not only the people but the places and things I know enlarge my Self in a sort of metaphoric way," James wrote (p. 308).

A good deal of research supports James's intuitions regarding the close connection between possessions and the self (see Belk, 1988). First, people spontaneously men-

---

[1] [I will quote liberally from James throughout this chapter. It should be noted, however, that James always uses the male personal pronoun "he," a practice inconsistent with contemporary standards. In this instance, I judged fidelity to be more important than political correctness and have reproduced his words without editing them.]

tion their possessions when asked to describe themselves (Gordan, 1968). People also amass possessions. Young children, for example, are avid collectors. They have bottle-cap collections, rock collections, shell collections, and so forth. These collections are not simply treasured for their material value (which is often negligible); instead, they represent important aspects of self. The tendency to treat possessions as part of the self continues throughout life, perhaps explaining why so many people have difficulty discarding old clothes or other possessions that have long outlived their usefulness.

There seem to be several reasons for this. First, possessions serve a symbolic function; they help people define themselves. The clothes we wear, the cars we drive, and the manner in which we adorn our homes and offices signal to ourselves (and others) who we think we are and how we wish to be regarded. People may be particularly apt to acquire and exhibit such signs and symbols when their identities are tenuously held or threatened (Wicklund & Gollwitzer, 1982). A recent Ph.D., for example, may prominently display his diploma in an attempt to convince himself (and others) that he is the erudite scholar he aspires to be. These functions support Sartre's (1958) claim that people accumulate possessions to enlarge their sense of self.

Possessions also extend the self in time. Most people take steps to ensure that their letters, photographs, possessions, and mementos are distributed to others at the time of their death. Although some of this distribution reflects a desire to allow others to enjoy the utilitarian value of these artifacts, Unruh (1983, cited in Belk, 1988) has argued that this dispersal also has a symbolic function. People seek immortality by passing their possessions on to the next generation.

People's emotional responses to their possessions also attest to their importance to the self. A person who loses a wallet often feels greater anguish over a lost photograph than over any money that is missing. Similarly, many car owners react with extreme anger (and often rage) when their cars are damaged, even when the damage is only slight in physical terms. Finally, many people who lose possessions in a natural disaster go through a grieving process similar to the process people go through when they lose a person they love (McLeod, 1984, cited in Belk, 1988).

Further evidence that possessions become part of the extended self comes from a series of investigations by Beggan (1992). In an initial study, participants were shown a variety of inexpensive objects (e.g., a key ring, plastic comb, playing cards). They were then given one object and told it was theirs to keep. Later, participants evaluated *their* object more favorably than the objects they didn't receive. A follow-up investigation found that this tendency was especially pronounced after participants had previously failed at an unrelated experimental test. There are several explanations for this "mere ownership effect," but one possibility is that once possessions become part of the self, we imbue them with value and use them to promote positive feelings of self-worth.

Finally, the tendency to value self-relevant objects and entities even extends to letters of the alphabet. When asked to judge the pleasantness of various letters, people show enhanced liking for the letters that make up their own name particularly their own initials (Greenwald & Banaji, 1995; Nuttin, 1985, 1987). This "name letter effect" provides further support for James's assertion that our sense of self extends far beyond our physical bodies to include those objects and entities we call *ours*.

Social Self

James called the second category of the empirical self the social self. The social self refers to how we are regarded and recognized by others. (I will refer to these aspects of self as a person's *social identities*.) As before, James's analysis was very broad.

> ...*a man has as many social selves as there are individuals who recognize him* and carry an image of him in their mind.... But as the individuals who carry the images fall naturally into classes, we may practically say that he has as many different social selves as there are distinct *groups* of persons about whose opinion he cares. (p. 294)

Deaux, Reid, Mizrahi, and Ethier (1995) distinguished five types of social identities: personal relationships (e.g., husband, wife), ethnic/religious (e.g., African-American, Muslim), political affiliation (e.g., Democrat, pacifist), stigmatized groups (e.g., alcoholic, criminal), and vocation/avocation (e.g., professor, artist). Some of these identities are ascribed identities (ones we are born with, such as son or daughter) and others are attained identities (ones we acquire in life, such as professor or student).

Each of thee identities is accompanied by a specific set of expectations and behaviors. We act differently in the role of "father" than in the role of "professor." Sometimes these differences are minor and unimportant; other times they are considerable and consequential.

> Many a youth who is demure enough before his parents and teachers, swears and swaggers like a pirate among his "tough" young friends. We do not show ourselves to our children as to our club-companions, to our customers as to the laborers we employ, to our own masters and employers as to our intimate friends. From this there results what practically is a division of the man into several selves; and this may be a discordant splitting, as where one is afraid to let one set of acquaintances know him as he is elsewhere; or it may be a perfectly harmonious division of labor, as where one tender to his children is stern to the soldiers or prisoners under his command. (p. 294)

The larger point James made here is a critical one. To a great extent, how we think of ourselves depends on the social roles we are playing (Roberts & Donahue, 1994). We are different *selves* in different social situations.

This can cause difficulties when we are confronted with situations in which two or more social selves are relevant. Anyone who has simultaneously been both a parent and a child at a family reunion can attest to the difficulties such situations create. We are also surprised to encounter people we typically see in only one role or situation outside of that usual setting. Students, for example, are often flustered when they see their teachers outside of the classroom (e.g., at a movie, restaurant, or sporting event). They aren't used to seeing their teachers dressed so casually and acting so informally.

The tendency for people to show different sides of themselves in different social settings raises an important question: Is there a stable, core sense of self that transcends these various social roles? Some theorists have answered this question with an emphatic "no." They have maintained that the self is comprised entirely of our various social roles, and that there is no real, true, or genuine self that exists apart from these social roles (Gergen, 1982; Sorokin, 1947). Many (if not most) other theorists reject this position as too extreme. While acknowledging that people behave differently in different social settings, these theorists also contend that there is a common sense of self that runs through these various social identities. William James was one adherent of this position. James believed that our social roles are one important aspect of self, but they are by no means the sole aspect of self nor the most important.

James went on to make an additional point about these social selves. He posited an instinctive drive to be noticed and recognized by others. We affiliate, James argued, not simply because we like company, but because we crave recognition and status.

> *A man's Social Self* is the recognition which he gets from his mates. We are not only gregarious animals, liking to be in sight of our fellows, but we have an innate propensity to get ourselves noticed, and noticed favorably, by our kind. No more fiendish punishment could be devised, were such a thing physically possible, than that one should be turned loose in society and remain absolutely unnoticed by all the members thereof. (p. 293)

To summarize, the social self includes the various social positions we occupy and the social roles we play. But it is not simply these identities, per se. It is more importantly the way we think we are regarded and recognized by others. It is how we think others *evaluate* us. These perceptions will figure prominently in our discussion of the reflected appraisal process in Chapter 3.

Spiritual Self

The third category in James's scheme is the spiritual self. The spiritual self is our *inner* self or our *psychological* self. It is comprised of everything we call *my* or *mine* that is not a tangible object, person, or place, or a social role.

Our perceived abilities, attitudes, emotions, interests, motives, opinions, traits, and wishes are all part of the spiritual self. (I will refer to these aspects of the spiritual self as our *personal identities*.) In short, the spiritual self refers to our perceived inner psychological qualities. It represents our subjective experience of ourselves—how it feels to be us.

> By the spiritual self . . . I mean a man's inner or subjective being, his psychic faculties or dispositions. . . . These psychic dispositions are the most enduring and intimate part of the self, that which we most verily seem to be. We take a purer self-satisfaction when we think of our ability to argue and discriminate, of our moral sensibility and conscience, of our indomitable will, than when we survey any of our other possessions. (p. 296)

James proposed two different ways of thinking about the spiritual self. One way (which he called the abstract way) is to consider each attribute in isolation, as distinct from the others. The other way (which he called the concrete way) is to consider the attributes as united in a constant stream.

> . . . this spiritual self may be considered in various ways. We may divide it into faculties, . . . isolating them one from another, and identifying ourselves with either in turn. This is an abstract way of dealing with consciousness . . . ; or we may insist on a concrete view, and then the spiritual self in us will be either the entire stream of our personal consciousness, or the present "segment" or "section" of that stream. . . . But whether we take it abstractly or concretely, our understanding the spiritual self at all is a reflective process, . . . the result of our abandoning the outward-looking point of view, and . . . [coming] *to think ourselves as thinkers.* (p. 296)

Finally, it's of interest to note the close connection between our possessions (which are aspects of the material self) and our emotions, attitudes, and beliefs (which are components of the spiritual self). As Abelson (1986) observed, this similarity is captured in our language. A person is said to *have* a belief, from the time the belief is first *acquired*, to the time it is *discarded* or *lost*. We also say things like "I *inherited* a view" or "I can't *buy* that!" Finally, we speak of people who have *abandoned* their convictions or *disowned* an earlier position. These terms imply that possessions and attitudes share an underlying conceptual property: They are both owned by the self (see Gilovich, 1991; Heider, 1956 for an elaboration of this view).

Tests and Refinements of James's Ideas

Does James's classification scheme describe the way you think about yourself? To answer this question, try to match the responses you gave to the questionnaire in my classes at the University of Washington, and I have found that students' answers do reliably fall into one of these three categories. The only trick is deciding which of the

TABLE 2. Gordon's (1968) Identity Classification Scheme

A. Ascribed Identities
    1. Age
    2. Sex
    3. Name
    4. Race/Ethnicity
    5. Religion

B. Roles and Memberships
    6. Kinship (family—son, daughter, brother, sister)
    7. Occupation
    8. Student
    9. Political affiliation
    10. Social status (part of the middle class; an aristocrat)
    11. Territoriality/Citizenship (from Minneapolis; an American)
    12. Actual group memberships (Boy Scout; Shriner)

C. Abstract
    13. Existential (me; an individual)
    14. Abstract (a person; a human)
    15. Ideological and belief references (liberal; environmentalist)

D. Interests and Activities
    16. Judgments, tastes, likes (a jazz fan)
    17. Intellectual concerns (interested in literature)
    18. Artistic activities (a dancer; a painter)
    19. Other activities (a stamp collector)

E. Material Possessions
    20. Possessions
    21. Physical body

F. Major Senses of Self
    22. Competence (intelligent; talented; creative)
    23. Self-determination (ambitious; hardworking)
    24. Unity (mixed up; together)
    25. Moral worth (trustworthy; honest)

G. Personal Characteristics
    26. Interpersonal style (friendly; fair; nice; shy)
    27. Psychic style (happy; sad; curious; calm)

H. External References
    28. Judgments imputed to others (admired; well-liked)
    29. Immediate situation (hungry; bored)
    30. Uncodable

three categories is applicable. One way to make this determination is to consider whether the response is a noun or an adjective. Rosenberg (1979) notes that social identities are generally expressed as nouns and serve to place us in a broader social context (e.g., I am an American; I am a Democrat). In contrast, personal identities (aspects of what James called the spiritual self) are usually expressed as adjectives and serve to distinguish us from others (e.g., I am moody; I am responsible).

Gordon (1968) elaborated on James's scheme and produced a coding procedure with 8 major categories and 30 subcategories. This scheme is described in Table 2, and it is illustrated with a sample (composite) questionnaire in Table 3. You can compare the responses you gave with the ones shown there.

The Collective Self

James wrote at a time when psychology was the exclusive province of highly educated (and, by extension, well-to-do) males of European descent. His analysis is therefore somewhat parochial and narrow in scope. This limitation is apparent in the lack of attention James gave to people's ethnic, religious, and racial identities. These identities (termed the collective self by modern researchers) are of great significance to people, particularly those who occupy a minority status. For example, people place great importance on being "Irish," "Jewish," "an African-American," and so forth.

Two related issues regarding these collective identities have received attention. One line of research has focused

TABLE 3. Sample Response to "What Would You Tell Them" Questionnaire

Response	James	Gordon
1. smart	spiritual	competence
2. brown hair, brown eyes	material	physical body
3. friendly	spiritual	interpersonal style
4. the daughter of Italian immigrants	material	kinship
5. am a junior at the UW	social	student
6. like psychology	spiritual	interests and activities
7. am Catholic	social	religion
8. work at a daycare	social	occupation
9. love theater	spiritual	interests and activities
10. own a red Honda Accord	material	possessions
11. a member of Greenpeace	social	actual group
12. plan to become a school teacher	social (future)	occupation
13. am 22	material	age
14. am an only child	social	kinship
15. love laughing and smiling	spiritual	judgments, tastes, likes
16. responsible	spiritual	self-determination
17. a dancer	social	artistic activities
18. trustworthy	spiritual	moral worth
19. moody	spiritual	psychic style; personality
20. petite	material	physical body

on how people evaluate these specific identities. Historically, minority status has carried a negative connotation. Minorities have been stigmatized and subject to discrimination. This state of affairs led some minority group members to resent, disavow, or even turn against their ethnic identity (Lewin, 1948).

Recent years have seen a shift in these tendencies. Beginning with the Black Pride movement in the 1960s, minority groups have worked to improve the way their members evaluate their minority status. Rather than viewing their minority status as a stigma, group members are encouraged to celebrate their heritage and view their minority status as a source of pride. These efforts appear to be meeting with success. Most minority group members now evaluate their ethnic identity in positive terms (Crocker, Luhtanen, Blaine, & Broadnax, 1994; Phinney, 1990).

A second line of research has looked at how people maintain their ethnic identities when exposed to a dominant majority culture. Consider children of Latin-American descent who live in the United States today. Their

Latin identity is apt to be paramount during their early (pre-school) years, as a result of housing and friendship patterns. Later, when they begin to attend school, they come into contact with the broader American culture. What happens to their ethnic identity then?

Table 4 describes four possible outcomes based on the strength of the children's identification with the majority and minority group (Phinney, 1990). Children who adopt the identity of the dominant culture, while still retaining a strong identification with their cultural background, are said to be acculturated, integrated, or bicultural. Those who abandon their ethnic identity for an American identity are said to be assimilated. Separation occurs among those who refuse to identify with the dominant culture, and those who lose their ties to both cultural groups are said to be marginalized.

Assimilation was the desired outcome for many turn-of-the century immigrants. These newly arrived Americans sought to completely immerse themselves in American culture and shed their ethnic identity. In so

TABLE 4. Four Identity Orientations Based on Degree of Identification with One's Ethnic Group and the Majority Group

		Identification with Ethnic Group	
		Strong	Weak
Identification with Majority Group	Strong	Acculturated Integrated Bicultural	Assimilated
	Weak	Separated Dissociated	Marginalized

Source: Adapted from Phinney, 1990, *Psychological Bulletin, 108,* 499–514. Copyright 1990. Adapted by permission of The American Psychology Association.

doing, many changed their names, tried to lose their accents, and studiously adopted the customs and mores of American culture.

The situation today is quite different. Cultural diversity and pluralism are celebrated, and many minority group members strive to become acculturated, not assimilated. Phinney (1990) describes several behaviors that facilitate this goal, including participation in ethnic activities, continued use of one's native language, and the forging of friendship patterns with other minority group members. Ethier and Deaux (1994) found that behaviors of this sort helped Hispanic students retain their ethnic identity during their first year in predominantly Anglo universities.

Cultural Differences in Identity Importance

Cultural differences in the importance people attach to their various identities have also been the subject of research. James argued that personal identities (aspects of the spiritual self) are more important to people than are their social identities (aspects of the social self).

> . . . men have arranged the various selves . . . in an hierarchical scale according to their worth. (p. 314) . . . with the bodily Self at the bottom, the spiritual Self at top, and the extracorporeal material selves and the various social selves between. (p. 313)

This hierarchical scheme varies across cultures (Markus & Kitayama, 1991; Triandis, 1989). Western countries (e.g., United States, Canada, and Western European countries) are very individualistic. They are competitive in orientation and emphasize ways in which people are different from one another. This emphasis leads citizens of these countries to place great importance on their personal identities. Eastern cultures (e.g., Japan, China, India), in contrast, tend to be more cooperative, collective, and interdependent. Instead of emphasizing the ways people are different from one another, these cultures emphasize ways in which people are linked together. Accordingly, people raised in these cultures emphasize their social identities.

An investigation by Cousins (1989) documents these tendencies. In this investigation, American and Japanese college students completed a questionnaire similar to the one you filled out earlier, and then placed a check mark next to the five responses they regarded as most self-descriptive. Researchers then classified each of the five responses according to whether it referred to a personal identity (a perceived trait, ability, or disposition), a social identity (a social role or relationship), or something else (e.g., physical characteristic). Figure 1 presents the results of this investigation. The figure shows that the American students listed personal identities (e.g., I am honest; I am smart) 59 percent of the time, but Japanese students did so only 19 percent of the time. In contrast, Japanese students listed social identities (e.g., I am a student; I am a daughter)

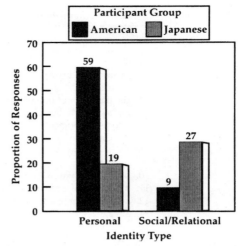

FIGURE 1. Identity statements by American and Japanese students in response to a "Who am I?" questionnaire. The data show that American students were more likely than Japanese students to describe themselves in terms of their personal attributes, whereas Japanese students were more likely than American students to describe themselves in terms of their social attributes. These findings document cross-cultural differences in the self-concept.

(Adapted from Cousins, 1989, *Journal of Personality and Social Psychology, 56,* 124–131. Copyright 1989. Adapted by permission of The American Psychological Association.)

27 percent of the time, but American students did so only 9 percent of the time. These findings document cross-cultural differences in the way people think about themselves (see also Trafimow, Triandis, & Goto, 1991).

Cousins (1989) documented another important cultural difference. People from Western cultures think of themselves as having psychological attributes that transcend particular situations. For example, when asked to describe herself, a person from a Western culture might say "I'm polite." People from Eastern cultures tend to think of themselves in relation to specific others and in specific situations; when asked to describe herself, a person from an Eastern culture might say "I'm polite at school," or "I'm polite with my father." The key difference is that the response of the person from a Western cultural background is unbounded by the situation, but the response of the person from an Eastern cultural background specifies the relational or situational context.

Individual Differences in Identity Importance

Even within cultures, people differ in the importance they attach to their various identities (Cheek, 1989; Dollinger, Preston, O'Brien, & Dilalla, 1996). Before reading further, take a moment to complete the questionnaire shown in Table 5. This questionnaire, adapted from one designed by Cheek, Tropp, Chen, and Underwood (1994), measures the weight people give to their various identities. The scale distinguishes three types of identities: personal identities (our perceived inner or psycho-

We're like a cube

TABLE 5. Identity Questionnaire

These items describe different aspects of identity. Please read each item carefully and consider how it applies to you. Fill in the blank next to each item by choosing a number from the scale below:

1 = Not important to my sense of who I am
2 = Slightly important to my sense of who I am
3 = Somewhat important to my sense of who I am
4 = Very important to my sense of who I am
5 = Extremely important to my sense of who I am

1. _____ My dreams and imagination.

2. _____ My attractiveness to other people.

3. _____ Being a part of the many generations of my family.

4. _____ My emotions and feelings.

5. _____ My popularity with other people.

6. _____ My race or ethnic background.

7. _____ My personal self-evaluations; the private opinion I have of myself.

8. _____ My reputation; what others think of me.

9. _____ My religion.

10. _____ My personal values and moral standards.

11. _____ The ways in which other people react to what I say and do.

12. _____ My feeling of belonging to my community.

Source: Adapted from Cheek, Tropp, Chen, & Underwood, 1994. Paper presented at the 102nd Annual Convention of The American Psychological Association, Los Angeles. Reprinted by permission of Jonathan M. Cheek.

logical qualities), social identities (the way we think we are regarded and recognized by others), and collective identities (our sense of belonging to a larger social group such as our race, ethnic heritage, and religion).

To determine your score, average your responses to the four items that refer to personal identities (items 1, 4, 7, and 10), the four items that refer to social identities (items 2, 5, 8, and 11), and the four items that measure collective identities (items 3, 6, 9, and 12). Most American college students score highest on the personal identity items, but not all do. Moreover, Asian-American students place more importance on their collective identities than do European-American students, further demonstrating how cultures shape the way people think about themselves. Finally, there is evidence that, across cultures, the tendency to see oneself in relational terms (which is a component of collectivism in this scale) is more characteristic of women than of men (Kashima et al., 1995; Markus & Oyserman, 1989).

The Personal Narrative

One more issue regarding the nature of the *ME* merits consideration. To this point, we have discussed the *ME* as

if it consists of a haphazard collection of perceived possessions, social roles, and traits. This is rarely the case. Most (if not all) individuals organize the various aspects of their empirical self into a coherent pattern.

McAdams (1996) has argued that this organization is generally accomplished in the context of a personal narrative. A personal narrative is a story a person (implicitly) constructs about her life. The narrative includes the ways the person thinks of herself, as well as the person's memories, feelings, and experiences. This ongoing story contains many of the literary devices that characterize works of fiction (e.g., plots and subplots, character descriptions). Many stories also feature a critical turning point or self-defining juncture (e.g., to really know me, you need to know why I abandoned a lucrative career as a taxi driver in favor of getting a Ph.D. in psychology). In short, a personal narrative unifies and makes sense of the various aspects of a person's life, including aspects of the empirical self.

*Editor's note: This is Chapter 2 in *The Self* by Jonathan D. Brown. Other chapters that are referenced in this article may be found in that book (The McGraw-Hill Companies, 1998).

Race and the Schooling of Black Americans

Claude Steele's article from the Atlantic Monthly *is a perceptive and troubling analysis of why black children are more likely than their white counterparts to fail in school. Steele notes the subtle and not-so-subtle ways that lead young blacks to "disidentify" with school, to resist measuring themselves against the values and goals of the classroom. He advocates the concept of "wise schooling," in which teachers and classmates see value and promise in black children rather than the opposite. Although he does not refer directly to them, note how Steele's analysis fits very well with modern social psychological theories about the development and maintenance of self-esteem.*

Claude M. Steele

My former university offered minority students a faculty mentor to help shepherd them into college life. As soon as I learned of the program, I volunteered to be a mentor, but by then the school year was nearly over. Undaunted, the program's eager staff matched me with a student on their waiting list—an appealing nineteen-year-old black woman from Detroit, the same age as my daughter. We met finally in a campus lunch spot just about two weeks before the close of her freshman year. I realized quickly that I was too late. I have heard that the best way to diagnose someone's depression is to note how depressed you feel when you leave the person. When our lunch was over, I felt as gray as the snowbanks that often lined the path back to my office. My lunchtime companion was a statistic brought to life, a living example of one of the most disturbing facts of racial life in America today: the failure of so many black Americans to thrive in school. Before I could lift a hand to help this student, she had decided to do what 70 percent of all black Americans at four-year colleges do at some point in their academic careers—drop out.

I sense a certain caving-in hope of America that problems of race can be solved. Since the sixties, when race relations held promise for the dawning of a new era, the issue has become one whose persistence causes "problem fatigue"—resignation to an unwanted condition of life.

This fatigue, I suspect, deadens us to the deepening crisis in the education of black Americans. One can enter any desegregated school in America, from grammar school to high school to graduate or professional school, and meet a persistent reality: blacks and whites in largely separate worlds. And if one asks a few questions or looks at a few records, another reality emerges: these worlds are not equal, either in the education taking place there or in the achievement of the students who occupy them.

As a social scientist, I know that the crisis has enough possible causes to give anyone problem fatigue. But at a personal level, perhaps because of my experience as a black in American schools, or perhaps just as the hunch of a myopic psychologist, I have long suspected a particular culprit—a culprit that can undermine black achievement as effectively as a lock on a schoolhouse door. The culprit I see is *stigma*, the endemic devaluation many blacks face in our society and schools. This status is its own condition of life, different from class, money, culture. It is capable, in the words of the late sociologist Erving Goffman, of "breaking the claim" that one's human attributes have on people. I believe that its connection to school achievement among black Americans has been vastly underappreciated.

This is a troublesome argument, touching as it does on a still unhealed part of American race relations. But it leads us to a heartening principle: if blacks are made less racially vulnerable in school, they can overcome even substantial obstacles. Before the good news, though, I must at least sketch in the bad: the worsening crisis in the education of black Americans.

Despite their socioeconomic disadvantages as a group, blacks begin school with test scores that are fairly close to the test scores of whites their age. The longer they

From *Psychology Is Social: Readings and Conversations in Social Psychology, 3/e,* edited by Edward Krupat, pp. 54–66, published by HarperCollins, 1994. Originally from *The Atlantic Monthly,* April 1992, pp. 68–78. © 1992 by Claude Steele. Reprinted by permission.

stay in school, however, the more they fall behind; for example, by the sixth grade blacks in many school districts are two full grade levels behind whites in achievement. This pattern holds true in the middle class nearly as much as in the lower class. The record does not improve in high school. In 1980, for example, 25,500 minority students, largely black and Hispanic, entered high school in Chicago. Four years later only 9,500 graduated, and of those only 2,000 could read at grade level. The situation in other cities is comparable.

Even for blacks who make it to college, the problem doesn't go away. As I noted, 70 percent of all black students who enroll in four-year colleges drop out at some point, as compared with 45 percent of whites. At any given time nearly as many black males are incarcerated as are in college in this country. And the grades of black college students average half a letter below those of their white classmates. At one prestigious university I recently studied, only 18 percent of the graduating black students had grade averages of B or above, as compared with 64 percent of the whites. This pattern is the rule, not the exception, in even the most elite American colleges. Tragically, low grades can render a degree essentially "terminal" in the sense that they preclude further schooling.

Blacks in graduate and professional schools face a similarly worsening or stagnating fate. For example, from 1977 to 1990, though the number of Ph.D.s awarded to other minorities increased and the number awarded to whites stayed roughly the same, the number awarded to American blacks dropped from 1,116 to 828. And blacks needed more time to get those degrees.

Standing ready is a familiar set of explanations. First is societal disadvantage. Black Americans have had, and continue to have, more than their share: a history of slavery, segregation, and job ceilings; continued lack of economic opportunity; poor schools; and the related problems of broken families, drug-infested communities, and social isolation. Any of these factors—alone, in combination, or through accumulated effects—can undermine school achievement. Some analysts point also to black American culture, suggesting that, hampered by disadvantage, it doesn't sustain the values and expectations critical to education, or that it fosters learning orientations ill suited to school achievement, or that it even "opposes" mainstream achievement. These are the chestnuts, and I had always thought them adequate. Then several facts emerged that just didn't seem to fit.

For one thing, the achievement deficits occur even when black students suffer no major financial disadvantage—among middle-class students on wealthy college campuses and in graduate school among black students receiving substantial financial aid. For another thing, survey after survey shows that even poor black Americans value education highly, often more than whites. Also, as I will demonstrate, several programs have improved black school achievement without addressing culturally specific learning orientations or doing anything to remedy socioeconomic disadvantage.

Neither is the problem fully explained, as one might assume, by deficits in skill or preparation which blacks might suffer because of background disadvantages. I first doubted that such a connection existed when I saw flunk-out rates for black and white students at a large, prestigious university. Two observations surprised me. First, for both blacks and whites the level of preparation, as measured by Scholastic Aptitude Test scores, didn't make much difference in who flunked out; low scorers (with combined verbal and quantitative SATs of 800) were no more likely to flunk out than high scorers (with combined SATs of 1,200 to 1,500). The second observation was racial: whereas only two percent to 11 percent of the whites flunked out, 18 percent to 33 percent of the blacks flunked out, even at the highest levels of preparation (combined SATs of 1,400). Dinesh D'Souza has argued recently that college affirmative-action programs cause failure and high dropout rates among black students by recruiting them to levels of college work for which they are inadequately prepared. That was clearly not the case at this school; black students flunked out in large numbers even with preparation well above average.

And, sadly, this proved the rule, not the exception. From elementary school to graduate school, something depresses black achievement *at every level of preparation, even the highest.* Generally, of course, the better prepared achieve better than the less prepared, and this is about as true for blacks as for whites. But given any level of school preparation (as measured by tests and earlier grades), blacks somehow achieve less in subsequent schooling than whites (that is, have poorer grades, have lower graduation rates, and take longer to graduate), no matter how strong that preparation is. Put differently, the same achievement level requires better preparation for blacks than for whites—far better: among students with a C+ average at the university I just described, the mean American College Testing Program (ACT) score for blacks was at the 98th percentile, while for whites it was at only the 34th percentile. This pattern has been documented so broadly across so many regions of the country, and by so many investigations (literally hundreds), that it is virtually a social law in this society—as well as a racial tragedy.

Clearly, something is missing from our understanding of black underachievement. Disadvantage contributes, yet blacks underachieve even when they have ample resources, strongly value education, and are prepared better than adequately in terms of knowledge and skills. Something else has to be involved. That something else could be of just modest importance—a barrier that simply adds its effect to that of other disadvantages—or it could be pivotal, such that were it corrected, other disadvantages would lose their effect.

That something else, I believe, has to do with the process of identifying with school. I offer a personal example:

I remember conducting experiments with my research adviser early in graduate school and awaiting the results with only modest interest. I struggled to meet deadlines. The research enterprise—the core of what one does as a social psychologist—just wasn't *me* yet. I was in school for other reasons—I wanted an advanced degree, I was vaguely ambitious for intellectual work, and being in graduate school made my parents proud of me. But as time passed, I began to like the work. I also began to grasp the value system that gave it meaning, and the faculty treated me as if they thought I might even be able to do it. Gradually I began to think of myself as a social psychologist. With this change in self-concept came a new accountability; my self-esteem was affected now by what I did as a social psychologist, something that hadn't been true before. This added a new motivation to my work; self-respect, not just parental respect, was on the line. I noticed changes in myself. I worked without deadlines. I bored friends with applications of arcane theory to their daily lives. I went to conventions. I lived and died over how experiments came out.

Before this transition one might have said that I was handicapped by my black working-class background and lack of motivation. After the transition the same observer might say that even though my background was working-class, I had special advantages: achievement-oriented parents, a small and attentive college. But these facts alone would miss the importance of the identification process I had experienced: the changes in self-definition and in the activities on which I based my self-esteem. They would also miss a simple condition necessary for me to make this identification: treatment as a valued person with good prospects.

I believe that the "something else" at the root of black achievement problems is the failure of American schooling to meet this simple condition for many of its black students. Doing well in school requires a belief that school achievement can be a promising basis of self-esteem, and that belief needs constant reaffirmation even for advantaged students. Tragically, I believe, the lives of black Americans are still haunted by a specter that threatens this belief and the identification that derived from it at every level of schooling.

The Specter of Stigma and Racial Vulnerability

I have a good friend, the mother of three, who spends considerable time in the public school classrooms of Seattle, where she lives. In her son's third-grade room, managed by a teacher of unimpeachable good will and competence, she noticed over many visits that the extraordinary art work of a small black boy named Jerome was ignored—or, more accurately perhaps, its significance was ignored. As a genuine art talent has a way of doing—even in the third grade—his stood out. Yet the teacher seemed hardly to notice. Moreover, Jerome's reputation, as it was passed along from one grade to the next, included only the slightest mention of his talent. Now, of course, being ignored like this could happen to anyone—such is the overload in our public schools. But my friends couldn't help wondering how the school would have responded to this talent had the artist been one of her own, middle-class white children.

Terms like "prejudice" and "racism" often miss the full scope of racial devaluation in our society, implying as they do that racial devaluation comes primarily from the strongly prejudiced, not from "good people" like Jerome's teacher. But the prevalence of racists—deplorable though racism is—misses the full extent of Jerome's burden, perhaps even the most profound part.

He faces a devaluation that grows out of our images of society and the way those images catalogue people. The catalogue need never be taught. It is implied by all we see around us: the kinds of people revered in advertising (consider the unrelenting racial advocacy of Ralph Lauren ads) and movies (black women are rarely seen as romantic partners, for example); media discussions of whether a black can be President; invitation lists to junior high school birthday parties; school curricula; literary and musical canons. These details create an image of society in which black Americans simply do not fare well. When I was a kid, we captured it with the saying "If you're white you're right, if you're yellow you're mellow, if you're brown stick around, but if you're black get back."

In ways that require no fueling from strong prejudice or stereotypes, these images expand the devaluation of black Americans. They act as mental standards against which information about blacks is evaluated: that which fits these images we accept; that which contradicts them we suspect. Had Jerome had a reading problem, which fits these images, it might have been accepted as characteristic more readily than his extraordinary art work, which contradicts them.

These images do something else as well, something especially pernicious in the classroom. They set up a jeopardy of double devaluation for blacks, a jeopardy that does not apply to whites. Like anyone, blacks risk devaluation for a particular incompetence, such as a failed test or a flubbed pronunciation. But they further risk that such performances will confirm the broader, racial inferiority they are suspected of. Thus, from the first grade through graduate school, blacks have the extra fear that in the eyes of those around them their full humanity could fall with a poor answer or a mistaken stroke of the pen.

Moreover, because these images are conditioned in all of us, collectively held, they can spawn racial devaluation in all of us, not just in the strongly prejudiced. They can do this even in blacks themselves: a majority of black children recently tested said they like and prefer to play with white rather than black dolls—almost fifty years after Kenneth and Mamie Clark, conducting similar experiments, documented identical findings and so paved the way for *Brown v. Topeka Board of Education*. Thus Jerome's devaluation can come from a circle of people in his world far greater than the expressly prejudiced—a circle that apparently includes his teacher.

In ways often too subtle to be conscious but sometimes overt, I believe, blacks remain devalued in American schools, where, for example, a recent national survey shows that through high school they are still more than twice as likely as white children to receive corporal punishment, be suspended from school, or be labeled mentally retarded.

Tragically, such devaluation can seem inescapable. Sooner or later it forces on its victims two painful realizations. The first is that society is preconditioned to see the worst in them. Black students quickly learn that acceptance, if it is to be won at all, will be hard-won. The second is that even if a black student achieves exoneration in one setting—with the teacher and fellow students in one classroom, or at one level of schooling, for example—this approval will have to be rewon in the next classroom, at the next level of schooling. Of course, individual characteristics that enhance one's value in society—skills, class status, appearance, and success—can diminish the racial devaluation one faces. And sometimes the effort to prove oneself fuels achievement. But few from any group could hope to sustain so daunting and everlasting a struggle. Thus, I am afraid, too many black students are left hopeless and deeply vulnerable in America's classrooms.

"Disidentifying" with School

I believe that in significant part the crisis in black Americans' education stems from the power of this vulnerability to undercut identification with schooling, either before it happens or after it has bloomed.

Jerome is an example of the first kind. At precisely the time when he would need to see school as a viable source of self-esteem, his teachers fail to appreciate his best work. The devalued status of his race devalues him and his work in the classroom. Unable to entrust his sense of himself to this place, he resists measuring himself against its values and goals. He languishes there, held by the law, perhaps even by his parents, but not allowing achievement to affect his view of himself. This psychic alienation—the act of not caring—makes him less vulnerable to the specter of devaluation that haunts him. Bruce Hare, an educational researcher, has documented this process among fifth-grade boys in several schools in Champaign, Illinois. He found that although the black boys had considerably lower achievement-test scores than their white classmates, their overall self-esteem was just as high. This stunning imperviousness to poor academic performance was accomplished, he found, by their deemphasizing school achievement as a

basis of self-esteem and giving preference to peer-group relations—a domain in which their esteem prospects were better. They went where they had to go to feel good about themselves.

But recall the young reader whose mentor I was. She had already identified with school, and wanted to be a doctor. How can racial vulnerability break so developed an achievement identity? To see, let us follow her steps onto campus: Her recruitment and admission stress her minority status perhaps more strongly than it has been stressed at any other time in her life. She is offered academic and social support services, further implying that she is "at risk" (even though, contrary to common belief, the vast majority of black college students are admitted with qualifications well above the threshold for whites). Once on campus, she enters a socially circumscribed world in which blacks—still largely separate from whites—have lower status; this is reinforced by a sidelining of minority material and interests in the curriculum and in university life. And she can sense that everywhere in this new world her skin color places her under suspicion of intellectual inferiority. All of this gives her the double vulnerability I spoke of: she risks confirming a particular incompetence, at chemistry or a foreign language, for example; but she also risks confirming the racial inferiority she is suspect of—a judgment that can feel as close at hand as a mispronounced word or an ungrammatical sentence. In reaction, usually to some modest setback, she withdraws, hiding her troubles from instructors, counselors, even other students. Quickly, I believe, a psychic defense takes over. She *disidentifies* with achievement; she changes her self-conception, her outlook and values, so that achievement is no longer so important to her self-esteem. She may continue to feel pressure to stay in school from her parents, even from the potential advantages of a college degree. But now she is psychologically insulated from her academic life, like a disinterested visitor. Cool, unperturbed. But, like a painkilling drug, disidentification undoes her future as it relieves her vulnerability.

The prevalence of his syndrome among black college students has been documented extensively, especially on predominantly white campuses. Summarizing this work, Jacqueline Fleming, a psychologist, writes, "The fact that black students must matriculate in an atmosphere that feels hostile arouses defensive reactions that interfere with intellectual performance. . . . They display academic demotivation and think less of their abilities. They profess losses of energy." Among a sample of blacks on one predominantly white campus, Richard Nisbett and Andrew Reaves, both psychologists, and I found that attitudes related to disidentification were more strongly predictive of grades than even academic preparation (that is, SATs and high school grades).

To make matters worse, once disidentification occurs in a school, it can spread like the common cold. Blacks who identify and try to achieve embarrass the strategy by valuing the very thing the strategy denies the value of. Thus pressure to make it a group norm can evolve quickly and become fierce. Defectors are called "oreos" or "incognegroes." One's identity as an authentic black is held hostage, made incompatible with school identification. For black students, then, pressure to disidentify with school can come from the already demoralized as well as from racial vulnerability in the setting.

Stimatization of the sort suffered by black Americans is probably also a barrier to the school achievement of other groups in our society, such as lower-class whites, Hispanics, and women in male-dominated fields. For example, at a large midwestern university I studied women match men's achievement in the liberal arts, where they suffer no marked stigma, but underachieve compared with men (get lower grades than men with the same ACT scores) in engineering and premedical programs, where they, like blacks across the board, are more vulnerable to suspicions of inferiority.

"Wise" Schooling

"When they approach me they see ... everything and anything except me.... [This] invisibility occurs because of a peculiar disposition of the eyes...."

Ralph Ellison, *Invisible Man*

Erving Goffman, borrowing from gays of the 1950s, used the term "wise" to describe people who don't themselves bear the stigma of a given group but who are accepted by the group. These are people in whose eyes the full humanity of the stigmatized is visible, people in whose eyes they feel less vulnerable. If racial vulnerability undermines black school achievement, as I have argued, then this achievement should improve significantly if schooling is made "wise"—that is, made to see value and promise in black students and to act accordingly.

And yet, although racial vulnerability at school may undermine black achievement, so many other factors seem to contribute—from the debilitations of poverty to the alleged dysfunctions of black American culture—that one might expect "wiseness" in the classroom to be of little help. Fortunately, we have considerable evidence to the contrary. Wise schooling may indeed be the missing key to the schoolhouse door.

In the mid-seventies black students in Philip Uri Treisman's early calculus courses at the University of California at Berkeley consistently fell to the bottom of every class. To help, Treisman developed the Mathematics Workshop Program, which, in a surprisingly short time, reversed their fortunes, causing them to outperform their white and Asian counterparts. And although it is only a freshman program, black students who take it graduate at a rate comparable to the Berkeley average. Its central technique is group study of calculus concepts. But it is also wise; it does things that allay the racial vulnerabili-

ties of these students. Stressing their potential to learn, it recruits them to a challenging "honors" workshop tied to their first calculus course. Building on their skills, the workshop gives difficult work, often beyond course content, to students with even modest preparation (some of their math SATs dip to the 300s). Working together, students soon understand that everyone knows something and nobody knows everything, and learning is speeded through shared understanding. The wisdom of these tactics is their subtext message: "You are valued in this program because of your academic potential—regardless of your current skill level. You have no more to fear than the next person, and since the work is difficult, success is a credit to your ability, and a setback is a reflection only of the challenge." The black students' double vulnerability around failure—the fear that they lack ability, and the dread that they will be devalued—is thus reduced. They can relax and achieve. The movie *Stand and Deliver* depicts Jaime Escalante using the same techniques of assurance and challenge to inspire advanced calculus performance in East Los Angeles Chicano high schoolers. And, explaining Xavier University's extraordinary success in producing black medical students, a spokesman said recently, "What doesn't work is saying, 'You need remedial work.' What does work is saying, 'You may be somewhat behind at this time but you're a talented person. We're going to help you advance at an accelerated rate.' "

The work of James Comer, a child psychiatrist at Yale, suggests that wiseness can minimize even the barriers of poverty. Over a fifteen-year period he transformed the two worst elementary schools in New Haven, Connecticut, into the third and fifth best in the city's thirty-three-school system without any change in the type of students—largely poor and black. His guiding belief is that learning requires a strongly accepting relationship between teacher and student. "After all," he notes, "what is the difference between scribble and a letter of the alphabet to a child? The only reason the letter is meaningful, and worth learning and remembering, is because a *meaningful* other wants him or her to learn and remember it." To build these relationships Comor focuses on the over-all school climate, shaping it not so much to transmit specific skills, or to achieve order per se, or even to improve achievement, as to establish a valuing and optimistic atmosphere in which a child can—to use his term—"identify" with learning. Responsibility for this lies with a team of ten to fifteen members, headed by the principal and made up of teachers, parents, school staff, and child-development experts (for example, psychologists or special-education teachers). The team develops a plan of specifics: teacher training, parent workshops, coordination of information about students. But at base I believe it tries to ensure that the students—vulnerable on so many counts—get treated essentially like middle-class students, with conviction about their value and promise. As this happens, their vulnerability diminishes, and with it the companion defenses of disidentification and misconduct. They achieve, and apparently identify, as their achievement gains persist into high school. Comer's genius, I believe, is to have recognized the importance of these vulnerabilities as barriers to *intellectual* development, and the corollary that schools hoping to educate such students must learn first how to make them feel valued.

These are not isolated successes. Comparable results were observed, for example, in a Comer-type program in Maryland's Prince Georges County, in the Stanford economist Henry Levin's accelerated-schools program, and in Harlem's Central Park East Elementary School, under the principalship of Deborah Meier. And research involving hundreds of programs and schools points to the same conclusion: black achievement is consistently linked to conditions of schooling that reduce racial vulnerability. These include relatively harmonious race relations among students; a commitment by teachers and schools to seeing minority-group members achieve; the instructional goal that students at all levels of preparation achieve; desegregation at the classroom as well as the school level; and a de-emphasis on ability tracking.

That erasing stigma improves black achievement is perhaps the strongest evidence that stigma is what depresses it in the first place. This is no happy realization. But it lets in a ray of hope: whatever other factors also depress black achievement—poverty, social isolation, poor preparation—they may be substantially overcome in a schooling atmosphere that reduces racial and other vulnerabilities, not through unrelenting niceness or ferocious regimentation but by wiseness, by *seeing* value and acting on it.

What Makes Schooling Unwise

But if wise schooling is so attainable, why is racial vulnerability the rule, not the exception, in American schooling?

One factor is the basic assimilationist offer that schools make to blacks: You can be valued and rewarded in school (and society), the schools say to these students, but you must first master the culture and ways of the American mainstream, and since that mainstream (as it is represented) is essentially white, this means you must give up many particulars of being black—styles of speech and appearance, value priorities, preferences—at least in mainstream settings. This is asking a lot. But is has been the "color-blind" offer to every immigrant and minority group in our nation's history, the core of the melting-pot ideal, and so I think it strikes most of us as fair. Yet non-immigrant minorities like blacks and Native Americans have always been here, and thus are entitled, more than new immigrants, to participate in the defining images of the society projected in school. More important, their exclusion from these images denies their contributive history and presence in society. Thus, whereas immigrants can tilt toward assimilation in pursuit of the opportunities for which they came, American blacks may find it harder to assimilate. For them, the offer of acceptance in return for assimilation carries a primal insult: it asks them to join in something that has made them invisible.

Now, I must be clear. This is not a criticism of Western civilization. My concern is an omission of image-work. In his incisive essay "What America Would Be Like Without Blacks," Ralph Ellison showed black influence on American speech and language, the themes of our finest literature, and our most defining ideals of personal freedom and democracy. In *The World They Made Together*, Mechal Sobel described how African and European influences shaped the early American South in everything from housing design and land use to religious expression. The fact is that blacks are not outside the American mainstream but, in Ellison's words, have always been "one of its major tributaries." Yet if one relied on what is taught in America's schools, one would never know this. There blacks have fallen victim to a collective self-deception, a society's allowing itself to assimilate like mad from its constituent groups while representing itself to itself as if the assimilation had never happened, as if progress and good were almost exclusively Western and white. A prime influence of American society on world culture is the music of black Americans, shaping art forms from rock-and-roll to modern dance. Yet in American schools, from kindergarten through graduate school, these essentially black influences have barely peripheral status, are largely outside the canon. Thus it is not what is taught but what is *not* taught, what teachers and professors have never learned the value of, that reinforces a fundamental unwiseness in American schooling, and keeps black disidentification on full boil.

Deep in the psyche of American educators is a presumption that black students need academic remediation, or extra time with elemental curricula to overcome background deficits. This orientation guides many efforts to close the achievement gap—from grammar school tutoring to college academic-support programs—but I fear it can be unwise. Bruno Bettelheim and Karen Zelan's article "Why Children Don't Like to Read" comes to mind: apparently to satisfy the changing sensibilities of local school boards over this century, many books that children like were dropped from school reading lists; when children's reading scores also dropped, the approved texts were replaced by simpler books; and when reading scores dropped again, these were replaced by even simpler books, until eventually the children could hardly read at all, not because the material was too difficult but because they were bored stiff. So it goes, I suspect, with a great many of these remediation efforts. Moreover, because so many such programs target blacks primarily, they virtually equate black identity with substandard intellectual status, amplifying racial vulnerability. They can even undermine students' ability to gain confidence from their achievement, by sharing credit for their successes while implying that their failures stem from inadequacies beyond the reach of remediation.

The psychologist Lisa Brown and I recently uncovered evidence of just how damaging this orientation may be. At a large, prestigious university we found that whereas the grades of black graduates of the 1950s improved during the students' college years until they virtually matched the school average, those of blacks who graduated in the 1980s (we chose only those with above-average entry credentials, to correct for more-liberal admissions policies in that decade) worsened, ending up considerably below the school average. The 1950s graduates faced outward discrimination in everything from housing to the classroom, whereas the 1980s graduates were supported by a phalanx of help programs. Many things may contribute to this pattern. The Jackie Robinson, "pioneer spirit" of the 1950s blacks surely helped them endure. And in a pre-affirmative-action era, they may have been seen as intellectually more deserving. But one cannot ignore the distinctive fate of the 1980s blacks: a remedial orientation put their abilities under suspicion, deflected their ambitions, distanced them from their successes, and painted them with their failures. Black students on today's campuses may experience far less overt prejudice than their 1950s counterparts but, ironically, may be more racially vulnerable.

The Elements of Wiseness

For too many black students school is simply the place where, more concertedly, persistently, and authoritatively than anywhere else in society, they learn how little valued they are.

Clearly, no simple recipe can fix this, but I believe we now understand the basics of a corrective approach. Schooling must focus more on reducing the vulnerabilities that block identification with achievement. I believe that four conditions, like the legs of a stool, are fundamental.

- If what is meaningful and important to a teacher is to become meaningful and important to a student, the student must feel valued by the teacher for his or her potential and as a person. Among the more fortunate in society, this relationship is often taken for granted. But it is precisely the relationship that race can still undermine in American society. As Comer, Escalante, and Treisman have shown, when one's students bear race and class vulnerabilities, building this relationship is the first order of business—at all levels of schooling. No tactic of instruction, no matter how ingenious, can succeed without it.
- The challenge and the promise of personal fulfillment, not remediation (under whatever guise), should guide the education of those students. Their present skills should be taken into account, and they should be moved along at a pace that is demanding but doesn't defeat them. Their ambitions should never be scaled down but should instead be guided to inspiring goals even when extraordinary dedication is called for. Frustration will be less crippling than alienation. Here psychology is everything: remediation defeats, challenge strengthens—affirming their potential, crediting them with their achievements, inspiring them.

    But the first condition, I believe, cannot work without the second, and vice versa. A valuing teacher-student relationship goes nowhere without challenge, and challenge will always be resisted outside a valuing relationship. (Again, I must be careful about something: in criticizing remediation I am not opposing affirmative-action recruitment in the schools. The success of this policy, like that of school integration before it, depends, I believe, on the tactics of implementation. Where students are valued and challenged, they generally succeed.)
- Racial integration is a generally useful element in this design, if not a necessity. Segregation, whatever its purpose, draws out group differences and makes people feel more vulnerable when they inevitably cross group lines to compete in the larger society. This vulnerability, I fear, can override confidence gained in segregated schooling unless that confidence is based on strongly competitive skills and knowledge—something that segregated schooling, plagued by shortages of resources and access, has difficulty producing.
- The particulars of black life and culture—art, literature, political and social perspective, music—must be presented in the mainstream curriculum of American schooling, not consigned to special days, weeks, or even months of the year, or to special-topic courses and programs aimed essentially at blacks. Such channeling carries the disturbing message that the material is not of general value. And this does two terrible things: it wastes the power of this material to alter our images of the American mainstream—continuing to frustrate black identification with it—and it excuses in whites and others a huge ignorance of their own society. The true test of democracy, Ralph Ellison has said, is "the inclusion—not assimilation—of the black man."

Finally, if I might be allowed a word specifically to black parents, one issue is even more immediate: our children may drop out of school before the first committee meets to accelerate the curriculum. Thus, although we, along with all Americans, must strive constantly for wise schooling, I believe we cannot wait for it. We cannot yet forget our essentially heroic challenge: to foster in our children a sense of hope and entitlement to mainstream American life and schooling, even when it devalues them.

CHARLES PEALE

For millions of people, finding the right partner, achieving professional success, and acquiring wealth are all means to a single end: being happy.

In this special section, THE FUTURIST ... attempt[s] to shed light on happiness and on what we can do to become more happy in the future.

In "The Science of Happiness," psychologists David Myers and Ed Diener discuss scientific research data that reveal who is happy, who is not, and why. The authors identify the traits of happy people and the impact of relationships, debunking myths along the way.

The Science of *Happiness*

By David G. Myers and Ed Diener

Does happiness favor those of a particular age, sex, or income level? Does happiness come with satisfying close relationships? With religious faith? What attitudes, activities, and priorities engender a sense of well-being?

Such questions not only went unanswered during psychology's first century, they went largely unasked. Psychology has focused more on negative emotions than on positive ones. From 1967 through 1995, *Psychological Abstracts* included 5,119 abstracts mentioning anger, 38,459

mentioning anxiety, and 48,366 mentioning depression—but only 1,710 mentioning happiness, 2,357 mentioning life satisfaction, and 402 mentioning joy. This 21 to 1 ratio of negative to positive emotions studied is changing, and researchers are offering fresh insights on an old puzzle: Who is happy and why?

Although the scientific pursuit of happiness has recently mushroomed, speculations about happiness are ages-old. Ancient philosophers believed that happiness accompanied a life of intelligent reflection. "There

> Scientists zero in on who is happy and why. Their findings may help more people find happiness in the years ahead.

Originally appeared in *The Futurist*, September/October 1997, pp. 1–7. © 1997 by the World Future Society, 7910 Woodmont Avenue, Suite 450, Bethesda, MD 20814. Tel. 301/656-8274; fax 301/951-0394; http://www.wfs.org/wfs. Reprinted by permission.

is no fool who is happy, and no wise man who is not," said the Roman philosopher Cicero. In the centuries since, some sages have suggested that happiness comes from living a virtuous life, and others, from indulging pleasures; some that it comes from knowing the truth, and others, from preserving illusions; some, that it comes from restraint, and others, from purging oneself of pent-up rage and misery. The list goes on, but the implication is clear: To discover the truth about happiness, we must ask how these competing ideas relate to reality. In short, we must study happiness scientifically.

Assessing Happiness

To probe people's "subjective well-being," researchers have asked them to report their *feelings* of happiness or unhappiness along with their *thoughts* about how satisfying their lives are. Like tangerines and oranges, happiness and life satisfaction are subtly different, yet they have much in common.

Sometimes researchers probe with simple questions, such as, "Taking all things together, how would you say things are these days? Would you say that you are very happy, pretty happy, or not too happy?" and, "How satisfied are you with your life as a whole these days? Are you very satisfied? Satisfied? Not very satisfied? Not at all satisfied?

Other researchers use tests that measure the relative frequencies of people's positive, happy feelings and their negative, depressed feelings. Surprisingly, the amount of good feeling a person experiences over time does not predict how much bad feeling the person experiences. Some people experience intense good moods but also intense bad moods. High highs alternate with low lows. Others are characteristically happy, or melancholy, or unemotional.

Although swayed by temporary moods, people's self-reported well-being on such measures is moderately consistent over years of retesting. The stability suggests the influence of enduring traits and circumstances, and the change indicates the influence of recent life events.

Do the measures have validity as well as reliability? Or are "happy" people merely "in denial" of their actual misery? Those who report

I enjoy being with friends and experiencing new things. My average mood is a feeling of inner contentment. I don't have great mood swings. I have pleasant feelings about my future." Another, who scored low, explained, "In 1985 I wrote a will and planned my suicide, but a motorcycle accident scared me out of it. My average mood is pretty poor. I'm often irri-

"No matter how dull, or how mean, or how wise a man is, he feels that happiness is his indisputable right."—Helen Keller

PHOTOS: © PHOTODISC

themselves happy and satisfied do *seem* happy to their close friends, family members, and a psychologist-interviewer. Their daily mood ratings reveal more positive emotions. They smile more. Their ratings are responsive to good and bad events and to therapy. Self-reported happiness also predicts other indicators of well-being. Compared with depressed people, happy people are less self-focused, less hostile and abusive, and less vulnerable to disease. They are also more loving, forgiving, trusting, energetic, decisive, creative, sociable, and helpful.

One person who scored high on a happiness scale explained, "Worry and guilt have little part in my life.

table and usually don't care what other people feel or think. It's a chore to be pleasant."

Dozens of researchers across the world have now asked more than a million people—a representative sample of the human race—to reflect on their happiness and life satisfaction. By taking their self-reports seriously, we can offer tentative answers to the age-old questions, How happy are most people? And who are the happiest?

Are Most People Unhappy?

There is a long tradition of viewing life as tragedy. It extends from Sophocles' writing (in *Oedipus at Colonus*) that "Not to be born is, past all prizing, best" to Woody Allen's discerning (in *Annie Hall*) two kinds of lives—the horrible and the merely miserable. Albert Camus, Tennessee Williams, Allen Drury, and other playwrights and novelists echo their unhappy picture of humanity.

So have many social observers. "Our pains greatly exceed our pleasures," it seemed to Rousseau, "so that, all things considered, human life is not at all a valuable gift." We are "not born for happiness," agreed Samuel Johnson. Recent warm-hearted books for the would-be-happy, mostly written by people who spend their days counseling the

But a much rosier picture emerges from careful surveys of ordinary people, using random-sample methods. In national surveys, three in 10 Americans say they are "very happy." Only one in 10 says "not too happy." The remainder—the majority—describe themselves as "pretty happy."

Asked about their "satisfaction with life," most people are similarly upbeat: In western Europe and North America, eight in 10 rate themselves as "satisfied" or "very satisfied" with their lives. Likewise, some three-fourths of people say that they've felt excited, proud, or pleased at some point during the

ents, South African blacks during apartheid, and students living under conditions of economic and political suppression.) This positivity contradicts many people's negative perceptions: Among psychology students, for example, half erroneously believe the elderly are "mostly unhappy"; a third wrongly guess that African-Americans are "mostly unhappy," and nine in 10 guess that unemployed men are.

But aren't depression rates on the rise? They are. Yet clinical researcher Ian Gotlib estimates that less than 2% of the world's population suffers clinically recognizable depression each year. In a recent multinational census of psychiatric disorders, the lifetime rate of depression was only 9% in the most vulnerable group.

Who is Happy?

Social scientists have exploded some myths about who's happy and who's not by identifying predictors of happiness and life satisfaction.

Many people believe there are unhappy times of life—typically the stress-filled teen years, the "mid-life crisis" years, or the declining years of old age. But interviews with people of all ages reveal that no time of life is notably happier or unhappier. The emotional terrain does change with age: Satisfaction with social relations and health becomes more important in later life. And teens, unlike adults, typically rebound from either gloom or elation within an hour's time. Yet knowing someone's age gives no clue to the person's enduring sense of well-being. Moreover, rates of depression, suicide, and divorce show no increase during the mythical mid-life crisis years.

Does happiness have a favorite sex? Are men happier because of their greater incomes and social power? Are women happier because of their reputedly greater capacity for intimacy and social connection? Like age, gender gives no clue to subjective well-being. There are gender gaps in misery: When troubled,

"There is no duty we so much underrate as the duty of being happy." —Robert Louis Stevenson

unhappy, concur. Dennis Wholey, in *Are You Happy?* (Houghton Mifflin, 1986), reports that the experts he interviewed believe perhaps 20% of Americans are happy. He remarks: "I would have thought the proportion was much lower!" In *Happiness Is an Inside Job* (Tabor, 1989), Father John Powell agrees: "One-third of all Americans wake up depressed every day. Professionals estimate that only 10% to 15% of Americans think of themselves as truly happy."

past few weeks; no more than a third say they've felt lonely, bored, or depressed.

These above-neutral reports characterize all age groups, virtually all economic groups, and all races studied, and hold for all strategies for assessing subjective well-being, including those that sample people's experience by "beeping" them at random times. (The few exceptions include hospitalized alcoholics, newly incarcerated inmates, new therapy climen more often become alcoholic, while women more often ruminate and get depressed or anxious. Yet men and women are equally likely to declare themselves "very happy" and "satisfied" with life. This conclusion is grounded in scores of studies around the world.

Wealth and Well-Being

Still in pursuit of an elusive happiness, we might wonder whether wealth predicts well-being. Although few agree that money can literally buy happiness, many agree that a *little* more money would make them a *little* happier. Moreover, the American dream since 1970 seems increasingly to have become life, liberty, and the purchase of happiness. In 1995, 74% of America's entering collegians declared that an "essential" or "very important" life goal was "being very well off financially"—nearly double the 39% who said the same in 1970. This topped a list of 19 rated life objectives, exceeding even "raising a family" and "helping others in difficulty."

Are wealth and well-being indeed connected? Let's ask three more-specific questions about happiness and wealth between countries, within countries, and over time.

First, are people in rich countries happier than people in not-so-rich countries? There are striking national differences in well-being: In Portugal, one in 10 people reports being very happy; in the Netherlands, four in 10 people say the same. Economic wealth might account for these variations. The correlation between national wealth and well-being is positive (despite curious reversals, such as the Irish during the 1980s consistently reporting greater life satisfaction than the wealthier West Germans). But national wealth is confounded with other factors, such as civil rights, literacy, and number of continuous years of democracy, which also correlate with average life satisfaction.

Second, within any country, are rich individuals happiest? In poor countries, such as Bangladesh and India, satisfaction with finances is a moderate predictor of well-being. But once an individual is able to afford life's necessities, increasing affluence matters surprisingly little. In the United States and in Europe, the correlation between income and happiness is, as University of Michigan political scientist Ronald Inglehart has noted, "surprisingly weak

(indeed, virtually negligible)." Even very rich people—those surveyed among Forbes' 100 wealthiest Americans— are only slightly happier than the average American. Those whose income has increased over a 10-year period are not happier than those whose income has not increased. And studies suggest that lottery winners gain but a temporary jolt of joy. Wealth, it seems, is like health: Although its utter absence can breed misery, possessing it is no guarantee of happiness. Happiness seems less a matter of getting what we want than of wanting what we have.

At the other end of life's circumstances are the victims of tragedies. We have been astonished by the negligible long-term emotional impact of negative as well as positive life

circumstances. People with disabilities usually report a near-normal level of well-being. Even the trauma of a paralyzing car accident typically gives way to a return of normal happiness. Within four months of his tragic, paralyzing accident, actor Christopher Reeve reported "genuine joy in being alive." So great is our adaptive capacity that, within three months, the emotional impact

"A merry heart doeth good like a medicine."—Proverbs 17:22

 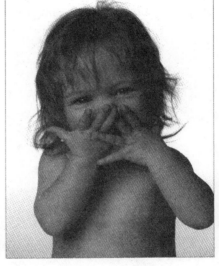

of most good and bad events wanes and emotions again fluctuate with more recent events.

As Benjamin Franklin surmised, happiness "is produc'd not so much by great Pieces of good Fortune that seldom happen, as by little Advantages that occur every day." Feeling the short-run influence of events and circumstances, people use such to explain their happiness, all the while missing subtler but bigger influences on their long-run well-being. Noticing that an influx of cash feels good, they may therefore mistakenly accept the Hollywood image of who is happy—the rich, famous, and beautiful. (Despite the presumptions underlying the billions of dollars spent on cosmetics, clothes, and diets, even the very attractive are barely happier than the unattractive.)

Third, have people become happier over time as their cultures have become more affluent? In 1957, when economist John Galbraith was about to describe the United States as *The Affluent Society*, Americans' per person income, expressed in today's dollars, was about $9,000 per year. Today it is more than $18,000, defining a "doubly affluent society"—with double what money buys, including twice as many cars per person. Moreover, we eat out more than twice as often and have vastly more abundant air conditioning, dishwashers, CD sound systems, and color TVs.

real incomes have *not* been accompanied by increasing happiness.

The findings lob a bombshell at modern Western culture's materialism: *Economic growth in affluent countries provides no apparent boost to human morale.*

The Traits of Happy People

If happiness is similarly available to those of any age, sex, or race, and to those of all but the lowest income levels, then who are the very happy people? Through life's ups and downs, some people's capacity for

people do report positive self-esteem. Indeed, they usually exhibit a self-service bias: They believe themselves to be more ethical, more intelligent, less prejudiced, better able to get along with others, and healthier than the average person. (Such findings bring to mind Freud's joke about the man who told his wife, "If one of us should die, I think I would go live in Paris.")

Second, happy people typically feel **personal control.** Feeling empowered rather than helpless, they also do better in school, achieve more at work, and cope better with stress. Deprived of control over one's life—an experience studied in prisoners, nursing-home patients, and people living under totalitarian regimes—people suffer lower morale and worse health. Severe poverty demoralizes when it erodes people's sense of control over their life circumstances.

Third, happy people are usually **optimistic.** One could reason that pessimists, whose low expectations are so often exceeded, would constantly be surprised by joy. "Blessed is he who expects nothing, for he shall never be disappointed," counseled poet Alexander Pope in a 1727 letter. Nevertheless, positive-thinking optimists—those who agree, for example, that "when I undertake something new, I expect to succeed"—tend to be more successful, healthier, and happier.

Fourth, happy people tend to be **extroverted.** Although we might have expected that introverts would live more happily in the serenity of their less-stressed contemplative lives, extroverts are happier—whether living alone or with others, whether living in rural or metropolitan areas, and whether working in solitary or social occupations.

With each of these trait-happiness correlations, the causal arrows are uncertain. For example, does happiness make people more outgoing? Or are outgoing people temperamentally more high-spirited and less anxious about reaching out to others? Such tendencies may explain

"We all live with the objective of being happy; our lives are all different and yet the same."—Anne Frank

So are Americans happier now than 38 years ago? From 1957 to 1996, the proportion of those telling the University of Chicago's National Opinion Research Center that they are "very happy" has declined slightly, from 35% to 30%. Meanwhile, divorce has doubled, teen suicide has tripled, arrests for juvenile violent crime have increased sixfold, and depression rates have soared. The same is true of European countries and Japan: Although people in affluent countries enjoy better nutrition, health care, education, and science—and are somewhat happier than people in very poor countries—increasing

joy persists undiminished. In one National Institute on Aging study of 5,000 adults, the happiest of people in 1973 were still relatively happy a decade later, despite changes in their work, their residence, and their family status.

In study after study, four traits characterize happy people. First, happy people, especially in individualistic Western cultures, like themselves. On **self-esteem** tests, they agree with statements such as "I'm a lot of fun to be with" and "I have good ideas." As we might expect from the typically better-than-neutral levels of well-being, most their marrying sooner, getting better jobs, and making more friends. If these traits indeed predispose happiness, people might become happier by acting as if they had the desired traits. In experiments, people who feign high self-esteem begin feeling better about themselves, and people manipulated into a smiling expression feel happier.

Yet happiness seems modifiable only within limits imposed by our genetic leash. From their study of 254 identical and fraternal twins, psychologists David Lykken and Auke Tellegen estimate that 50% of the difference among people's happiness ratings is heritable. Even identical twins raised apart often are similarly happy. Depending on our outlooks and recent experiences, our happiness fluctuates around our happiness set point, which disposes some people to be every upbeat, and others dour.

The Relationships of Happy People

Close relationships also mark happy lives. One could easily imagine why the stress of close relationships might exacerbate illness and misery. "Hell is other people," mused Jean-Paul Sartre. Thankfully, however, the benefits of close relationships with friends and family usually outweigh the strains. Compared with people bereft of such relationships, those who can name several intimate friends are healthier, less likely to die prematurely, and happier. Psychologist William Pavot has found that people report happier feelings when with others.

For more than nine in 10 people, the most significant alternative to aloneness is marriage. Although broken marital relationships are a source of much misery, a supportive, intimate, committed relationship is among life's greatest satisfactions. To paraphrase Henry Ward Beecher, "Well-married a person is winged; ill-matched, shackled." Fortunately, National Opinion Research Center

Years of Happy Life, By Country

Nation	Average number of happy years
Iceland	62.0
Sweden	61.5
Switzerland	59.8
Australia	59.5
United States	57.8
Japan	53.0
Israel	47.9
China	43.8
Brazil	42.9
South Africa	38.2
India	36.4
Russia	34.5

To compare the quality of life in different countries, Dutch social psychologist Ruut Veenhoven combines the average life expectancy with public-opinion polls in which citizens report their level of happiness and satisfaction with life. "Happy life expectancy" levels ranked highest in northwestern Europe and lowest in Africa and in former Soviet-bloc countries.

Source: *Washington Post*

surveys reveal that three in four married Americans say their spouse is their best friend, and four out of five say they would marry the same person again. Such feelings help explain why, during the 1970s and 1980s, more married adults said they were "very happy" than did never-marrieds (39% vs. 24%).

Is marriage, as is so often supposed, more strongly associated with men's happiness than women's? In both European and North American national surveys, the happiness gap between the married and never-married is similar for women and men. A digest of nearly a hundred such studies confirms this: Although a bad marriage may be more depressing to a woman than to a man, the myth that single women report greater happiness than married women can be laid to rest.

The Faith of Happy People

"Joy is the serious business of heaven," said C. S. Lewis. Freud had the opposite opinion: Religion, he said, is an illusion that *erodes* happiness or even becomes a sort of sickness—an "obsessional neurosis" accompanied by guilt, repressed sexuality, and suppressed emotions.

Accumulating data contradict Freud's surmise. Actively religious people are much less likely to become delinquent, to abuse drugs and alcohol, to divorce, and to commit suicide. In Europe and North America, religiously active people also report greater happiness. In one Gallup Poll, highly spiritual people were twice as likely as those lowest in spiritual commitment to declare themselves very happy. Other surveys find that happiness and life satisfaction rise with strength of religious affiliation and frequency of worship attendance. One statistical digest of research among the elderly found that one of the best predictors of life satisfaction is religiousness.

Studies have probed the connection between faith and coping with a crisis. Recently widowed women who worship regularly report more joy in their lives than do religiously inactive widows. Deeply religious mothers of disabled children are less vulnerable to depression than are their irreligious counterparts. Those with a strong faith also recover greater happiness after suffering divorce, unemployment, or serious illness.

attenders. A religious world view may offer people answers to life's deepest questions and an optimistic appraisal of life events. Faith offers hope when people face the terror of death. Such proposed explanations await further exploration.

So, knowing people's age, sex, and income (assuming they have

satisfying work and leisure experiences—those that typically engage an unselfconscious "flow" state in which challenges examine happy people's exercise patterns, cultural world views, and goal-strivings.

This new research on subjective well-being is a welcome complement both to societal emphases on physical and material well-being and to psychology's historic preoccupation with negative emotions. By asking who is happy, and why, the scientific study of well-being can help people rethink their priorities. And it can help us all better understand how to build a world that enhances human well-being.

"Joy, beautiful spark of the gods! . . . All people become brothers where you abide."—Friedrich Schiller

What explains these positive links between faith and well-being? Possible explanations include the supportive close relationships often enjoyed by those active in faith communities, the sense of meaning and purpose that many people derive from their faith, and the motivation to focus beyond self. The Gallup Organization consistently finds doubled rates of volunteerism and quadrupled rates of charitable giving among weekly church attenders compared with non-

enough to afford life's necessities) hardly clues us to their happiness. William Cowper's 1782 hunch has proven right: "Happiness depends, as Nature shows, Less on exterior things than most suppose." Better clues come from knowing a person's traits, whether the person enjoys a supportive network of close relationships, and whether the person has a faith that entails social support, purpose, and hope. Additional studies have defined the marks of

About the Authors
David G. Myers is professor of psychology at Hope College and author of *The Pursuit of Happiness: Who Is Happy—And Why* (Avon, 1993). His address is Department of Psychology, Hope College, Holland, Michigan 49422. Telephone 1-616-395-7730; fax 1-616-395-7121; e-mail myers@hope.edu.

Ed Diener is professor of psychology at the University of Illinois, where he and his collaborators have studied subjective well-being (happiness and life-satisfaction) for more than a decade. He is president of the International Society of Quality of Life Studies. His address is University of Illinois, Department of Psychology, 603 East Daniel Street, Champaign, Illinois 61820. Telephone 1-217-333-4804; fax 1-217-244-5876; e-mail ediener@s.psych.uiuc.edu.

Making Sense of Self-Esteem

Mark R. Leary[1]

Department of Psychology, Wake Forest University, Winston-Salem, North Carolina

Abstract

Sociometer theory proposes that the self-esteem system evolved as a monitor of social acceptance, and that the so-called self-esteem motive functions not to maintain self-esteem per se but rather to avoid social devaluation and rejection. Cues indicating that the individual is not adequately valued and accepted by other people lower self-esteem and motivate behaviors that enhance relational evaluation. Empirical evidence regarding the self-esteem motive, the antecedents of self-esteem, the relation between low self-esteem and psychological problems, and the consequences of enhancing self-esteem is consistent with the theory.

Keywords

self-esteem; self; self-regard; rejection

Self-esteem has been regarded as an important construct since the earliest days of psychology. In the first psychology textbook, William James (1890) suggested that the tendency to strive to feel good about oneself is a fundamental aspect of human nature, thereby fueling a fascination—some observers would say obsession—with self-esteem that has spanned more than a century. During that time, developmental psychologists have studied the antecedents of self-esteem and its role in human development, social psychologists have devoted attention to behaviors that appear intended to maintain self-esteem, personality psychologists have examined individual differences in the trait of self-esteem, and theorists of a variety of orientations have discussed the importance of self-regard to psychological adjustment. In the past couple of decades, practicing psychologists and social engineers have suggested that high self-esteem is a remedy for many psychological and social problems.

Yet, despite more than 100 years of attention and thousands of published studies, fundamental issues regarding self-esteem remain poorly understood. Why is self-esteem important? Do people really have a need for self-esteem? Why is self-esteem so strongly determined by how people believe they are evaluated by others? Is low self-esteem associated with psychological difficulties and, if so, why? Do efforts to enhance self-esteem reduce personal and social problems as proponents of the self-esteem movement claim?

PERSPECTIVES ON THE FUNCTION OF SELF-ESTEEM

Many writers have assumed that people seek to maintain their self-esteem because they possess an inherent "need" to feel good about themselves. However, given the apparent importance of self-esteem to psychological functioning, we must ask why self-esteem is so important and what function it might serve. Humanistic psychologists have traced high self-esteem to a congruency between a person's real and ideal selves and suggested that self-esteem signals people as to when they are behaving in self-determined, autonomous ways. Other writers have proposed that people seek high self-esteem because it facilitates goal achievement. For example, Bednar, Wells, and Peterson (1989) proposed that self-esteem is subjective feedback about the adequacy of the self. This feedback—self-esteem—is positive when the individual copes well with circumstances but negative when he or she avoids threats. In turn, self-esteem affects subsequent goal achievement; high self-esteem increases coping, and low self-esteem leads to further avoidance.

The ethological perspective (Barkow, 1980) suggests that self-esteem is an adaptation that evolved in the service of maintaining dominance in social relationships. According to this theory, human beings evolved mechanisms for monitoring dominance because dominance facilitated the acquisition of mates and other reproduction-enhancing resources. Because attention and favorable reactions from others were associated with being dominant, feelings of self-esteem became tied to social approval and deference. From this perspective, the motive to evaluate oneself positively reduces, in evolutionary terms, to the motive to enhance one's relative dominance.

One of the more controversial explanations of self-esteem is provided by terror management theory, which suggests that the function of self-esteem is to buffer people against the existential terror they experience at the prospect of their own death and annihilation (Solomon, Greenberg, & Pyszczynski, 1991). Several experiments have supported aspects of the theory, but not the strong argument that the function of the self-esteem system is to provide an emotional buffer specifically against death-related anxiety.

All of these perspectives offer insights into the nature of self-esteem, but each has conceptual and empirical difficulties (for critiques, see Leary, 1999; Leary & Baumeister, in press). In the past few years, a novel perspective—sociometer theory—has cast self-esteem in a somewhat different light as it attempts to address lingering questions about the nature of self-esteem.

SOCIOMETER THEORY

According to sociometer theory, self-esteem is essentially a psychological meter, or gauge, that monitors the quality of people's relationships with others (Leary, 1999; Leary & Baumeister, in

From *Current Directions in Psychological Science*, February 1999, pp. 32-35. © 1999 by the American Psychological Society. Reprinted by permission of Blackwell Publishers.

press; Leary & Downs, 1995). The theory is based on the assumption that human beings possess a pervasive drive to maintain significant interpersonal relationships, a drive that evolved because early human beings who belonged to social groups were more likely to survive and reproduce than those who did not (Baumeister & Leary, 1995). Given the disastrous implications of being ostracized in the ancestral environment in which human evolution occurred, early human beings may have developed a mechanism for monitoring the degree to which other people valued and accepted them. This psychological mechanism—the *sociometer*—continuously monitors the social environment for cues regarding the degree to which the individual is being accepted versus rejected by other people.

The sociometer appears to be particularly sensitive to changes in relational evaluation—the degree to which others regard their relationship with the individual as valuable, important, or close. When evidence of low relational evaluation (particularly, a decrement in relational evaluation) is detected, the sociometer attracts the person's conscious attention to the potential threat to social acceptance and motivates him or her to deal with it. The affectively laden self-appraisals that constitute the "output" of the sociometer are what we typically call self-esteem.

Self-esteem researchers distinguish between *state self-esteem*—momentary fluctuations in a person's feelings about him- or herself—and *trait self-esteem*—the person's general appraisal of his or her value; both are aspects of the sociometer. Feelings of state self-esteem fluctuate as a function of the degree to which the person perceives others currently value their relationships with him or her. Cues that connote high relational evaluation raise state self-esteem, whereas cues that connote low relational evaluation lower state self-esteem. Trait self-esteem, in contrast, reflects the person's general sense that he or she is the sort of person who is valued and accepted by other people. Trait self-esteem may be regarded as the resting state of the sociometer in the absence of incoming information relevant to relational evaluation.

SELF-ESTEEM AND ITS RELATIONSHIP TO BEHAVIOR

Sociometer theory provides a parsimonious explanation for much of what we know about self-esteem. Here I examine how sociometer theory answers four fundamental questions about self-esteem raised earlier.

The Self-Esteem Motive

As noted, many psychologists have assumed that people possess a motive or need to maintain self-esteem. According to sociometer theory, the so-called self-esteem motive does not function to maintain self-esteem but rather to minimize the likelihood of rejection (or, more precisely, relational devaluation). When people behave in ways that protect or enhance their self-esteem, they are typically acting in ways that they believe will increase their relational value in others' eyes and, thus, improve their chances of social acceptance.

The sociometer perspective explains why events that are known (or potentially known) by other people have much greater effects on self-esteem than events that are known only by the individual him- or herself. If self-esteem involved only private self-judgments, as many psychologists have assumed, public events should have no greater impact on self-esteem than private ones.

Antecedents of Self-Esteem

Previous writers have puzzled over the fact that self-esteem is so strongly tied to people's beliefs about how they are evaluated by others. If self-esteem is a *self*-evaluation, why do people judge themselves by *other* people's standards? Sociometer theory easily explains why the primary determinants of self-esteem involve the perceived reactions of other people, as well as self-judgments on dimensions that the person thinks are important to significant others. As a monitor of relational evaluation, the self-esteem system is inherently sensitive to real and potential reactions of other people.

Evidence shows that state self-esteem is strongly affected by events that have implications for the degree to which one is valued and accepted by other people (Leary, Haupt, Strausser, & Chokel, 1998; Leary, Tambor, Terdal, & Downs, 1995). The events that affect self-esteem are precisely the kinds of things that, if known by other people, would affect their evaluation and acceptance of the person (Leary, Tambor, et al., 1995). Most often, self-esteem is lowered by failure, criticism, rejection, and other events that have negative implications for relational evaluation; self-esteem rises when a person succeeds, is praised, or experiences another's love—events that are associated with relational appreciation. Even the mere possibility of rejection can lower self-esteem, a finding that

makes sense if the function of the self-esteem system is to warn the person of possible relational devaluation in time to take corrective action.

The attributes on which people's self-esteem is based are precisely the characteristics that determine the degree to which people are valued and accepted by others (Baumeister & Leary, 1995). Specifically, high trait self-esteem is associated with believing that one possesses socially desirable attributes such as competence, personal likability, and physical attractiveness. Furthermore, self-esteem is related most strongly to one's standing on attributes that one believes are valued by significant others, a finding that is also consistent with sociometer theory.

In linking self-esteem to social acceptance, sociometer theory runs counter to the humanistic assumption that self-esteem based on approval from others is false or unhealthy. On the contrary, if the function of self-esteem is to avoid social devaluation and rejection, then the system must be responsive to others' reactions. This system may lead people to do things that are not always beneficial, but it does so to protect their interpersonal relationships rather than their inner integrity.

Low Self-Esteem and Psychological Problems

Research has shown that low self-esteem is related to a variety of psychological difficulties and personal problems, including depression, loneliness, substance abuse, teenage pregnancy, academic failure, and criminal behavior. The evidence in support of the link between low self-esteem and psychological problems has often been overstated; the relationships are weaker and more scattered than typically assumed (Mecca, Smelser, & Vasconcellos, 1989). Moreover, high self-esteem also has notable drawbacks. Even so, low self-esteem tends to be more strongly associated with psychological difficulties than high self-esteem.

From the standpoint of sociometer theory, these problems are caused not by low self-esteem but rather by a history of low relational evaluation, if not outright rejection. As a subjective gauge of relational evaluation, self-esteem may parallel these problems, but it is a coeffect rather than a cause. (In fact, contrary to the popular view that low self-esteem causes these problems, no direct evidence exists to document that self-esteem has any causal role in thought, emotion, or behavior.) Much research shows that interpersonal rejection results in emotional problems, difficulties relating with others, and maladaptive efforts to be accepted (e.g., excessive dependency, membership in deviant groups), precisely the concomitants of low self-esteem (Leary, Schreindorfer, & Haupt, 1995). In addition, many personal problems lower self-esteem because they lead other people to devalue or reject the individual.

Consequences of Enhancing Self-Esteem

The claim that self-esteem does not cause psychological outcomes may appear to fly in the face of evidence showing that interventions that enhance self-esteem do, in fact, lead to positive psychological changes. The explanation for the beneficial effects of programs that enhance self-esteem is that these interventions change people's perceptions of the degree to which they are socially valued individuals. Self-esteem programs always include features that would be expected to increase real or perceived social acceptance; for example, these programs include components aimed at enhancing social skills and interpersonal problem solving, improving physical appearance, and increasing self-control (Leary, 1999).

CONCLUSIONS

Sociometer theory suggests that the emphasis psychologists and the lay public have placed on self-esteem has been somewhat misplaced. Self-esteem is certainly involved in many psychological phenomena, but its role is different than has been supposed. Subjective feelings of self-esteem provide ongoing feedback regarding one's relational value vis-à-vis other people. By focusing on the monitor rather than on what the monitor measures, we have been distracted from the underlying interpersonal processes and the importance of social acceptance to human well-being.

Recommended Reading

Baumeister, R. F. (Ed.). (1993). *Self-esteem: The puzzle of low self-regard.* New York: Plenum Press.
Colvin, C. R., & Block, J. (1994). Do positive illusions foster mental health? An examination of the Taylor and Brown formulation. *Psychological Bulletin, 116,* 3–20.
Leary, M. R. (1999). (See References)
Leary, M. R., & Downs, D. L. (1995). (See References)
Mecca, A. M., Smelser, N. J., & Vasconcellos, J. (Eds.). (1989). (See References)

Note

1. Address correspondence to Mark Leary, Department of Psychology, Wake Forest University, Winston-Salem, NC 27109; e-mail: leary@wfu.edu.

References

Barkow, J. (1980). Prestige and self-esteem: A biosocial interpretation. In D. R. Omark, F. F. Strayer, & D. G. Freedman (Eds.), *Dominance relations: An ethological view of human conflict and social interaction* (pp. 319–332). New York: Garland STPM Press.
Baumeister, R. F., & Leary, M. R. (1995). The need to belong: Desire for interpersonal attachments as a fundamental human motivation. *Psychological Bulletin, 117,* 497–529.
Bednar, R. L., Wells, M. G., & Peterson, S. R. (1989). *Self-esteem: Paradoxes and inno-vations in clinical theory and practice.* Washington, DC: American Psychological Association.
James, W. (1890). *The principles of psychology* (Vol. 1). New York: Henry Holt.
Leary, M. R. (1999). The social and psychological importance of self-esteem. In R. M. Kowalski & M. R. Leary (Eds.), *The social psychology of emotional and behavioral problems: Interfaces of social and clinical psychology* (pp. 197–221). Washington, DC: American Psychological Association.
Leary, M. R., & Baumeister, R. F. (in press). The nature and function of self-esteem: Sociometer theory. *Advances in Experimental Social Psychology.*
Leary, M. R., & Downs, D. L. (1995). Interpersonal functions of the self-esteem motive: The self-esteem system as a sociometer. In M. H. Kernis (Ed.), *Efficacy, agency, and self-esteem* (pp. 123–144). New York: Plenum Press.
Leary, M. R., Haupt, A. L., Strausser, K. S., & Chokel, J. L. (1998). Calibrating the sociometer: The relationship between interpersonal appraisals and state self-esteem. *Journal of Personality and Social Psychology, 74,* 1290–1299.
Leary, M. R., Schreindorfer, L. S., & Haupt, A. L. (1995). The role of self-esteem in emotional and behavioral problems: Why is low self-esteem dysfunctional? *Journal of Social and Clinical Psychology, 14,* 297–314.
Leary, M. R., Tambor, E. S., Terdal, S. J., & Downs, D. L. (1995). Self-esteem as an interpersonal monitor. The sociometer hypothesis. *Journal of Personality and Social Psychology, 68,* 518–530.
Mecca, A. M., Smelser, N. J., & Vasconcellos, J. (Eds.). (1989). *The social importance of self-esteem.* Berkeley: University of California Press.
Solomon, S., Greenberg, J., & Pyszczynski, T. (1991). A terror management theory of social behavior: The psychological functions of self-esteem and cultural worldviews. *Advances in Experimental Social Psychology, 24,* 93–159.

In Forecasting Their Emotions, Most People Flunk Out

By PHILIP J. HILTS

Everyone is a forecaster, says Dr. Daniel Gilbert, a psychologist at Harvard University, trafficking not in the day-to-day weather, but in individual emotional barometers.

And in making decisions, any decisions, people rely on their individual forecasts to determine how their choices will make them feel in the future, and then use those forecasts to guide their choices. But, like some weather forecasts, it appears those predictions are often wrong, according to an array of data from a small but growing field of psychology.

Beginning a recent scientific paper in The Journal of Personality and Social Psychology, Dr. Gilbert wrote: "Imagine that one morning your telephone rings and you find yourself talking to the King of Sweden, who informs you in surprisingly good English that you have been selected as this year's recipient of a Nobel Prize. How would you

feel and how long would you feel that way?"

Then, he continued: "Now imagine that the telephone call is from your college president, who regrets to inform you (in surprisingly good English) that the Board of Regents has dissolved your department, revoked your appointment and stored your books in little cardboard boxes in the hallway. How would you feel and how long would you feel that way?"

In the second instance, Dr. Gilbert wrote, "Losing one's livelihood has all the hallmarks of a major catastrophe, and most people would expect this news to have an enduring negative impact on their emotional lives."

But, he added, "Such expectations are often important and often wrong."

Dr. Gilbert studied more than 100 college professors before and after

they found out whether they had achieved tenure. He found that the educators expected to be quite happy if chosen, and quite unhappy if not. But those predictions were wrong. Those who got tenure were happy, but not as happy as they themselves had predicted. And those who were denied tenure did not become very unhappy.

There is a now a long list of such experiments.

Lottery winners, for example, were interviewed several times after they won big jackpots (averaging almost $500,000). While people expected to feel considerably happier for a long time, the winners, after a very brief euphoria, in fact found their level of happiness settling quickly back to average.

Students, asked whether they would be happier going to school in California or in a colder climate, predicted they would be happier in

California, both because of the climate, and over all. In fact, students were equally happy in different parts of the country, despite the climate.

And people who were tested for Huntington's disease or H.I.V. infection expected to be devastated if the news was bad, but most often they were not; in fact, those who remained most anxious were those who decided not to be tested or, in the case of testing for Huntington's, were not to be told their test results.

People are aware that they are bad at some predictions. Dr. George Loewenstein of the Center for the

---

A study's lesson: You never know how you'll feel later on.

Advanced Study in the Behavioral Sciences at Carnegie Mellon University offered some well-known examples of the results of poor forecasting: "Besides marrying too young, there is shopping for groceries on an empty stomach; professions of love during moments of lust; believing you can 'eat just one chip.' "

There is a pattern to the way people get predictions wrong, and understanding the pattern may be useful, researchers say.

For example, people are most often right when they describe what makes them feel good or bad, but are often wrong when asked to predict how strongly they will feel that way, and how long the feeling will last.

The problem comes with the nature of feelings, caused by strong chemical events in the brain that occur after an experience. The feeling itself quickly dies, as the mind shifts attention and the surge of chemicals subsides. When the event is recalled later, the rush of the feeling recurs, but to a lesser degree.

Dr. Gilbert points out that this is not just the gradual lessening of vividness, but that the mind has a number of active processes that alter the memory and blunt the feeling on purpose. Beginning almost immediately, we obscure the irritating or humiliating in the same way an oyster covers a grain of sand with a layer of smooth pearl.

Studies have shown that even severe life events have a negative impact on people's sense of well-being and satisfaction for no more than three months, after which their feelings at least go back to normal.

"Most people are reasonably happy most of the time, and most events do little to change that for long," Dr. Gilbert said.

He quotes Sir Thomas Browne, a 17th-century writer, who said: "I am the happiest man alive. I have that in me that can convert poverty into riches, adversity into prosperity, and I am more invulnerable than Achilles; fortune hath not one place to hit me."

Dr. Gilbert said that whatever that thing was that Browne claimed to have, "most ordinary people seem to have it, too."

"In science, literature and folklore," Dr. Gilbert said, "people are famous for making the best of bad situations, remembering their successes and overlooking their excesses, trumpeting their triumphs and excusing their mistakes. Psychologists from Freud to Festinger have described the artful methods by which the human mind ignores, augments, transforms and rearranges information in its unending battle" against the bad feelings produced by the world and things in it.

One primary reason people do not get predictions right about their own future feelings and tastes is that people forget these powers, this "immune system" that blunts bad feeling and helps them adjust.

In experiments, the researchers found that when people tried to predict future feelings, they most often failed to take into account their capacity to discount bad events. But as

soon as the bad events occurred, they made full use of those powers.

In one example, students were given personality ratings by two methods—a rating by computerized test and a rating by a panel of qualified and experienced psychologists. They said they expected that they would feel equally bad if given the lowest rating by either method. But when the scores came in, within seconds, those given the lowest rating by computer felt better and commented on the unreliability of the computer method.

Dr. Daniel Kahneman of Princeton University said that different areas of scholarship, and economics in particular, built their descriptions of behavior on the assumptions that people were both rational in making choices and were able to predict how they would feel in the future.

The most obvious import of the new research came when people were asked to predict their future states and to make decisions based on those predictions—in giving informed consent to become part of medical experiments, or in signing directives about what medical treatment they might want near death.

Peter Ditto, a psychologist at the University of California at Irvine who has studied the matter, pointed out that people changed their minds about these issues. In his studies, he said, "Even people who say they 'definitely want' or 'definitely don't want' treatment often change their wishes."

The researchers also noted that in trying to devise treatment for criminals, research of the past made the mistake of assuming that criminals' choices to commit crimes were rational. In fact, Dr. Loewenstein reported, a large part of criminal decision-making was emotional and criminals were unable to predict that effectively ahead of time.

When ordinary students were asked how likely they were to commit certain sexual acts, their predictions changed radically if they were sexually aroused prior to having the questions asked. Their own sexual aggressiveness changed and when sexually aroused the students "were more likely to imagine that they would behave in a sexually forceful manner on a date." What is more, the students did not expect this difference to occur.

Dr. Kahneman of Princeton pointed out that new findings across the field challenged the economic theories on which government and commercial policies were made. If people do not really predict what is good even for themselves, then it becomes important to measure the consequences of social and political decisions, to measure how much a policy improves citizens' well-being.

He first wrote about the utility of doubting one's own predictive powers about eight years ago, he said, after having learned what he called the "squeaking door" lesson.

"Twenty years ago, my wife and I moved, and we quarreled about bedroom curtains," Dr. Kahneman said in a telephone interview. She had curtains that he thought were "truly dreadful." (They were brown with vertical stripes.)

The fight escalated as each became more entrenched, until finally it became a question of who would yield and why. He knew he did not like the curtains, but he asked himself if he would always feel that way. "Would they remain forever like a squeaking door that you never get used to?" he said. "I decided that if I would always dislike them, I shouldn't yield. But if I could get used to them, I should probably yield."

He did yield, and discovered later that not only had he become used to the curtains, but he had actually come to like them. They had the opposite experience buying a house, he said, when they had to decide whether to pay much more for a water view. If they got used to it and ended up paying little attention, it was not worth the money.

"We have never gotten used to it," he said. "The pleasure we get from the view is unending. It was worth it."

Unit 2

Key Points to Consider

❖ Why does the representativeness heuristic so strongly affect our judgments? Why would such a heuristic even exist? Can you think of any ways to counteract its effects?

❖ Thomas Gilovich demonstrates in his article how we can sometimes perceive patterns where none exist—even in the apparent "hot hand" of basketball players. Can you think of any examples from your own life in which you misperceived essentially random events as being connected?

❖ What does it mean to say that some parts of the social inference process are "automatic" and some are "controlled"? Why is that distinction important for our understanding of the perception process?

❖ How would you summarize the phenomenon known as "behavioral confirmation"? What is actually being "confirmed"? What circumstances make behavioral confirmation more likely to occur? Less likely? Why?

 **Links** www.dushkin.com/online/

6. **Cognitive and Psychological Sciences on the Internet**
   http://matia.stanford.edu/cogsci/
7. **Nonverbal Behavior and Nonverbal Communication**
   http://zen.sunderland.ac.uk/~hb5jma/1stbersn.htm

These sites are annotated on pages 4 and 5.

Pretend that I have just asked you your position on gun control, the name of your favorite television program, and how many children you plan on having. Now assume that I also ask you to estimate what proportion of the U.S. population holds the same attitude about guns, likes the same program, or plans on having that same number of children. If you are like most people, there is a good chance that your estimates of what the general population thinks on an issue will be influenced by your own opinion. In short, most of us believe that our own attitudes and preferences are relatively common in the population, and that alternate attitudes and preferences are less common. This tendency to see our own preferences as being widely shared by others is referred to as the "false consensus effect."

This phenomenon is just one example of the kinds of topics that fall under the heading of social cognition, a broad area that may loosely be defined as how people think about the social world. That is, the emphasis in this area is on the thought processes people engage in when they think about others. The emphasis in social cognition research, then, is usually on how people think, rather than on the content of those thoughts. For example, one issue of importance to those who study social cognition is what happens to the information we acquire about other people. How is such information about people stored and organized in memory? How is it accessed and retrieved later on? After retrieval, how is it used to help us understand and interpret the world?

Pretend that you are the personnel director of a large company and have the job of interviewing hundreds of prospective employees for that company every year. The total amount of time and money that will be invested in these new employees will be enormous; thus, the consequences of hiring the wrong people will be serious. In each interview, you must try to answer a number of important questions: How honest is this candidate? How dependable? How will he or she fit in with the other employees?

This hypothetical situation is an example of social perception, or the process by which one individual makes inferences about another individual. As you might imagine, this is a very important ability for humans to have, because there are many times when it is important to reach an accurate understanding about what kind of person someone else is. When the behavior of others, such as employees and spouses, has important implications for us, then the ability to successfully predict how such people will act in the future can be critical. It should not be surprising, then, to discover that social psychology has been interested in this topic for decades.

One approach to this topic has been to study "impression formation"—the process by which we form an initial impression of someone with whom we are not familiar. Research indicates that we form such impressions quite quickly, often on the basis of very little information. One kind of information that

is often available in such situations—and that is therefore frequently used—is group membership, that is, the person's sex, race, age, social class, etc. Beyond such obvious kinds of information, we also use the person's words and actions to reach an initial impression.

The three articles included in the first part of this unit illustrate the variety of issues that have been addressed within the area of social cognition. The first selection, "Like Goes with Like: The Role of Representativeness in Erroneous and Pseudoscientific Beliefs," describes how a common mental shortcut that we all use—the representativeness heuristic—can actually lead us to accept incorrect beliefs. Because certain things just seem to us to "go together," we are at risk of ignoring real evidence that they do not. The next selection addresses an important issue in contemporary social psychology, the distinction between automatic and controlled mental processes. In "The Seed of Our Undoing," Daniel Wegner describes some research he has done on the phenomenon of "ironic" mental processes—when our attempts to control our thoughts in a particular way lead to the *opposite* result. Wegner argues that this occurs because "ironic" processes automatically operate whenever we also engage in deliberate efforts at thought control. Finally, in "Something Out of Nothing: The Misperception and Misinterpretation of Random Data," Thomas Gilovich describes the almost overwhelming tendency that people have to look for pattern and order in the world. As he illustrates with an interesting example, this tendency can lead us to see order where none really exists.

The second subsection in this unit deals with social perception. In the first article, "Inferential Hopscotch: How People Draw Social Inferences from Behavior," the authors review recent research that indicates that drawing inferences actually consists of multiple steps. The initial step is typically rather quick and automatic; in it, the behavior is immediately interpreted as evidence of an underlying trait. In the more conscious and effortful second step, however, we deliberately try to take into account other factors that might have influenced the behavior. The second article, "Face It!" by Deborah Blum, describes how we read the split-second expressions that cross people's faces all day long to help us know others. Then "Motivational Approaches to Expectancy Confirmation," deals with an interesting phenomenon known as the self-fulfilling prophecy—when our expectancies about people lead us to act differently toward them, and this behavior then prompts them to act in ways that confirm the expectancy. In this selection, John Copeland reviews recent research on motivational factors that can either make this phenomenon more likely or less likely to occur. The fourth selection in this subsection, "Culture, Ideology, and Construal," describes how some social perception processes, especially attribution, can be affected by cultural and regional factors.

Like Goes with Like:

The Role of Representativeness in Erroneous and Pseudoscientific Beliefs

The misguided premise that effects should resemble their causes under-lies a host of erroneous beliefs, from folk wisdom about health and the human body to elaborate pseudoscientific belief systems.

THOMAS GILOVICH and KENNETH SAVITSKY

It was in 1983, at an infectious-disease conference in Brussells, that Barry Marshall, an internal-medicine resident from Perth, Australia, first staked his startling claim. He argued that the peptic ulcer, a painful crater in the lining of the stomach or duodenum, was not caused by a stressful lifestyle as everyone had thought. Instead, the malady that afflicts millions of adults in the United States alone was caused by a simple bacterium, and thus could be cured using antibiotics (Hunter 1993; Monmaney 1993; Peterson 1991; Wandycz 1993).

Although subsequent investigations have substantiated Marshall's claim (e.g., Hentschel et al. 1993), his colleagues initially were highly skeptical. Martin Blaser, director of the Division of Infectious Diseases at the Vanderbilt University

School of Medicine, described Marshall's thesis as "the most preposterous thing I'd every heard" (Monmaney 1993).

What made the idea so preposterous? Why were the experts so resistant to Marshall's suggestion? There were undoubtedly many reasons. For one, the claim contradicted what most physicians, psychiatrists, and psychologists knew (or thought they knew): Ulcers were caused by stress. As one author noted, "No physical ailment has ever been more closely tied to psychological turbulence" (Monmaney 1993, p. 64). In addition, science is necessarily and appropriately a rather conservative enterprise. Although insight, creativity, and even leaps of faith are vital to the endeavor, sound empirical evidence is the true coin of the realm. Much of the medical establishment's hesitation doubtless stemmed from the same healthy skepticism that readers of the SKEPTICAL INQUIRER have learned to treasure. After all, Marshall's results at the time were suggestive at best—no cause-effect relationship had yet been established.

But there may have been a third reason for the reluctance to embrace Marshall's contention, a reason we explore in this article. The belief that ulcers derive from stress is particularly seductive—for physicians and laypersons alike—because it flows from a general tendency of human judgment, a tendency to employ what psychologists Amos Tversky and Daniel Kahneman have called the "representativeness heuristic" (Kahneman and Tversky 1972, 1973; Tversky and Kahneman 1974, 1982). Indeed, we believe that judgment by representativeness plays a role in a host of erroneous beliefs, from beliefs about health and the human body to handwriting analysis and astrology (Gilovich 1991). We consider a sample of these beliefs in this article.

The Representativeness Heuristic

Representativeness is but one of a number of heuristics that people use to render complex problems manageable. Heuristics are often described

BRAD

Brad Marshall

as judgmental shortcuts that generally get us where we need to go—and quickly—but at the cost of occasionally sending us off course. Kahneman and Tversky liken them to perceptual cues, which generally enable us to perceive the world accurately, but occasionally give rise to misperception and illusion. Consider their example of using clarity as a cue for distance. The clarity of an object is one cue people use to decide how far away it is. The cue typically works well because the farther away something is, the less distinct it appears. On a particularly clear day, however, objects can appear closer than they are, and on hazy days they can appear farther away. In some circumstances, then, this normally accurate cue can lead to error.

Representativeness works much the same way. The representativeness heuristic involves a reflexive tendency to assess the similarity of objects and events along salient dimensions and to organize them on the basis of one overarching rule: "Like goes with like." Among other things, the representativeness heuristic reflects the belief that a member of a given category ought to resemble the cause that produced it. Thus, the representativeness heuristic is often used to assess

Thomas Gilovich, professor of psychology at Cornell University and a Fellow of CSICOP, is the author of How We Know What Isn't So: The Fallibility of Human Reason in Everyday Life. *Kenneth Savitsky is a doctoral student in social psychology at Cornell University.*

"Heuristics are often described as judgmental shortcuts that generally get us where we need to go—and quickly—but at the cost of occasionally sending us off course."

whether a given instance belongs to a particular category, such as whether an individual is likely to be an accountant or a comedian. It is also used in assigning causes to effects, as when deciding whether a meal of spicy food caused a case of heartburn or determining whether an assassination was the product of a conspiracy.[1]

Note that judgment by representativeness often works well. Instances often resemble their category prototypes and causes frequently resemble their effects. Members of various occupational groups, for example, frequently do resemble the group prototype. Likewise, "big" effects (such as the development of the atomic bomb) are often brought about by "big" causes (such as the Manhattan Project).

Still, the representativeness heuristic is only that—a heuristic or shortcut. As with all shortcuts, the representativeness heuristic should be used with caution. Although it can help us to make some judgments with accuracy and ease, it can also lead us astray. Not all members fit the category prototype. Some comedians are shy or taciturn, and some accountants are wild and crazy. And although causes are frequently representative of their effects, this relationship does not always hold: Tiny viruses give rise to devastating epidemics like malaria or AIDS; and splitting the nucleus of an atom releases an awesome amount of energy. In some cases, then, representativeness yields inaccuracy and error. Or even superstition. A nice example is provided by craps shooters, who roll the dice gently to coax a low number, and more vigorously to encourage a high one (Hanslin 1967). A small effect (low number) requires a small cause (gentle roll), and a big effect (high number) requires a big cause (vigorous roll).

How might the belief in a stress-ulcer link derive from the conviction that like goes with like? Because the burning feeling of an ulcerated stomach is not unlike the gut-wrenching, stomach-churning feeling of extreme stress (albeit more severe), the link seems natural: Stress is a representative cause of an ulcer.[2] But as Marshall suggested (and subsequent research has borne out), the link may be overblown. Stress alone does not appear to cause ulcers (Glavin and Szabo 1992; Soll 1990).

Representativeness and the Conjunction Fallacy

One of the most compelling demonstrations of how the representativeness heuristic can interfere with sound judgment comes from a much-discussed experiment in which participants were asked to consider the following description (Tversky and Kahneman 1982, 1983):

> Linda is 31 years old, single, outspoken, and very bright. She majored in philosophy. As a student, she was deeply concerned with issues of discrimination and social justice, and also participated in anti-nuclear demonstrations.
>
> Now, based on the above description, rank the following statements about Linda, from most to least likely:
> a. Linda is an insurance salesperson.
> b. Linda is a bank teller.
> c. Linda is a bank teller and is active in the feminist movement.

If you are like most people, you probably thought it was more likely that "Linda is a bank teller and is active in the feminist movement" than that "Linda is a bank teller." It is easy to see why: A feminist bank teller is much more representative of the description of Linda that is "just" a bank teller. It reflects the political activism, social-consciousness, and left-of-center politics implied in the description.

It may make sense, but it cannot be. The category "bank teller" subsumes the category "is a bank teller and is active in the feminist movement." The latter therefore cannot be more likely than the former. Anyone who is a bank teller and is active in the feminist movement is automatically also a bank teller. Indeed, even if one thinks it is impossible for someone with Linda's description to be solely a bank teller (that is, one who is not a feminist), being a bank teller is still *as* likely as being both. This error is referred to as the "conjunction fallacy" because the probability of two events co-occurring (i.e., their conjunction) can never exceed the individual probability of either of the constituents (Tversky and Kahneman 1982, 1983; Dawes and Mulford 1993).

Such is the logic of the situation. The psychology we bring to bear on it is something else. If we start with an unrepresentative outcome (being

"In ancient Chinese medicine, for example, people with vision problems were fed ground bat in the mistaken belief that bats had particularly keen vision and that some of this ability might be transferred to the recipient."

a bank teller) and then add a representative element (being active in the feminist movement), we create a description that is at once more psychologically compelling but objectively less likely. The rules of representativeness do not follow the laws of probability. A detailed description can seem compelling precisely because of the very details that, objectively speaking, actually make it less likely. Thus, someone may be less concerned about dying during a trip to the Middle East than about dying in a terrorist attack while there, even though the probability of death due to a *particular* cause is obviously lower than the probability of death due to the set of all possible causes. Likewise, the probability of global economic collapse can seem remote until one sketches a detailed scenario in which such a collapse follows, say, the destruction of the oil fields in the Persian Gulf. Once again, the additional details make the outcome less likely at the same time that they make it more psychologically compelling.

Representativeness and Causal Judgments

Most of the empirical research on the representativeness heuristic is similar to the work on the conjunction fallacy in that the judgments people make are compared to a normative standard—in this case, to the laws of probability. The deleterious effect of judgment by representativeness is thereby established by the failure to meet such a standard. Previous work conducted in this fashion has shown, for example, that judgment by representativeness leads people to commit the "gambler's fallacy," to overestimate the reliability of small samples of data, and to be insufficiently "regressive" in making predictions under conditions of uncertainty.

The ulcer example with which we began this article does not have this property of being obviously at variance with a clear-cut normative standard. The same is true of nearly all examples of the impact of representativeness on causal judgments: It can be difficult to establish with certainty that a judgmental error has been made. Partly for this reason, there has been less empirical research on representativeness and causal judgments than on other areas, such as representativeness and the conjunction fallacy. This is

not because representativeness is thought to have little impact on causal judgments, but because without a clear-cut normative standard it is simply more difficult to conduct research in this domain. The research that has been conducted, furthermore, is more suggestive than definitive. Nonetheless, the suggestive evidence is rather striking, and it points to the possibility that representativeness may exert at least as much influence over causal judgments as it does over other, more exhaustively researched types of judgments. To see how much, we discuss some examples of representativeness-thinking in medicine, in pseudo-scientific systems, and in psychoanalysis.

Representativeness and Medical Beliefs

One area in which the impact of representativeness on causal judgments is particularly striking is the domain of health and medicine. Historically, people have often assumed that the symptoms of a disease should resemble either its cause or its cure (or both). In ancient Chinese medicine, for example, people with vision problems were fed ground bat in the mistaken belief that bats had particularly keen vision and that some of this ability might be transferred to the recipient (Deutsch 1977). Evans-Pritchard (1937) noted many examples of the influence of representativeness among the African Azande (although he discussed them in the context of magical-thinking, not representativeness). For instance, the Azande used the ground skull of the red bush monkey to cure epilepsy. Why? The cure should resemble the disease, so the herky-jerky movements of the monkey make the essence of monkey appear to be a promising candidate to settle the violent movements of an epileptic seizure. As Evans-Pritchard (quoted in Nisbett and Ross 1980, p. 116) put it:

> Generally the logic of therapeutic treatment consists in the selection of the most prominent external symptoms, the naming of the disease after some object in nature it resembles, and the utilization of the object as the principal ingredient in the drug administered to cure the disease. The circle may even be completed by belief that the external symptoms not only yield to treatment by the object which resembles them but are caused by it as well.

"The representativeness heuristic should be used with caution. Although it can help us to make some judgments with accuracy and ease, it can also lead us astray."

Western medical practice has likewise been guided by the representativeness heuristic. For instance, early Western medicine was strongly influenced by what was known as the "doctrine of signatures," or the belief that "every natural substance which possesses any medicinal virtue indicates by an obvious and well-marked external character the disease for which it is a remedy, or the object for which it should be employed" (quoted in Nisbett and Ross 1980, p. 116). Thus, physicians prescribed the lungs of the fox (known for its endurance) for asthmatics, and the yellow spice turmeric for jaundice. Again, disease and cure are linked because they resemble one another.

Or consider the popularity of homeopathy, which derives from the eighteenth century work of the German physician Samuel Hahnemann (Barrett 1987). One of the bedrock principles of homeopathy is Hahnemann's "law of similars," according to which the key to discovering what substance will cure a particular disorder lies in noting the effect that various substances have on healthy people. If a substance causes a particular reaction in an unafflicted person, then it is seen as a likely cure for a disease characterized by those same symptoms. As before, the external symptoms of a disease are used to identify a cure for the disease—a cure that manifests the same external characteristics.

Of course, there are instances in which substances that cause particular symptoms *are* used effectively as part of a therapeutic regimen to cure, alleviate, or prevent those very symptoms. Vaccines deliver small quantities of disease-causing viruses to help individuals develop immunities. Likewise, allergy sufferers sometimes receive periodic doses of the exact substance to which they are allergic so that they will develop a tolerance over time. The problem with the dubious medical practices described above is the *general* assumption that the symptoms of a disease should resemble its cause, its cure, or both. Limiting the scope of possible cures to those that are representative of the disease can seriously impede scientific discovery. Such a narrow focus, for example, would have inhibited the discovery of the two most significant developments of modern medicine: sanitation and antibiotics.

Representativeness-thinking continues to abound in modern "alternative" medicine, a pursuit that appears to be gaining in perceived legitimacy. (Cowley, King, Hager, and Rosenberg 1995). An investigation by Congress into health fraud and quackery noted several examples of what appear to be interventions inspired by the superficial appeal of representativeness (U.S. Congress, House Subcommittee on Health and Long-Term Care 1984). In one set of suggested treatments, patients are encouraged to eat raw organ concentrates corresponding to the dysfunctional body part: e.g., brain concentrates for mental disorders, heart concentrates for cardiac conditions, and raw stomach lining for ulcers. Similarly, the fingerprints of representativeness are all over the practice of "rebirthing," a New Age therapeutic technique in which individuals attempt to reenact their own births in an effort to correct personality defects caused by having been born in an "unnatural" fashion (Ward 1994). One person who was born breech (i.e., feet first) underwent the rebirthing procedure to cure his sense that his life was always going in the wrong direction and that he could never seem to get things "the right way round." Another, born Caesarean, sought the treatment because of a lifelong difficulty with seeing things to completion, and always relying on others to finish tasks for her. As one author quipped, "God knows what damage forceps might inflict . . . a lifelong neurosis that you're being dragged where you don't want to go?" (Ward 1994, p. 90).

A more rigorous examination of the kind of erroneous beliefs about health and the human body that can arise from the appeal of representativeness has dealt with the adage, "You are what you eat." Just how far do people take this idea? In certain respects, the saying is undeniably true: Bodies are composed to a large extent of the molecules that were once ingested as food. Quite literally, we are what we have eaten. Indeed, there are times when we take on the character of what we ingest: People gain weight by eating fatty foods, and a person's skin can acquire an orange tint from the carotene found in carrots and tomatoes. But the notion that we develop the characteristics of the food we eat sometimes goes beyond such examples to almost magical extremes. The Hua of Papua New Guinea, for example, believe that individuals will grow quickly if they eat rapidly growing food (Meigs 1984, cited by Nemeroff and Rozin 1989).

But what about a more "scientifically minded" population? Psychologists Carol Nemeroff and Paul Rozin (1989) asked college students to consider a hypothetical culture known as the "Chandorans," who hunt wild boar and marine turtles. Some of the students learned that the Chandorans hunt turtles for their shells, and wild boar for their meat. The others heard the opposite: The tribe hunts turtles for their meat, and boar for their tusks.

After reading one of the two descriptions of the Chandorans, the students were asked to rate the tribe members on numerous characteristics. Their responses reflected a belief that the characteristics of the food that was eaten would "rub off" onto the tribe members. Boar-eaters were thought to be more aggressive and irritable than their counterparts—and more likely to have beards! The turtle-eaters were thought to live longer and be better swimmers.

However educated a person may be (the participants in Nemeroff and Rozin's experiment were University of Pennsylvania undergraduates), it can be difficult to get beyond the assumption that like goes with like. In this case, it leads to the belief that individuals tend to acquire the attributes of the food they ingest. Simple representativeness.

Representativeness and Pseudoscientific Beliefs

A core tenet of the field of astrology is that an individual's personality is influenced by the astrological sign under which he or she was born (Huntley 1990). A glance at the personality types associated with the various astrological signs reveals an uncanny concordance between the supposed personality of someone with a particular sign and the characteristics associated with the sign's namesake (Huntley 1990; Howe 1970; Zusne and Jones 1982). Those born under the sign of the goat (Capricorn) are said to be tenacious, hardworking, and stubborn; whereas those born under the lion (Leo) are proud, forceful leaders. Likewise, those born under the sign of Cancer (the crab) share with their namesake a tendency to appear hard on the outside; while inside their "shells" they are soft and vulnerable. One treatment of astrology goes so far as to suggest that, like the crab, those born under the sign of Cancer tend to be "deeply attached to their homes" (Read et al. 1978).

What is the origin of these associations? They are not empirically derived, as they have been shown time and time again to lack validity (e.g., Carlson 1985; Dean 1987; for reviews see Abell 1981; Schick and Vaughn 1995; Zusne and Jones 1982). Instead, they are conceptually driven by simple, representativeness-based assessments of the personalities that *should* be associated with various astrological signs. After all, who is more likely to be retiring and modest than a Virgo (the virgin)? Who better to be well balanced, harmonious, and fair than a Libra (the scales)? By taking advantage of people's reflexive associations, the system gains plausibility among those disinclined to dig deeper.

And it doesn't stop there. Consider another elaborate "scientific" system designed to assess the "secrets" of an individual's personality—graphology, or handwriting analysis. Corporations pay graphologists sizable fees to help screen job applicants by developing personality profiles of those who apply for jobs (Neter and Ben-Shakhar 1989). Graphologists are also called upon to provide "expert" testimony in trial proceedings, and to help the Secret Service determine if any real danger is posed by threatening letters to government officials (Scanlon and Mauro 1992). How much stock can we put in the work of handwriting analysts?

Unlike astrology, graphology is not worthless. It has been, and continues to be, the subject of careful empirical investigation (Nevo 1986), and it has been shown that people's handwriting can reveal certain things about them. Particularly shaky writing can be a clue that an individual suffers from some neurological disorder that causes hand tremors; whether a person is male or female is often apparent from his or her writing. In general, however, what handwriting analysis can determine most reliably tends to be things that can be more reliably ascertained through other means. As for the "secrets" of an individual's personality, graphology has yet to show that it is any better than astrology.

This has not done much to diminish the popularity of handwriting analysis, however. One reason for this is that graphologists, like astrologers, gain some surface plausibility or "face validity" for their claims by exploiting the tendency for people to employ the representativeness heuristic. Many of their claims have a superficial "sensible" quality, rarely violating the principle that like goes with like. Consider, for instance, the "zonal theory" of graphology, which divides a person's handwriting into the upper, middle, and lower regions. A person's "intellectual," "practical," and "instinctual" qualities supposedly correspond to the dif-

"Although skepticism is a vital component of critical thought, it should not be based on an excessive adherence to the principle that like goes with like."

ferent regions (Basil 1989). Can you guess which is which? Could our "lower" instincts be reflected anywhere other than the lower region, or our "higher" intellect anywhere other than the top?

The list of such representativeness-based "connections" goes on and on. Handwriting slants to the left? The person must be holding something back, repressing his or her true emotions. Slants to the right? The person gets carried away by his or her feelings. A signature placed far below a paragraph suggests that the individual wishes to distance himself or herself from what was written (Scanlon and Mauro 1992). Handwriting that stays close to the left margin belongs to individuals attached to the past, whereas writing that hugs the right margin comes from those oriented toward the future.

What is ironic is that the very mechanism that many graphologists rely upon to argue for the persuasive value of their endeavor—that the character of the handwriting resembles the character of the person—is what ultimately betrays them: They call it "common sense"; we call it judgment by representativeness.

Representativeness and Psychoanalysis

Two prominent social psychologists, Richard Nisbett and Lee Ross, have argued that "the enormous popularity of Freudian theory probably lies in the fact that, unlike all its competitors among contemporary views, it encourages the layperson to do what comes naturally in causal explanation, that is, to use the representativeness heuristic" (Nisbett and Ross 1980, p. 244). Although this claim would be difficult to put to empirical test, there can be little doubt that much of the interpretation of symbols that lies at the core of psychoanalytical theory is driven by representativeness. Consider the interpretation of dreams, in which the images a client reports from his or her dreams are considered indicative of underlying motives. An infinite number of potential relationships exist between dream content and underlying psychodynamics, and it is interesting that virtually all of the "meaningful" ones identified by psychodynamically oriented clinicians are ones in which there is an obvious fit or resemblance between the reported image and inner dynamics. A man

who dreams of a snake or a cigar is thought to be troubled by his penis or his sexuality. People who dream of policemen are thought to be concerned about their fathers or authority figures. Knowledge of the representativeness heuristic compels one to wonder whether such connections reflect something important about the psyche of the client, or whether they exist primarily in the mind of the therapist.

One area of psychodynamic theorizing in which the validity of such superficially plausible relationships has been tested and found wanting is the use of projective tests. The most widely known projective test is the Rorschach, in which clients report what they "see" in ambiguous blotches of ink on cards. As in all projective tests, the idea is that in responding to such an unstructured stimulus, a person must "project," and thus reveal, some of his or her inner dynamics. Countless studies, however, have failed to produce evidence that the test is valid—that is, that the assessments made about people on the basis of the test correspond to the psychopathological conditions from which they suffer (Burros 1978).[3]

The research findings notwithstanding, clinicians frequently report the Rorschach to be extremely helpful in clinical practice. Might representativeness contribute to this paradox of strongly held beliefs coexisting with the absence of any real relationship? You be the judge. A person who interprets the whole Rorschach card, and not its specific details, is considered by clinicians to suffer from a need to form a "big picture," and a tendency toward grandiosity, even paranoia. In contrast, a person who refers only to small details of the ink blots is considered to have an obsessive personality—someone who attends to detail at the expense of the more important holistic aspects (Dawes 1994). Once again, systematic research has failed to find evidence for these relationships, but the sense of representativeness gives them some superficial plausibility.

Conclusion

We have described numerous erroneous beliefs that appear to derive from the overuse of the representativeness heuristic. Many of them arise in domains in which the reach for solutions to important problems exceeds our gasp—such as the attempt to uncover (via astrology or handwriting analysis) simple cues to the complexities of human motivation and personality. In such domains in which no simple solutions exist, and yet the need or desire for such solutions remains strong, people often let down their guard. Dubious cause-effect links are then uncritically accepted because they satisfy the principle of like goes with like.

Representativeness can also have the opposite effect, inhibiting belief in valid claims that violate the expectation of resemblance. People initially scoffed at Walter Reed's suggestion that malaria was carried by the mosquito. From a representativeness standpoint, it is easy to see why: The cause (a tiny mosquito) is not at all representative of the result (a devastating disease). Reed's claim violated the notion that big effects should have big causes, and thus was difficult to accept (Nisbett and Ross 1980). Although skepticism is a vital component of critical thought, it should not be based on an excessive adherence to the principle that like goes with like.

Indeed, it is often those discoveries that violate the expected resemblance between cause and effect that are ultimately hailed as significant breakthroughs, as with the discovery of *Helicobacter pylori,* as the ulcer-causing bacterium is now named. As one author put it, "The discovery of *Helicobacter* is no crummy little shift. It's a mind-blower—tangible, reproducible, unexpected, and, yes, revolutionary. Just the fact that a bug causes peptic ulcers, long considered the cardinal example of a psychosomatic illness, is a spear in the breast of New Age medicine" (Monmaney 1993, p. 68). Given these stakes, one might be advised to avoid an overreliance on the shortcut of representativeness, and instead to devote the extra effort needed to make accurate judgments and decisions. (But not too much effort—you wouldn't want to give yourself an ulcer.)

Notes

We thank Dennis Regan for his helpful comments on an earlier draft of this article.

1. The reason that the heuristic has been dubbed "representativeness" rather than, say, "resemblance" or "similarity" is that it also applies in circumstances in which the assessment of "fit" is not based on similarity. For example, when assessing whether a series of coin flips was produced by tossing a fair coin, people's judgments are influenced in part by whether the sequence is representative of one produced by a fair coin. A sequence of five heads and five tails is a representative outcome, but a sequence of nine heads

and one tail is not. Note, however, that a fifty-fifty split does not make the sequence "similar" to a fair coin, but it does make it representative of one.

2. Some theories of the link between stress and ulcers are even more tinged with representativeness. Since the symptoms of an ulcer manifest themselves in the stomach, the cause "should" involve something that is highly characteristic of the stomach as well, such as hunger and nourishment. Thus, one theorist asserts, "The critical factor in the development of ulcers is the frustration associated with the wish to receive love—when this wish is rejected, it is converted into a wish to be fed," leading ultimately "to an ulcer." Echoing such ideas, James Masterson writes in his book *The Search for the Real Self* that ulcers affect those who are "hungering for emotional supplies that were lost in childhood or that were never sufficient to nourish the real self" (both quoted in Monmaney 1993).

3. Actually, a nonprojective use of the Rorschach, called the Exner System, has been shown to have some validity (Exner 1986). The system is based on the fact that some of the inkblots *do* look like various objects, and a person's responses are scored for the number and proportion that fail to reflect this correspondence. Unlike the usual Rorschach procedure, which is subjectively scored, the Exner system is a standardized test.

References

Abell, G. O. 1981. Astrology. In *Science and the Paranormal: Probing the Existence of the Supernatural,* ed. by G. O. Abell and B. Singer. New York: Charles Scribner's Sons.

Barrett, S. 1987. Homeopathy: Is it medicine? SKEPTICAL INQUIRER 12 (1) (Fall): 56–62.

Basil, R. 1989. Graphology and personality; Let the buyer beware. SKEPTICAL INQUIRER 13 (3) (Spring): 241–243.

Burros, O. K. 1978. *Mental Measurement Yearbook.* 8th ed. Highland Park, N.J.: Gryphon Press.

Carlson, S. 1985. A double-blind test of astrology. *Nature* 318: 419–425.

Cowley, G., P. King, M. Hager, and D. Rosenberg. 1995. Going mainstream. *Newsweek* June 26: 56–57.

Dawes, R. M. 1994. *House of Cards: Psychology and Psychotherapy Built on Myth.* New York: Free Press.

Dawes, R. M., and M. Mulford. 1983. Diagnoses of alien kidnappings that result from conjunction effects in memory. SKEPTICAL INQUIRER 18 (1) (Fall): 50–51.

Dean, G. 1987. Does astrology need to be true? Part 2: The answer is no. SKEPTICAL INQUIRER 11 (3) (Spring): 257–273.

Deutsch, R. M. 1977. *The New Nuts among the Berries: How Nutrition Nonsense Captured America.* Palo Alto, Calif.: Ball Publishing.

Evans-Pritchard, E. E. 1937. *Witchcraft, Oracles and Magic among the Azande.* Oxford: Clarendon.

Exner, J. E. 1986. *The Rorschach: A Comprehensive System.* 2d ed. New York: John Wiley.

Gilovich, T. 1991. *How We Know What Isn't So: The Fallibility of Human Reason in Everyday Life.* New York: The Free Press.

Glavin, G. B., and S. Szabo. 1992. Experimental gastric mucosal injury: Laboratory models reveal mechanisms of pathogenesis and new therapeutic strategies. *FASEB Journal* 6: 825–831.

Hanslin, J. M. 1967. Craps and magic. *American Journal of Sociology* 73: 316–330.

Hentschel, E., G. Brandstatter, B. Dragosics, A. M. Hirschel, H. Nemec, K. Schutze, M. Taufer, and H. Wurzer. 1993. Effect of rantidine and amoxicillin plus metronidazole on the eradication of Helicobacter pylori and the recurrence of duodenal ulcer. *New England Journal of Medicine* 328: 308–312.

Howe, E. 1970. Astrology. In *Man, Myth, and Magic: An Illustrated Encyclopedia of the Supernatural,* ed. by R. Cavendish, New York: Marshall Cavendish.

Hunter, B. T. 1993. Good news for gastric sufferers. *Consumer's Research* 76 (October): 8–9.

Huntley, J. 1990. *The Elements of Astrology.* Shaftesbury, Dorset, Great Britain: Element Books.

Kahneman, D., and A. Tversky. 1972. Subjective probability: A judgment of representativeness. *Cognitive Psychology* 3: 430–454.

Kahneman, D., and A. Tversky. 1973. On the psychology of prediction. *Psychological Review* 80: 237–251.

Meigs, A. S. 1984. *Food, Sex, and Pollution: A New Guinea Religion.* New Brunswick, N.J.: Rutgers University Press.

Monmaney, T. 1993. Marshall's hunch. *The New Yorker* 69 (September 20): 64–72.

Nemeroff, C., and P. Rozin. 1989. 'You are what you eat': Applying the demand-free 'impressions' technique to an unacknowledged belief. *Ethos* 17: 50–69.

Neter, E., and G. Ben-Shakhar. 1989. The predictive validity of graphological inferences: A meta-analytic approach. *Personality and Individual Differences* (10): 737–745.

Nevo, B. 1986. ed. *Scientific Aspects of Graphology: A Handbook.* Springfield, Ill.: Charles C. Thomas.

Nisbett, R., and L. Ross. 1980. *Human Inference: Strategies and Shortcomings of Social Judgment.* Englewood Cliffs, N.J.: Prentice-Hall.

Peterson, W. L. 1991. Helicobacter pylori and peptic ulcer disease. *New England Journal of Medicine* 324: 1043–1048.

Read, A. W. et al. eds. 1978. *Funk and Wagnall's New Comprehensive International Dictionary of the English Language.* New York: Publishers Guild Press.

Scanlon, M., and J. Mauro. 1992. The lowdown on handwriting analysis: Is it for real? *Psychology Today* (November/December): 46–53; 80.

Schick, T., and L. Vaughn. 1995. *How to Think about Weird Things: Critical Thinking for a New Age.* Mountain View, Calif.: Mayfield Publishing Company.

Soll, A. H. 1990. Pathogenesis of peptic ulcer and implications for therapy. *New England Journal of Medicine* 322: 909–916.

Tversky, A., and D. Kahneman. 1974. Judgment under uncertainty: Heuristics and biases. *Science* 185: 1124–1131.

Tversky, A., and D. Kahneman. 1982. Judgments of and by representativeness. In *Judgment under Uncertainty: Heuristics and Biases,* ed. by D. Kahneman, P. Slovic, and A. Tversky. Cambridge: Cambridge University Press.

Tversky, A., and D. Kahneman. 1983. Extensional versus intuitive reasoning: The conjunction fallacy in probability judgment. *Psychological Review* 90: 293–315.

U.S. Congress. 1984. *Quackery; A $10 Billion Scandal: A Report by the Chairman of the (House) Subcommittee on Health and Long-Term Care.* Washington, D.C.: United States Government Printing Office.

Wandycz, K. 1993. The H. pylori factor. *Forbes* 152 (August 2): 128.

Ward, R. 1994. Maternity ward. *Mirabella* (February): 89–90.

Zusne, L. and W. H. Jones 1982. *Anomalistic Psychology.* Hillsdale, N.J.: Lawrence Erlbaum Associates.

The Seed of Our Undoing

by Daniel M. Wegner, University of Virginia

Daniel M. Wegner is Professor of Psychology at the University of Virginia. His doctorate in psychology is from Michigan State University (1974), and his work is on the role of thought in self-control and social life. Author of *White Bears and Other Unwanted Thoughts* (1989), he also wrote *Implicit Psychology* (1977) and *A Theory of Action Identification* (Erlbaum, 1985), both with Robin R. Vallacher, and edited *The Self in Social Psychology* (1980) with Vallacher and the *Handbook of Mental Control* (1993) with James W. Pennebaker. His research has been funded by NSF and is currently funded by NIMH. He has been a Fellow of the Center for Advanced Study in the Behavioral Sciences (1996–1997), and has served as associate editor of *Psychological Review*. References to his research are available on his home page: http://wsrv.clas.Virginia.EDU/~dmw2m/

According to Aristotle, the classic Greek tragedies tell stories of good people whose nature contains the seed of their own undoing. The research that my colleagues, students, and I have been conducting on *mental control* reveals the outline of just such a seed in the psychological processes that operate when people try to control their own minds. This seed is not quite tragic, as it does not always lead to wholesale undoing. However, it is certainly ironic—and we have been using the term "ironic process" to describe it.

The Irony of Not Thinking

The possibility that there might be an ironic process in mental control is easy to grasp in the case of thought suppression. A person who is asked to stop thinking about a white bear, for example, will typically think about it repeatedly as a result. In the first studies of this phenomenon (conducted with David Schneider, Sam Carter, and Teri White), we used stream-of-consciousness reports during suppression to measure this recurrence, but this suppression-induced preoccupation has now been found with less conspicuous methods. People who are trying not to think of an emotional thought such as sex, for example, show an increase in electrodermal response—as much as they do when they are specifically trying to focus on that thought.

Under some conditions, suppression yields even more intense levels of preoccupation with a thought than does concentration. People trying not to think about a target thought show such *hyperaccessibility*—the tendency for the thought to come to mind more readily even than a thought that is the focus of intentional concentration—when they are put under an additional mental load or stress. In several studies using the Stroop color-word paradigm (conducted with Ralph Erber and Sophia Zanakos), for example, we have found that trying not to think about a target word under conditions of mental load makes people unusually slow at identifying the color in which the word is presented. The word jumps into mind before the color and interferes with naming it. By this measure, unwanted thoughts are found to be more accessible than other comparison thoughts. And the ironic effect announces itself with a reversal of this finding under load for concentration: On average, any thought at all is more accessible than the concentration target.

Both of these observations can be explained by an ironic automatic process in the mind. The attempt to suppress a thought seems to conjure up an ironic psychological process that then works against the very intention that set it in motion. The suppressed thought is brought to mind in sporadic intrusions because of this sensitivity. The attempt to concentrate on a thought, in turn, seems to introduce an ironic psychological process that works against the intention to concentrate, and that therefore enhances the accessibility of everything other than the concentration target.

Why might such ironic processes occur? One way of accounting for these findings is to suggest that ironic processes are part of the machinery of mental control. It may be that in any attempt to control our minds, two processes are instituted—an *operating process* that works quite consciously and effortfully to carry out our desire, and an *ironic process* that works unconsciously and less effortfully to check on whether the operating process is failing and needs renewal. In the case of thought suppression, for instance, the operating process involves the conscious and labored search for distracters—as we try to fasten our minds on anything other than the unwanted thought—whereas the ironic process is an automatic search for the unwanted thought itself. The ironic process is a monitor of sorts, a checker that determines whether the operating process is needed, but that also has a tendency to influence the accessibility of conscious mental contents. It ironically enhances the sensitivity of the mind to the very thought that is being suppressed.

Varieties of Irony

An ironic process theory can explain far more than the paradox of thought suppression—indeed, something like this might vex most everything we try to do with our minds. If the ironic process is inherent in the control system whereby we secure whatever mental control we do enjoy, then it ought to be evident across many domains in which we do have some success in controlling our minds. However, because the operating process requires conscious effort and mental resources, it can be undermined by distraction and evidence of ironic processes will then arise. When people undertake to control their minds while they are burdened by mental loads—such as distracters, stress, or time pressure—the result should often be the opposite of what they intend.

Studies in my laboratory have uncovered evidence of ironic effects in several domains. Ironic mood effects occur, for example, when people attempt to control their moods while they are under mental load. Individuals following instructions to try to make themselves happy become sad, whereas those trying to make themselves sad actually experience buoyed mood. Ironic effects also surface in the self-control of anxiety. People trying to relax under load show psychophysiological indications of anxiousness, whereas those not trying to relax show fewer such indications. And ironic effects also occur in the control of sleep. People who are encouraged to "fall asleep as quickly as you can" as they listen to raucous, distracting music stay awake longer than those who are not given such encouragement. Ironic effects also accrue in the control of movement, arising when people try to keep a handheld pendulum from moving in a certain direction, or when they try to keep from overshooting a golf putt. In both cases, an imposition of mental load makes individuals more likely to commit exactly the unwanted action.

Research in other laboratories has revealed further ironic effects. Studies by Neil Macrae, Galen Bodenhausen, Alan Milne, and their colleagues, for instance, have established several remarkable ironic effects in the mental control of stereotyping and prejudice. People who are trying not to stereotype a skinhead as they form an impression of him, for example, show greater stereotyping under mental load. Individuals in this circumstance have been found to avoid even sitting near the skinhead as well. And people under mental load who are specifically trying to forget the stereotypical characteristics of a person (in a directed forgetting study) have been found more likely to recall those characteristics than are people without such load.

Ironic effects observed in yet other laboratories lend further credence to the basic idea. In work by Jeff Greenberg, Tom Pyszczynski, Sheldon Solomon, Jamie Arndt and their colleagues, for example, distraction tasks imposed after people have been asked to reflect for a while on their own death have revealed high levels of accessibility of death-related thoughts. This series of experiments suggests that people who are prompted to think about death turn shortly thereafter to the strategy of suppressing such thoughts even without instruction to do so—and thus suffer ironic returns of the thought. Related findings reported by Leonard Newman, Kimberly Duff, and Roy Baumeister indicate that people under mental load who are forming impressions of a person will project a personality trait onto the target when they are suppressing thoughts of the trait—whether in response to suppression instructions, or

spontaneously because they dislike the trait in themselves.

Cultivating the Seed

These studies illustrate how it is that we can, on occasion, cultivate the seed of our own undoing. To begin with, we apparently need good intentions. Like Aristotle's tragic hero, the individual attempting mental control often does so for good cause—in hopes of achieving high performance, moral ends, or at least mental peace. People often begin on the path toward ironic effects when they try to exercise good intentions—to behave effectively, to avoid prejudice, to be happy, to relax, to avoid negative thoughts or thoughts of personal shortcomings, or even just to sleep. The simple adoption of a goal is no sin, but this turns out to be the first step toward ironic effects.

The next step in cultivating the seed, as illustrated in this research, is the pursuit of such noble goals in the face of a shortage of mental resources. When there is insufficient time and thought available to achieve the chosen intention, people do not merely fail to produce the mental control they desire. Rather, the ironic process goes beyond "no change" to produce an actual reversal. The opposite happens. These studies indicate, in sum, that ironic effects are precipitated when we try to do more than we can with our minds.

Why would we do such a thing? At the extreme, we do this when we are desperate: We will try to achieve a particular sort of mental control even though we are mentally exhausted. These traits are, of course, highly reminiscent of the circumstances of many people suffering from various forms of psychological disorder. It makes sense that people who are anxious, depressed, traumatized, obsessed, or those with disorders of sleep, eating, movement, or the like, might frequently try to overcome their symptoms—and might also be inclined to

attempt such control even under adverse conditions of stress or distraction. Evidence from correlational studies conducted in my laboratory and elsewhere suggests a possible role for ironic processes in several such forms of psychopathology.

We know from such relations that attempts to avoid unwanted symptoms are often highly associated with those symptoms. The most obvious explanation of these associations is that people who experience unwanted mental states attempt to control them. But the more subtle possibility, as yet untested in large-scale studies, is that the attempt to control unwanted mental states plays a role in perpetuating them. The experiments showing that mental control attempts can yield laboratory analogs of unwanted mental states provide one basis for this conclusion.

Another line of evidence suggesting a role for ironic processes in the etiology of some disorders comes from studies of what happens when mental control is rescinded. The best examples of such work are the series of experiments by James Pennebaker and colleagues. When people in these studies are encouraged to express their deepest thoughts and feelings in writing, they experience subsequent improvements in psychological and physical health. Expressing oneself in this way involves relinquishing the pursuit of mental control, and so eliminates a key requirement for the production of ironic effects. After all, as suggested in other studies conducted in my lab with Julie Lane and Laura Smart, the motive to keep one's thoughts and personal characteristics secret is strongly linked with mental control. Disclosing these things to others, or even in writing to oneself, is the first step toward abandoning what may be an overweening and futile quest to control one's own thoughts and emotions.

When we relax the desire for the control of our minds, the seeds of our undoing may remain uncultivated, perhaps then to dry up and blow away.

Something Out of Nothing

The Misperception and Misinterpretation of Random Data

Thomas Gilovich

> The human understanding supposes a greater degree of order and equality in things than it really finds; and although many things in nature be sui generis and most irregular, will yet invest parallels and conjugates and relatives where no such thing is.
>
> Francis Bacon, *Novum Organum*

In 1677, Baruch Spinoza wrote his famous words, "Nature abhors a vacuum," to describe a host of physical phenomena. Three hundred years later, it seems that his statement applies as well to human nature, for it too abhors a vacuum. We are predisposed to see order, pattern, and meaning in the world, and we find randomness, chaos, and meaninglessness unsatisfying. Human nature abhors a lack of predictability and the absence of meaning. As a consequence, we tend to "see" order where there is none, and we spot meaningful patterns where only the vagaries of chance are operating.

People look at the irregularities of heavenly bodies and see a face on the surface of the moon or a series of canals on Mars. Parents listen to their teenagers' music backwards and claim to hear Satanic messages in the chaotic waves of noise that are produced.[1] While praying for his critically ill son, a man looks at the wood grain on the hospital room door and claims to see the face of Jesus; hundreds now visit the clinic each year and confirm the miraculous likeness.[2] Gamblers claim that they experience hot and cold streaks in random rolls of the dice, and they alter their bets accordingly.

The more one thinks about Spinoza's phrase, the better it fits as a description of human nature. Nature does not "abhor" a vacuum in the sense of "to loathe" or "to regard with extreme repugnance" (Webster's definition). Nature has no rooting interest. The same is largely true of human nature as well. Often we impose order even when there is no motive to do so. We do not "want" to see a man in the moon. We do not profit from the illusion. We just see it.

The tendency to impute order to ambiguous stimuli is simply built into the cognitive machinery we use to apprehend the world. It may have been bred into us through evolution because of its general adaptiveness: We can capitalize on ordered phenomena in ways that we cannot on those that are random. The predisposition to detect patterns and make connections is what leads to discovery and advance. The problem, however, is that the tendency is so strong and so automatic that we sometimes detect coherence even when it does not exist.

This touches on a theme that will be raised repeatedly in this book. Many of the mechanisms that distort our judgments stem from basic cognitive processes that are usually quite helpful in accurately perceiving and understanding the world. The structuring and ordering of stimuli is no exception. Ignaz Semmelweis detected a pattern in the occurrence of childbed fever among women who were assisted in giving birth by doctors who had just finished a dissection. His observation led to the practice of antisepsis. Charles Darwin saw order in the distribution of different species of finches in the

Galapagos, and his insight furthered his thinking about evolution and natural selection.

Clearly, the tendency to look for order and to spot patterns is enormously helpful, particularly when we subject whatever hunches it generates to further, more rigorous test (as both Semmelweis and Darwin did, for example). Many times, however, we treat the products of this tendency not as hypotheses, but as established facts. The predisposition to impose order can be so automatic and so unchecked that we often end up believing in the existence of phenomena that just aren't there.

To get a better sense of how our structuring of events can go awry, it is helpful to take a closer look at a specific example. The example comes from the world of sports, but the reader who is not a sports fan need not dismay. The example is easy to follow even if one knows nothing about sports, and the lessons it conveys are quite general.

THE MISPERCEPTION OF RANDOM EVENTS

"If I'm on, I find that confidence just builds . . . you feel nobody can stop you. It's important to hit that first one, especially if it's a swish. Then you hit another, and . . . you feel like you can do anything."

—World B. Free

I must caution the reader not to construe the sentences above as two distinct quotations, the first a statement about confidence, and the second an anti-imperialist slogan. Known as Lloyd Free before legally changing his first name, World B. Free is a professional basketball player. His statement captures a belief held by nearly everyone who plays or watches the sport of basketball, a belief in a phenomenon known as the "hot hand." The term refers to the putative tendency for success (and failure) in basketball to be self-promoting or self-sustaining. After making a couple of shots, players are thought to become relaxed, to feel confident, and to "get in a groove" such that subsequent success becomes more likely. In contrast, after missing several shots a player is considered to have "gone cold" and is thought to become tense, hesitant, and less likely to make his next few shots.

The belief in the hot hand, then, is really one version of a wider conviction that "success breeds success" and "failure breeds failure" in many walks of life. In certain areas it surely does. Financial success promotes further financial success because one's initial good fortune provides more capital with which to wheel and deal. Success in the art world promotes further success because it earns an artist a reputation that exerts a powerful influence over people's judgments of inherently ambiguous stimuli. However, there are other areas—gambling games immediately come to mind—where the belief may be just as strongly held, but where the phenomenon simply does not exist. What about the game of basketball? Does success in this sport tend to be self-promoting?

My colleagues and I have conducted a series of studies to answer this question.[3] The first step, as always, involved translating the idea of the hot hand into a testable hypothesis. If a player's performance is subject to periods of hot and cold shooting, then he should be more likely to make a shot after making his previous shot (or previous several shots) than after missing his previous shot. This implies, in turn, that a player's hits (and misses) should cluster together more than one would expect by chance. We interviewed 100 knowledgeable basketball fans to determine whether this constitutes an appropriate interpretation of what people mean by the hot hand. Their responses indicated that it does: 91% thought that a player has "a better chance of making a shot after having just made his last two or three shots than he does after having just missed his last two or three shots." In fact, when asked to consider a hypothetical player who makes 50% of his shots, they estimated that his shooting percentage would be 61% "after having just made a shot," and 42% "after having just missed a shot." Finally, 84% of the respondents thought that "it is important to pass the ball to someone who has just made several shots in a row."

To find out whether players actually shoot in streaks, we obtained the shooting records of the Philadelphia 76ers during the 1980–81 season. (The 76ers are the only team, we were told, who keep records of the *order* in which a player's hits and misses occurred, rather than simple cumulative totals.) We then analyzed these data to determine whether players' hits tended to cluster together more than one would expect by chance. Table 1 presents the relevant data. Contrary to the expectations

Table 1 Probability of Making a Shot Conditioned on the Outcome of Previous Shots for Nine Members of the 76ers

Player	P(x|ooo)	P(x|oo)	P(x|o)	P(x)	P(x|x)	P(x|xx)	P(x|xxx)	r
C. Richardson	.50	.47	.56	.50	.49	.50	.48	−.02
J. Erving	.52	.51	.51	.52	.53	.52	.48	.02
L. Hollins	.50	.49	.46	.46	.46	.46	.32	.00
M. Cheeks	.77	.60	.60.	.56	.55	.54	.59	−.04
C. Jones	.50	.48	.47	.47	.45	.43	.27	−.02
A. Toney	.52	.53	.51	.46	.43	.40	.34	−.08
B. Jones	.61	.58	.58	.54	.53	.47	.53	−.05
S. Mix	.70	.56	.52	.52	.51	.48	.36	−.02
D. Dawkins	.88	.73	.71	.62	.57	.58	.51	−.14
Mean =	.56	.53	.54	.52	.51	.50	.46	−.04

NOTE: x = a hit; o = a miss. r = the correlation between the outcomes of consecutive shots expressed by our sample of fans, players were *not* more likely to make a shot after making their last one, two, or three shots than after missing their last one, two, or three shots. In fact, there was a slight tendency for players to shoot better after *missing* their last shot. They made 51% of their shots after making their previous shot, compared to 54% after missing their previous shot; 50% after making their previous two shots, compared to 53% after missing their previous two; 46% after making three in a row, compared to 56% after missing three in a row. These data flatly contradict the notion that "success breeds success" in basketball and that hits tend to follow hits and misses tend to follow misses.

We also examined each player's performance record to determine whether the number of streaks of various lengths exceeded the number to be expected if individual shots were statistically independent. Were there more streaks of, say, 4, 5, or 6 hits in a row than chance would allow? Were there more, for example, than the number of streaks of 4, 5, or 6 heads in a row that one observes when flipping coins? The relevant statistical tests indicated that there was no such tendency. A variety of additional, more complicated, analyses led to the same conclusion: A player's performance on a given shot is independent of his performance on previous shots. (It is interesting to note that an interview with eight members of the 76ers that year revealed that these *very* players believed that they tended to shoot in streaks.)

How can we reconcile the widespread belief in the hot hand with the startling disconfirmation provided by these data? Most people's first response is to insist that the belief is valid and the data are not. The hot hand exists, the argument goes, it just did not show up in our sample of data. Perhaps it did not appear because being hot is perfectly compensated for by a hot player's tendency to take more difficult shots or receive more attention by the defensive team. The hot hand may have been masked, in other words, by other phenomena that work in the opposite direction. To test such an alternative interpretation, one must examine players' performance records when the difficulty of the shot and the amount of defensive pressure have been held constant. The most direct way of doing so is to examine players' "free-throw" records—penalty shots taken in pairs from the same distance and without defensive pressure. If success promotes success, then we would expect a player's shooting percentage on his second shot to be higher after making his first shot than after missing his first. It is not. Our analysis of two seasons of free-throw statistics by the Boston Celtics indicate that the outcomes of consecutive free throws are independent. On average, the players made 75% of their second free throws after making their first, and 75% after missing their first.

Still unconvinced, a number of people have tried to salvage their belief in the hot hand by suggesting that perhaps we have not adequately captured what is meant by the term (our initial survey results notwithstanding).

Perhaps players' hits and misses do not cluster together more than do heads and tails, but, unlike coin flips, the player can predict in advance whether he is likely to make the next shot. In other words, maybe the hot hand really refers to the predictability of hits and misses rather than the clustering together of success with success and failure with failure.

This too was tested and found wanting. We asked a group of college basketball players to take 100 shots from along an arc that was everywhere an equal distance from the basket. Before each shot the players chose either a risky or conservative bet corresponding to whether they felt more or less likely to make their upcoming shot. The results indicated that the players believed that they shot in streaks: They tended to make risky bets after hitting their previous shot and conservative bets after missing their previous shot. However, there was no correlation between the outcome of consecutive shots, and hence no connection between their bets and the outcome of the next shot. In other words, not only do players fail to shoot in streaks, but they cannot predict in advance whether they are likely to make a given shot. Even according to this revised definition, the hot hand does not seem to exist.

Why Players Seem *to Shoot in Streaks.* It is important to note that although a player's performance record does not contain more or longer streaks than chance would allow, it does not mean that the player's performance is chance *determined.* It is not. Whether a given shot is hit or missed is determined by a host of non-chance factors, foremost among them being the skill of the offensive and defensive players involved. However, one factor that does *not* influence the outcome, or does not have any *predictable* influence, is the outcome of the previous shot(s). That is what our research shows.

This qualification aside, why do people believe in the hot hand when it does not exist? There are at least two possible explanations. The first involves the tendency for people's preconceptions to bias their interpretations of what they see. Because people have theories about how confidence affects performance, they may expect to see streak shooting even before watching their first basketball game. This preconception could then influence their interpretation and memory of the game's events. Streaks of successive hits or misses may stand out and be remembered, while sequences of frequent alternation between the two may go unnoticed and be forgotten. Or, the common occurrence of a shot popping out of the basket after having seemingly been made might be counted as a "near miss" if the player had made his last several shots, but as evidence of being extremely cold if the player had missed his last several shots.[4] . . .

A second explanation involves a process that appears to be more fundamental, and thus operates even in the absence of any explicit theories people might have. Psychologists have discovered that people have faulty intuitions about what chance sequences look like.[5] People expect sequences of coin flips, for example, to alternate between heads and tails more than they actually do. Because chance produces less alternation than our intuition leads us to expect, truly random sequences look too ordered or "lumpy." Streaks of 4, 5, or 6 heads in a row clash with our expectations about the behavior of a fair coin, although in a series of 20 tosses there is a 50–50 chance of getting 4 heads in a row, a 25 percent chance of five in a row, and a 10 percent chance of a streak of six. Because the average basketball player makes about 50% of his shots, he has a reasonably good chance of looking like he has the hot hand by making four, five, or even six shots in a row if he takes 20 shots in a game (as many players do).

To determine whether this general misconception of the laws of chance might be responsible for the belief in the hot hand, we showed basketball fans sequences of X's and 0's that we told them represented a player's hits and misses in a basketball game. We also asked them to indicate whether each sequence constituted an example of streak shooting. For instance, one of the sequences was 0XXX0XXX0XX000X00XX00, a sequence in which the order of hits and misses is perfectly random.* Nevertheless, 62% of our subjects thought that it constituted streak shooting.

Note that although these judgments are wrong, it is easy to see why they were made. The sequence above does *look* like streak shooting. Six of the first eight shots were hits, as were eight of the first eleven! Thus, players and fans are not mistaken in what they see: Basketball players do shoot in streaks. But the length and frequency of such streaks do not exceed the laws of chance and thus do not warrant an explanation involving factors like confidence and relaxation that comprise the mythical concept of the hot hand. Chance works in strange ways, and the mistake made by players and fans lies in how they interpret what they see.

The Clustering Illusion. The intuition that random events such as coin flips should alternate between heads and tails more than they do has been described by statisticians as a "clustering illusion." Random distributions seem to us to have too many clusters or streaks of consecutive outcomes of the same type, and so we have difficulty accepting their true origins. The term illusion is well-chosen because, like a perceptual illusion, it is not eliminated by repeated examination.[6]

Consider the picture of St. Louis's Gateway Arch depicted in Figure 1.[7] The arch is one of the world's largest optical illusions: It appears to be much taller than it is wide, although its height and base are equal in length. More important, even when one is told that the height and base are equal, they still do not seem to be. The

illusion cannot be overcome simply by taking another look; only an objective measurement will do. (The reader is encouraged to make the necessary measurements.)

The reaction of the professional basketball world to our research on the hot hand is instructive in this regard. Do those close to the game give up their belief in the hot hand when confronted with the relevant data? Hardly. Red Auerbach, the brains behind what is arguably the most successful franchise in American sports history, the Boston Celtics, had this to say upon hearing about our results: "Who is this guy? So he makes a study. I couldn't care less." Another prominent coach, Bobby Knight of the 1987 NCAA champion Indiana Hoosiers, responded by saying " . . . there are so many variables involved in shooting the basketball that a paper like this really doesn't mean anything." These comments are not terribly surprising. Because a truly random arrangement of hits and misses contains a number of streaks of various lengths, the belief in the hot hand should be held most strongly by those closest to the game. Furthermore, simply hearing that the hot hand does not exist, or merely taking another look at the game is not sufficient to disabuse oneself of this belief. It is only through the kind of objective assessment we performed that the illusion can be overcome.

Figure 1 Gateway Arch

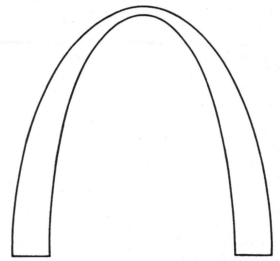

Judgment by Representativeness. In the grand scheme of things, whether or not basketball players shoot in streaks is not particularly important. What is important is the suggestion—conveyed with unusual clarity by the basketball example—that people chronically misconstrue random events, and that there may be other cases in which truly random phenomena are erroneously thought to be ordered and "real." If so, we arrive at the more critical question of why people expect random sequences to alternate more than they do. Why, beyond noting that human nature abhors a vacuum, do people fall prey to the clustering illusion?

---

* The sequence is random in the sense that there is no correlation between the outcomes of consecutive shots. The number of adjacent shots with the same outcome (i.e., XX or 00) in the sequence is equal to the number of adjacent shots with different outcomes (i.e., X0 or 0X).

The best explanation to date of the misperception of random sequences is offered by psychologists Daniel Kahneman and Amos Tversky, who attribute it to people's tendency to be overly influenced by judgments of "representativeness."[8] Representativeness can be thought of as the reflexive tendency to assess the similarity of outcomes, instances, and categories on relatively salient and even superficial features, and then to use these assessments of similarity as a basis of judgment. People assume that "like goes with like": Things that go together should look as though they go together. We expect instances to look like the categories of which they are members; thus, we expect someone who is a librarian to resemble the prototypical librarian. We expect effects to look like their causes; thus, we are more likely to attribute a case of heartburn to spicy rather than bland food, and we are more inclined to see jagged handwriting as a sign of a tense rather than a relaxed personality.

Judgment by representativeness is often valid and helpful because objects, instances, and categories that go together often do in fact share a resemblance. Many librarians fit the prototype of a librarian—after all, the prototype came from somewhere. Causes often resemble their effects: All else being equal, "bigger" effects require "bigger" causes, complex effects stem from complex causes, etc. It is the *overapplication* of representativeness that gets us into trouble. All else is not always equal. Not all librarians are prototypical; Some big effects (e.g., an epidemic) have humble causes (e.g., a virus) and some complex effects (e.g., the alteration of a region's ecological balance) have simple causes (e.g., the introduction of a single pesticide).

It is easy to see how judgment by representativeness could contribute to the clustering illusion. In the case of coin flipping, one of the most salient features of a fair coin is the set of outcomes it produces—an approximate 50–50 split of heads and tails. In examining a sequence of coin flips, this 50–50 feature of the coin is automatically compared to the sequence of outcomes itself. If the sequence is split roughly 50–50, it strikes us as random because the outcome appears representative of a random generating process. A less even split is harder to accept. These intuitions are correct, but only in the long term. The law of averages (called the "law of large numbers" by statisticians) ensures that there will be close to a 50–50 split after a large number of tosses. After only a few tosses, however, even very unbalanced splits are quite likely. There is no "law of small numbers."

The clustering illusion thus stems from a form of over-generalization: We expect the correct proportion of heads and tails or hits and misses to be present not only globally in a long se-quence, but also locally in each of its parts. A sequence like the one shown previously with 8 hits in the first 11 shots does not look random because it deviates from the expected 50–50 split. In such a short sequence, however, such a split is not terribly unlikely.

Misperceptions of Random Dispersions. The hot hand is not the only erroneous belief that stems from the compelling nature of the clustering illusion. People believe that fluctuations in the prices of stocks on Wall Street are far more patterned and predictable than they really are. A random series of changes in stock prices simply does not look random; it seems to contain enough coherence to enable a wily investor to make profitable predictions of future value from past performance. People who work in maternity wards witness streaks of boy births followed by streaks of girl births that they attribute to a variety of mysterious forces like the phases of the moon. Here, too, the random sequences of births to which they are exposed simply do not look random.

The clustering illusion also affects our assessments of spatial dispersions. As noted earlier, people "see" a face on the surface of the moon and a series of canals on Mars, and many people with a religious orientation have reported seeing the likeness of various religious figures in unstructured stimuli such as grains of wood, cloud formations, even skillet burns. A particularly clear illustration of this phenomenon occurred during the latter stages of World War II, when the Germans bombarded London with their "vengeance weapons"—the V-1 buzz bomb and the V-2 rocket. During this "Second Battle of London," Londoners asserted that the weapons appeared to land in definite clusters, making some areas of the city more dangerous than others.[9] However, an analysis carried out after the war indicated that the points of impact of these weapons were randomly dispersed throughout London.[10] Although with time the Germans became increasingly accurate in terms of having a higher percentage of these weapons strike London, within this general target area their accuracy was sufficiently limited that any location was as likely to be struck as any other.

Figure 2 Points of Impact of 67 V-1 Bombs in Central London

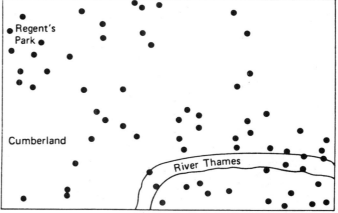

Still, it is hard not to empathize with those who thought the weapons fell in clusters. A random dispersion of events often does not look random, as Figure 2 indicates. This figure shows the points of impact of 67 V-1 bombs in Central London.[11] Even after learning the results of the proper statistical analysis, the points do not look randomly dispersed. The lower right quadrant looks devastated and the upper left quadrant also looks rather hard hit; the upper right and lower left quadrants, however, appear to be relatively tranquil. We can easily imagine how the presence of special target areas could have seemed to Londoners to be an "irresistible product of their own experience."

A close inspection of Figure 2 sheds further light on why people "detect" order in random dispersions. Imagine Figure 2 being bisected both vertically and horizontally, creating four quadrants of equal area. As already discussed, this results in an abundance of points in the upper-left and lower-right quadrants, and a dearth of points in the other two areas. In fact, the appropriate statistical test shows this clustering to be a significant departure from an independent, random dispersion.[*] In other words, when the dispersion of points is carved up in this particular way, non-chance clusters can be found. It is the existence of such clusters, no doubt, that creates the impression that the bombs did not fall randomly over London.

But why carve the map this way? (Indeed, why conduct the statistical analysis only on the data from this particular area of London?) Why not bisect this figure with two diagonal lines? Bisected that way, there are no significant clusters.

The important point here is that with *hindsight* it is always possible to spot the most anomalous features of the data and build a favorable statistical analysis around them. However, a properly trained scientist (or simply a wise person) avoids doing so because he or she recognizes that constructing a statistical analysis retrospectively capitalizes too much on chance and renders the

analysis meaningless. To the scientist, such apparent anomalies merely suggest hypotheses that are subsequently tested on other, *independent* sets of data. Only if the anomaly persists is the hypothesis to be taken seriously.

Unfortunately, the intuitive assessments of the average person are not bound by these constraints. Hypotheses that are formed on the basis of one set of results are considered to have been proven by those very same results. By retrospectively and selectively perusing the data in this way, people tend to make too much of apparent anomalies and too often end up detecting order where none exists. . . .

Notes

1. J. R. Vokey & J. D. Read (1985) Subliminal messages: Between the devil and the media. *American Psychologist, 40,* 1231–39.
2. J. W. Connor (1984) Misperception, folk belief, and the occult: A cognitive guide to understanding. *Skeptical Inquirer, 8,* 344–54.
3. T. Gilovich, R. Vallone, & A. Tversky (1985) The hot hand in basketball: On the misperception of random sequences. *Cognitive Psychology, 17,* 295–314.
4. T. Gilovich (1983) Biased evaluation and persistence in gambling. *Journal of Personality and Social Psychology, 44,* 1110–26.
5. R. Falk (1981) The perception of randomness. In *Proceedings, Fifth International Conference for the Psychology of Mathematics Education,* Grenoble, France: Wagenaar, W. A. (1972) Generation of random sequences by human subjects: A critical survey of literature. *Psychological Bulletin, 77,* 65–72.
6. A. Tversky & D. Kahneman (1974) Judgment under uncertainty: Heuristics and biases. *Science, 185,* 1124–31.
7. Taken from R. Thaler (1983) Illusions and mirages in public policy. *The Public Interest, 73,* 60–74.
8. D. Kahneman & A. Tversky (1971) Subjective probability: A judgment of representativeness. *Cognitive Psychology, 3,* 430–54; D. Kahneman & A. Tversky (1973) On the psychology of prediction. *Psychological Review, 80,* 237–51; A. Tversky & D. Kahneman (1971) Belief in the law of small numbers. *Psychological Bulletin, 76,* 105–110; A. Tversky & D. Kahneman (1974) Judgment under uncertainty: Heuristics and biases. *Science, 185,* 1124–31.
9. R. D. Clarke (1946) An application of the poisson distribution. *Journal of the Institute of Actuaries (London), 72,* p. 72; D. Johnson (1981) *V-1, V-2: Hitler's vengeance on London.* New York: Stein & Day.
10. R. D. Clarke (1946) An application of the poisson distribution. *Journal of the Institute of Actuaries (London, 72,* p. 72; W. Feller (1968) *An introduction to probability theory and its applications.* New York: Wiley.
11. D. Johnson (1981) *V-1, V-2: Hitler's vengeance on London.* New York: Stein & Day, p. 144–45.

* The appropriate test in this case is the chi-square test, and the obtained chi-square value is 20.69. The probability of obtaining a chi-square value this large by chance alone is less than 1 in 1,000.

Inferential Hopscotch: How People Draw Social Inferences From Behavior

Douglas S. Krull and Darin J. Erickson

Douglas S. Krull is an Assistant Professor of Psychology at Northern Kentucky University, Highland Heights. **Darin J. Erickson** is a graduate student at the University of Missouri, Columbia. Address correspondence to Douglas S. Krull, Department of Psychology, Northern Kentucky University, Highland Heights, KY 41099; e-mail: Krull@nku.edu.

Tim and Sue observe an anxious-looking man in a dentist's waiting room. Tim decides that the man must have an anxious personality (a trait inference). In contrast, Sue decides that the man is anxious because he is waiting to see the dentist (a situational inference). Why might Tim and Sue have drawn such different inferences? Social inference researchers have long been interested in the different inferences that people draw when they view the same behavior. Early work on social inference focused on the tendency for peoples' inferences to be biased in favor of trait inferences. For example, when members of a debate team are assigned to argue for a particular political position, observers often infer that the debaters' true attitudes match their assigned position.[1] More recently, research has focused not only on *what* people infer (i.e., the final inference), but also on *how* they infer (i.e., the process by which inferences are drawn).

THE TRAIT INFERENCE PROCESS

The vast majority of recent work on social inference has investigated the process by which people draw inferences about an actor's personality. Research suggests that the trait inference process can be thought of as composed of three states: behavior interpretation, trait inference, and situational revision.[2] First, people interpret, or derive meaning from, the actor's behavior ("John seems to be behaving in a very anxious manner"); next, they draw a trait inference that corresponds to the behavior ("John must have a very anxious personality"); finally, they may revise this inference to a greater or lesser degree by taking into account the situational forces that may have contributed to the actor's behavior ("John is waiting to see the dentist; perhaps he isn't such an anxious person after all"). These three stages seem to differ in the amount of effort required. Behavior interpretation and trait inference seem to be relatively spontaneous and effortless, whereas situational revision seems to be relatively effortful.[3] This process is depicted in Figure 1.

Stage 1: Behavior Interpretation

People tend to see what they expect to see.[4] Thus, many people in American society tend to interpret an ambiguous shove as more hostile when given by a black person than by a white person. However, people's expectations have less impact on their interpretations of behavior if the behavior is unambiguous. Trope[5] conducted an experiment in which participants interpreted facial expressions after being informed about the context in which the expressions took place. If the facial expressions were ambiguous, participants' context-based expectations influenced their interpretations of the emotions (e.g., participants interpreted a facial expression as happier if the context was "winning in a TV game show" and more fearful if the context was "a swarm of bees flying into the room"). If the facial expressions were unambiguous, participants' expectations had significantly less impact.

Stage 2: Trait Inference

People often think that you can judge a book by its cover, that people's actions reflect their personalities. Uleman, Winter, and their colleagues[6] conducted a series of investigations which suggest that when people view behavior, they may spontaneously draw inferences about the actor's personality. In these studies, participants read sentences (e.g., "The secretary solved the mystery halfway through the book") that suggest a particular trait (e.g., clever). Uleman and Winter proposed that if people spontaneously draw trait inferences upon reading the sentences (at encoding), then these traits should facilitate recall for the sentences (at retrieval). Studies of this hypothesis have found repeatedly that participants' recall is superior with trait cues than with no cues, and occasionally better with trait cues than with other types of cues (semantic), even when participants were not aware when reading the sentences that their memory for the sentences would be tested.

In a similar paradigm, Lupfer, Clark, and Hutcherson[7] conducted an experiment which suggests that trait inferences may be substantially effortless as well as spontaneous. If trait inference is substantially effortless, then people should be able to perform it even when their conscious resources are limited (i.e.,

From *Current Directions in Psychological Science,* April 1995, pp. 35–38. © 1995 by the American Psychological Society. Reprinted by permission of Blackwell Publishers.

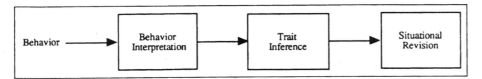

Fig. 1. The trait inference process.

when they are cognitively busy). Participants read sentences while they simultaneously rehearsed an easy set of numbers (which should not make people cognitively busy) or a difficult set of numbers (which should make people cognitively busy). Not only did trait-cued participants recall more sentences than noncued participants, but the trait-cued recall of participants in the difficult condition was not significantly different from the trait-cued recall of participants in the easy condition. This and other research suggests that when people view behavior, they may spontaneously and effortlessly interpret the behavior and infer that the actor's personality corresponds to the behavior ("John behaved in an anxious manner; John must have an anxious personality") even when they are distracted or preoccupied.

A relearning paradigm developed by Carlston and Skowronski[8] looks particularly promising for the further investigation of spontaneous trait inferences. These researchers first presented participants with person photos paired with personal statements that implied traits. For example, the following statement implies that the person in the photo is cruel: "I hate animals. Today I was walking to the pool hall and I saw this puppy. So I kicked it out of my way." Some participants were instructed to draw a trait inference (specific-impression condition), others were instructed to form an impression (general-impression condition), and others were told to simply look at the photos and statements (ostensibly to familiarize themselves with these materials for a later phase of the experiment; no-instruction condition). If these latter participants inferred traits, this would be evidence for spontaneity.

After a filler task, all participants were given photo–trait pairs and were instructed explicitly to memorize the trait associated with each photo. In some cases (relearning trials), these pairs corresponded to the photo–statement pairs presented earlier (e.g., the photo previously presented with the statement about kicking the puppy was paired with the word *cruel*). Thus, if the participants had previously inferred traits from the statements, they would be relearning the associations between the photos and the traits instead of learning these asso-

ciations for the first time. In other cases, the photo–trait pairs did not correspond to the previous photo–statement pairs (control trials). Finally, participants were shown the photos and asked to recall the traits. Recall was higher for relearning trials than for control trials, suggesting that participants had inferred traits from the initial photo–statement paris. In addition, this finding was similar across all three conditions (specific impression, general impression, no instruction), which suggests that trait inferences had occurred in the impression conditions, and spontaneous trait inferences had occurred in the no-instruction condition. Carlston and Skowronski also ruled out several alternative explanations. Thus, these results provide strong evidence that trait inferences can be drawn spontaneously.

Stage 3: Situational Revision

People may consider the situation in which the behavior took place when they draw trait inferences, but it is not easy for them to do so. Unlike behavior interpretation and trait inference, situational revision seems to be a relatively effortful process, and so people may not complete it when they lack either the ability or the motivation to do so. A program of research conducted by Gilbert and his colleagues[3] suggests that people may be unable to complete the situational revision stage sufficiently when they are cognitively busy (when they have limited conscious resources). In one study, participants viewed several videotape clips of an anxious-appearing woman who was ostensibly discussing anxiety-provoking topics (sexual fantasies) or calm topics (world travel) with an interviewer. The film was silent, but the discussion topics appeared in subtitles. Half the participants were required to memorize these topics (cognitively busy participants), and half were not. One might expect that participants would recognize that most people would be more anxious when discussing anxiety-provoking topics than calm topics, but, remarkably, participants who attempted to memorize the discussion topics were less able than the other participants to consider the effects of the topics when drawing inferences about the target. Thus, this study

suggests that when people are preoccupied or distracted, they may draw biased trait inferences because they fail to sufficiently consider the situation in which the behavior took place.

An experiment by Webster[9] suggests that people may also revise their trait inferences insufficiently when they are unmotivated. Participants expected to answer questions about their impression of a speaker who expressed a negative view toward student exchange programs. Before viewing the speaker, participants were informed that she was required to express a negative view, but Webster predicted that unmotivated participants would be less likely than motivated participants to consider this fact, and would be more likely to infer that the speaker's view reflected her true attitude. Half of the participants expected to perform a task involving multivariate statistics after the impression formation task, whereas the other half expected to perform a task involving comedy clips after the impression formation task. Webster predicted that participants who expected to view the statistics lecture would be motivated to "stretch the fun" on the (comparatively attractive) impression formation task, whereas participants who expected to view the comedy clips would be motivated to "get the (comparatively boring) impression formation task over with." As Webster predicted, participants in the statistics conditions were better able to revise their inferences than were participants in the comedy clips condition, and were less likely to infer that the speaker's expressed view reflected her true attitude.

THE SITUATIONAL INFERENCE PROCESS

When people want to know about people, they seem to infer traits. What if people want to know about situations? Social inference researchers have learned much about the process by which people infer traits. Considerably less work has investigated how social inference proceeds when people are interested in learning about a situation, but some work suggests that situational inference may be a mirror image of the trait inference process.[10] In an experiment very similar to Gilbert's aforementioned anxious-woman experiment, participants viewed a silent videotape of an anxious-appearing interviewee. Half the participants attempted to estimate the interviewee's trait anxiety (trait goal); half attempted to estimate the degree of anxiety provoked by the interview topics (situational goal). Half of the participants in each of these conditions were made

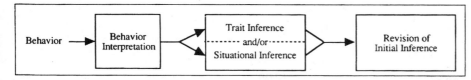

Fig. 2. The social inference process.

cognitively busy. For people with a trait goal, the results mirrored Gilbert's; that is, in an analysis that combined the dispositional and situational anxiety measures, busy participants inferred more dispositional anxiety than did nonbusy participants. However, the results were reversed for participants with a situational goal; that is, busy participants in this condition inferred more situational anxiety than did nonbusy participants. These results suggest that when people are interested in situations (rather than traits, they may spontaneously and effortlessly draw situational inferences (rather than trait inferences) from behavior. If people have the ability and motivation, they may revise these inferences by considering the actor's personality.

THE SOCIAL INFERENCE PROCESS

Considerable research suggests that when people have a trait goal, they interpret the actor's behavior, spontaneously and effortlessly draw a trait inference, and, if they have sufficient conscious resources and motivation, revise this inference by considering the situation in which the behavior took place. When people have a situational goal, they interpret the actor's behavior, may spontaneously and effortlessly draw a situational inference, and, if they have sufficient conscious resources and motivation, revise this inference by considering the actor's personality (see Fig. 2). It seems that people are able to draw either trait inferences or situational inferences from behavior when they are given either trait goals or situational goals, but what might create these goals in people's day-to-day lives? Social inference researchers have long maintained that people draw inferences to increase their ability to predict other people's behavior. Thus, a trait goal may be invoked when someone expects to interact with a person in the future ("I just met our new neighbors. They seem like friendly people"). When someone expects to enter a situation, a situational goal may be invoked ("Did you hear those people laughing? I can hardly wait to see that movie").

Even when goals are not invoked by the immediate circumstances or people's

current needs and motives, people may be predisposed to either trait inference or situational inference by their culture or personality.[11] A number of cross-cultural investigations have found that non-Westerners tend to form judgments that are more situational than those of Westerners. Shweder and Bourne[12] have suggested that non-Western people may be "culturally primed to see context and social relationships as a necessary condition for behavior," whereas Westerners may be "culturally primed to search for abstract summaries of the autonomous individual." Thus, Westerners' default process may be the trait inference process, whereas non-Westerners' default process may be the situational inference process. Even within a culture, some types of individuals may think more in terms of traits, and others may think more in terms of situational forces. For instance, Newman[13] has found that people who are high in idiocentrism (an individualist view) are more likely than people who are low in idiocentrism to infer traits spontaneously from behavior.

CONCLUSION

In the past decade or so, social inference researchers have increased their attention on the process by which people draw inferences from behavior, particularly the trait inference process. This research suggests that when people are interested in learning about another person, they may spontaneously and effortlessly interpret behavior and draw an inference about the actor's personality. They may then revise their initial inference by considering the situation in which the behavior took place if they have the ability and motivation to do so. Less research has investigated how people draw inferences when they are interested in learning about situations. However, people with a situational goal may spontaneously and effortlessly interpret behavior and draw an inference about the situation, and may revise this inference by considering the actor's personality if they have the ability and motivation to do so. Thus, it seems that the social inference process may be flexible in that people may not be compelled to always travel the same inferential road. Social inference researchers have be-

gun to investigate factors that might influence people's tendency to initially draw either trait or situational inferences (or perhaps both); some research suggests that people's current goals and motives may influence the process, and that individual differences and cultural factors may predispose people to either trait or situational inferences.

Further advances in the understanding of social inference processes and the influence of cultural factors and individual differences will have important implications at many levels of social science. Important benefits will accrue for psychologists, but also for political scientists and sociologists. For example, in politics, it may be that the tendency for conservatives to blame the poor for their plight and for liberals to blame the system reflects differences in social inference. Similarly, the default social inference process for an entire culture may influence its members' inferences and proposed solutions with regard to such ubiquitous social problems as homelessness, injustice, and violence.

Acknowledgments—We wish to thank Craig A. Anderson, Lori A. Krull, Jody C. Dill, and David Dubois for their valuable comments on earlier drafts of this manuscript.

Notes

1. This tendency to draw unwarranted trait inferences has been called correspondence bias, the fundamental attribution error, and overattribution bias. For a review, see E. E. Jones, *Interpersonal Perception* (Macmillan, New York, 1990).
2. See, e.g., D. T. Gilbert, B. W. Pelham, and D. S. Krull, On cognitive busyness: When person perceivers meet persons perceived, *Journal of Personality and Social Psychology, 54*, 733–740 (1988); Y. Trope, Identification and inferential processes in dispositional attribution, *Psychological Review, 93*, 239–257 (1986).
3. See, e.g., D. T. Gilbert, Thinking lightly about others: Automatic components of the social inference process, in *Unintended Thought: Limits of Awareness, Intention, and Control*, J. S. Uleman and J. A. Bargh, Eds. (Guilford Press, New York, 1989).
4. See, e.g., H. A. Sagar and J. W. Schofield, Racial and behavioral cues in black and white children's perceptions of ambiguously aggressive acts, *Journal of Personality and Social Psychology, 39*, 590–598 (1980). Note that contrast effects may also occur; e.g., L. L. Martin, J. J. Seta, and R. A. Crelia, Assimilation and contrast as a function of people's willingness and ability to expend effort in forming an impression, *Journal of Personality and Social Psychology, 59*, 27–37 (1990).
5. Trope, note 2.
6. For a review, see J. S. Uleman, Consciousness and control: The case of spontaneous trait inferences, *Personality and Social*

Psychology Bulletin, 13, 337–354 (1987). Note that more recent work suggests that these spontaneous inferences may often be better thought of as summaries of behavior; e.g., J. N. Bassili, Traits as action categories versus traits as person attributes in social cognition, in *On-Line Cognition in Person Perception,* J. N. Bassili, Ed. (Erlbaum, Hillsdale, NJ, 1989).

7. M. B. Lupfer, L. F. Clark, and H. W. Hutcherson, Impact of context on spontaneous trait and situational attributions, *Journal of Personality and Social Psychology, 58,* 239–249 (1990). Note that trait inferences do require some conscious resources; see J. S. Uleman, L. S. Newman, and L. Winter, Can personality traits be inferred automatically? Spontaneous inferences require cognitive capacity at encoding, *Consciousness and Cognition, 1,* 72–90 (1992). See Bassili, note 6.

8. D. E. Carlston and J. J. Skowronski, Savings in the relearning of trait information as evidence for spontaneous inference generation, *Journal of Personality and Social Psychology, 66,* 840–856 (1994).

9. D. M. Webster, Motivated augmentation and reduction of the overattribution bias, *Journal of Personality and Social Psychology, 65,* 261–271 (1993).

10. D. S. Krull, Does the grist change the mill?: The effect of perceiver's goal on the process of social inference, *Personality and Social Psychology Bulletin, 19,* 340–348 (1993). See also G. A. Quattrone, Overattribution and unit formation: When behavior engulfs the person, *Journal of Personality and Social Psychology, 42,* 593–607 (1982); J. D. Vorauer and M. Ross, Making mountains out of molehills: An informational goals analysis of self- and social perception, *Personality and Social Psychology Bulletin, 19,* 620–632 (1993).

11. See, e.g., G. J. O. Fletcher and C. Ward, Attribution theory and processes: A cross-cultural perspective, in *The Cross-Cultural Challenge to Social Psychology,* M. H. Bond, Ed. (Sage, Beverly Hills, CA, 1988); J. G. Miller, Culture and the development of everyday social explanation, *Journal of Personality and Social Psychology, 46,* 961–978 (1984). Although the terms Western and non-Western have been used for simplicity, the cultural difference is perhaps better thought of as a distinction between cultures with an independent and with an interdependent view of the self.

12. R. A. Shweder and E. Bourne, Does the concept of the person vary cross-culturally? in *Cultural Conceptions of Mental Health and Therapy,* A. J. Marsella and G. White, Eds. (Reidel, Boston, 1982), pp. 129–130.

13. L. S. Newman, How individualists interpret behavior: Idiocentrism and spontaneous trait inference, *Social Cognition, 11,* 243–269 (1993). See Bassili, note 6.

Recommended Reading

Trope, Y., and Higgins, E. T., Eds. (1993). Special issue: On Inferring Personal Dispositions from Behavior. *Personality and Social Psychology Bulletin, 19.*

Face It!

How we make and read the fleeting split-second expressions that slip across our countenances thousands of times each day is crucial to our emotional health as individuals and to our survival as a species. BY DEBORAH BLUM

Who hasn't waited for an old friend at an airport and scanned faces impatiently as passengers come hurrying through the gate? You can recognize instantly the travelers with no one to meet them, their gaze unfocused, their expressions carefully neutral; the people expecting to be met, their eyes narrowed, their lips poised on the edge of a smile; the children returning home to their parents, their small laughing faces turned up in greeting. Finally, your own friend appears, face lighting up as you come into view. If a mirror suddenly dropped down before you, there'd be that same goofy smile on your face, the same look of uncomplicated pleasure.

Poets may celebrate its mystery and artists its beauty, but they miss the essential truth of the human countenance. As scientists now are discovering, the power of the face resides in the fleeting split-second expressions that slip across it thousands of times each day. They guide our lives, governing the way we relate to each other as individuals and the way we connect together as a society. Indeed, scientists assert, the ability to make faces—and read them—is vital both to our personal health and to our survival as a species.

Growing out of resurging interest in the emotions, psychologists have been poring over the human visage with the intensity of cryptographers scrutinizing a hidden code. In fact, the pursuits are strikingly similar. The face is the most extraordinary communicator, capable of accurately signaling emotion in a bare blink of a second, capable of concealing emotion equally well. "In a sense, the face is equipped to lie the most and leak the most, and thus can be a very confusing source of information,"

observes Paul Ekman, Ph.D., professor of psychology at the University of California in San Francisco and a pioneer in studying the human countenance.

"The face is both ultimate truth and fata morgana, declares Daniel McNeill, author of the new book *The Face* (Little Brown & Company), a vivid survey of face-related lore from the history of the nose to the merits of plastic surgery. "It is a magnificent surface, and in the last 20 years, we've learned more about it than in the previous 20 millennia."

Today, scientists are starting to comprehend the face's contradiction, to decipher the importance of both the lie and leak, and to puzzle out a basic mystery. Why would an intensely social species like ours, reliant on communication, be apparently designed to give mixed messages? By connecting expression to brain activity with extraordinary precision, researchers are now literally going beyond "skin deep" in understanding how the face connects us, when it pulls us apart. "The face is a probe, a way of helping us see what's behind people's interactions," explains psychology professor Dacher Keltner, Ph.D., of the University of California-Berkeley. Among the new findings:

• With just 44 muscles, nerves, and blood vessels threaded through a scaffolding of bone and cartilage, all layered over by supple skin, the face can twist and pull into 5,000 expressions, all the way from an outright grin to the faintest sneer.

> SMILES, the most recognizable signal of HAPPINESS in the world, are so important that we can SEE them far more clearly than any other EXPRESSION—even at 300 feet, the length of a FOOTBALL field.

• There's a distinct anatomical difference between real and feigned expressions—and in the biological effect they produce in the creators of those expressions.

• We send and read signals with lightning-like speed and over great distances. A browflash—the lift of the eyebrow common when greeting a friend—lasts only a sixth of a second. We can tell in a blink of a second if a stranger's face is registering surprise or pleasure—even if he or she is 150 feet away.

• Smiles are such an important part of communication that we see them far more clearly than any other expression. We can pick up a smile at 300 feet—the length of a football field.

• Facial expressions are largely universal, products of biological imperatives. We are programmed to make and read faces. "The abilities to express and recognize emotion are inborn, genetic, evolutionary," declares George Rotter, Ph.D., professor of psychology at Montclair University in New Jersey.

• Culture, parenting, and experience can temper our ability to display and interpret emotions. Abused children may be prone to trouble because they cannot correctly gauge the meaning and intent of others' facial expressions.

Making FACES

Deciphering facial expressions first entails understanding how they are created. Since the 1980s, Ekman and Wallace Friesen, Ph.D., of the University of California in San Francisco, have been painstakingly inventorying the muscle movements that pull our features into frowns, smiles, and glares. Under their Facial Action Coding System (FACS), a wink is Action Unit 46, involving a twitch of a single muscle, the *obicularis oculi*, which wraps around the eye. Wrinkle your nose (Action Unit 09), that's a production of two muscles, the *levator labii superioris* and the *alaeque nasi*.

The smile, the most recognizable signal in the world, is a much more complex endeavor. Ekman and colleagues have so far identified 19 versions, each engaging slightly different combinations of muscles. Consider two: the beam shared by lovers reunited after a long absence and the smile given by a teller passing back the deposit slip to a bank patron.

The old phrase "smiling eyes" is exactly on target. When we are genuinely happy, as in the two lovers' re-

union, we produce what Ekman and Richard Davidson of the University of Wisconsin-Madison call a "felt" smile. The *zygomatic major* muscles, which run from cheekbone to the corner of the mouth, pull the lips upward, while the *obicularis oculi* crinkle the outer corner of the eyes. In contrast, the polite smile offered by the bank teller (or by someone hearing a traveling salesman joke for the hundredth time) pulls up the lips but, literally, doesn't reach the eyes.

It doesn't reach the brain either. Felt smiles, it seems, trigger a sort of pleasurable little hum, a scientifically measurable activity in their creators' left frontal cortex, the region of the brain where happiness is registered. Agreeable smiles simply don't produce that buzz.

Are we taught to smile and behave nicely in social situations? Well, certainly someone instructs us to say, "Have a nice day." But we seem to be born with the ability to offer both felt and social smiles. According to studies by Davidson and Nathan Fox of the University of Maryland, ten-month-old infants will curve their lips in response to the coo of friendly strangers, but they produce happy, felt smiles only at the approach of their mother. The babies' brains light with a smile, it appears, only for those they love.

Evolution's IMPERATIVE

Why are we keyed in so early to making faces? Charles Darwin argued in his 1872 book, *The Expression of the Emotions in Man and Animals*, that the ability to signal feelings, needs, and desires is critical to human survival and thus evolutionarily based. What if infants could not screw up their faces to communicate distress or hunger? Or if foes couldn't bare their teeth in angry snarls as a warning and threat? And what if we couldn't grasp the meaning of those signals in an instant but had to wait minutes for them to be decoded?

Everything known about early hominid life suggests that it was a highly social existence," observes Ekman, who has edited a just-published new edition of Darwin's classic work. "We had to deal with prey and predators; we had a very long period of child rearing. All of that would mean that survival would depend on our being able to respond quickly to each other's emotional states."

> **We can move PEOPLE from culture to culture and they KNOW how to make and read the same basic expressions: anger, fear, sadness, disgust, surprise, and happiness. The six appear to be HARDWIRED in our brains. EMBARRASSMENT, some suspect, may be a seventh.**

Today, the need is just as great. As Ekman points out, "Imagine the trouble we'd be in, if when an aunt came to visit, she had to be taught what a newborn baby's expression meant—let alone if she was going to be a caretaker." Or if, in our world of non-stop far-flung travel, an expression of intense pain was understood in one society but not in another. "And yet," says Ekman, "we can move people from one culture to another and they just know."

Researchers have identified six basic or universal expressions that appear to be hardwired in our brains, both to make and to read: anger, fear, sadness, disgust, surprise, and happiness. Show photos of an infuriated New Yorker to a high-mountain Tibetan or of a miserable New Guinea tribeswoman to a Japanese worker, and there's no translation problem. Everyone makes the same face—and everyone gets the message.

One of the expressions that hasn't made the universal list but probably should is embarrassment. It reflects one of our least favorite emotions: who doesn't loathe that red-faced feeling of looking like a fool? Yet such displays are far less self-centered than has been assumed. Rather than marking a personal humiliation, contends Keltner, embarrassment seems designed to prompt social conciliation.

Think about it. If we accidentally spill a drink on a colleague, stumble into a stranger in the hall, what's the best way to defuse the tension and avoid an escalation into battle? Often, notes Keltner, even before offering a verbal apology, we appease the injured party by showing embarrassment.

When we're embarrassed, our hands tend to come up, partly covering the face. We rub the side of the nose. We cast our eyes downward. We also try to appear smaller, to shrink into ourselves. These behaviors aren't uniquely ours. In awkward social situations, chimpanzees and monkeys do the same thing—and accomplish the same end. The actions defuse hostility, offer a tacit apology, even elicit sympathy in viewers. (When Keltner first tentatively introduced his chosen topic at research meetings, even jaded scientists let out immediate empathetic "oohs" at the slides of people with red faces).

There are physiological changes associated with this," notes Keltner. "If people see an angry face staring at them, they have a heightened autonomic response—rising stress hormones, speeding pulse—all the signs of fear. When they see an embarrassment response, fear is reduced."

A reddened face and downward glance typically start a rapid de-escalation of hostility among children involved in playground quarrels, says Keltner. Parents go easier on youngsters who show visible embarrassment after breaking a household rule, such as playing handball on the living room wall or chasing the dog up and downstairs throughout the house. Adults also go easier on adults. In one of Keltner's studies, jurors in a hypothetical trial meted out much lighter sentences when convicted drug dealers displayed the classic signs of embarrassment.

Cultural RULES

Expressions aren't dictated by biology alone, however; they are deeply influenced by cultural attitudes. De Paul University psychologist Linda Camras, Ph.D., has been exploring why European-American adults seem so much more willing than Asians to express emotion in public. In one experiment, she studied the reactions of European-American and Asian infants, age 11 months, to being restrained by having one arm lightly grasped by a researcher.

European-American and Japanese babies were remarkably similar in their visible dislike of being held still by a stranger's grip. (The scientists let go if the babies cried for seven seconds straight.) Since infants show no apparent inborn difference in the willingness to publicly express dismay, it stands to reason that they must eventually learn the "appropriate" way to express themselves from their families and the society in which they are reared.

Ekman's work clearly shows how culture teaches us to subdue our instinctive emotional reactions. In one set of studies, he asked American and Japanese college students to watch nature films of streams tumbling down mountainsides and trees rustling in the wind, and also graphic tapes of gory surgeries, including limb amputations. Everyone grimaced at the spurting blood at first. But when a note-taking scientist clad in a white coat—the ultimate authority figure—sat in on watching the films, the Japanese students' behavior altered radically. Instead

When it comes to READING the subtleties of emotion, women are the stronger SEX. While men almost always correctly recognize happiness in a female face, they pick up DISTRESS just 70% of the time. A WOMAN'S face has to be really sad for men to see it.

of showing revulsion, they greeted the bloody films with smiles.

"No wonder that foreigners who visit or live among the Japanese think that their expressions are different from Americans," says Ekman. "They see the results of the cultural display rules, masking and modifying the underlying universal expressions of emotion."

Blank **LOOKS**

Mental or physical illness, too, can interfere with the ability to make faces—with profound consequences for relationships, researchers are learning. Neurophysiologist Jonathan Cole, of Poole Hospital at the University of Southampton, Great Britain, and author of the new book *About Face* (MIT Press), points out that people with Parkinson's disease are often perceived as boring or dull because their faces are rigid and immobile.

Consider also depression. As everyone knows, it shuts down communication. But that doesn't mean only that depressed people withdraw and talk less. The normal expressiveness of the face shuts down as well.

In one experiment, psychologist Jeffrey Cohn, Ph.D., of the University of Pittsburgh had healthy mothers mimic a depressed face while holding their infants. The women were told not to smile. Their babies responded with almost instant dismay. At first they tried desperately to recruit a response from their mother, smiling more, gurgling, reaching out. "The fact that the babies were trying to elicit their mother's response shows that at an early age, we do have the beginnings of a social skill for resolving interpersonal failures," Cohn notes.

But equally important, the infants simply could not continue to interact without receiving a response. They stopped their efforts. The experiment lasted only three minutes, but by that time, the babies were themselves withdrawn. "When mothers again resumed normal behavior, babies remained distant and distressed for up to a minute," says Cohn. "You can see that maternal depression, were it chronic, could have developmental consequences."

In fact, children of depressed parents tend to become very detached in their relationships with others. They often fail to connect with other people throughout their life and experience difficulties in romantic relationships and marriage, in large part, researchers suspect, because they have trouble producing and picking up on emo-

tional signals. "We think that the lack of facial animation interferes with forming relationships," says Keltner.

Reading **FACES**

Displays of emotion are only half the equation, of course. How viewers interpret those signals is equally important. "We evolved a system to communicate and a capacity to interpret," observes Keltner. "But much less is known about the interpreting capacity."

What scientists do know for certain is that we are surprisingly bad at discerning the real emotions or intentions behind others' facial expressions. "One of the problems that people don't realize is how complicated face reading is," notes Pollak. "At first glance, it seems very straightforward. But if you break it down—think of all the information in the face, how quickly the brain has to comprehend and analyze it, memories come in, emotions, context, judgments—then you realize that we really can't do it all."

Or can't do it all well. What we seem to have done during our evolution is to learn shortcuts to face reading. In other words, we make snap judgments. "It's not actually a conscious decision," Pollak explains. "But decisions are being made in the brain—What am I going to pay attention to? What am I going to clue into?"

Most of us are pretty good at the strong signals—sobbing, a big grin—but we stumble on the subtleties. Some people are better than others. There's some evidence that women are more adept than men at picking up the weaker signals, especially in women's faces.

In an experiment conducted by University of Pennsylvania neuroscientists Ruben and Raquel Gur, men and women were shown photos of faces. Both genders did well at reading men's expressions. Men also were good at picking up happiness in female faces; they got it right about 90% of the time. But when it came to recognizing distress signals in women's faces, their accuracy fell to 70%.

"A woman's face had to be really sad for men to see it," says Ruben Gur. The explanation may lie in early human history. Charged with protecting their tribes, men had to be able to quickly read threats from other males, suggests Gur. Women, in contrast, en-

Abused children are so POISED to detect anger that they often will READ it into others' faces even when it isn't there. That tendency may serve them well at HOME, where they need all the self defenses they can muster, but it can lead to TROUBLE outside.

trusted with child-rearing, became more finely-tuned to interpreting emotions.

We may be biologically primed to grasp certain expressions, but our individual experiences and abilities also filter the meaning. Mental disorders, apparently, can swamp the biology of facial recognition. People with schizophrenia, for instance, are notoriously bad at face reading; when asked to look at photographs, they struggle to separate a happy face from a neutral one.

Mistaking CUES

Seth Pollak, Ph.D., a psychologist at the University of Wisconsin-Madison, has been exploring how children who have suffered extreme parental abuse—broken bones, burn scarring—read faces. In his studies, he asks these youngsters and those from normal homes to look at three photographs of faces which display classic expressions of fear, anger, and happiness. Mean-

while, electrodes attached to their heads measure their brain activity.

Battered children seem to sustain a damaging one-two punch, Pollak is finding. Overall, they have a subdued level of electrical activity in the brain. (So, in fact, do people suffering from schizophrenia or alcoholism. It seems to be a sign of trouble within.) However, when abused youngsters look at the photo of an angry face, they rapidly generate a rising wave of electrical energy, sharper and stronger than anything measured in children who live in less threatening homes.

When Pollak further analyzed the brain activity readings, he found that abused children generate that panicky reaction even when there's no reason to, misreading as angry some of the other pictured faces. They are so primed to see anger, so poised for it, that when making split-second judgments, they tilt toward detection of rage.

This falls in line with findings from DePaul's Camras and other psychologists, which show that abused children struggle significantly more in deciphering ex-

Face SHAPE

Since ancient times, human beings have been making judgments about each other based not just on the expressions that cross the face but on its very structure. The practice of finding meaning in anatomy is enjoying a remarkable renaissance today.

A plethora of pop books ponder the significance of chins, eye slant, and eyebrows. One popular magazine has even started a new face-reading feature. First to be analyzed: President William Jefferson Clinton. His triangular face apparently indicates a dynamic and—big surprise—sexual personality. Among the theories now being trotted out: heavy eyelids denote jealousy, a rosebud mouth promises fidelity, and a hairy brow line ensures restlessness.

Scientists dismiss these readings as no more than facial astrology. "There is as yet no good data to support this practice," observes Lesley Zebrowitz, professor of psychology at Brandeis University.

While many may regard it as a sort of harmless parlor game, face reading does have a more pernicious effect. Charles Darwin noted that he was almost barred from voyaging on the H.M.S. Beagle because the captain thought his nose suggested a lazy nature. In the 1920s, Los Angeles judge Edward Jones insisted that he could, with over 90% accuracy, determine someone was a "born criminal" by his protruding lips and too-close-together eyes.

Though today no one would make such a blatant assessment of character based on anatomy, facial shape at least

subconsciously does appear to figure into our judgments. In her book, *Reading Faces*, Zebrowitz meticulously documents her research showing that baby-faced adults, with big eyes and full cheeks and lips, bring out in the rest of us a nurturing protective response, the kind we give to children.

In one remarkable study, she tracked proceedings in Boston small claims court for more than 500 cases and found that, whatever the evidence, chubby-cheeked plaintiffs were more apt to prevail than claimants with more mature-looking faces. Says Zebrowitz: "Although our judicial system talks about 'blind justice,' it's impossible to control the extra-legal factor of stereotyping based on physical appearance."—D.B.

pression. "Overall, there's a relationship between the expressive behavior of the mother and the child's recognition ability," Camras says. "And it's an interesting kind of a difference."

Identifying negative expressions seems to be essential in human interaction; four of the six universal expressions are negative. In most homes, notes Camras, mothers use "mild negative expressions, little frowns, tightening of the mouth." Children from such families are very good at detecting early signs of anger. But youngsters from homes with raging furious moms have trouble recognizing anger. "If the mom gets really angry, it's so frightening, it's so disorganizing for children that it seems they can't learn anything from it."

The Best DEFENSE

So, out of sheer self-protection, if the children from abusive homes are uncertain about what a face says—as they often are—they'll fall back on anger as the meaning and prepare to defend themselves. "They overdetect rage," says Pollak. Does this create problems in their relationships outside the home? It's a logical, if as yet unproven, conclusion.

"What Darwin tells us is that emotions are adaptations," Pollak explains. "If a child is physically abused, I'd put my money on an adaptation toward assuming hostile intent. Look at the cost for these kids of missing a threat. So what happens is, they do better in the short run—they're very acute at detecting anger and threat because unfortunately they have to be. But take them out of those maltreating families and put them with other people and their reactions don't fit."

One of Pollak's long-term goals is to find out if such harmful effects can be reversed, if abused children can regain or reconstruct the social skills—that is, reading faces—that are evidently so critical to our design.

Failure to read signals accurately may also figure in juvenile delinquency. "There are studies that have found that juvenile delinquents who are prone to aggression have trouble deciphering certain expressions," says Keltner. "They're not as good as other kids at it. Is that because they're particularly bad at reading appeasement signals like embarrassment? That's something we'd really like to know."

Truth OR LIES?

One area where *everyone* seems to have trouble in reading faces is in detecting deception. We average between 45 and 65% accuracy in picking up lies—pretty dismal when one considers that chance is 50%. Secret Service agents can notch that up a bit to about 64%; sci-

entists suspect that improvement comes only after years of scanning crowds, looking for the faces of potential assassins.

Con artists, too, seem to be especially adept at reading expressions. The latter are also skilled at faking emotions, a trait they share with actors. Not surprising, since success in both careers depends on fooling people.

We seem to be duped particularly easily by a smile. In fact, we tend to implicitly trust a smiling face, just as we do a baby-faced one. In one experiment, Rotter cut out yearbook photos of college students and then asked people to rate the individuals pictured for trustworthiness. In almost every instance, people chose the students with smiling faces as the most honest. Women with the biggest grins scored the best; men needed only a slight curve of the lips to be considered truthful. "Smiles are an enormous controller of how people perceive you," says Rotter. "It's an extremely powerful communicator, much more so than the eyes."

> **We do a better job of detecting falsehoods if we listen to a voice or examine body stance than if we read a face.**

Incidentally, we aren't suckered only by human faces. We can be equally and easily tricked by our fellow primates. In one classic story, a young lowland gorilla gently approached a keeper, stared affectionately into his face, gave him a hug—and stole his watch. Chimpanzees, too, are famous for their friendly-faced success in luring lab workers to approach, and then triumphantly spraying them with a mouthful of water.

There *are* clues to insincerity. We tend to hold a simulated expression longer than a real one. If we look carefully, a phony smile may have the slightly fixed expression that a child's face gets when setting a smile for a photograph. As we've discussed, we also use different muscles for felt and fake expressions. And we are apt to blink more when we're lying. But not always—and that's the problem. When Canadian researchers Susan Hyde, Kenneth Craig, and Chrisopher Patrick asked people to simulate an expression of pain, they found that the fakers used the same facial muscles—lowering their brows, tightening their lips—as did those in genuine pain. In fact, the only way to detect the fakers was that the expressions were slightly exaggerated and "blinking occurred less often, perhaps because of the cognitive demands to act as if they were in pain," the scientists explain.

We do a better job of finding a falsehood by listening to the tone of a voice or examining the stance of a body than by reading the face, maintains Ekman, who has served as a consultant for police departments, intelligence agencies, and antiterrorist groups. He's even been approached by a national television network—"I can't tell you which one"—eager to train its reporters to better recognize when sources are lying.

Which brings us to perhaps the most provocative mystery of the face: why are we so willing to trust in what the face tells us, to put our faith in a steady gaze, a smiling look? With so much apparently at stake in reading facial cues correctly, why are we so prone to mistakes?

Living SMOOTHLY

Most of us don't pick up lies and, actually, most of us don't care to," declares Ekman. "Part of the way politeness works is that we expect people to mislead us sometime—say, on a bad hair day. What we care about is that the person goes through the proper role."

Modern existence, it seems, is predicated to some extent on ignoring the true meaning of faces: our lives run more smoothly if we don't know whether people really find our jokes funny. It runs more smoothly if we don't know when people are lying to us. And perhaps it runs more smoothly if men can't read women's expressions of distress.

Darwin himself told of sitting across from an elderly woman on a railway carriage and observing that her mouth was pulled down at the corners. A proper British Victorian, he assumed that no one would display grief while traveling on public transportation. He began musing on what else might cause her frown.

While he sat there, analyzing, the woman's eyes suddenly overflowed with tears. Then she blinked them away, and there was nothing but the quiet distance between two passengers. Darwin never knew what she was thinking. Hers was a private grief, not to be shared with a stranger.

There's a lesson in that still, for all of us airport face-watchers today. That we may always see only part of the story, that what the face keeps secret may be as valuable as what it shares.

Motivational Approaches to Expectancy Confirmation

John T. Copeland

John Copeland is an Assistant Professor of Psychology at Wabash College. Address correspondence to John T. Copeland, Wabash College, Crawfordsville, IN 47933; e-mail: copelanj@wabash.bitnet.

For some time now, social, personality, and cognitive psychologists have been interested in how our interpersonal expectations affect our thoughts, feelings, and behavior. A provocative finding in this research suggests that people often act in ways that preferentially confirm their expectations of others. Specifically, an individual who holds some expectation (who is generally referred to as a perceiver) about some other person (who is generally referred to as a target), through the course of their interaction, will often form expectancy-confirming impressions of the target (a phenomenon referred to as *perceptual confirmation*) and elicit expectancy-confirming behavior from the target (a phenomenon referred to as *behavioral confirmation*). Thus, expecting Jody to be a warm and friendly person, I may elicit warm and friendly behavior from her and form similar impressions of her. This expectancy confirmation is the essence of Merton's self-fulfilling prophecy and has been the subject of considerable laboratory and field studies by social psychologists.[1]

In a widely cited investigation of expectancy confirmation, Snyder, Tanke, and Berscheid had male perceivers engage in a dyadic, getting-acquainted conversation with female targets.[2] Before the conversation, each man was given a randomly assigned photograph, ostensibly of his woman partner. For half of the men, the picture portrayed the target woman as physically attractive; for the

other half of the men, the picture portrayed the target as physically unattractive. In reality, the pictures were not of the targets, but of women who had participated in an earlier study. Snyder, Tanke, and Berscheid wanted to see if the beliefs, expectations, and stereotypes associated with physical attractiveness—namely, "what is beautiful is good"—would have an influence on the conversations between perceivers and targets.

Perceivers' reports indicated that the photo-induced expectations did indeed affect perceivers' postconversation impressions of targets. Men given attractive photos found their women partners to be more warm, open, and friendly than did men given unattractive photos—evidence of the perceptual confirmation of the men's physical attractiveness-based expectations. Additionally, independent judges, blind to experimental conditions, listened to only the targets' portion of the conversations. Judges' reports of targets' behavior indicated that the women in the attractive-photo condition actually behaved in a more warm and friendly manner than the women in the unattractive-photo condition—providing evidence of behavioral confirmation of perceivers' expectations. Analyses of perceivers' portions of the conversation, also by independent judges, indicated that the observed confirmation effects were due to differential behavior of the perceivers during the conversations. Specifically, men who expected to interact with attractive, warm, and friendly women behaved in a warm and friendly manner themselves, thus helping to elicit such behavior from those women. Thus, Snyder, Tanke, and Berscheid demonstrated that a "what is beautiful is good" stereotype can be self-fulfilling—behaviorially

confirmed by targets because of perceivers' biased behavior.

Although this expectancy confirmation effect has important moderators and boundary conditions, it has been demonstrated in a variety of social settings, including the classroom, the workplace, and the psychological clinic. In addition to physical appearance, researchers have examined the confirmatory effects of other interpersonal expectations, such as those based on gender, race, and academic ability.[1] Although recent reviews and theoretical models have questioned the pervasiveness and extent of behavioral expectancy effects, most accounts of expectancy-influenced social encounters affirm the potential of such expectancies for producing biased outcomes.[3] Furthermore, expectancy confirmation phenomena have been linked to important deleterious social phenomena such as prejudice, discrimination, and the perpetuation of stereotypes. Thus, previous work on expectancy confirmation has focused on questions of the process, outcomes, and boundary conditions of the phenomenon—the "how" and "how much" of expectancy confirmation.

The purpose of this review is to highlight a newly emerging theme in theory and research on expectancy confirmation. Recently, researchers interested in expectancy confirmation processes have turned their attention toward understanding the motivational antecedents of these processes—the "why" of expectancy confirmation. These efforts reflect an attempt to understand and explain, at a more parsimonious level, the diverse psychological and behavioral mechanisms that affect expectancy-influenced social interactions. Additionally, this motivational focus coincides with a renewed

From *Current Directions in Psychological Science*, August 1993, pp. 117–121. © 1993 by the American Psychological Society. Reprinted by permission of Blackwell Publishers.

interest in motivational theories of social thinking and social behavior—theories being developed and explored in many psychological domains. Such theories postulate that much of thinking and behavior is purposeful and directed at achieving some more or less specific end. Thus, understanding psychological and behavioral processes requires understanding the needs, motives, goals, and plans that underlie such processes.

This review presents a sample of the emerging theory and research on the motivational moderators of expectancy confirmation. First, the role of impression formation goals—the extent to which people are concerned with gathering and integrating information about other people—is considered. Work on motives dealing with the regulation and facilitation of social interaction is then presented, including work on the moderating effects of self-presentation (e.g., ingratiation, self-promotion). Finally, the motivational and confirmatory implications of the social relationship between interactants is considered. Although covering the steps in the expectancy confirmation process and the pervasiveness of that process is beyond the scope of the current review, it does represent a taste of the current motivational work in this area.

PERSON PERCEPTION AND IMPRESSION FORMATION

Impression formation is generally defined as the process of perceiving pieces of information about an individual (e.g., prior expectations, verbal and nonverbal behaviors) and integrating them into some coherent summary impression. Already a process of considerable study by cognitive and social psychologists for some time, impression formation as a motivational goal has recently become a focus of researchers interested in expectancy confirmation processes. These researchers postulate that social interactants' person perception and impression formation concerns moderate the extent of expectancy influences.

Snyder and his colleagues have taken a functional approach to studying the motivational foundations of expectancy confirmation.[4] At a general level, a functional approach is concerned with understanding the psychological functions served by an individual's beliefs and behaviors. A functional analysis of expectancy confirmation focuses on the psychological functions served by the beliefs and behaviors of a perceiver and a target. According to Snyder, perceivers motivated to form stable, predictable impressions of their target partners—perceivers whose behaviors serve the

psychological function of acquiring and using social knowledge—are likely to confirm their expectations of targets.

In one study, Snyder and Haugen had male perceivers engage in a getting-acquainted conversation with female targets.[5] This was a conceptual replication of the earlier study by Snyder, Tanke, and Berscheid, but with a focus on obesity stereotypes. Each man was given a photograph, ostensibly of his partner, but, again, in reality, obtained in an earlier study. The picture portrayed the partner as being either obese or of normal weight. Independent of the picture manipulation, each man was given one of three sets of motivational instructions. One third of the men were told to try to "get to know" their partners during their conversations—to form stable, predictable impressions of their partners. Another third of the men were told to "get along" well with their partners—to have smooth and pleasant conversations with them and try to avoid awkward points during their talk. Finally, one third of the men were given no specific motivational instructions for the conversations (a motivational control condition consisting of the traditional paradigmatic components but without any specific interaction objectives delivered to perceivers).

Analyses of perceivers' postconversation impression ratings revealed that relative to the men in the other motivational conditions, the men who were instructed to form stable, predictable impressions of their partners were more likely to form expectancy-confirming impressions of those targets. Specifically, for the men in this motivational condition, those given a picture of an obese target found their partners to be more unfriendly, reserved, and unenthusiastic than those given a picture of a normal-weight target found their partners. Additionally, the behavior of the women in this motivational condition was found by independent judges to be expectancy-consistent. In contrast, there was no evidence of either perceptual or behavioral confirmation in the other two motivational conditions. Perceivers who were instructed to "get along" with their targets as well as perceivers lacking any specific motivational instructions for their interaction neither formed confirming impressions nor elicited confirming behavior. Thus, perceivers whose behaviors served the psychological function of acquiring and using social knowledge were more likely to confirm their preinteraction expectations of targets.

Neuberg has focused on how accuracy motives in person perception moderate expectancy confirmation.[6] Neuberg contrasts the goal of forming an accurate impression of a person with the goal of

forming a rapid impression of a person. He believes that a perceiver motivated to form an accurate impression of a target will be less biased in information gathering about the target than will a perceiver motivated to form a rapid impression. As a result, the tendency for expectancy-confirming outcomes will be reduced for the former perceiver.

In a test of this hypothesis, Neuberg had perceivers serve as interviewers for a hypothetical job, with targets serving as applicants. Each interviewer talked with two targets, one at a time, and assessed their suitability for the job. Prior to the conversations, perceivers were led to believe that one of the targets was not well suited for the job, but no such information was given about the other target. Independent of the expectations, perceivers were given instructions either to form accurate impressions of the targets (accuracy goal) or to form impressions sufficient to decide on their suitability for the job (sufficiency goal).

Results indicated that accuracy motives had the predicted effects. Perceivers' postinterview impressions showed that expectancy confirmation occurred only in the sufficiency-goal condition, in which negative-expectancy targets were assessed less favorably than control targets. In contrast, perceivers motivated to form accurate impressions did not differ significantly in their impressions of the two targets. A substantially similar pattern of results was found from analyses of targets' actual behavior. Behavioral confirmation of perceivers' expectations occurred only in the sufficiency-goal condition. Indeed, in the accuracy-goal condition, there was evidence of behavioral disconfirmation: In the eyes of the independent judges, negative-expectancy targets performed better than the control targets.

These researchers have demonstrated that the extent to which perceivers are concerned with arriving at some understanding of their target partners will moderate expectancy effects. One distinction within this research seems to be between forming a stable, predictable impression of a target, as in the work of Snyder and Haugen, and forming an accurate impression of a target, as in Neuberg's work. When perceivers are motivated to form stable, predictable impressions of targets, we see the traditional expectancy confirmation effects. However, when perceivers are motivated to form accurate impressions, the effects are attenuated. The distinction between stability and accuracy appears to be important and has drawn the attention of these researchers.[5] Indeed, some recent theoretical accounts of expectancy confirmation highlight the potential accuracy of expectations and call into question the degree of confirmatory biases in social interaction.[7]

SELF-PRESENTATION AND INTERACTION FACILITATION

Researchers interested in the motivational antecedents of expectancy confirmation are also examining how interactants' self-presentational concerns and concerns with facilitating their social interactions affect the expectancy confirmation process. Briefly, self-presentational motives are concerns associated with managing one's image, one's appearance in the eyes of other people, or one's self-perception. Concerns about interaction facilitation center on having pleasant interactions with others, interactions unencumbered by awkward or uncomfortable exchanges. Both types of motives appear to play important roles in the moderation of expectancy effects.

In the previously discussed study by Snyder and Haugen, one third of the perceivers were instructed to get along well with their target partners.[5] As a result of this manipulation, there was no evidence of expectancy confirmation either in perceivers' postinteraction impressions of targets or in judges' ratings of targets' behavior. Perceivers whose behaviors served the psychological function of regulating and facilitating their social interaction avoided the cognitive and behavioral processes that generally lead to expectancy-confirming interaction outcomes.

In an investigation of the moderating role of ingratiation—a self-presentational goal—Neuberg, Judice, Virdin, and Carrillo had perceivers interview targets for a hypothetical job.[8] Half of the targets were portrayed in a negative light, and the other half were given no such portrayal. Independent of the expectancy manipulation, half of the interviewers were encouraged to get the applicants to like them (self-presentation), while the other half of the interviewers were given no explicit goal.

In the no-goal condition, the traditional expectancy confirmation effects were obtained. Interviewers were relatively cold and more challenging toward the negative-expectancy targets, causing these targets to perform less favorably during the interviews. However, in the liking-goal condition, interviewers behaved in a more warm and friendly manner toward the negative-expectancy targets than toward the no-expectancy targets, which led these interviewers to form expectancy-disconfirming impressions of the negatively labeled targets.

These studies suggest that perceivers motivated either to manage the impressions they give to targets or to have enjoyable social encounters will be less likely to effect a self-fulfilling prophecy than perceivers motivated to form impressions of targets. The interactions seem to be qualitatively different. Self-presentational and facilitative motives appear to inhibit both the tendency for perceivers to engage in expectancy-biased information seeking and targets' behavioral confirmation of perceivers' expectations.

THE PERCEIVER—TARGET RELATIONSHIP

Other researchers interested in the motivational underpinnings of expectancy confirmation focus on the relationship between a perceiver and a target in a particular interaction setting. These researchers claim that the interactants' roles, their relative power in the interaction setting, and the formality and structure of the interaction setting may affect both the motives of the interactants and the likelihood of expectancy-confirming outcomes.

Elsewhere, I have suggested that the relative power of perceiver and target moderates both motivation and expectancy confirmation.[9] In an investigation of this hypothesis, each perceiver was given one of two expectations about the target. Independent of the expectancy manipulation, one of the participants (either the perceiver or the target, as determined by random assignment to experimental conditions) had the power to choose whether the other would be a participant in a subsequent reward-laden phase of the study. When the perceivers had the power to affect the targets' outcomes, perceivers reported they were motivated primarily to acquire knowledge about targets, and targets reported they were motivated primarily to facilitate favorable interaction outcomes. These interactions resulted in both the perceptual and the behavioral confirmation of perceivers' experimentally delivered expectations about targets. However, when targets had control over perceivers' outcomes, the motive reports were reversed: Perceivers reported a primary concern with facilitating favorable interaction outcomes, and targets reported a primary concern with the acquisition of knowledge about perceivers. In these interactions, there were no signs of perceptual or behavioral confirmation. Thus, power affected both subjects' motivations (at least, self-reported motivations) and the likelihood of subsequent expectancy confirmation.

In her situational taxonomy of expectancy situations, Harris has suggested that the formality and degree of structure in an interaction setting affect the extent to which expectancies will be influential.[10] Formality refers to the social formality of an interaction setting, the extent of adherence to explicit and fixed customs or social rules. Structure refers to how highly scripted an interaction is, the extent to which the roles are highly specified and articulated. Although these two dimensions are related, they are probably not redundant, as not all socially structured situations are formal (e.g., the players of a board game have structured roles, but they need not be formal roles).

Indirect support for Harris's hypothesis about the degree of structure was found in a study in which grade-school boys were paired for two different tasks.[11] For the structured task, the boys worked together to complete a color-by-number picture; for the less structured task, the boys worked together to plan and build their own Lego block design. Perceiver boys in this study also either were told that their partner would be difficult to work with or were given no such expectancy. Expectancy effects were weaker in the more structured task. During the color-by-number task, perceivers were less likely to form expectancy-confirming impressions and elicit expectancy-confirming behavior from targets than during the Lego task. From a motivational perspective, this result may have been due to perceivers' greater concern with completing the formal requirements of the more structured task. This concern may have kept perceivers too cognitively and behaviorally busy to engage in the expectancy confirmation processes that the less structured Lego task afforded.

Thus, aspects of the social relationship between a perceiver and a target can have motivational ramifications and subsequent moderating effects on expectancy influences. The effects of these relationship factors are important to a thorough understanding of expectancy confirmation phenomena. Perceivers' and targets' motives may often be induced specifically because of the nature of the social relationship in a given interaction setting. When perceivers and targets will be concerned with impression formation or self-presentation may depend in large part on the nature of their social setting and the roles they are required to play.

DISCUSSION

Although most of the work covered in this review focuses on a perceiver's motives, other work not covered here focuses on the moderating role of a target's motives. To the extent that the same motives operate in other social contexts, these motivational approaches may add not only to our understanding of expectancy confirmation processes in particular, but also to what we know about social thinking and social behavior in general.

Acknowledgments—Support for the author's research described in this article was provided by a Dissertation Research Award from the American Psychological Association. The author would like to thank the anonymous reviewer who provided valuable comments on an earlier version of the manuscript. Preparation of the manuscript was aided through a Byron K. Trippet stipend.

Notes

1. J. M. Darley and R. H. Fazio, Expectancy-confirmation processes arising in the social interaction sequence, *American Psychologist, 35,* 867–881 (1980); R. Rosenthal, *On the Social Psychology of the Self-Fulfilling Prophecy: Further Evidence for Pygmalion Effects and Their Mediating Mechanisms* (M.S.S. Information Corporation Modular Publications, New York, 1974); M. Snyder, When belief creates reality, in *Advance in Experimental Social Psychology,* Vol. 18, L. Berkowitz, Ed. (Academic Press, Orlando, FL, 1984).

2. M. Snyder, E. D. Tanke, and E. Bersheid, Social perception and interpersonal behavior: On the self-fulfilling nature of social stereotypes, *Journal of Personality and Social Psychology, 35,* 656–666 (1977).

3. L. Jussim, Social perception and social reality: A reflection-construction model, *Psychological Review, 98,* 54–73 (1991); E. E. Jones, *Interpersonal Perception* (W. H. Freeman, New York, 1990).

4. M. Snyder, Motivational foundations of behavior confirmation, in *Advances in Experimental Social Psychology,* Vol. 25, M. Zanna, Ed. (Academic Press, San Diego, 1992).

5. M. Snyder and J. A. Haugen, *Why does behavioral confirmation occur? A functional perspective,* paper presented at the annual meeting of the American Psychological Association, Boston (August 1990).

6. S. L. Neuberg, The goal of forming accurate impressions during social interactions: Attenuating the impact of negative expectancies, *Journal of Personality and Social Psychology, 56,* 374–386 (1989).

7. Jussim, note 3.

8. S. L. Neuberg, T. N. Judice, L. M. Virdin, and M. A. Carrillo, Perceiver self-presentational goals as moderators of expectancy influences: Ingratiation and the disconfirmation of negative expectancies, *Journal of Personality and Social Psychology, 64,* 409–420 (1993).

9. J. T. Copeland, *Motivational implications of social power for behavioral confirmation,,* paper presented at the annual meeting of the Midwestern Psychological Association, Chicago (May 1992).

10. M. J. Harris, Issues in studying the mediation of interpersonal expectancy effects: A taxonomy of expectancy situations, in *Interpersonal Expectations: Theory, Research, and Applications,* P. D. Blank, Ed. (Cambridge University Press, London, in press).

11. M. J. Harris, R. Milich, E. M. Corbitt, D. W. Hoover, and M. Brady, Self-fulfilling effects of stigmatizing information on children's social interactions, *Journal of Personality and Social Psychology, 63,* 41–50 (1992).

Recommended Reading

Hilton, J. L., and Darley, J. M. (1991). The effects of interaction goals on person perception. In *Advances in Experimental Social Psychology,* Vol. 24, M. P. Zanna, Ed. (Academic Press, San Diego).

Jussim, L. (1991). Social perception and social reality: A reflection-construction model. *Psychological Review, 98,* 54–73.

Snyder, M. (1992). Motivational foundations of behavioral confirmation. In *Advances in Experimental Social Psychology,* Vol. 25, M. Zanna, Ed. (Academic Press, San Diego).

CULTURE, IDEOLOGY, AND CONSTRUAL

Lee Ross and Richard E. Nisbett

Social Context and Attribution in East and West

North American social psychologists have been preoccupied, over the last two decades, with attempts to describe strategies and biases in the way people make trait inferences and behavioral attributions. Recent cross-cultural work suggests that we may have been guilty of some ethnocentrism, or at least of a failure to consider variability across cultures and subcultures, in our efforts. Some contrasts between subjects showing the individualistic orientation of culture and those from more collectivist cultures provide an instructive starting point.

Importance of self relative to others. An interesting demonstration by Kitayama and his colleagues (1989) suggests that collectivist Japanese subjects may be less inclined than individualistic Americans to see themselves as the focal point of attention in their dealings with their peers. The evidence for this conclusion is a bit indirect, but ingenious in the way that it proceeds from a classic finding on similarity assessment.

In 1977, Amos Tversky reported the surprising finding that assessments of similarity between objects of judgment often are asymmetric—that is, that subjects tend to judge Madrid to be more similar to New York than New York is to Madrid, or judge jackals to be more similar to dogs than dogs are to jackals. The reason for this asymmetry apparently lies in the tendency for subjects to treat the more salient, important, and cognitively rich object as the implicit reference or standard of comparison, and thus judge the less salient and significant object to be more similar to the highly salient and significant one than vice versa. Consistent with this generalization, Holyoak and Gordon (1979) found that

American subjects judged the similarity of others to themselves to be substantially greater than the similarity of themselves to others—that is, the relatively nonsignificant, nonsalient, cognitively impoverished other was deemed rather similar to the significant, salient, cognitively rich self, but not vice versa. What Kitayama and colleagues showed was a literal reversal of this pattern among Japanese—a result suggesting that the relatively collectivist Japanese may deem their peers more important and salient objects of attention and contemplation, and themselves less important and salient objects, than do individualistic "self-centered" Americans.

Generalized versus contextualized views of personal attributes. A related demonstration was reported by Cousins (1989), who used the "Who Am I" test to show that the collectivist Japanese are less inclined than Americans to claim that they possess broad, cross-situational, personal attributes. Thus, when a free-response version of the test stipulated no specific contexts, the Japanese listed only a fourth as many abstract, psychological attributes (for example, "I am optimistic") as did American subjects, but three times as many social roles and contexts (for example, "I am a member of the drama club"). When specific contexts were stipulated, however, it was the Japanese who were more likely to use psychological attributes to describe themselves (for example, "at home I am sometimes lazy" or "in school I am hard-working"). Cousins argues that this pattern makes sense in terms of the Japanese understanding that their behavior is dependent on social context. In contrast, Americans like to think of themselves as having a set of personal attributes that is independent of any particularized relations with other people or specified situational contexts.

No fundamental attribution error for Hindus? The weight that collectivist Asian subjects give to social context may also influence the way they account for social behavior. In particular, Joan Miller (1984) has shown that Hindus are more likely than Americans to explain events in terms of situational or contextual factors. As noted in Chapter 5 (where we discussed only the results for American subjects), Miller asked her subjects to describe, and then to account for, "good" or "wrong" things that someone they knew well had recently done. Their explanations were coded into broad categories of which the most relevant, in terms of our concerns, were those corresponding to general dispositions (for example, "generosity" or "clumsiness") versus context (for example, "there was no one else there to help" or "it was dark"). Individualistic, person-oriented U.S. sub-

jects invoked general dispositions 45 percent of the time to explain negative or deviant behaviors, while Hindu subjects invoked them only 15 percent of the time. Similarly, U.S. subjects invoked dispositional explanations 35 percent of the time to explain positive or prosocial behaviors, while Hindu subjects invoked them only 22 percent of the time. In contrast, Hindu subjects invoked contextual reasons 32 percent of the time for deviant behaviors, while U.S. subjects invoked them only 14 percent of the time; and Hindu subjects invoked contextual explanations 49 percent of the time for prosocial behaviors, while U.S. subjects invoked them only 22 percent of the time. Miller also made use of an elegant control comparison to show that the differing American versus Hindu explanations were not the result of any differences in the actions to be explained. She asked her U.S. subjects to explain behavior generated by her Hindu subjects. Consistent with Miller's cultural difference hypothesis, the American subjects explained the Hindu-generated behaviors with virtually the same proportions of dispositional and contextual explanations that they applied to behaviors they generated themselves.

Does this mean that Hindus are free of the fundamental attribution error, thereby calling into question how "fundamental" the error really is? Perhaps, but Miller's study alone cannot establish this; for it is possible that situational factors really do play more of a role in determining behavior in the East than in the West. Indeed, this is a basic assumption of scholars who contrast individualist and collectivist cultures. Accordingly, the Hindus may not be showing greater situationist insight, they simply may be explaining more situationally determined behavior. We suspect, however, that the truth involves both factors. That is, situational influences, in non-Western contexts, may be both more powerful determinants of behavior and more salient explanations of behavior. Thus we suspect that Hindus and many other collectivist people really are less susceptible than Americans to the fundamental attribution error.

The studies just described represent some of the clearest evidence available that different cultures construe the world in ways that are truly different at base. And they suggest that marked cognitive differences may have fundamentally social origins.

Social Class and Locus of Control

Just as there is a "horizontal" dimension of difference among the world's cultures in preference for explanation, there is a cross-cutting and somewhat related "vertical" dimension of difference corresponding to social class. People of lower socioeconomic status (SES) are more likely to explain events pertaining to them by reference to external causes than are higher SES people (P. Gurin, G. Gurin, & Morrison, 1978). For example, lower SES subjects are more likely to believe that "many of the unhappy things in people's lives are partly due to bad luck," while higher SES subjects are more likely to believe that "people's misfortunes result from the mistakes they make." Lower SES subjects are also more likely to believe that "knowing the right people is important in deciding whether a person will get ahead," while higher SES subjects are more likely to believe that people will get ahead in life if they have talent and do a good job: "knowing the right people has nothing to do with it."

This explanation preference is correlated with a value preference. Higher SES people value autonomy and personal causation more than do lower SES people, probably for the good and sufficient reason that their livelihoods are more dependent on the efficaciousness of their personal decisions than are those of lower SES people (Kohn & Schooler, 1969). For example, higher SES subjects, more than lower SES subjects, value independent judgment, self-reliance, and being interested in how and why things happen. Lower SES subjects, more than higher SES subjects, value respectability and ability to get along well with people. In their child-rearing, higher SES parents claim to emphasize responsibility and self-control, while lower SES parents claim to emphasize good manners and obedience to parents.

Thus higher and lower SES people differ in the assumptions they make about causality and in their values related to locus of causality. Higher SES people assume that people's outcomes are primarily a direct reflection of their behavior, while lower SES people are more likely to assume that people's outcomes are beyond their control. To a substantial extent, of course, these explanation preferences are a reflection of reality. Higher SES people in fact have more control over outcomes, both in professional life and personal life, than do lower SES people. The values of the two groups can be seen as a response to their objective situation. Higher SES parents prefer inquisitiveness and control orientation in their peers, their children, and themselves, as befits managers and professionals. Lower SES parents prefer obedience and getting along with others, attributes that will be valued by employers and friends. (Though it should be noted that the differences between social classes are not large in any of the terms we have discussed in this book. Whether this is because the differences, in fact, are not great

or whether the methodology of verbal survey responses mutes real differences is not clear. Participant observation work by Heath, 1983, suggests there are truly substantial social-class differences in socialization practices related to independence, self-reliance, and personal efficacy.)

The discovery of differences between the social classes in expressed ideology and values constitutes a victory for the situationist, economic determinism view of culture. The differences between classes, for the most part, are highly understandable in terms of the jobs that members of a class hold and for which they are tacitly preparing their children. Nevertheless, these differences in perspective, once established, may have objective as well as subjective consequences—creating additional constraints for lower SES people and additional advantages for higher SES people.

Regional Differences in the United States as Cultural Differences

Regional differences in explanation style. There is another cultural difference in explanatory style, one related to the type of national and class differences just discussed, that can be detected by comparing two different regions of the United States. Sims and Baumann (1972) have found that Southerners believe more in external control of events than do Northerners. To document and explore this difference, the investigators presented their subjects, all of whom were middle class, with sentence stems that they were to complete as they saw fit. Thus, for example, when subjects were given the stem "As far as my own life is concerned, God . . . ," Southern informants were likely to provide the ending "controls it," while Northern subjects were more likely to write "watches over me." In other words, Southern subjects were assigning God an active role and effectively denying their own responsibility for their fate, while Northern subjects were assigning God a benign but essentially passive role and assigning primary responsibility to themselves. Similarly, Southern subjects were more likely to finish the sentence stem "I believe that luck . . ." with a phrase implying that luck holds great importance, (for example, "can make a man rich or poor"), while Northern subjects were more likely to finish it with a phrase denying its existence or significance ("there's no such thing"). And Southern subjects were more likely to finish the sentence stem "Getting ahead in the world results from . . ." with a view reflecting the importance of a moral stance or God's will, while Northern subjects were more likely to finish it with a view reflecting the importance of work.

What made Sims and Baumann's work particularly provocative, however, was their attempt to demonstrate how such differences in attributional stance can have life-and-death consequences. They began their argument by noting the puzzling fact that there are many more deaths from tornadoes in the South than in the North, a discrepancy that cannot be accounted for by any difference in the number or strength of tornadoes in the two areas, or by differences in the extent to which tornadoes' paths take them through densely populated areas, or by any other plausible physical explanation. They argued that the difference in death rates, which actually appear to be several times higher in the South, stems from differences in preventive measures taken by Northerners and Southerners—a difference fully compatible with the differing outlooks shown in their sentence completions. That is, Northerners, who are more likely to believe that their outcomes depend on their own actions, might be expected to pay attention to weather reports and to take cover when a tornado is in the vicinity. Southerners, who are more likely to believe that fate or God controls their outcomes, might be expected to pay less attention to weather reports and to be less likely to take cover when the reports are unfavorable.

To support these contentions, Sims and Baumann gave their subjects sentence stems directly relevant to tornadoes, for example, "During the time when a tornado watch is out, I . . ." Consistent with the investigators' hypothesis, Northern subjects proved more likely to say that they "listened closely" to the news media, while Southern subjects proved more likely to say that they "watched the sky." (Watching the sky is, of course, much less likely to reveal the real degree of danger, and to suggest appropriate precautions, than attending to news media.) Similarly, when they also gave their subjects such stems as "The survivors of a tornado . . . ," Northern subjects were likely to offer endings indicating the survivors' need for assistance, Southern subjects to offer endings emphasizing the negative emotions the survivors would feel.

It should be ntoed that the stance characteristic of Southerners, like that characterizing collectivists, is a two-edged sword. Several investigators have examined what happens when disaster, for example, in the form of sudden infant death syndrome or a traffic fatality, strikes families. Those with a more external, religious orientation rebound more quickly and more readily return to productive lives (Bahr & Harvey, 1979; Bornstein, Clayton, Hlikas, Maurice, & Robins, 1973; McIntosh, Silver, & Wortman, 1989; Sanders, 1980).

Unit Selections

13. **Mindless Propaganda, Thoughtful Persuasion,** Anthony R. Pratkanis and Elliot Aronson
14. **How to Sell a Pseudoscience,** Anthony R. Pratkanis
15. **A Social Psychological Perspective on the Role of Knowledge about AIDS in AIDS Prevention,** Marie Helweg-Larsen and Barry E. Collins

Key Points to Consider

❖ When someone is paying careful attention to a persuasive message, what implications does this have for the message's success? That is, what factors will be especially important, or unimportant, in such cases? What are the implications when the audience is not carefully attending to the message? Could persuasion still occur? What would determine whether it did or not?

❖ How would you go about "selling" a pseudoscientific belief system to someone? Which techniques do you think would be most effective? Least effective? Can you think of any examples from real life of such techniques being used? How could you use the individual's own behaviors as a means of increasing commitment?

❖ Why does providing information about AIDS, its transmission, and ways to avoid it have such a small impact on actual attitudes and behavior? Can this be explained by the traditional theories about attitudes and attitude change? Are there other factors at play as well?

 **Links** ## www.dushkin.com/online/

8. **Propaganda and Psychological Warfare Research Resource**
   http://www.lafayette.edu/mcglonem/prop.html
9. **The Psychology of Cyberspace**
   http://www.rider.edu/users/suler/psycyber/psycyber.html

These sites are annotated on pages 4 and 5.

Every year during professional football's Super Bowl, advertisers pay untold millions of dollars in order to show their commercials for beer, chips, beer, tires, beer, computers, and beer. The network showing the game also takes the opportunity to air countless advertisements promoting other programs on that network.

Every 4 years, during the presidential election, the airwaves are crowded with political advertisements in which candidates tout their own accomplishments, pose with cute children and cheering crowds, and display ominous, unflattering, black and white photographs of their opponents as grim-voiced announcers catalog the opponents' shortcomings.

The underlying reason for both of these phenomena is that the advertisers, networks, and candidates all share a common assumption: that attitudes are important. If attitudes toward a particular brand of beer can be made more favorable through cute commercials involving talking frogs, then people will buy more of that beer. If attitudes toward a television program can be made more favorable by showing funny clips from it every 12 minutes, then more people will watch the program. If attitudes toward a candidate can be made more positive—or attitudes toward the opponent more negative—then people will be more likely to vote for the candidate. To change someone's behavior, this argument goes, you must first change that person's attitude.

To one degree or another, social psychology has shared this view for decades. The study of attitudes and attitude change has been a central concern of the field for half a century—in fact, for a while that seemed to be all that social psychology studied. One major approach during this time has been to focus on where attitudes come from. The evidence from this research suggests that we acquire attitudes not only from careful consideration of the facts, but also through processes that are much less conscious and deliberate. Merely being exposed to some object frequently enough, for example, generally leads to a more favorable attitude toward it. It also appears that we sometimes arrive at our attitudes by looking at our behaviors, and then simply inferring what our attitudes must be based on our actions.

Another approach to the topic of attitudes has been to examine directly the basic assumption mentioned above, namely that attitudes are strongly associated with actual behavior. As it turns out, the link between attitudes and behavior is not as powerful or reliable as you might think, although under the right circumstances it is still possible to predict behavior from attitudes with considerable success. In fact, it is because of this link between attitudes and behavior that the last major approach to the topic—studying the factors that influence

attitude *change*—has been popular for so long. Two of the three articles in this unit, in fact, focus explicitly on the issue of persuasion; in short, how does one person convince others to change their attitudes?

In "Mindless Propaganda, Thoughtful Persuasion," Anthony Pratkanis and Elliot Aronson discuss an influential theory in contemporary social psychology, the elaboration likelihood model. According to this approach, audiences react to persuasion attempts in two basic ways—either by thinking carefully about the message and attending to its arguments, or through a much more superficial processing of the message and its content. In "How to Sell a Pseudoscience," Anthony Pratkanis outlines how someone could use social psychological principles to persuade others to accept as valid a pseudoscientific belief system. It is his belief that existing pseuodsciences use precisely these techniques in their quest for new members. The final selection in this section, "A Social Psychological Perspective on the Role of Knowledge about AIDS in AIDS Prevention," examines an approach frequently used in attempts to alter nonhealthy behaviors—providing information in order to change attitudes toward the behavior. As the authors note, there is little evidence that providing such information has much influence on attitudes or behavior in the case of AIDS.

Mindless Propaganda, Thoughtful Persuasion

Anthony Pratkanis and
Elliot Aronson

Here are a five facts that professional persuaders have learned about modern propaganda:[1]

Ads that contain the words *new, quick, easy, improved, now, suddenly, amazing, and introducing* sell more products.

In supermarkets, merchandise placed on shelves at eye level sells best. Indeed, one study found that sales for products at waist level were only 74% as great and sales for products at floor level were only 57% as great as for those products placed at eye level.

Ads that use animals, babies, or sex appeal are more likely to sell the product than those that use cartoon characters and historical figures.

Merchandise placed at the end of a supermarket aisle or near the checkout aisle is more likely to be purchased.

Bundle pricing—for example, selling items at 2 for $1 instead of 50¢ each—often increases the customer's perception of product "value."

Why do these five techniques work? When you think about it, it makes little sense to purchase an item because it happens to be placed at the end of a supermarket aisle or on a shelf at eye level. You may not really need this conveniently located product, or the item you really want may be located on a top shelf. It makes little sense to be convinced by an ad because it uses a baby or contains certain words; such "information" is of little value in determining the quality of the product. A subtle rewording of the price does not add any value to the product. But that is the point—we consumers often don't think about the reasons we make the decisions we do. Studies show that about half of purchases in a supermarket are impulse buys and that upwards of 62% of all shoppers in discount stores buy at least one item on an unplanned basis.[2]

We often respond to propaganda with little thought and in a mindless fashion. Consider the experiments on mindlessness conducted by Ellen Langer and her colleagues.[3] Langer's collaborators walked up to persons busily using a university copy machine and said: "Excuse me: may I use the Xerox machine?" What would you do in such a situation? If you are like most people, it would depend on your mood. On some occasions you might think: "*Sure, why not? I'm a helpful person.*" At other times, you might say to yourself: "*Is this person nuts or what? I got here first and have lots of work to do.*" Indeed Langer's results indicate that both types of thinking were going on—a little over half of the people complied with this request.

Now, here's the interesting part. Langer found that she could get almost everyone to agree to let another person cut in front of them at the copy machine by adding one detail to the request—a *reason* for why the machine was needed. This makes sense. It takes a cold heart to deny someone, perhaps panic-stricken with an urgent need, the simple use of a copy machine. The odd thing about Langer's study is that although some of the reasons given made no sense at all, nearly everyone let the person cut in. For example, on some occasions Langer's collaborators would say, "Excuse me: May I use the Xerox machine, because I have to make copies." When you think about it, this is a pretty silly thing to say" Why would you need a copy machine if you were not planning to make copies? It is the same as no reason at all. But that is the point. Most of the people in the study did not think about it and mindlessly complied with the request.

We can also be influenced when we are being thoughtful. For example, most of us, at one time or another, have been panhandled, that is, stopped on the street by a passerby who asks for a quarter or any spare change. A common response is to ignore the request and continue to walk *mindlessly* down the street. Recently, we were panhandled in a novel manner. The panhandler asked, "Excuse me, do you have 17 cents that I could have?" What thoughts would run through your head in this situation? When it happened to us, our immediate thought was: *"Why does this person need exactly 17 cents? Is it for bus fare? Is it for a specific food purchase? Maybe the person came up short at the market."* Suddenly the panhandler was a real individual with real needs, not someone we could mindlessly pass by. We were persuaded to part with a handful of change. Intrigued, we later sent our students out on the streets to panhandle for a local charity. They found that almost twice as many people contributed when asked for 17 or 37 cents compared to those who were asked for a quarter or any spare change.[4]

People can be persuaded both when they are in a mindless state *and* when they are thoughtful, but exactly how they are influenced in either of these two states differs considerably. Richard Petty and John Cacioppo argue that there are two routes to persuasion—*peripheral* and *central*.[5] In the peripheral route, a message recipient devotes little attention and effort to processing a communication. Some examples might include watching television while doing something else or listening to a debate on an issue that you don't care much about. In the peripheral route, persuasion is determined by simple cues, such as the attractiveness of the communicator, whether or not the people around you agree with the position presented, or the pleasure and pain associated with agreeing with the position. In contrast, in the central route, a message recipient engages in a careful and thoughtful consideration of the true merits of the information presented. For example, in the central route the person may actively argue against the message, may want to know the answer to additional questions, or may seek out new information. The persuasiveness of the message is determined by how well it can stand up to this scrutiny.

Let's see how the two routes to persuasion could be used to process one of the most influential and controversial television ads of the 1988 presidential election. This ad, prepared by the Bush campaign, told the story of Willie Horton, a black man who had been sent to prison for murder. During the time when Michael Dukakis, Bush's Democratic opponent, was governor of Massachusetts, Horton was released on a prison furlough program. While on furlough, Horton fled to Maryland, where he raped a white woman after stabbing her male companion.

The ad was influential because it required little thought for a person in the peripheral route to get the point. A typical response elicited by the ad went something like this: *"Dukakis let Horton out of prison to rape and kill. Dukakis is weak on crime, especially those committed by bad, black guys."* Although the response is simple, it was nonetheless effective for George Bush. Michael Dukakis was painted as a weak leader who was soft on crime; by comparison, George Bush

looked strong and tough, capable of protecting us from the likes of Willie Horton.

However, no one was forced to think about this ad in the peripheral route. For example, in the central route to persuasion, the viewer might have asked *"Just how unusual is the Massachusetts prison furlough program? Do other states have similar programs? What is the success rate of such programs? Have instances like the Horton case happened in other states and with other governors? Can Dukakis really be held personally responsible for the decision to release Horton? How many prisoners were furloughed in Massachusetts without incident? Given that the cost of imprisoning someone for four years is approximately $88,000, or equal to the cost of four years of tuition for a student at Harvard with enough left over to buy the student a BMW upon graduation, is the furlough release program worth trying?"* In the central route, the Horton ad is potentially less effective (and might even have had the potential to damage the Bush campaign). The ad addressed few questions that a thoughtful viewer might raise.

This raises a crucial question: What determines which route to persuasion will be adopted? One factor identified by Petty and Cacioppo is the recipient's motivation to think about the message. In one experiment, Petty and Cacioppo, along with their student Rachel Goldman,[6] investigated the role of personal involvement in determining how we think about a message. Students at the University of Missouri heard a message. Students at the University of Missouri heard a message advocating that their university adopt an exam that all students would need to pass in their senior year in order to graduate. Half of the students were told that their university's chancellor was considering adopting the comprehensive exam the following year, thereby making the issue of adopting the exam personally relevant for these students. The other half were told that the changes would not take effect for ten years and thus would not affect them personally.

To see how the personal relevance of an issue influenced thinking about a communication, Petty, Cacioppo, and Goldman prepared four different versions of the comprehensive exam message. Half of the messages were attributed to a source low in expertise—a local high school class. The other half of the messages were attributed to a source high in expertise—the Carnegie Commission on Higher Education. The researchers also varied the quality of arguments in the message, with half of the messages containing weak arguments (personal opinions and anecdotes) and the other half consisting of strong arguments (statistics and other data about the value of the exam).

This simple study can tell us a lot about the way people think about a persuasive message. Suppose someone was operating in the central route to persuasion and was carefully scrutinizing the communication. When would that person be most persuaded?

Given that the person was thinking carefully, he or she would not be persuaded by weak arguments and the source of the communication would not matter much; however, a strong message that stood up to close examination would be very effective. In contrast, the content of the message would not matter much to someone who was not thinking too much about the issue; instead, someone using the peripheral route would be most persuaded by a simple device such as a source that appears to be expert.

What did Petty, Cacioppo, and Goldman find? The personal relevance of the issue determined the route to persuasion. For those students for whom the issue of comprehensive exams was personally relevant, the strength of the message's argument was the most important factor determining whether or not they were persuaded. In contrast, for those students for whom the issue of the comprehensive exam was not personally relevant, the source of the communication mattered—the source high in expertise convinced; the one from the high school class failed to do so.

Petty and Cacioppo's two routes to persuasion should alert us to two important points—one about ourselves as human beings and one about propaganda in our modern world. In many ways, we are *cognitive misers*—we are forever trying to conserve our cognitive energy.[7] Given our finite ability to process information, we often adopt the strategies of the peripheral route for simplifying complex problems; we mindlessly accept a conclusion or proposition—not for any good reason but because it is accompanied by a simplistic persuasion device.

Modern propaganda promotes the use of the peripheral route to persuasion and is designed to take advantage of the limited processing capabilities of the cognitive miser. The characteristics of modern persuasion—the message-dense environment, the thirty-second ad, the immediacy of persuasion—make it increasingly more difficult to think deeply about important issues and decisions. Given that we often operate in the peripheral route, professional propagandists have free rein to use the type of tactics described at the beginning of this chapter and throughout this book to achieve, with impunity, whatever goal they may have in mind.

We have a state of affairs that may be called the *essential dilemma of modern democracy*. On the one hand, we, as a society, value persuasion; our government is based on the belief that free speech and discussion and exchange of ideas can lead to fairer and better decision making. On the other hand, as cognitive misers we often do not participate fully in this discussion, relying instead not on careful thought and scrutiny of a message, but on simplistic persuasion devices and limited reasoning. Mindless propaganda, not thoughtful persuasion, flourishes.

The antidote to the dilemma of modern democracy is not a simple one. It requires each of us to take steps to minimize the likelihood of our processing important information in the peripheral route. This might include increasing our ability to think about an issue through education or improving our ability to detect and understand propaganda by learning more about persuasion. It may mean alerting others to the personal importance of an issue so that many more citizens are encouraged to think deeply about a proposition. It could involve restructuring the way information is presented in our society so that we have the time and the ability to think before we decide. . . . Given the stakes, it behooves each of us to think carefully about how this dilemma can best be resolved.

Notes

1. Burton, P. W. (1981). *Which ad pulled best?* Chicago: Crain; Caples, J. (1974). *Tested advertising methods.* Englewood Cliffs, NJ: Prentice-Hall; Loudon, D. L., & Della Bitta, A. J. (1984). *Consumer behavior.* New York: McGraw-Hill; Ogilvy, D. (1983). *Ogilvy on advertising.* New York: Crown.

2. Ibid.

3. Langer, E., Blank, A., & Chanowitz, B. (1978). The mindlessness of ostensibly thoughtful action: The role of "placebic" information in interpersonal interaction. *Journal of Personality and Social Psychology, 36,* 635–642.

4. Santos, M., Leve, C., & Pratkanis, A. R. (August 1991). *Hey buddy, can you spare 17 cents? Mindfulness and persuasion.* Paper presented at the annual meeting of the American Psychological Association, San Francisco.

5. Petty, R. E., & Cacioppo, J. T. (1986). The elaboration likelihood model of persuasion. In L. Berkowitz (Ed.), *Advances in experimental social psychology* (Vol. 19; pp. 123–205). New York: Academic Press; Petty, R. E., & Cacioppo, J. T. (1986). *Communication and persuasion: Central and peripheral routes to attitude change.* New York: Springer-Verlag. See also Chaiken, S. (1980). Heuristic versus systematic information processing and the use of source versus message cues in persuasion. *Journal of Personality and Social Psychology, 39,* 752–766; Chaiken, S., Liberman, A., & Eagly, A. (1989). Heuristic versus systematic information processing within and beyond the persuasion context. In J. S. Uleman & J. A. Bargh (Eds.), *Unintended thought* (pp. 212–252). New York: Guilford.

6. Petty, R. E., Cacioppo, J. T., & Goldman, R. (1981). Personal involvement as a determinant of argument-based persuasion. *Journal of Personality and Social Psychology, 41,* 847–855.

7. Fiske, S. T., & Taylor, S. E. (1991). *Social cognition.* New York: McGraw-Hill.

How to Sell a Pseudoscience

ANTHONY R. PRATKANIS

Want your own pseudoscience? Here are nine effective persuasion tactics for selling all sorts of filmflam.

Every time I read the reports of new pseudosciences in the SKEPTICAL INQUIRER or watch the latest "In Search Of"-style television show I have one cognitive response, "Holy cow, how can anyone believe that?" Some recent examples include: "Holy cow, why do people spend $3.95 a minute to talk on the telephone with a 'psychic' who has never foretold the future?" "Holy cow, why do people believe that an all uncooked vegan diet is natural and therefore nutritious?" "Holy cow, why would two state troopers chase the planet Venus across state lines thinking it was an alien spacecraft?" "Holy cow, why do people spend millions of dollars each year on subliminal tapes that just don't work?"

There are, of course, many different answers to these "holy cow" questions. Conjurers can duplicate pseudoscientific feats and thus show us how slights of hand and misdirections can mislead (e.g., Randi 1982a, 1982b, 1989). Sociologists can point to social conditions that increase the prevalence of pseudoscientific beliefs (e.g., Lett 1992; Padgett and Jorgenson 1982; Victor 1993). Natural scientists can describe the physical properties of objects to show that what may appear to be supernatural is natural (e.g., Culver and Ianna 1988; Nickell 1983, 1993). Cognitive psychologists have identified common mental biases that often lead us to misinterpret social reality and to conclude in favor of supernatural phenomena (e.g., Blackmore 1992; Gilovich 1991; Hines 1988). These perspectives are useful in addressing the "holy cow" question; all give us a piece of the puzzle in unraveling this mystery.

I will describe how a social psychologist answers the holy cow question. Social psychology is the study of social influence—how human beings and their institutions influence and affect each other (see Aronson 1992; Aronson and Pratkanis 1993). For the past seven decades, social psychologists have been developing theories of social influence and have been testing the effectiveness of various persuasion tactics in their labs (see Cialdini 1984; Pratkanis and Aronson, 1992). It is my thesis that many persuasion tactics discovered by social psychologists are used

Anthony R. Pratkanis is associate professor of psychology, University of California, Santa Cruz, CA 95064. *This article is based on a paper presented at the conference of the Committee for the Scientific Investigation of Claims of the Paranormal, June 23–26, 1994, in Seattle, Washington.*

From *The Skeptical Inquirer*, July/August 1995, pp. 19–25. © 1995 by the Committee for the Scientific Investigation of Claims of the Paranormal (CSICOP). Reprinted by permission.

every day, perhaps not totally consciously, by the promoters of pseudoscience (see Feynman 1985 or Hines 1988 for a definition of pseudoscience).

To see how these tactics can be used to sell flimflam, let's pretend for a moment that we wish to have our very own pseudoscience. Here are nine common propaganda tactics that should result in success.

1. Create a Phantom

The first thing we need to do is to create a phantom—an unavailable goal that looks real and possible; it looks as if it might be obtained with just the right effort, just the right belief, or just the right amount of money, but in reality it can't be obtained. Most pseudosciences are based on belief in a distant or phantom goal. Some examples of pseudoscience phantoms: meeting a space alien, contacting a dead relative at a séance, receiving the wisdom of the universe from a channeled dolphin, and improving one's bowling game or overcoming the trauma of rape with a subliminal tape.

Phantoms can serve as effective propaganda devices (Pratkanis and Farquhar 1992). If I don't have a desired phantom, I feel deprived and somehow less of a person. A pseudoscientist can take advantage of these feelings of inferiority by appearing to offer a means to obtain that goal. In a rush to enhance self-esteem, we suspend better judgment and readily accept the offering of the pseudoscience.

The trick, of course, is to get the new seeker to believe that the phantom is possible. Often the mere mention of the delights of a phantom will be enough to dazzle the new pseudoscience recruit (see Lund's 1925 discussion of wishful thinking). After all, who wouldn't want a better sex life, better health, and peace of mind, all from a $14.95 subliminal tape? The fear of loss of a phantom also can motivate us to accept it as real. The thought that I will never speak again to a cherished but dead loved one or that next month I may die of cancer can be so painful as to cause me to suspend my better judgment and hold out hope against hope that the medium can contact the dead or that Laetrile works. But at times the sell is harder, and that calls for our next set of persuasion tactics.

Gerald Fried

2. Set a Rationalization Trap

The rationalization trap is based on the premise: Get the person committed to the cause as soon as possible. Once a commitment is made, the nature of thought changes. The committed heart is not so much interested in a careful evaluation of the merits of a course of action but in proving that he or she is right.

To see how commitment to a pseudoscience can be established, let's look at a bizarre case—mass suicides at the direction of cult leader Jim Jones. This is the ultimate "holy cow" question: "Why kill yourself and your children on another's command?" From outside the cult, it appears strange, but from the inside it seems natural. Jones began by having his followers make easy commitments (a gift to the church, attending Wednesday night service) and then increased the level of commitment—more tithes, more time in service, loyalty oaths, public admission of sins and punishment, selling of homes, forced sex, moving to Guyana, and then the suicide. Each step was really a small one. Outsiders saw the strange end-product; insiders experienced an ever increasing spi-

> **"Source credibility can stop questioning. After all, what gives you the right to question a guru, a prophet, the image of the Mother Mary, or a sincere seeker of life's hidden potentials?"**

ral of escalating commitment. (See Pratkanis and Aronson 1992 for other tactics used by Jones.)

This is a dramatic example, but not all belief in pseudoscience is so extreme. For example, there are those who occasionally consult a psychic or listen to a subliminal tape. In such cases, commitment can be secured by what social psychologists call the foot-in-the-door technique (Freedman and Fraser 1966). It works this way: You start with a small request, such as accepting a free chiropractic spine exam (Barrett 1993a), taking a sample of vitamins, or completing a free personality inventory. Then a larger request follows—a $1,000 chiropractic realignment, a vitamin regime, or an expensive seminar series. The first small request sets the commitment: Why did you get that bone exam, take those vitamins, or complete that test if you weren't interested and didn't think there might be something to it? An all too common response, "Well gosh, I guess I am interested." The rationalization trap is sprung.

Now that we have secured the target's commitment to a phantom goal, we need some social support for the newfound pseudoscientific beliefs. The next tactics are designed to bolster those beliefs.

3. Manufacture Source Credibility and Sincerity

Our third tactic is to manufacture source credibility and sincerity. In other words, create a guru, leader, mystic, lord, or other generally likable and powerful authority, one who people would be just plain nuts if they didn't believe. For example, practitioners of alternative medicine often have "degrees" as chiropractors or in homeopathy. Subliminal tape sellers claim specialized knowledge and training in such arts as hypnosis. Advocates of UFO sightings often become directors of "research centers." "Psychic detectives" come with long résumés of police service. Prophets claim past successes. For example, most of us "know" that Jeane Dixon predicted the assassination of President Kennedy but probably don't know that she also predicted a Nixon win in 1960. As modern public relations has shown us, credibility is easier to manufacture than we might normally think (see Ailes 1988; Dilenschneider 1990).

Source credibility is an effective propaganda device for at least two reasons. First, we often process persuasive messages in a half-mindless state—either because we are not motivated to think, don't have the time to consider, or lack the abilities to understand the issues (Petty and Cacioppo 1986). In such cases, the presence of a credible source can lead one to quickly infer that the message has merit and should be accepted.

Second, source credibility can stop questioning (Kramer and Alstad 1993). After all, what gives you the right to question a guru, a prophet, the image of the Mother Mary, or a sincere seeker of life's hidden potentials? I'll clarify this point with an example. Suppose I told you that the following statement is a prediction of the development of the atomic bomb and the fighter aircraft (see Hines 1988):

> They will think they have seen the Sun at night
>
> When they will see the pig half-man:
>
> Noise, song, battle fighting in the sky perceived,
>
> And one will hear brute beasts talking.

You probably would respond: "Huh? I don't see how you get the atomic bomb from that. This could just as well be a prediction of an in-flight showing of the Dr. Doolittle movie or the advent of night baseball at Wrigley field." However, attribute the statement to Nostradamus and the dynamics change. Nostradamus was a man who supposedly cured plague victims, predicted who would be pope, foretold the future of kings and queens, and even found a poor dog lost by the king's page (Randi 1993). Such a great seer and prophet can't be wrong. The implied message: The problem is with you; instead of questioning, why don't you suspend your faulty, linear mind until you gain the needed insight?

4. Establish a Granfalloon

Where would a leader be without something to lead? Our next tactic supplies the answer: Establish what Kurt Vonnegut (1976) terms a "granfalloon," a proud and meaningless association of human beings. One of social psychology's most remarkable findings is the ease with which granfalloons can be created. For example, the social psychologist Henri Tajfel merely brought subjects into his lab, flipped a coin, and randomly assigned them to be labeled either Xs or Ws (Tajfel 1981; Turner 1987). At the end of the study, total strangers were acting as if those in their granfalloon were their close kin and those in the other group were their worse enemies.

Granfalloons are powerful propaganda devices because they are easy to create and, once established, the granfalloon defines social reality and maintains social identities. Information is dependent on the granfalloon. Since most granfalloons quickly develop outgroups, criticisms can be attributed to those "evil ones" outside the group, who are thus stifled. To maintain a desired social identity, such as that of a seeker or a New Age rebel, one must obey the dictates of the granfalloon and its leaders.

The classic séance can be viewed as an ad-hoc granfalloon. Note what happens as you sit in the dark and hear a thud. You are dependent on the group led by a medium for the interpretation of this sound. "What is it? A knee against the table or my long lost Uncle Ned? The group believes it is Uncle Ned. Rocking the boat would be impolite. Besides, I came here to be a seeker."

Essential to the success of the granfalloon tactic is the creation of a shared social identity. In creating this identity, here are some things you might want to include:

(a) rituals and symbols (e.g., a dowser's rod, secret symbols, and special ways of preparing food): these not only create an identity, but provide items for sale at a profit.

(b) jargon and beliefs that only the in-group understands and accepts (e.g., thetans are impeded by engrams, you are on a cusp with Jupiter rising): jargon is an effective means of social control since it can be used to frame the interpretation of events.

(c) shared goals (e.g., to end all war, to sell the faith and related products, or to realize one's human potential): such goals not only define the group, but motivate action as believers attempt to teach them.

(d) shared feelings (e.g., the excitement of a prophecy that might appear to be true or the collective rationalization of strange beliefs to others): shared feelings aid in the *we* feeling.

(e) specialized information (e.g., the U.S. government is in a conspiracy to cover up UFOs): this helps the target feel special because he or she is "in the know."

(f) enemies (e.g., alternative medicine opposing the AMA and the FDA, subliminal-tape companies spurning academic psychologists, and spiritualists condemning Randi and other investigators): enemies are very important because you as a pseudoscientist will need scapegoats to blame for your problems and failures.

5. Use Self-Generated Persuasion

Another tactic for promoting pseudoscience and one of the most powerful tactics identified by social psychologists is self-generated persuasion—the subtle design of the situation so that the targets persuade themselves. During World War II, Kurt Lewin (1947) was able to get Americans to eat more sweetbreads (veal and beef organ meats) by having them form groups to discuss how they could persuade others to eat sweetbreads.

Retailers selling so-called nutritional products have discovered this technique by turning customers into salespersons (Jarvis and Barrett 1993). To create a multilevel sales organization, the "nutrition" retailer recruits customers (who recruit still more customers) to serve as sales agents for the product. Customers are recruited as a test of their belief in the product or with the hope of making lots of money (often to buy more products). By trying to sell the product, the customer-turned-salesperson becomes more convinced of its worth. One multilevel leader tells his new sales agents to "answer all objections with testimonials. That's the secret to motivating people" (Jarvis and Barrett 1993), and it is also the secret to convincing yourself.

6. Construct Vivid Appeals

Joseph Stalin once remarked: "The death of a single Russian soldier is a tragedy. A million deaths is a statistic." (See Nisbett and Ross 1980.) In other words, a vividly presented case study or example can make a lasting impression. For example, the pseudosciences are replete with graphic stories of ships and planes caught in the Bermuda Triangle, space aliens examining the sexual parts of humans, weird goings-on in Borley Rectory or Amityville, New York, and psychic surgeons removing cancerous tumors.

A vivid presentation is likely to be very memorable and hard to refute. No matter how many logical arguments can be mustered to counter the pseudoscience claim, there remains that one graphic incident that comes quickly to mind to prompt the response: "Yeah, but what about that haunted house in New York? Hard to explain that." By the way, one of the best ways to counter a vivid appeal is with an equally vivid counter appeal. For example, to counter stories about psychic surgeons in the Philippines, Randi (1982a) tells an equally vivid story of a psychic surgeon palming chicken guts and then pretending to remove them from a sick and now less wealthy patient.

7. Use Pre-persuasion

Pre-persuasion is defining the situation or setting the stage so you win, and sometimes without raising so much as a valid argument. How does one do this? At least three steps are important.

First, establish the nature of the issue. For example, to avoid the wrath of the FDA, advocates of alternative medicine define the issue as health freedom (you should have the right to the health alternative of your choice) as opposed to consumer protection or quality care. If the issue is defined as freedom, the alternative medicine advocate will win because "Who is opposed to freedom?" Another example of this technique is to create a problem or disease, such as reactive hypoglycemia or yeast allergy, that then just happens to be "curable" with whatever quackery you have to sell (Jarvis and Barrett 1993).

Another way to define an issue is through differentiation. Subliminal-tape companies use product differentiation to respond to negative subliminal-tape studies. The claim: "Our tapes have a special technique that makes them superior to other tapes that have been used in studies that failed to show the therapeutic value of subliminal tapes." Thus, null results are used to make a given subliminal tape look superior. The psychic network has taken a similar approach—"Tired of those phoney psychics? Ours are certified," says the advertisement.

Second, set expectations. Expectations can lead us to interpret ambiguous information in a way that supports an original hypothesis (Greenwald, Pratkanis, Leippe, and Baumgardner 1986). For example, a belief in the Bermuda Triangle may lead us to interpret a plane crash off the coast of New York City as evidence for the Triangle's sinister effects (Kusche 1986; Randi 1982a). We recently conducted a study that showed how an expectation can lead people to think that subliminal tapes work when in fact they do not (Greenwald, Spangenberg, Pratkanis, and Eskenazi 1991; Pratkanis, Eskenazi, and Greenwald 1994; for a summary see Pratkanis 1992). In our study, expectations were established by mislabeling half the tapes (e.g., some subjects thought they had a subliminal tape to improve memory but really had one designed to increase self-esteem). The results showed that about half the subjects thought they improved (though they did not) based on how the tape was labeled (and not the actual content). The label led them to interpret their behavior in support of expectations, or what we termed an "illusory placebo" effect.

A third way to pre-persuade is to specify the decision criteria. For example, psychic supporters have developed guidelines on what should be viewed as acceptable evidence for paranormal abilities—such as using personal experiences as data, placing the burden of proof on the critic and not the claimant (see Beloff 1985), and above all else keeping James Randi and other psi-inhibitors out of the testing room. Accept these criteria and one must conclude that psi is a reality. The collaboration of Hyman and Honorton is one positive attempt to establish a fair playing field (Hyman and Honorton 1986).

8. Frequently Use Heuristics and Commonplaces

My next recommendation to the would-be pseudoscientist is to use heuristics and commonplaces. Heuristics are simple if-then rules or norms that are widely accepted; for example, if it costs more it must be more valuable. Commonplaces are widely accepted beliefs that can serve as the basis of an appeal; for example, government health-reform should be rejected because politicians are corrupt (assuming political corruption is a widely accepted belief). Heuristics and commonplaces gain their power because they are widely accepted and thus induce little thought about whether the rule or argument is appropriate.

To sell a pseudoscience, liberally sprinkle your appeal with heuristics and commonplaces. Here are some common examples.

(a) The *scarcity heuristic,* or if it is rare it is valuable. The Psychic Friends Network costs a pricey $3.95 a minute and therefore must be valuable. On the other hand, an average University of California professor goes for about 27 cents per minute and is thus of little value.[1]

(b) The *consensus or bandwagon* heuristic, or if everyone agrees it must be true. Subliminal tapes, psychic phone ads, and quack medicine (Jarvis and Barrett 1993) feature testimonials of people who have found what they are looking for (see Hyman 1993 for a critique of this practice).

(c) The *message length* heuristic, or if the message is long it is strong. Subliminal-tape brochures often list hundreds of subliminal studies in support of their claims. Yet most of these studies do not deal with subliminal influence and thus are irrelevant. An uninformed observer would be impressed by the weight of the evidence.

(d) The *representative* heuristic or if an object resembles another (on some salient dimension) then they act similarly. For example, in folk medicines the cure often resembles the apparent cause of the disease. Homeopathy is based on the notion that small amounts of substances that can cause a disease's symptoms will cure the disease (Barrett 1993b). The Chinese Doctrine of Signatures claims that similarity of shape and form determine therapeutic value; thus rhinoceros horns, deer antlers, and ginseng root look phallic and supposedly improve vitality (Tyler 1993).

(e) The *natural* commonplace, or what is natural is good and what is made by humans is bad. Alternative medicines are promoted with the word "natural." Psychic abilities are portrayed as natural, but lost, abilities. Organic food is natural. Of course mistletoe berries are natural too, and I don't recommend a steady diet of these morsels.

(f) The *goddess-within* commonplace, or humans have a spiritual side that is neglected by modern materialistic science. This commonplace stems from the medieval notion of the soul, which was modernized by Mesmer as animal magnetism and then converted by psychoanalysis into the powerful, hidden unconscious (see Fuller 1982, 1986). Pseudoscience plays to this commonplace by offering ways to tap the unconscious, such as subliminal tapes, to prove this hidden power exists through extrasensory perception (ESP) and psi, or to talk with the remnants of this hidden spirituality through channeling and the séance.

(g) The *science* commonplaces. Pseudosciences use the word "science" in a contradictory manner. On the one hand, the word "science" is sprinkled liberally throughout most pseudosciences: subliminal tapes make use of the "latest scientific technology"; psychics are "scientifically tested"; health fads are "on the cutting edge of science." On the other hand, science is often portrayed as limited. More in one article in *Self* magazine (Sharp 1993) reported our subliminal-tapes studies (Greenwald et al. 1992; Pratkanis et al. 1994) showing no evidence that the tapes worked and then stated: "Tape makers dispute the objectivity of the studies. They also point out that science can't always explain the results of mainstream medicine either" (p. 194). In each case a commonplace about science is used: (1) "Science is powerful" and (2) "Science is limited and can't replace the personal." The selective use of these commonplaces allows a pseudoscience to claim the power of science but have a convenient out should science fail to promote the pseudoscience.

9. Attack Opponents Through Innuendo and Character Assassination

Finally, you would like your pseudoscience to be safe from harm and external attack. Given that the best defense is a good offense, I offer the advice of Cicero: "If you don't have a good argument, attack the plaintiff."

Let me give a personal example of this tactic in action. After our research showing that subliminal tapes have no therapeutic value was reported, my co-authors, Tony Greenwald, Eric Spangenberg, and Jay Eskenazi, and I were the target of many innuendoes. One subliminal newsletter edited by Eldon Taylor, Michael Urban, and others (see the *International Society of Peripheral Learning Specialists Newsletter*, August 1991) claimed that our research was a marketing study designed not to test the tapes but to "demonstrate the influence of marketing practices on consumer perceptions." The article points out that the entire body of data presented by Greenwald represents a marketing dissertation by Spangenberg and questions why Greenwald is even an author. The newsletter makes other attacks as well, claiming that our research design lacked a control group, that we really found significant effects of the tapes, that we violated American Psychological Association ethics with a hint that an investigation would follow, that we prematurely reported our findings in a manner similar to those who prematurely announced cold fusion, and that we were conducting a "Willie Horton"-style smear campaign against those who seek to help Americans achieve their personal goals.

Many skeptics can point to similar types of attacks. In the fourteenth century, Bishop Pierre d'Arcis, one of the first to contest the authenticity of the Shroud of Turin, was accused by shroud promoters as being motivated by jealousy and a desire to possess the shroud (Nickell 1983: 15). Today, James Randi is described by supporters of Uri Geller as "a powerful psychic trying to convince the world that such powers don't exist so he can take the lead role in the psychic world" (Hines 1988: 91).

Why is innuendo such a powerful propaganda device? Social psychologists point to three classes of answers. First, innuendoes change the agenda of discussion. Note the "new" discussion on subliminal types isn't about whether these tapes are worth your money or not. Instead, we are discussing whether I am ethical or not, whether I am a competent researcher, and whether I even did the research.

Second, innuendoes raise a glimmer of doubt about the character of the person under attack. That doubt can be especially powerful when there is little other information on which to base a judgment. For example, the average reader of the subliminal newsletter I quoted probably knows little about me—knows little about the research and little about the peer review process that evaluated it, and doesn't know that I make my living from teaching college and not from the sale of subliminal tapes. This average reader is left with the impression of an unethical and incompetent scientist who is out of control. Who in their right mind would accept what that person has to say?

Finally, innuendoes can have a chilling effect (Kurtz 1992). The recipient begins to wonder about his or her reputation and whether the fight is worth it. The frivolous lawsuit is an effective way to magnify this chilling effect.

Can Science Be Sold with Propaganda?

I would be remiss if I didn't address one more issue: Can we sell science with the persuasion tactics of pseudoscience? Let's be honest; science sometimes uses these tactics.

For example, I carry in my wallet a membership card to the Monterey Bay Aquarium with a picture of the cutest little otter you'll ever see. I am in the otter granfalloon. On some occasions skeptics have played a little loose with their arguments and their name-calling. As just one example, see George Price's (1955) *Science* article attacking Rhine's and Soal's work on ESP—an attack that went well beyond the then available data. (See Hyman's [1985] discussion.)

I can somewhat understand the use of such tactics. If a cute otter can inspire a young child to seek to understand nature, then so be it. But we should remember that such tactics can be ineffective in promoting science if they are not followed up by involvement in the process of science—the process of questioning and discovering. And we should be mindful that the use of propaganda techniques has its costs. If we base our claims in cheap propaganda tactics, then it is an easy task for the pseudoscientist to develop even more effective propaganda tactics and carry the day.

More fundamentally, propaganda works best when we are half mindless, simplistic thinkers trying to rationalize our behavior and beliefs to ourselves and others. Science works best when we are thoughtful and critical and scrutinize claims carefully. Our job should be to promote such thought and scrutiny. We should be careful to select our persuasion strategies to be consistent with the goal.

Notes

I thank Craig Abbott, Elizabeth A. Turner, and Marlene E. Turner for helpful comments on an earlier draft of this article.

1. Based on 50 weeks a year at an average salary of $49,000 and a work week of 61 hours (as reported in recent surveys of the average UC faculty work load). Assuming a work week of 40 hours, the average faculty makes 41 cents a minute.

References

Ailes, R. 1988. *You Are the Message.* New York: Doubleday.

Aronson, E. 1992. *The Social Animal,* 6th ed. New York: W. H. Freeman.

Aronson, E., and A. R. Pratkanis. 1993. "What Is Social Psychology?" In *Social Psychology*, vol. 1, ed. by E. Aronson and A. R. Pratkanis, xiii–xx. Cheltenham, Gloucestershire: Edward Elgar Publishing.

Barrett, S. 1993a. "The Spine Salesmen." In *The Health Robbers,* ed. by S. Barrett and W. T. Jarvis, 161–190. Buffalo, N.Y.: Prometheus Books.

———. 1993b. "Homeopathy: Is It Medicine?" In *The Health Robbers,* ed. by S. Barrett and W. T. Jarvis, 191–202. Buffalo, N.Y.: Prometheus Books.

Beloff, J. 1985. "What Is Your Counter-Explanation? A Plea to Skeptics to Think Again." In *A Skeptic's Handbook of Parapsychology,* ed. by P. Kurtz, 359–377. Buffalo, N.Y.: Prometheus Books.

Blackmore, S. 1992. Psychic experiences: Psychic illusions. SKEPTICAL INQUIRER, 16: 367–376.

Cialdini, R. B. 1984. *Influence.* New York; William Morrow.

Culver, R. B., and P. A. Ianna. 1988. *Astrology: True or False?* Buffalo, N.Y.: Prometheus Books.

Dilenschneider, R. L. 1990. *Power and Influence.* New York: Prentice-Hall.

Feynman, R. P. 1985. *Surely You're Joking Mr. Feynman.* New York: Bantam Books.

Freedman, J., and S. Fraser. 1966. Compliance without pressure: The foot-in-the-door technique. *Journal of Personality and Social Psychology,* 4: 195–202.

Fuller, R. C. 1982. *Mesmerism and the American Cure of Souls.* Philadelphia: University of Pennsylvania Press.

_____. 1986. *Americans and the Unconscious.* New York: Oxford University Press.

Gilovich, T. 1991. *How We Know What Isn't So.* New York: Free Press.

Greenwald, A. G., E. R. Spangenberg, A. R. Pratkanis, and J. Eskenazi. 1991. Double-blind tests of subliminal self-help audiotapes. *Psychological Science,* 2: 119–122.

Greenwald, A. G., A. R. Pratkanis, M. R. Leippe, and M. H. Baumgardner.1986. Under what conditions does theory obstruct research progress? *Psychological Review,* 93: 216–229.

Hines, T. 1988. *Pseudoscience and the Paranormal.* Buffalo, N.Y.: Prometheus Books.

Hyman, R. 1985. "A Critical Historical Overview of Parapsychology." In *A Skeptic's Handbook of Parapsychology,* ed. by P. Kurtz, 3–96. Buffalo, N.Y.: Prometheus Books.

_____. 1993. Occult health practices. In *The Health Robbers,* ed. by S. Barrett and W. T. Jarvis, 55–66. Buffalo, N.Y.: Prometheus Books.

Hyman, R., and C. Honorton. 1986. A joint communique: The Psi Ganzfeld controversy. *Journal of Parapsychology,* 56: 351–364.

Jarvis, W. T., and S. Barrett. 1993. "How Quackery Sells." In *The Health Robbers,* ed. by S. Barrett and W. T. Jarvis, 1–22. Buffalo, N.Y.: Prometheus Books.

Kramer, J., and D. Alstad. 1993. *The Guru Papers: Masks of Authoritarian Power,* Berkeley, Calif.: North Atlantic Books/Frog Ltd.

Kurtz, P. 1992. On being sued: The chilling of freedom of expression. SKEPTICAL INQUIRER, 16: 114–117.

Kusche, L. 1986. *The Bermuda Triangle Mystery Solved.* Buffalo, N.Y.: Prometheus Books.

Lett, J. 1992. The persistent popularity of the paranormal. SKEPTICAL INQUIRER, 16, 381–388.

Lewin, K. 1947. "Group Decision and Social Change." In *Readings in Social Psychology,* ed. by T. M. Newcomb and E. L. Hartley, 330–344. New York: Holt.

Lund, F. H. 1925. The psychology of belief. *Journal of Abnormal and Social Psychology,* 20: 63–81, 174–196.

Nickell, J. 1983. *Inquest on the Shroud of Turin.* Buffalo, N.Y.: Prometheus Books.

_____. 1993. *Looking for a Miracle.* Buffalo, N.Y.: Prometheus Books.

Nisbett, R., and L. Ross. 1980. *Human Inference: Strategies and Shortcomings of Social Judgment.* Englewood Cliffs, N.J.: Prentice-Hall.

Padgett, V. R., and D. O. Jorgenson. 1982. Superstition and economic threat: Germany 1918–1940. *Personality and Social Psychology Bulletin,* 8: 736–741.

Petty, R. E., and J. T. Cacioppo. 1986. *Communication and Persuasion: Central and Peripheral Routes to Attitude Change.* New York: Springer-Verlag.

Pratkanis, A. R. 1992. The cargo-cult science of subliminal persuasion. SKEPTICAL INQUIRER, 16: 260–272.

Pratkanis, A. R., and E. Aronson. 1992. *Age of Propaganda; Everyday Use and Abuse of Persuasion.* New York: W. H. Freeman.

Pratkanis, A. R., J. Eskenazi, and A. G. Greenwald. 1994. What you expect is what you believe (but not necessarily what you get): A test of the effectiveness of subliminal self-help audiotapes. *Basic and Applied Social Psychology,* 15: 251–276.

Pratkanis, A. R., and P. H. Farquhar. 1992. A brief history of research on phantom alternatives: Evidence for seven empirical generalizations about phantoms. *Basic and Applied Social Psychology,* 13: 103–122.

Price, G. R. 1955. Science and the supernatural. *Science,* 122: 359–367.

Randi, J. 1982a. *Flim-Flam!* Buffalo, N.Y.: Prometheus Books.

_____. 1982b. *The Truth About Uri Geller.* Buffalo, N.Y.: Prometheus Books.

_____. 1989. *The Faith Healers.* Buffalo, N.Y.: Prometheus Books.

_____. 1993. *The Mask of Nostradamus.* Buffalo, N.Y.: Prometheus Books.

Sharp, K. 1993. The new hidden persuaders. *Self,* March, pp. 174–175, 194.

Tajfel, H. 1981. *Human Groups and Social Categories.* Cambridge, U.K.: Cambridge University Press.

Turner, J. C. 1987. *Rediscovering the Social Group.* New York: Blackwell.

Tyler, V. E. 1993. "The Overselling of Herbs." In *The Health Robbers,* ed. by S. Barrett and W. T. Jarvis, 213–224. Buffalo, N.Y.: Prometheus Books.

Victor, J. S. 1993. *Satanic Panic: The Creation of a Contemporary Legend.* Chicago, Ill.: Open Court.

Vonnegut, K. 1976. *Wampeters, Foma, and Granfalloons.* New York; Dell.

A Social Psychological Perspective on the Role of Knowledge About AIDS in AIDS Prevention

Marie Helweg-Larsen and Barry E. Collins[1]

Department of Psychology, University of California, Los Angeles, Los Angeles, California

Widespread ignorance regarding the transmission of HIV in the mid to late 1980s was, at once, a source of despair and optimism. It was discouraging that people knew so little about HIV prevention. At the same time, one could hope that an attack on the ignorance might amount to an attack on the virus itself. Today, many health educators still believe that ignorance is at the root of the spread of the disease and continue to focus on knowledge as a central causal variable in AIDS prevention. Many AIDS interventions are based on the idea that giving people the facts about transmission of HIV will lead to positive behaviors (and ultimately behavior change). In fact, some educational programs measure their success by assessing how much people learn about AIDS rather than by assessing people's changes in attitudes or behavior per se (e.g., Farley, Pompu-tius, Sabella, Helgerson, & Hadler, 1991; Ganz & Greenberg, 1990).

There are a number of philosophical and practical reasons for using infor-mation-based approaches to changing health-related behavior. The idea that people will change their behavior when they are informed about the logic of do-ing so is consistent with the Western worldview, which places individualism, enlightenment, and reason at the center of its value system. Knowledge-based behavior change is, in theory, internal-ized. Thus, the new behaviors will last longer, display a greater resistance to extinction, and generalize across more situations than will new behaviors arising from other forms of social influence (e.g., reward, coercion, and compliance with authority figures). Behaviors based on these other influences may be relatively situation specific and require surveil-lance for compliance.

Subscribing to an information-based view, many psychologists (and nonpsy-chologists) believe that knowledge about disease processes is a fundamental variable in any prevention theory or in-tervention program. Teaching the facts is seen as essential to changing attitudes or behaviors. For example, the author of one health psychology textbook argued that "health information is the first nec-essary component and a key ingredient in any attempt to bring about health be-havior" (DiMatteo, 1991, p. 88). Similarly, the term "AIDS knowledge" is frequently used synonymously with the term "AIDS prevention" in the public-health literature in general and the AIDS prevention lit-erature in particular.

Unfortunately, the evidence that sex education leads to changes in behaviors intended to prevent AIDS or pregnancy is disappointing. Similarly, the many re-search efforts aimed specifically at ex-amining the relation between knowledge about AIDS (including how AIDS is transmitted) and preventive behaviors suggest overwhelmingly that this relation is weak or nonexistent. A review of global perspectives on AIDS (Mann, Tar-antola, & Netter, 1992) concluded that "the failure of information to lead reliably, regularly, or predictably to behavior change has been documented repeat-edly in varying culture and contexts and underscores the need for a comprehen-sive approach to prevention" (p. 330). Surprisingly, some of the researchers who themselves have found no effects of knowledge about AIDS on AIDS-related attitudes or behaviors nevertheless have made recommendations suggest-ing that counselors, physicians, and other health care professionals ought to provide more information about AIDS, develop educational programs, and pro-vide sex education (Freeman et al., 1980). Our point is not that people might not benefit from or need such informa-tion (e.g., education might help reduce the stigma against persons with AIDS). Rather, we are saying that disease-related information about AIDS seems not to be an important cause of change in sexual behavior.

Surveys indicate that the absolute level of knowledge about AIDS, trans-mission routes, and preventive behaviors is quite high in some populations even while the frequency of behaviors that in-crease the risk of contamination remains high—a fact that would preclude a

Recommended Reading

Brandt, A.M. (1987). *No magic bullet: A history of venereal disease in the United States since 1880.* New York: Oxford University Press.

Cialdini, R.B. (1993). *Influence: Science and practice* (3rd ed.). Glenview, IL: Scott, Foresman/Little, Brown.

Eagley, A., & Chaiken, S. (1992). *The psychology of attitudes.* Orlando, FL: Harcourt, Brace, & Jovanovich.

From *Current Directions in Psychological Science,* April 1997, pp. 23–26. © 1997 by the American Psychological Society. Reprinted by permission of Blackwell Publishers.

strong relationship between knowledge and preventive behaviors. For example, in one study of injection drug users, participants were randomly assigned to an AIDS education group, an AIDS education group with optional HIV testing, or a wait-list control group (Calsyn, Saxon, Freeman, & Whittaker, 1992). Four months after the intervention, a structured interview could not detect any differences between the groups in either their knowledge about AIDS or their frequency of engaging in risky behaviors. Additionally, the injection drug users were very well informed about AIDS. Between 97% and 99% correctly identified routes of contracting HIV and knew that condoms could prevent its transmission. High absolute levels of knowledge about AIDS have also been found in heterosexual adolescents (e.g., DiClemente, Forrest, Mickler, & Principal Site Investigators, 1990) and gay men (e.g., Aspinwall, Kemeny, Taylor, Schneider, & Dudley, 1991). Thus, one might simply look to these high levels of knowledge to conclude that knowing the facts about AIDS is not sufficient to cause people to change their behavior. If it were, very few people in these populations would be engaging in risky behaviors.

One of the most common reactions to a failure to find a relationship between knowing the facts abut AIDS and engaging in risky behaviors is to conclude that information is a necessary, but not a sufficient, condition for behavior change (see J.D. Fisher & Fisher, 1992, for a review). However, as we discuss next, the route to changes in behaviors related to risk of contracting HIV does not (or does not always) pass through the acquisition of knowledge about AIDS.

SOCIAL PSYCHOLOGICAL THEORIES

Within social psychology, a wealth of research on persuasion and attitude change provides clues as to (a) why and under what circumstances information per se does not necessarily lead to behavior change and (b) why uninformed people nevertheless change their attitudes or behaviors. It is not our purpose to review the literature on persuasion and attitude change here, but we provide three illustrations.

First, consider the elaboration likelihood model of attitude change (Petty & Cacioppo, 1986). In this model, it is not knowledge per se but cognitive reactions to knowledge that cause changes in attitude and behavior. The model proposes that one cannot judge how effective a message is simply by examining the information learned—one must know how the recipient of the message reacts to that knowledge. Thus, the message may be ineffective if the person sees the information as irrelevant (e.g., "I'm young and have a strong immune system, so I need not worry") or reacts negatively rather than positively (e.g., "Condoms are too much trouble, and they make me think of death and disease"). Positive reactions, which are key to an effective message, may result from superficial cues in the message (the peripheral route to persuasion) rather than from elaborate, in-depth, thoughtful analysis of the issues (the central route to persuasion). However, research shows that peripheral routes to persuasion (such as having a famous actress promote condom use) result in attitudes that are relatively temporary, are susceptible to change, and have little impact on behavior. If the central route to persuasion does result in attitude change, such change may be relatively enduring, but the person may not have the necessary skills or self-worth to carry the belief into action (Petty, Gleicher, & Jarvis, 1993).

Ajzen's (1988) theory of planned behavior provides a second example in which increased knowledge may or may not produce behavior change. The theory of planned behavior—an extension of Ajzen and Fishbein's (1980) theory of reasoned action—suggests that a behavior follows from intention, which in turn follows from a person's attitude toward the behavior, the perceived opinions of other people (norms), and perceived control over the behavior (see W.A. Fisher, Fisher, & Rye, 1995, for an application of the theory of reasoned action to AIDS-related behavior). Based on this theory, one would predict that behavior change can be produced without attitude change if new norms can be created (e.g., "I'll start bleaching my needles, not because I personally believe it's important but because everyone wants me to") or if perceived control over the behavior changes (e.g., "Now that I can easily get condoms in vending machines in the restroom, I'll begin using them"). In sum, the theory of planned behavior and the theory of reasoned action suggest that a change in norms or perceived control might reduce the frequency of risky behaviors even if people do not learn more about AIDS.

Cognitive dissonance theory (Festinger, 1957) is a third example of a social psychological theory that suggests a mechanism for attitude and behavior change in which learning a message is not relevant. According to this theory, cognitive dissonance may be evoked when a person holds inconsistent attitudes or acts inconsistently with held attitudes. To reduce the resulting discomfort, the person is motivated to change an inconsistent behavior or attitude so as to eliminate the inconsistency. Using this paradigm, Stone, Aronson, Crain, and Winslow (1994) had students develop and videotape a persuasive speech about condom use and also asked the students to think about their own past inconsistent condom use. That is, cognitive dissonance was aroused by reminding students that they were being hypocritical (promoting use even though they had not used condoms consistently in the past). This cognitive dissonance in turn increased students' resolve to use condoms in the future, and more students in this condition (compared with three control conditions) bought condoms following the experiment. The important point here is that the change in intentions (and behaviors) occurred after an apparent inconsistency became clear, not because of new information.

In sum, then, many social psychological theories provide sound theoretical reasons for why information at times does not lead to learning, attitude change, or behavior change, and why attitude and behavior change may occur without new knowledge.

NEGATIVE CONSEQUENCES OF KNOWLEDGE ABOUT AIDS

Some people might argue that even if providing the facts about AIDS is not sufficient (or necessary) to change behaviors, it certainly could not hurt for people to learn more about AIDS as long as the education does not detract from other intervention methods. But in some cases, knowledge about AIDS may inhibit preventive behaviors, such as use of condoms. For example, one study (Berrenberg et al., 1993) measured the degree to which college students felt overwhelmed and irritated by information about AIDS and desired to avoid additional information (called degree of "AIDS information saturation"). The authors found that students with a high level of AIDS information saturation rated AIDS information that was provided as less valuable, less clear, and less disturbing than did students with a lower level of AIDS saturation. The students with a high level of AIDS information saturation also reported fewer intentions to change high-risk behaviors. This study hints at the possibility that there may be negative consequences of repeatedly telling people what they already know.

Health educators who believe that rational people make rational choices once they have all the information might create interventions in which they teach individuals to use disease information to persuade their partners to use condoms. However, this approach may be problematic for several related reasons. First, the failure to use condoms is more often related to concerns regarding how one appears to other people than to lack of information about the benefits of using condoms (Leary, Tchividjian, & Kraxberger, 1994). That is, people are embarrassed to buy condoms, are embarrassed about introducing the issue to their partners, and worry about the impression they give to their partners (Helweg-Larsen & Collins, 1994). Knowing the rational reasons for using a condom may not overcome these interpersonal concerns. Second, given the powerful images associated with AIDS (e.g., being gay, promiscuous, or "unclean"), AIDS might be exactly the reason one should not use to convince one's partner to use a condom. Research on attitudes and classical conditioning suggests that one should avoid linking a desired behavior (e.g., using condoms) with an image or word (AIDS) that, rightly or wrongly, carries negative connotations.

Third, there is also emerging empirical evidence that introducing disease information in a sexual situation might in fact have adverse effects on a potential partner's perceptions of a person trying to make a good impression (Collins & Karney, 1995). In one study, students who read a scenario about a college student who mentioned to his or her partner that he or she was "worried about AIDS" judged the student as nice (responsible, sincere, clean, and conscientious) but also unexciting (dull, boring, bland, uninteresting, weak, and passive). Even when these effects were controlled statistically (the effects of the nice and exciting dimensions were statistically removed), college students still perceived a person revealing concern about AIDS to his or her partner to be promiscuous, a poor long-term romantic prospect, and less sexually attractive and less heterosexual than a person who did not mention concern about AIDS.

In sum, providing the facts about disease processes might have negative consequences under certain circumstances, especially if the recipients feel they are already overloaded with such information or if they use (or are taught to use) such information to persuade their partners to use condoms or take other precautionary measures.

CONCLUSION

Not only is knowledge about AIDS an unreliable predictor of attitudes or be-

haviors, but the focus on knowledge-based approaches to behavior change might distract health educators from targeting other factors leading to risky sexual behavior—factors that predict risky behaviors better than does knowledge about AIDS. This is not to say that knowledge might not be important for purposes other than changing attitudes or behaviors. It is to say that researchers should consider a broad array of theories of behavior change, including those that do not focus on information as a determinant of such change. In addition, several social psychological theories of attitude change provide excellent information about when providing factual information is most likely to lead to changes in attitudes or behaviors. In the midst of the AIDS crisis, it is essential that specialists and nonspecialists alike become aware that knowledge is not sufficient, is not always necessary, and may in certain circumstances do more harm than good.

Acknowledgments—We thank James Shepperd and David Boninger for providing helpful comments on an earlier draft of this article. This work was supported by a California State Doctoral AIDS Research Training Grant (TG-LA022) awarded through the UCLA School of Public Health to the first author.

Note

1. Address correspondence to Marie Helweg-Larsen, University of Florida, Department of Psychology, Gainesville, FL 32611-2250, or to Barry Collins, Department of Psychology, UCLA, Los Angeles, CA 90024-1563; e-mail: helweg@psych.ufl.edu or collins@psych.ucla.edu.

References

Ajzen, I. (1988). *Attitudes, personality, and behavior.* Chicago: Dorsey Press.

Ajzen, I., & Fishbein, M. (1980). *Understanding attitudes and predicting social behavior.* Englewood Cliffs, NJ: Prentice-Hall.

Aspinwall, L.G., Kemeny, M.E., Taylor, S.E., Schneider, S.G., & Dudley, J.P. (1991). Psychosocial predictors of gay men's AIDS risk-reduction behavior. *Health Psychology, 10,* 432–444.

Berrenberg, J.L., Dougherty, K.L., Erikson, M.S., Lowe, J.L., Pacot, D.M., & Rousseau, C.N.S. (1993, April). *Saturation in AIDS education: Can we still make a difference?* Paper presented at the annual meeting of the Rocky Mountain and

Western Psychological Associations, Phoenix, AZ.

Calsyn, D.A., Saxon, A.J., Freeman, G., & Whittaker, S. (1992). Ineffectiveness of AIDS education and HIV antibody testing in reducing high-risk behaviors among injection drug users. *American Journal of Public Health, 82,* 573–575.

Collins, B.E., & Karney, B.P. (1995). *Behavior change and impression management: The case of safer sex.* Unpublished manuscript, University of California, Los Angeles.

DiClemente, R.J., Forrest, K.A., Mickler, S., & Principal Site Investigators. (1990). College students' knowledge and attitudes about AIDS and changes in HIV-preventive behaviors. *AIDS Education and Prevention, 2,* 201–212.

DiMatteo, M.R. (1991). *The psychology of health, illness, and medical care.* Pacific Grove, CA: Brooks/Cole.

Farley, T.A., Pomputius, P.F., Sabella, W., Helgerson, S.D., & Hadler, J.L. (1991). Evaluation of the effect of school-based education on adolescents' AIDS knowledge and attitudes. *Connecticut Medicine, 55,* 15–18.

Festinger, L. (1957). *A theory of cognitive dissonance.* Evanston, IL: Row, Peterson.

Fisher, J.D., & Fisher, W.A. (1992). Changing AIDS-risk behavior. *Psychological Bulletin, 111,* 455–474.

Fisher, W.A., Fisher, J.D., & Rye, B.J. (1995). Understanding and promoting AIDS-preventive behavior: Insights from the theory of reasoned action. *Health Psychology, 14,* 255–264.

Freeman, E.W., Rickels, k., Huggins, G. R., Mudd, E.H., Garcia, C.R., & Dickens, H.O. (1980). Adolescent contraceptive use: Comparisons of male and female attitudes and information. *American Journal of Public Health, 70,* 790–797.

Ganz, W., & Greenberg, B.S. (1990). The role of informative television programs in the battle against AIDS. *Health Communication, 2,* 199–215.

Helweg-Larsen, M., & Collins, B.E. (1994). The UCLA Multidimensional Condom Attitudes Scale: Documenting the complex determinants of condom use in college students. *Health Psychology, 13,* 224–237.

Leary, M.R., Tchividjian, L.R., & Kraxberger, B.E. (1994). Self-presentation can be hazardous to your health: Impression management and health risk. *Health Psychology, 13,* 461–470.

Mann, J.M., Tarantola, D.J.M., & Netter, T.W. (Eds.). (1992). *AIDS in the world.* Cambridge, MA: Harvard University Press.

Petty, R.E., & Cacioppo, J.T. (1986). *Communication and persuasion: Central and peripheral routes to attitude change.* New York: Springer-Verlag.

Petty, R.E., Gleicher, F., & Jarvis, W.B.G. (1993). Persuasion theory and AIDS prevention. In J.B. Pryor & J.D. Reeder (Eds.), *The social psychology of HIV infection* (pp. 155–182). Hillsdale, NJ: Erlbaum.

Stone, J., Aronson, E., Crain, A.L., & Winslow, M.P. (1994). Inducing hypocrisy as a means of encouraging young adults to use condoms. *Personality and Social Psychology Bulletin, 20,* 116–128.

Unit 4

Key Points to Consider

❖ Why are conformity pressures so powerful? What creates them? Can you think of any examples from your own life that are comparable to Bill Maxwell's? That is, are there any groups to which you belong that exert pressure on you to think, feel, or act in a particular way? How do you handle this?

❖ Why is the norm of reciprocity so powerful? Can you think of any other examples, besides the ones listed by Robert Cialdini in his selection, in which sales people use this norm to increase compliance? Which other compliance techniques used by salespeople can you identify? Why don't customers see through these techniques more frequently and refuse to fall for them? What steps could customers take to protect themselves from such techniques?

❖ Are the techniques described in "Suspect Confessions" fair tactics for the police to use? Why or why not? More generally, what sort of restrictions, if any, should be placed on the use of social influence techniques in our society?

 **Links**   **www.dushkin.com/online/**

These sites are annotated on pages 4 and 5.

After World War II, members of the Nazi high command were put on trial for war crimes, in particular, their genocidal slaughter of millions of "undesirables": Jews, Gypsies, and homosexuals, among others. One argument that they offered in their defense was that they were "only following orders"—that is, as soldiers during wartime they had no choice but to obey the orders of their superior officers. As a result, so the argument went, they did not bear the ultimate responsibility for their actions. This argument was not especially effective, however, and many of the defendants were convicted and, in some cases, executed for their crimes. In essence, then, the war crimes judges rejected the notion that people can give up their individual moral responsibility when they are given immoral orders.

A decade later, in one of the most famous social psychological investigations ever done, Stanley Milgram reexamined this issue, and his results were highly disturbing. Milgram found that normal everyday Americans—not Nazi monsters—would follow the orders of an experimenter to administer what they thought were extremely intense electric shocks to an innocent victim as part of a research project. In some cases, a substantial percentage of the participants would administer what they thought were 450-volt shocks to a man with a heart condition who was screaming hysterically to be released from the experiment. Although many of the participants were in a state of extreme anxiety and discomfort over their terrible behavior, they nevertheless continued to obey the experimenter. As had the Nazis during World War II, these American citizens seemed to give up their moral responsibility when they agreed to follow the orders of the experimenter.

This research is just one example, although a highly dramatic one, of the phenomenon that social psychologists call social influence—the ability of a person or group to change the behavior of others. Traditionally, a distinction has been drawn among three different types of social influence: conformity, compliance, and obedience. *Conformity* refers to those times when individuals will change their attitudes or behaviors because of perceived group pressure—that is, they feel pressure to conform to the attitude or behavior of some group that is at least somewhat important to them. If, for instance, everyone in your group of friends adopts a particular style of clothing, or adopts a particular attitude toward another group, you may feel some pressure to conform to their behavior, even if no one in the group ever asks you to. *Compliance*, on the other hand, refers to those times when individuals change their behavior in response to a direct request from others. We are often faced with direct requests intended to change our behavior, whether they come from family, friends, teachers, bosses, or door-to-door salesmen. Considerable research has been conducted to determine what kinds of strategies by "requesters" are the most effective in prompting actual compliance. Finally, *obedience* refers to those times when individuals change their behavior in response to a direct order from another person; thus, unlike compliance, in which you are asked to make a behavioral change, in obedience you are commanded to do so. The research by Milgram is a good example of an obedience situation.

The four selections in this unit illustrate, sometimes dramatically, the powerful ways in which social influence operates. In the first, "The Heavy Burden of Black Conformity," journalist Bill Maxwell gives a vivid example of how powerful conformity pressures can be. Maxwell describes the pressure he feels from what he calls the "Soul Patrol": fellow African Americans who discourage any attempts to criticize their own ethnic group. In "Obedience in Retrospect," Alan Elms gives an insider's perspective on what it was like to work with Milgram on his famous studies of obedience, and on the initial reaction from other psychologists when the findings were first made known.

In the next selection, "Reciprocation: The Old Give and Take . . . and Take," Robert Cialdini describes a particular compliance-inducing strategy: the use of the reciprocity norm. By doing something for you initially (such as giving you a flower), other people can invoke the powerful reciprocity norm, which holds that we should return favors that are done for us. As a result, we become more likely to comply with a subsequent request from the one who has done us the favor.

In the final selection, "Suspect Confessions," Richard Jerome profiles a social psychologist who specializes in investigating a particular kind of compliance situation—the police interrogation. The work of social psychologist Richard Ofshe suggests that some of the techniques used by police during questioning can be so powerful that suspects will sometimes comply (confess) even when they are innocent of the crimes! This article provides a fascinating glimpse into just how powerful some compliance-inducing tactics can be.

The heavy burden of black conformity

BILL MAXWELL

COLUMNIST

Four weeks ago, I spoke to a group in the Tampa Bay area about the need for blacks and whites to cooperate for the good of future generations of young people. A prominent black civil rights activist stormed from the room after I said that blacks must stop seeing racism in the ordinary "comings and goings" of human relations and that "some things are the inescapable hazards of living in a pluralistic society."

A week later, I was showing social service professionals how to write effective letters and guest columns to the editor and how to arrange meetings with the editorial board of their local newspaper when a black man interrupted. He demanded, inappropriately for the topic at hand, that I explain why the *St. Petersburg Times,* the newspaper for which I work, has not employed more black executives and has not appointed a black to the board of directors.

After I said that the paper is slowly changing for the better, that blacks cannot force themselves into executive jobs or onto the board, he stormed out, but not before suggesting that I am an Uncle Tom.

A week ago, as I told a group interested in crime prevention that young blacks—especially males—must learn the practical virtues of citizenship, Perkins T. Shelton, former St. Petersburg NAACP president and one of the self-anointed seers of black esprit, marched out of the auditorium.

Although these acts of rudeness and ugly manners were not directly related, they show that monolithism—the compulsion for sameness and oneness—thrives in black society despite loud cries to the contrary. Certainly, all black Americans are free to speak their minds. But woe unto the errant fool who bucks prevailing thought, who dares to think *un-black,* as it were. Blacks wanting to enjoy an unmolested life must conform to the tenets of the unwritten

manifesto of the Soul Patrol, the group to which the three men who walked out on my speeches belong.

What is the Soul Patrol? What are its tenets? And, of course, how do the patrol and its manifesto affect black society in general? The Soul Patrol is not an organized body. Rather, it consists of loosely connected opinion leaders—elected and appointed officials, preachers, journalists, gangsta rappers, business owners, teachers, school administrators and others—who wield considerable influence, who possess the "right" attitude and use coded rhetoric.

These mind cops, practicing the ancient art of saving face for their ethnic group, are said to *think black.* They include the likes of O.J. Simpson attorney Johnny Cochran, U.S. Rep. Maxine Waters, former NAACP Executive Director Benjamin Chavis, Nation of Islam leader Louis Farrakhan. The list does not include the likes of O.J. prosecutor Christopher Darden, Harvard intellectual Henry Louis Gates Jr., English professor Shelby Steele, retired Gen. Colin Powell.

In the broadest sense, the manifesto of the Soul Patrol is the centuries-old prohibition against saying or writing anything negative about fellow blacks in the presence of whites or for their consideration. Its rationale, framed by the instinct of self-preservation, is that negative observations by blacks about other blacks only aid and abet the enemy by justifying racism and other forms of malevolence and by validating ugly stereotypes.

True brethren of color, therefore, do not air the race's dirty linen in public, a stricture that has created the pseudonegritude—false consciousness of and false pride in the cultural and physical aspects of our African heritage—that diminishes the quality of black life. Negritude itself, genuine consciousness and pride, is desir-

able, undergirding the positive aspects of African-American society.

Genuine negritude realistically assesses our heritage, actively makes our own personal behavior a shining example of the positive and publicly rejects self-immolation. The pseudonegritude of the Soul Patrol's manifesto, however, has produced a pernicious and dangerous cult of silence that embraces unwholesome sacred cows, unsavory personalities, self-defeating behavior and rationalizes various forms of criminality.

So, when I said that young black males often are their own worst enemies, that they should not be permitted to terrorize their neighborhoods, that they must learn to be good citizens, the protectors of negritude saw me as a traitor.

Outsiders would think that because blacks do not discuss their intrarace problems in public, we surely must discuss these problems behind closed doors. The truth is that, because we often are too busy heaping blame on others, we rarely discuss among ourselves the root causes of our own self-destructiveness.

And we see the ugly results of this silence everywhere: in the squalid conditions of our neighborhoods; in the high number of our young men behind bars; in the high incidence of teen pregnancy; in the excessive school dropout rates; in the alarming suspension and expulsion trends; in the crime statistics; in the number of unemployable blacks.

Is the silence of saving face a sensible trade-off for such personal, spiritual and societal carnage? I think not. The real enemies of African-Americans are not the self-critics who speak out publicly, but the blindly loyal soul brothers and sisters who storm out of auditoriums, who bite their tongues even as black life implodes.

Obedience in Retrospect

Alan C. Elms
University of California, Davis

Milgram's original paradigm for studying obedience to authority is briefly described, and the main results are summarized. Personal observations of the conduct of the initial studies give added context for interpreting the results. Psychologists' reactions to the Milgram experiments are discussed in terms of (1) rejecting the research on ethical grounds, (2) explaining away the results as expressions of trivial phenomena, (3) subsuming obedience to destructive authority under other explanatory rubrics, and (4) endorsing or rejecting the results in terms of their perceived social relevance or irrelevance.

The problem of obedience to authority may well be the crucial issue of our time. The experiments you took part in represent the first efforts to understand this phenomenon in an objective, scientific manner. (Stanley Milgram, *Report to Memory Project Subjects,* 1962b)

Introduction

Obedience to destructive authority was indeed a crucial social issue in 1962. The Holocaust had ended less than two decades earlier. Adolf Eichmann recently had been sentenced to death for expediting it, despite his plea that he had just been "following orders." American military advisers were being ordered to Vietnam in increasing numbers to forestall Communist control of Southeast Asia. Whether destructive obedience could reasonably be described as *the* crucial issue of the time is a

Quotations from unpublished correspondence of Stanley Milgram are used by permission of Alexandra Milgram.

Correspondence regarding this article should be addressed to Alan C. Elms, Department of Psychology, University of California, Davis, California 95616-8686.

judgment call; surely other issues offered competition for that status. But there can be little argument that Stanley Milgram's experiments were indeed "the first efforts to understand this phenomenon in an objective, scientific manner."

Milgram was not seeking to develop a grand theory of obedience. His main concern was with the phenomenon itself. He advised his graduate students that as they began their own research, "First decide what questions you want to answer." For him those first questions were typically substantive, not theoretical. He also told his students he sought to collect data that would still be of interest 100 years later, whatever theoretical interpretations might be made of the data. For his data on obedience, we are a third of the way through that 100 years. Those data remain of high interest indeed, offering continual challenges to our theories and to our confidence as psychologists that we really understand important aspects of human social behavior.

Milgram eventually proposed his own theoretical interpretations. But what most people still remember are the data themselves, the sheer numbers of research volunteers who obeyed every order to the very end. Before Milgram, creative writers had incorporated striking incidents of obedience into novels, poems, and screenplays. Historians had written factual accounts of remarkably obedient individuals and groups. Psychologists had developed F- and other scales to measure inclinations toward authoritarian tyranny and subservience. Milgram instead established a realistic laboratory setting where actual obedience and its circumstances might be closely studied.

The Obedience Paradigm

For those who have forgotten the details, and for the few who have never read them, here is the basic situation that Milgram devised. First, he advertised in the New Haven (Connecticut) daily newspaper and through direct mail for volunteers for a study of memory and learning. Volunteers were promised $4.00 for an hour of their time, plus 50 cents carfare. (At the time, $4 was well above minimum wage for an hour of work; 50 cents would have paid for a round-trip bus ride to and from most areas of New Haven.) Most of those who volunteered were scheduled by telephone to come at a given time to a laboratory on the Yale University campus.

In the basic experiments, two volunteers arrived at the laboratory at about the same time. Both were invited into the lab by the experimenter. The experimenter explained that one volunteer would be assigned the role of teacher and the other would become the learner. The teacher would administer an electric shock to the learner whenever the learner made an error, and each additional shock would be 15 volts higher than the previous one. By drawing slips of paper from a hat, one volunteer became the teacher. His first task was to help strap the arms of the other volunteer to the arms of a chair, so the electrodes from the shock generator would not fall off accidentally. The teacher was given a sample 45 volt electric shock from the shock generator, a level strong enough to be distinctly unpleasant. Then the experimenter asked the teacher to begin teaching the learner a list of word pairs. The learner did fairly well at first, then began to make frequent errors. Soon the teacher found himself administering higher and higher shock levels, according to the experimenter's instructions. (Male pronouns are used here because most volunteers were male; in only one experimental condition out of 24 were female subjects used.)

After a few shocks the learner began to object to the procedure. After more shocks and more objections, he loudly refused to participate further in the learning task, and stopped responding. If the teacher stopped giving him electric shocks at this point, the experimenter ordered the teacher to continue, and to administer stronger and stronger shocks for each failure to respond—all the way to the end of the graded series of levers, whose final labels were "Intense Shock," "Extreme Intensity Shock," "Danger: Severe Shock," and "XXX," along with voltage levels up to 450 volts. In the first experimental condition, the teacher was separated from the learner by a soundproofed wall; the learner could communicate his distress only by kicking on the wall. In subsequent conditions, teachers could hear the learner's voice through a speaker system, or sat near the learner in the same room while the learning task proceeded, or sat next to the learner and had to force his hand down onto a shock grid if he refused to accept the shocks voluntarily.

Teachers were not told several important pieces of information until their participation in the experiment was finished. Number one, the experiment was a study of obedience to authority, not a study of memory and learning. Number two, the volunteer who assumed the role of learner was actually an experimental confederate. Number three, the only shock that anyone ever got was the 45 volt sample shock given to each teacher; the shock generator was not wired to give any shocks to the learner. Number four, the learner's kicks against the wall, his screams, his refusals to continue, were all carefully scripted and rehearsed, as were the experimenter's orders to the teacher. A number of variables could be (and were) added to the research design in different conditions, but these aspects were constant.

Observations from the Inside

The basic series of obedience experiments took place in the summer of 1961. Milgram was at that time a very junior assistant professor, 27 years old, with no professional publications yet in print. I had just finished my first year of graduate school when he hired me to be his research assistant for the summer. Stanley sent me a letter on June 27, a week before I was scheduled to return to New Haven from a brief summer vacation:

> Matters have been proceeding apace on the project. The apparatus is almost done and looks thoroughly professional; just a few small but important pieces remain to be built. It may turn out that you will build them, but that depends on factors at present unknown.
>
> The advertisement was placed in the *New Haven Register* and yielded a disappointingly low response. There is no immediate crisis, however, since we do have about 300 qualified applicants. But before long, in your role as Solicitor General, you will have to think of ways to deliver more people to the laboratory. This is a very important practical aspect of the research. I will admit it bears some resemblance to Mr. Eichmann's position, but *you* at least should have no misconceptions of what *we* do with our daily quota. We give them a chance to resist the commands of malevolent authority and assert their alliance with morality.
>
> . . . The goal this summer is to run from 250–300 subjects in nine or ten experimental conditions. Only if this is accomplished can the summer be considered a success. Let me know if there is something I have overlooked.

The summer was a success by any reasonable standards, if not fully by Milgram's. He had not overlooked anything procedural; even at that early state in his career, he was already the most well-organized researcher I have ever encountered. But he had hardly come close to anticipating the degree to which his subjects would yield to the commands of malevolent authority, or how readily they would abrogate their alliance with morality. Milgram knew he would get *some* obedience; in a pilot study the previous winter, he had found Yale undergraduates disturbingly willing to shock their victims. But he recognized that Yale undergraduates were a special sample in many ways; that the prototype shock generator was rather crude and perhaps not altogether convincing; and that the simulated victim's displays of pain were fairly easy to ignore. For the main experiments, Milgram auditioned and rehearsed a victim whose cries of agony were truly piercing. He recruited a larger and diverse sample of nonstudent adults from the New Haven area, ranging from blue-collar workers to professionals and from 20 to 50 years in age. He constructed a professional-looking shock generator and purchased other high-quality equipment, including a 20-pen Esterline Angus Event Recorder that registered the duration and latency of each "shock" administration to the nearest hundredth of a second. He had decided that his main dependent variable would be the mean shock level at which subjects refused to go further in each experimental condition, but he wanted to be able to examine more subtle differences in their performance as well.

In early August the curtains went up on the first official obedience experiment. (More accurately, the curtains were drawn aside; Yale's new Social Interaction Laboratory, on temporary loan from the Sociology Department, was enclosed by two-way-mirrors and heavy soundproofing curtains.) Would subjects be convinced of the reality of the learning-and-memory experiment, the shock generator, the victim's suffering? They were. Would subjects obey the experimenter? They did. How far would they go? On and on up the sequence of shock levels. Would any subjects go all the way to the end of the shock board? Yes indeed.

Behind the two-way mirrors, Stanley Milgram and I (as well as occasional visitors) watched each early subject with fascination and with our own share of tension. Stanley had made broad predictions concerning the relative amounts of obedience in different conditions, but we paid little attention to the gradual confirmation of those predictions. Instead we tried to predict the behavior of each new subject, based on his initial demeanor and the little we knew about his background. We were gratified when any subject resisted authority. Sometimes it was quiet resistance, sometimes noisy, but it was exciting each time it happened. As more and more subjects obeyed every command, we felt at first dismayed, then cynically confirmed in our bleakest views of humanity. We were distressed when some volunteers wept, appalled when others laughed as they administered shock after shock. The experimenter gave each subject a standard debriefing at the end of the hour, to minimize any continuing stress and to show that the "victim" had not been injured by the "shocks." When a subject appeared especially stressed, Milgram often moved out from behind the curtains to do an especially thorough job of reassurance and stress reduction. When a subject did something truly unexpected during the experiment—an especially resolute show of resistance, for instance, or a long laughing jag—Milgram would join the experimenter in giving the subject a detailed cross-examination about why he had displayed such behavior. For us as well as the subjects, the situation quickly became more than an artificially structured experiment. Instead it presented slice after slice of real life, with moral decisions made and unmade very evening.

The Most Prominent Results

As matters turned out, Milgram did not need equipment sensitive enough to measure shock intervals in hundredths of a second. By the end of the second run of 40 subjects, if not before, his main dependent variable had become simply the percentage of subjects who obeyed the experimenter's commands all the way to the end of the shock series, contrasted with the percentage who disobeyed by quitting at *any* point in the whole long sequence of shock levels. In the first condition, a substantial majority of subjects (26 out of 40, or 65%) obeyed completely. That was the condition with minimal feedback from the learner—a few vigorous kicks on the wall. But wouldn't obedience drop substantially if the teacher could actually hear the learner screaming and demanding to be set free? It didn't. Twenty-five out of 40 were fully obedient in this second condition. Even when Milgram tried to encourage disobedience by having the learner claim a preexisting heart condition ("It's bothering me now!"), obedience remained at a high level: 26 of 40 subjects again (Milgram, 1974, pp. 56–57). Putting the victim in the same room and near the teacher reduced obedience somewhat, but 40% still obeyed fully. Indeed, even when teachers were ordered to press the hand of the screaming victim down onto a shock plate to complete the electrical circuit, a majority did so at least twice before quitting, and 30% obeyed in this fashion to the end of the shock board (Milgram, 1974, p. 35).

Milgram ran approximately a thousand subjects through various obedience conditions in less than a year. (The National Science Foundation, which financed the research, got its money's worth from two grants totaling about $60,000.) Each subject was run through the procedure individually, then was subjected to both immediate and follow-up questionnaires of various kinds. Milgram looked at the effects not only of the victim's physical proximity to the subject but of the experimenter's proximity, the amount of group support either for obedience or for defiance, and the learning experiment's apparent institutional backing. He made a variety of interesting findings—enough to fill a book, and more. But the data that carried the greatest impact, on other psychologists and on the general public, came from those first few experimental conditions: two-thirds of a sample of average Americans were willing to shock an innocent victim until the poor man was screaming for his life, and to go on shocking him well after he had lapsed into a perhaps unconscious silence, all at the command of a single experimenter with no apparent means of enforcing his orders.

Reactions to the Research

Once these data appeared in professional psychological journals (after initial resistance from editors), they were rather quickly disseminated through newspaper and magazine stories, editorials, sermons, and other popular media. With few exceptions, the nonprofessional citations of the experiments emphasized their social relevance: Milgram had revealed in ordinary Americans the potential for behavior comparable to that of the Nazis during the European Holocaust. (According to a *TV Guide* ad for a docudrama with William Shatner as a fictionalized Milgram, the research revealed "A world of evil so terrifying no one dares penetrate its secret. Until now!" [August 21, 1976, p. A-86].)

Psychologists responded in more diverse ways. Authors eager to enliven their introductory and social psychology textbooks soon made the obedience experiments a staple ingredient. Other psychologists seemed to regard Milgram's results as a challenge of one sort or another: conceptual, ethical, theoretical, political. The obedience studies were related, historically and procedurally, to earlier studies of social influence, but they did not fit readily into current theoretical models or research trends. Because of their rapidly achieved visibility inside and outside the field, they were soon treated as fair game for elucidation or attack by psychologists with a multitude of orientations.

Ethical Concerns

One type of response to the disturbing results of the obedience studies was to shift attention from the amounts of obedience Milgram obtained to the ethics of putting subjects through such a stressful experience. The first substantial published critique of Milgram's studies focused on the presumed psychic damage wreaked on his subjects by their ordeal (Baumrind, 1964). Milgram was not altogether surprised by such criticism; similar concerns had been expressed by several Yale faculty members during or soon after the experiments, and ethical questions had been raised about the research when Milgram first applied for American Psychological Association membership. But he was disappointed that his critics did not recognize the care he had put into responding to his subjects' high stress levels immediately after their participation, as well as into checking on any lingering effects over time (Milgram, 1964). Milgram was a pioneer in the debriefing procedures that are now a matter of course in psychological experiments on human subjects—debriefing in the sense not only of questioning the subject about his or her perception of the experiment, but of providing the subject with information and encouragement that will counteract any reactions to participation that might damage the subject's self-esteem. As Milgram told me later,

> My membership application to APA was held up for one year while they investigated the ethicality of the obedience experiment. In the end, they gave me a clean bill of health and admitted me to membership. Whenever any group has seriously considered the merits and problems of the experiment, they have concluded that it was an ethical experiment. Nonetheless, isolated individuals still feel strongly enough to attack it. (Personal communication, July 3, 1969)

One consequence of those individual attacks was a set of stringent federal regulations that made it virtually impossible ever again to conduct a close replication of the Milgram studies at any U.S. educational or research institution.

Many social scientists who have considered the ethics of the obedience studies in print have taken a neutral position or have come down on the side of Milgram. But outside the field, a similar perception of appropriate research and debriefing procedures is not widespread. When I participated in a conference on social science research ethics at the Kennedy Institute of Ethics 18 years after the obedience research was completed, several philosophers and professional ethicists devoted a large part of their energies to what struck me as rather crude Milgram bashing. The research scientists at the conference were not so inclined, but they had to work hard to communicate the virtues of a set of studies that had raised important issues about both the bad and the good in human nature (Beauchamp, Faden, Wallace, & Walters, 1982).

Questions of Belief

Among the early commentaries on the research, several psychologists argued that the results were not credible because the subjects did not believe they were actually harming the victim (e.g., Orne & Holland, 1968). Milgram's own data, showing that during the experiment a very high percentage of subjects believed the victim was receiving extremely painful shocks (1974, pp. 171–174), were ignored or dismissed as attempts by the subject to give Milgram the answers he wanted. Researchers' descriptions of many subjects' visible signs of high stress were also ignored, or were assumed to be evidence merely of the subjects' enthusiastic play acting. Even a filmed record of several actual subjects (Milgram, 1965a), displaying either great stress or extraordinary improvisational acting ability, did not convince psychologists who took this dismissive position. Some critics may have assumed that the four subjects shown at length in the film, plus several others who appeared more briefly, were the most convincingly emotional subjects Milgram could find among his thousand participants. In fact, Milgram chose all of them from the 14 subjects who happened to be "selected in the normal manner for recruitment" during the two days he brought movie cameras to the laboratory (Milgram, 1965c, p. 5).

Theoretical Alternatives

Many social psychologists have accepted the ethical appropriateness of Milgram's procedures and the believability of the experimental context. Even they, however, have often redirected attention away from the specific phenomenon of destructive obedience by subsuming it under a broader theoretical approach or alternative hypothetical constructs.

Milgram was slow to offer a comprehensive theoretical account of his own. His definitions of obedience to authority, from his first to his final writings on the subject, drew upon no theoretical assumptions. Rather, they were commonsense or dictionary definitions: "Every power system implies a structure of command and action in response to the command"

(Milgram, 1961, p. 2); "If *Y* follows the command of *X* we shall say that he has obeyed *X;* if he fails to carry out the command of *X,* we shall say that he has disobeyed *X*" (Milgram, 1965b, p. 58); "[I]t is only the man dwelling in isolation who is not forced to respond, through defiance or submission, to the commands of others" (Milgram, 1974, p. 1). In his grant proposals he referred to "internal restraints" or "internal resistances" that were pitted against the acceptance of authoritative commands, but he did not specify the nature of these internal processes (Milgram, 1961, p. 3; Milgram, 1962a, p. 1). He raised the possibility of predispositional factors and of "highly complex, and possibly, idiosyncratic motive structures" (1962z, p. 17), but in the research itself he directed his efforts mainly toward identifying situational factors that increased or decreased obedience. In his most extensive early discussion of his results (Milgram, 1965b, largely written in 1962), he cited such midlevel hypothetical constructs as "empathic cues," "denial and narrowing of the cognitive field," and a varying "sense of *relatedness* between his [the subject's] own actions and the consequences of those actions for the victim" (pp. 61–63; his italics).

Though it took Milgram less than a year to run all his subjects and not much longer than that to write several papers on the results, he worked on his book about obedience for over five years. He attributed the slowness of the book's writing in part to his becoming engaged in other sorts of research. But much of his struggle with the book appears to have centered on the difficulty of developing a general theory of obedience. The principal theoretical concepts he advanced in the book, including the agentic state (Milgram, 1974, pp. 133–134) and the evolution of a potential for obedience in humans (pp. 123–125), impressed many readers rather less than the results themselves—a reaction that both frustrated and pleased the data-centric Milgram. Though he had collected demographic information on all participants and had supported my collection of personality data from subsamples of obedient and disobedient subjects (Elms & Milgram, 1965), he gave short shrift to such data in his book, concluding that "It is hard to relate performance to personality because we really do not know very much about how to measure personality" (p. 205).

Others have usefully discussed the interaction of personality and situational variables in the obedience situations (e.g., Blass, 1991). A majority of the alternative explanations, however, have stressed cognitive processes, emphasizing ways in which the subject processed information about the situation that might have justified his obedience or strengthened his resistance. Milgram viewed such alternative explanations with interest, but took steps to rule out certain of them experimentally. One of the most obvious of these alternatives was the idea that subjects might be so awed by Yale University and so certain of its virtue that they would do anything they were told within those august halls, regardless of any general proclivity toward destructive obedience. Even before this environment-based explanation of his subjects' obedience was first offered in print, Milgram had largely vitiated it by moving the experiments from the awe-inspiring Interaction Laboratory to a rather less impressive basement facility and then to the in-

tentionally unimpressive office of a fly-by-night company in industrial Bridgeport, Connecticut. He got essentially the same results in all three locations. A number of alternative or additional explanations of Milgram's results remain as operable hypotheses, but none has decisively carried the day. Their very diversity ensures that the larger audience for the research will continue to be concerned primarily about the subjects' disturbing behavior rather than about the internal processes that may have produced it.

The Question of Relevance

Finally among ways in which psychologists have responded to Milgram's findings are arguments concerning the social relevance of the experiments. Many psychologists, at least in their textbooks, have embraced his findings as being highly relevant to important social phenomena, including destructive obedience not only in totalitarian states but among American soldiers, Bosnian combatants, and suicidal religious cults. But others (including some who also argued that the research was unethical or experientially unconvincing) have denied any real social relevance. Even if subjects believed they were really shocking the victim, these psychologists say, they knew the situation must not be as bad as it appeared, because somebody would have stopped them if it was. Or the subjects were in a situation where the experimenter accepted responsibility for the effects of their behavior, so their behavior is not really relevant to real-world situations where blame is less readily transferred to another individual. Or some other rationale is advanced, presumably peculiar to the Milgram obedience situation, that somehow does not translate into real-world social dynamics. Milgram rightly dismissed all such explanations that had been advanced up to the time of his final writings, and very likely would have dismissed all subsequent ones, for two simple reasons: Any effective authority figure in the real world always finds ways to justify imposing his or her will on underlings. The underlings who obey authoritative commands in the real world always find rationales for their obedience. In most prominent real-world cases of destructive obedience that have been compared (or discompared) to the Milgram studies, the authorities were able to call upon a social rationale for their commands that was at least as strong as or stronger than that available to any psychological experimenter. In addition, they were often able to promise their followers much greater rewards for obedience and punishments for disobedience.

Stanley Milgram's research on obedience tapped into psychological processes that ranked as neither new nor extreme in the history of human behavior. A "crucial issue of our time," perhaps *the* crucial issue, obedience, unfortunately remains. Though Milgram was proud that his studies were "the first efforts to understand this phenomenon in an objective, scientific manner," he did not want them to be the last. This issue of the *Journal of Social Issues* gives strong evidence that the efforts of other researchers to expand upon his groundbreaking work will continue unabated.

References

Baumrind, D. (1964). Some thoughts on ethics of research: After reading Milgram's "Behavioral Study of Obedience." *American Psychologist, 19,* 421–423.

Beauchamp, T. L., Faden, R. R., Wallace, R. J., Jr., & Walters, I., (Eds.). (1982) *Ethical issues in social science research.* Baltimore, MD: Johns Hopkins University Press.

Blass, T. (1991). Understanding behavior in the Milgram obedience experiment: The role of personality, situations, and their interactions. *Journal of Personality and Social Psychology, 60,* 398–413.

Elms, A. C., & Milgram, S. (1965). Personality characteristics associated with obedience and defiance toward authoritative command. *Journal of Experimental Research in Personality, 1,* 282–289.

Milgram, S. (1961) *Dynamics of obedience: Experiments in social psychology.* Application for National Science Foundation research grant, Yale University.

Milgram, S. (1962a). *Obedience to authority: Experiments in social psychology.* Application for National Science Foundation grant renewal, Yale University.

Milgram, S. (1962b). *Report to Memory Project subjects.* Unpublished manuscript, Yale University.

Milgram, S. (1964). Issues in the study of obedience: A reply to Baumrind. *American Psychologist, 19,* 848–852.

Milgram, S. (1965a). *Obedience* [Film]. (Available from the Pennsylvania State University Audiovisual Services.)

Milgram, S. (1965b). Some conditions of obedience and disobedience to authority. *Human Relations, 18,* 57–76.

Milgram, S. (1965c). Study notes for "Obedience." (Distributed by the New York University Film Library.)

Milgram, S. (1974). *Obedience to authority.* New York: Harper & Row.

Orne, M. T., & Holland, C. C. (1968). On the ecological validity of laboratory deceptions. *International Journal of Psychiatry, 6,* 282–293.

ALAN C. ELMS, while a graduate student at Yale University, worked with Stanley Milgram on the first obedience studies and earned his Ph.D. under the direction of Irving L. Janis. Dr. Elms did laboratory studies of role-play-induced attitude change and interview studies of right- and left-wing political activists before he focused his work on psychobiography. He has written *Social Psychology and Social Relevance* (1972), *Personality in Politics* (1976), and *Uncovering Lives: The Uneasy Alliance of Biography and Psychology* (1994). He has taught at Southern Methodist University, has been a visiting scholar at Trinity College, Dublin, and at Harvard University, and has been a faculty member at the University of California, Davis, since 1967.

Reciprocation

The Old Give and Take . . . and Take

Robert B. Cialdini

Karales/Peter Arnold, Inc.

"Pay every debt, as if God wrote the bill."
Ralph Waldo Emerson

A few years ago, a university professor tried a little experiment. He sent Christmas cards to a sample of perfect strangers. Although he expected some reaction, the response he received was amazing—holiday cards addressed to him came pouring back from people who had never met nor heard of him. The great majority of those who returned cards never inquired into the identity of the unknown professor. They received his holiday greeting card, *click*, and *whirr*, they automatically sent cards in return (Kuntz & Woolcott, 1976).

While small in scope, this study shows the action of one of the most potent of the weapons of influence around us—the rule of reciprocation. The rule says that we should try to repay, in kind, what another person has provided us. If a woman does us a favor, we should do her one in return; if a man sends us a birthday present, we should remember his birthday with a gift of our own;

if a couple invites us to a party, we should be sure to invite them to one of ours. By virtue of the reciprocity rule, then, we are *obligated* to the future repayment of favors, gifts, invitations, and the like. So typical is it for indebtedness to accompany the receipt of such things that a phrase like "much obliged" has become a synonym for "thank you," not only in the English language but in others as well.

The impressive aspect of reciprocation with its accompanying sense of obligation is its pervasiveness in human culture. It is so widespread that, after intensive study, Alvin Gouldner (1960), along with other sociologists, report that all human societies subscribe to the rule.[1] Within each society it seems pervasive also; it permeates exchanges of every kind. Indeed, it may well be that a developed system of indebtedness flowing from the rule of reciprocation is a unique property of human culture. The noted archaeologist Richard Leakey ascribes the essence of what makes us human to the reciprocity system. He claims that we are human because our ancestors learned to share food and skills "in an honored network of obligation" (Leakey & Lewin, 1978). Cultural anthropologists Lionel Tiger and Robin Fox (1971) view this "web of indebtedness" as a unique adaptive mechanism of human beings, allowing for the division of labor, the exchange of diverse forms of goods and different services, and the creation of interdependencies that bind individuals together into highly efficient units.

It is a sense of future obligation that is critical to produce social advances of the sort described by Tiger and

---

[1]Certain societies have formalized the rule into ritual. Consider for example the Vartan Bhanji, an institutionalized custom of gift exchange common to parts of Pakistan and India. In commenting upon the Vartan Bhanji, Gouldner (1960) remarks:

It is . . . notable that the system painstakingly prevents the total elimination of outstanding obligations. Thus, on the occasion of a marriage, departing guests are given gifts of sweets. In weighing them out, the hostess may say, "These five are yours," meaning "These are a repayment for what you formerly gave me," and then she adds an extra measure, saying, "These are mine." On the next occasion, she will receive these back along with an additional measure which she later returns, and so on.

From *Influence: Science and Practice, 3/e,* edited by Robert B. Cialdini, chapter 2, pp. 19–29. © 1993 by HarperCollins College Publishers. Reprinted by permission of Addison Wesley Educational Publishers, Inc.

Fox. A widely shared and strongly held feeling of future obligation made an enormous difference in human social evolution because it meant that one person could give something (for example, food, energy, care) to another with confidence that the gift was not being lost. For the first time in evolutionary history, one individual could give away any of a variety of resources without actually giving them away. The result was the lowering of the natural inhibitions against transactions that must be *begun* by one person's providing personal resources to another. Sophisticated and coordinated systems of aid, gift giving, defense, and trade became possible, bringing immense benefits to the societies that possessed them. With such clearly adaptive consequences for the culture, it is not surprising that the rule for reciprocation is so deeply implanted in us by the process of socialization we all undergo.

I know of no better illustration of the way reciprocal obligations can reach long and powerfully into the future than the perplexing story of $5,000 of relief aid that was exchanged between Mexico and Ethiopia. In 1985, Ethiopia could justly lay claim to the greatest suffering and privation in the world. Its economy was in ruin. Its food supply had been ravaged by years of drought and internal war. Its inhabitants were dying by the thousands from disease and starvation. Under these circumstances, I would not have been surprised to learn of a $5,000 relief donation from Mexico to that wrenchingly needy country. I remember my feeling of amazement, though, when a brief newspaper item I was reading insisted that the aid had gone in the opposite direction. Native officials of the Ethiopian Red Cross had decided to send the money to help the victims of that year's earthquakes in Mexico City.

It is both a personal bane and a professional blessing that whenever I am confused by some aspect of human behavior, I feel driven to investigate further. In this instance, I was able to track down a fuller account of the story. Fortunately, a journalist who had been as bewildered as I by the Ethiopians' actions had asked for an explanation. The answer he received offered eloquent validation of the reciprocity rule: Despite the enormous needs prevailing in Ethiopia, the money was being sent to Mexico because, in 1935, Mexico had sent aid to Ethiopia when it was invaded by Italy ("Ethiopian Red Cross," 1985). So informed, I remained awed, but I was no longer puzzled. The need to reciprocate had transcended great cultural differences, long distances, acute famine, many years, and immediate self-interest. Quite simply, a half-century later, against all countervailing forces, obligation triumphed.

HOW THE RULE WORKS

Make no mistake, human societies derive a truly significant competitive advantage from the reciprocity rule and, consequently, they make sure their members are trained to comply with and believe in it. Each of us has been taught to live up to the rule, and each of us knows the social sanctions and derision applied to anyone who violates it. Because there is a general distaste for those who take and make no effort to give in return, we will often go to great lengths to avoid being considered a moocher, ingrate, or welsher. It is to those lengths that we will often be taken in, in the process, be "taken" by individuals who stand to gain from our indebtedness.

To understand how the rule of reciprocation can be exploited by one who recognizes it as the weapon of influence it certainly is, we might closely examine an experiment conducted by psychologist Dennis Regan (1971). A subject who participated in the study rated, along with another subject, the quality of some paintings as part of an experiment on "art appreciation." The other rater—we can call him Joe—was only posing as a fellow subject and was actually Dr. Regan's assistant. For our purposes, the experiment took place under two different conditions. In some cases, Joe did a small, unsolicited favor for the true subject. During a short rest period, Joe left the room for a couple of minutes and returned with two bottles of Coca-Cola, one for the subject and one for himself, saying "I asked him [the experimenter] if I could get myself a Coke, and he said it was OK, so I bought one for you, too." In other cases, Joe did not provide the subject with a favor; he simply returned from the two-minute break empty-handed. In all other respects, however, Joe behaved identically.

Later on, after the paintings had all been rated and the experimenter had momentarily left the room, Joe asked the subject to do *him* a favor. He indicated that he was selling raffle tickets for a new car and that if he sold the most tickets, he would win a $50 prize. Joe's request was for the subject to buy some raffle tickets at 25 cents apiece: "Any would help, the more the better." The major finding of the study concerns the number of tickets subjects purchased from Joe under the two conditions. Without question, Joe was more successful in selling his raffle tickets to the subjects who had received his earlier favor. Apparently feeling that they owed him something, these subjects bought twice as many tickets as the subjects who had not been given the prior favor. Although the Regan study represents a fairly simple demonstration of the workings of the rule of reciprocation, it illustrates several important characteristics of the rule that, upon further consideration, help us to understand how it may be profitably used.

The Rule Is Overpowering

One of the reasons reciprocation can be used so effectively as a device for gaining another's compliance is its power. The rule possesses awesome strength, often producing a yes response to a request that, except for an existing feeling of indebtedness, would have surely been refused. Some evidence of how the rule's force can overpower the influence of other factors that normally determine compliance with a request can be seen in a second result of the Regan study. Besides his interest in the impact of the reciprocity rule on compliance, Regan was also investigating how liking for a person affects the tendency to comply with that person's request. To measure how liking toward Joe affected the subjects' decisions to buy his raffle tickets, Regan had them fill out several rating scales indicating how much they had liked Joe. He then compared their liking responses with the number of tickets they had purchased from Joe. There was a significant tendency for subjects to buy more raffle tickets from Joe the more they liked him. This alone is hardly a startling finding, since most of us would have guessed that people are more willing to do a favor for someone they like.

The interesting finding of the Regan experiment, however, was that the relationship between liking and compliance was completely wiped out in the condition under which subjects had been given a Coke by Joe. For those who owed him a favor, it made no difference whether they liked him or not; they felt a sense of obligation to repay him, and they did. The subjects who indicated that they disliked Joe bought just as many of his tickets as did those who indicated that they liked him. The rule for reciprocity was so strong that it simply overwhelmed the influence of a factor—liking for the requester—that normally affects the decision to comply.

Think of the implications. People we might ordinarily dislike—unsavory or unwelcome sales operators, disagreeable acquaintances, representatives of strange or unpopular organizations—can greatly increase the chance that we will do what they wish merely by providing us with a small favor prior to their requests. Let's take an example that, by now, many of us have encountered. The Hare Krishna Society is an Eastern religious sect with centuries-old roots traceable to the Indian city of Calcutta. Its spectacular modern-day story occurred in the 1970s when it experienced a remarkable growth, not only in followers, but also in wealth and property. The economic growth was funded through a variety of activities, the principal and still most visible of which is society members' requests for donations from passersby in public places. During the early history of the group in this country, the solicitation for contributions was attempted in a fashion memorable for anyone who saw it. Groups of Krishna devotees—often with shaved heads, and wearing ill-fitting robes, leg wrappings, beads, and bells—would canvass a city street, chanting and bobbing in unison while begging for funds.

Although highly effective as an attention-getting technique, this practice did not work especially well for fund raising. The average American considered the Krishnas weird, to say the least, and was reluctant to provide money to support them. It quickly became clear to the society that it had a considerable public-relations problem. The people being asked for contributions did not like the way the members looked, dressed, or acted. Had the society been an ordinary commercial organization, the solution would have been simple—change the things the public does not like. The Krishnas are a religious organization, however, and the way members look, dress, and act is partially tied to religious factors. Since religious factors are typically resistant to change because of worldly considerations, the Krishna leadership was faced with a real dilemma. On the one hand were beliefs, modes of dress, and hairstyles that had religious significance. On the other hand, threatening the organization's financial welfare, were the less-than-positive feelings of the American public toward these things. What's a sect to do?

The Krishnas' resolution was brilliant. They switched to a fund-raising tactic that made it unnecessary for their targets to have positive feelings toward the fund-raisers. They began to employ a donation-request procedure that engaged the rule for reciprocation, which, as demonstrated by the Regan study, was strong enough to overcome dislike for the requester. The new strategy still involved the solicitation of contributions in public places with much pedestrian traffic (airports are a favorite), but, before a donation was requested, the target person was given a "gift"—a book (usually the *Bhagavad Gita*), the *Back to Godhead* magazine of the society, or, in the most cost-effective version, a flower. The unsuspecting passersby who suddenly found flowers pressed into their hands or pinned to their jackets were under no circumstances allowed to give them back, even if they asserted that they did not want them. "No, it is our gift to you," said the solicitor, refusing to take it back. Only after the Krishna member had thus brought the force of the reciprocation rule to bear on the situation was the target asked to provide a contribution to the society. This benefactor-before-beggar strategy has been wildly successful for the Hare Krishna Society, producing large-scale economic gains and funding, the ownership of temples, businesses, houses, and property in 321 centers in the United States and abroad.

As an aside, it is instructive that the reciprocation rule has begun to outlive its usefulness for the Krishnas, not because the rule itself is any less potent societally, but because we have found ways to prevent the Krishnas from using it on us. After once falling victim to their tactic, many travelers are now alert to the presence of robed Krishna society solicitors in airports and train stations, adjusting their paths to avoid an encounter and preparing beforehand to ward off a solicitor's "gift." Although the society has tried to counter this increased vigilance by instructing members to be dressed and groomed in modern styles to avoid immediate recognition when soliciting (some actually carry flight bags or suitcases), even disguise has not worked especially well for the Krishnas. Too many individuals now know better than to accept unrequested offerings in public places such as airports.

As a result, the Krishnas have experienced a severe financial reversal over the past 10 years. In North America alone, nearly 30 percent of their temples have been closed for economic reasons, and the number of devotees staffing the remaining temples has plummeted from a high of 5,000 to an estimated 800. The Krishnas are a resilient group, though. Officials admit that the organization is struggling to maintain its long-standing presence in North America, but they report that it is thriving in the newly opened "markets" of Eastern Europe—where, apparently, people haven't yet caught on to the Krishnas' strategic benevolence.

It is a testament to the societal value of reciprocation that even those of us who know what the Krishnas are up to have chosen to avoid them or to deflect their flowers rather than to withstand the force of their gift giving directly by taking the flower and walking away with it. The reciprocation rule that empowers their tactic is too strong—and socially beneficial—for us to want to challenge head-on.

Politics Politics is another arena in which the power of the reciprocity rule shows itself. Reciprocation tactics appear at every level:

- At the top, elected officials engage in "logrolling" and the exchange of favors that makes politics the place of strange bedfellows, indeed. The out-of-character vote of one of our elected representatives on a bill or measure can often be understood as a favor returned to the bill's sponsor. Political analysts were amazed at Lyndon Johnson's success in getting so many of his programs through Congress during his early administration. Even congress-members who were thought to be strongly opposed to the proposals were voting for them. Close examination by political scientists has found the cause to be not so much Johnson's political savvy as the large score of favors he had been able to provide to other legislators during his many years of power in the House and Senate. As President, he was able to produce a truly remarkable amount of legislation in a short time by calling in those favors. It is interesting that this same process may account for the problems Jimmy Carter had in getting his programs through Congress during his early administration, despite heavy Democratic majorities in both the House and Senate. Carter came to the presidency from outside the Capitol Hill establishment. He campaigned on his outside-Washington identity, saying that he was indebted to no one. Much of his legislative difficulty upon arriving may be traced to the fact that no one there was indebted to *him*.

- At another level, we can see the recognized strength of the reciprocity rule in the desire of corporations and individuals to provide judicial and legislative officials with gifts and favors and in the series of legal restrictions against such gifts and favors. Even with legitimate political contributions, the stockpiling of obligations often underlies the stated purpose of supporting a favorite candidate. One look at the lists of companies and organizations that contribute to the campaigns of *both* major candidates in important elections gives evidence of such motives. A skeptic, requiring direct evidence of the *quid pro quo* expected by political contributors, might look to the remarkably bald-faced admission by Charles H. Keating, Jr., who was later convicted on multiple counts of fraud in this country's Savings & Loan disaster. Addressing the question of whether a connection existed between the $1.3 million he had contributed to the campaigns of five U.S. senators and their subsequent actions on his behalf against federal regulators, he asserted, "I want to say in the most forceful way I can: I certainly hope so."

- At the grass-roots level, local political organizations have learned that a principal way to keep their candidates in office is to make sure they provide a wide range of little favors to the voters. The "ward heelers" of many cities still operate effectively in this fashion. But ordinary citizens are not alone in trading political support for small personal favors. During the 1992 presidential primary campaign, actress Sally Kellerman was asked why she was lending her name and efforts to the candidacy of Democratic hopeful, Jerry Brown. Her reply: "Twenty years ago, I asked ten friends to help me move. He was the only one who showed up."

The Not-So-Free Sample Of course, the power of reciprocity can be found in the merchandising field as well. Although the number of examples is large, let's examine a pair of familiar ones. As a marketing technique, the free sample has a long and effective history. In most instances, a small amount of the relevant product is given to potential customers to see if they like it. Certainly this is a legitimate desire of the manufacturer—to expose the public to the qualities of the product. The beauty of the free sample, however, is that it is also a gift and, as such, can engage the reciprocity rule. In true jujitsu fashion, a promoter who provides free samples can release the natural indebting force inherent in a gift, while innocently appearing to have only the intention to inform.

A favorite place for free samples is the supermarket, where customers are frequently given small amounts of a certain product to try. Many people find it difficult to accept samples from the always smiling attendant, return only the toothpicks or cups, and walk away. Instead, they buy some of the product, even if they might not have liked it very much. A highly effective variation on this marketing procedure is illustrated in the case, cited by Vance Packard in *The Hidden Persuaders* (1957), of the Indiana supermarket operator who sold an astounding 1,000 pounds of cheese in a few hours one day by putting out the cheese and inviting customers to cut off slivers for themselves as free samples.

A different version of the free-sample tactic is used by the Amway Corporation, a rapid-growth company that manufactures and distributes household and personal-care products in a vast national network of door-to-door neighborhood sales. The company, which has grown from a basement-run operation a few years ago to a $1.5 billion yearly sales business, makes use of the free sample in a device called the BUG. The BUG consists of a collection of Amway products—bottles of furniture polish, detergent, or shampoo, spray containers of deodorizers, insect killers, or window cleaners—carried to a customer's home in a specially designed tray or just a polyethylene bag. The confidential Amway Career Manual then instructs the salesperson to leave the BUG with the customer "for 24, 48, or 72 hours, at no cost or obligation to her. Just tell her you would like her to try the products. . . . That's an offer no one can refuse." At the end of the trial period, the Amway representative is to return and pick up orders for the products the customer wishes to purchase. Since few customers use up the entire contents of even one of the product containers in such a short time, the salesperson may then take the remaining product portions in the BUG to the next potential customer down the line or across the street and start the process again. Many Amway representatives have several BUGS circulating in their districts at one time.

Of course, by now you and I know that the customer who has accepted and used the BUG products has been trapped by the reciprocity rule. Many such customers yield to a sense of obligation to order the products that they have tried and partially consumed—and, of course, by now the Amway Corporation knows that to be the case. Even in a company with as excellent a growth record as Amway, the BUG device has created a big stir. Reports by state distributors to the parent company record a remarkable effect:

> Unbelievable! We've never seen such excitement. Product is moving at an unbelievable rate, and we've only just begun. . . . Local distributors took the BUGS, and we've had an unbelievable increase in sales [from Illinois distributor]. The most fantastic retail idea we've ever had! . . . On the average, customers purchased about half the total amount of the BUG when it is picked up. . . . In one word, tremendous! We've never seen a response within our entire organization like this [from Massachusetts distributor].

The Amway distributors appear to be bewildered—happily so, but nonetheless bewildered—by the startling power of the BUG. Of course, by now you and I should not be.

The reciprocity rule governs many situations of a purely interpersonal nature where neither money nor commercial exchange is at issue. Perhaps my favorite illustration of the enormous force available from the reciprocation weapon of influence comes from such a situation. The European scientist Eibl-Eibesfeldt (1975) provides the account of a German soldier during World War I whose job was to capture enemy soldiers for interrogation. Because of the nature of the trench warfare at that time, it was extremely difficult for armies to cross the no-man's-land between opposing front lines, but it was not so difficult for a single soldier to crawl across and slip into an enemy trench position. The armies of the Great War had experts who regularly did so to capture enemy soldiers, who would then be brought back for questioning. The German expert had often successfully completed such missions in the past and was sent on another. Once again, he skillfully negotiated the area between fronts and surprised a lone enemy soldier in his trench. The unsuspecting soldier, who had been eating at the time, was easily disarmed. The frightened captive, with only a piece of bread in his hand, then performed what may have been the most important act of his life. He gave his enemy some of the bread. So affected was the German by this gift that he could not complete his mission. He turned from his benefactor and recrossed the no-man's-land empty-handed to face the wrath of his superiors.

An equally compelling point regarding the power of reciprocity comes from an account of a woman who saved her own life, not by *giving* a gift as did the captured soldier, but by *refusing* a gift and the powerful obligations that went with it. In November 1978 Jim Jones the leader of Jonestown, Guyana, called for the mass suicide of all residents, most of whom compliantly drank and died from a vat of poison-laced Kool-Aid. Diane Louie, a resident, however, rejected Jones's command and made her way out of Jonestown and into the jungle. She attributes her willingness to do so to her earlier refusal to accept special favors from him when she was in need. She turned down his offer of special food while she was ill, because "I knew once he gave me those privileges, he'd have me. I didn't want to owe him nothin' " (Anderson & Zimbardo, 1984). . . .

SUSPECT
CONFESSIONS

**He's made mincemeat of false memories.
But the social psychologist Richard Ofshe has a more pressing
question: Why do innocent people admit to crimes
they didn't commit?**

Richard Jerome

Richard Jerome is a senior writer at People *magazine.*

THROUGH A THICKENING FOG, RICHARD J. OFSHE WINDS HIS WHITE BMW homeward into the Oakland hills, leaving behind the University of California at Berkeley, where he is a professor of social psychology. In florid tones refined by 30 years at the lectern, Ofshe is expounding on his latest area of interest, the ways in which police interrogations can elicit false confessions. Specifically, he is bemoaning the case of Jessie Lloyd Misskelley Jr., a teen-ager from a squalid Arkansas trailer park who confessed—falsely, Ofshe maintains—to taking part in the ghastly murder of three 8-year-old boys. In spite of Ofshe's voluminous expert testimony on his behalf, Misskelley, who has an I.Q. in the 70's, was sentenced to life plus 40 years in prison.

"It was like walking straight into 'Deliverance,' " Ofshe says, casually veering around another hairpin turn. "The trial was a travesty. The conduct of the judge was outrageous."

At 54, Ofshe has acquired a muted celebrity for his work on extreme influence tactics and thought control. He shared in the 1979 Pulitzer Prize in public service after assisting The Point Reyes (Calif.) Light in its exposé of Synanon, a Bay Area drug rehabilitation group that evolved into an armed cult. More recently, Ofshe has been an aggressive and influential debunker of "recovered memory," the theory whereby long-repressed traumas are retrieved by patients undergoing what Ofshe calls exceedingly manipulative psychotherapy. As such, Ofshe is a vivid figure in "Remembering Satan," Lawrence Wright's book about the case of Paul Ingram, a former Olympia, Wash., sheriff's deputy now serving 20 years in prison primarily because he became convinced that the accusa-

tions of one of his daughters, who claimed that he had indulged in a 17-year binge of satanism, incest and infanticide, were true. Ofshe, a champion of Ingram, dissects the affair in his recent book, "Making Monsters: False Memories, Psychotherapy and Sexual Hysteria," written with Ethan Watters.

But for the most part, Ofshe has set aside violent cults and overzealous shrinks and is fixated on the third of his bêtes noires: false confessions. According to Ofshe and a considerable body of literature, modern interrogation tactics are so subtly powerful that police can—entirely unwittingly—coerce innocent suspects into admitting to the most heinous crimes. Sometimes, Ofshe says, a suspect admits guilt simply to escape the stress of the interrogation. More rarely, a suspect comes to believe that he actually committed the crime in question, though he has no memory of it.

For Ofshe, exorcising both kinds of false confession from the American justice system has become an almost obsessive quest. All told, he has consulted or testified in more than 80 criminal cases involving suspects from whom, he concluded, confessions were coerced; in most of these cases, the physical evidence strongly suggested innocence. Although he makes money at it overall—$40,000 in 1993—he sometimes works pro bono. With dark, disdaining eyes set against a shock of gray curls and a swirling beard, Ofshe looks vaguely sinister—a wily Renaissance pol, perhaps, or Claudius in a road company of Hamlet. Confession, he points out, is the anchor of a trial in which there is no hard evidence. "And false confession," he says, "ranks third after perjury and eyewitness error as a cause of wrongful convictions in American homicide cases."

His numbers are based on several studies, most recently work by the sociologist Michael L. Radelet of the University of Florida, Hugo Adam Bedau, professor of philosophy at Tufts University, and Constance E. Putnam, a Boston-based writer. In their 1992 book, "In Spite of Innocence," the authors review more than 400 cases in which innocent people were convicted of capital crimes in the United States. Fourteen percent were caused by false confession. "If it happened just one-half of 1 percent of the time," Ofshe says, "it still means that hundreds, or perhaps thousands, of people each year are being unjustly imprisoned. Even if one innocent man or woman is convicted, it's too many. And it's unnecessary because this is a fixable problem"—fixable, he adds, if only police interrogations were electronically recorded, a requirement now only in Alaska and Minnesota.

"Now I don't think for one second," Ofshe stresses, "that the detectives and prosecutors in cases of false confessions want to bring about that result. But because they don't understand the mistake as it is being made, the case moves forward and takes everyone along with it."

THE BMW IS NOW TUCKED SAFELY UNDER OFSHE'S RED FERRARI, which sits on a raised hoist in the garage of his hillside home, a quasi-Mediterranean mix of stone and stucco. Inside, rock music from a new stereo system tumbles down the coiled stairs of a three-and-a-half-story central rotunda, into a cherry-paneled library where Ofshe, propped like a pasha on a brown leather couch, surveys his domain with a reverent sigh: "I never thought I'd ever get to have a house like this."

It mirrors its inhabitant: spare, opulent, imposing yet accessible. One can well appreciate that Ofshe's fondest boyhood memory is of the austere charms of the Frick Collection mansion. His father, a dress designer, moved the family from the Bronx to Queens when Ofshe was a child. Ofshe attended Queens College, then went to graduate school at Stanford. "I honestly can't tell you now what led me to psychology," he says. "I suppose I'm a watcher. "I'm comfortable observing people and lecturing at them—but I am absolutely incapable of making small talk, a gift I consider one of the great mysteries of life."

During graduate school, Ofshe was married briefly and then, as he puts it, "got un-married." (He married his present wife, Bonnie Blair, a successful designer of sweaters, in 1981.) Ofshe gravitated toward social psychology; his work on cults grew out of a study of utopian societies he undertook in the early 1970's. One such community was Synanon, begun as a drug treatment center by Charles Dederich. But by 1978, Dederich had accumulated a substantial arsenal, as well as a large cadre of loyal followers. By this time, The Point Reyes Light, a weekly based near Ofshe's summer home, had begun an investigative series on Synanon, on which Ofshe collaborated. As a result of the media exposure, Synanon lost its tax-exempt status

and disintegrated. Dederich sued Ofshe three times unsuccessfully for libel, prompting him to retaliate with a malicious prosecution suit. " 'When this is over, I'll be the one driving the red Ferrari,' " Ofshe says he told people at the time. The Ferrari, he now confides, "accounts for a small percentage of my settlement. A very small percentage."

Material success aside, Ofshe seems to revel most in the validation of his work by respected media outlets. It takes little prodding for him to express his glee at Lawrence Wright's description of him as "Zeus-like" in "Remembering Satan"—which first appeared as an article in The New Yorker, a magazine Ofshe clearly reveres. And he is quick to point out that the television movie of Wright's book, currently being filmed, features him as the central character—as played by William Devane.

What saves this self-absorption from being insufferable is Ofshe's interest in helping people he considers innocent. He first focused on police interrogation in 1987, after a phone call from Joseph G. Donahey Jr., a veteran Florida attorney. Donahey was representing Thomas F. Sawyer, a Clearwater golf course groundskeeper who in 1986, after an uncommonly grueling 16-hour interrogation, confessed to the brutal murder of a neighbor; the police convinced Sawyer that he'd lost all memory of the incident during an alcoholic blackout. (Sawyer, against whom there was no physical evidence, had quickly recanted.) "Donahey realized something was terribly wrong with Tom's confession," Ofshe says. "At first I was skeptical. But once I read the transcript of the interrogation, it became obvious what had happened to Tom."

Ofshe spent 300 hours analyzing the Sawyer interrogation—which, by a lucky quirk, was taped in its entirety—and concluded it was "a tour de fore of psychological coercion." Sawyer's police interrogators, Peter Fire and John Dean, invited Sawyer to the station house on the premise that he was being asked to "assist" with their investigation. Then, Ofshe says, they flattered him into providing his own hypothetical murder scenario. The detectives then used leading questions to shape the groundskeeper's responses, eventually tossing his answers back as evidence of his guilt. Consider the following dialogue, slightly condensed, on the position of the victim's body:

FIRE: And he would put her in the bed how? Like she's doing what?
SAWYER: Sleeping.
FIRE: O.K. What would you put her on? Her. . . .
SAWYER: On her back.
FIRE: Put her on her back? . . .
SAWYER: I'd put her on her back sleeping.
FIRE: Put her on her back, sleeping?
SAWYER: Don't you sleep on your back?
FIRE: No. . . .
SAWYER: I don't sleep on my side.
FIRE: Well, what other way could you put her?
SAWYER: Face down.

FIRE: O.K. Face down. . . .

SAWYER: I'd put her on her stomach. . . .

FIRE: You hit the nail on the head. You put her on her stomach.

Deception, typically by lying about the presence of witnesses or physical evidence or about polygraph results, is a common interrogation tactic, Ofshe says, and it was used baldly against Sawyer. ("We found a lot of hairs and fibers on her body," Fire insisted at one point. "We have your hair. . . . There's a lot of evidence. There's a lot of evidence. A lot of evidence.")

"If you're dealing with middle-class types," Ofshe says, "or at least middle-class types socialized by my mother, they're hearing: 'It's inevitable that you'll be caught and punished to the max.' I have no interest in stripping police of tactics that make perfect sense—when those tactics are supported by compelling physical evidence. But the same things that can convince a guilty person that he's been caught can convince someone who's innocent that he's caught."

Under this intense barrage, Sawyer, who for hours steadfastly maintained his innocence, exhibited his first trace of self-doubt: "I honestly believe that I didn't do it. . . . I don't remember doing it. If I did, and I don't think I did. . . . You almost got me convinced I did, but. . . ."

"He went from straight denial to 'I couldn't have done something like this,'" Ofshe says. "And finally, when he confessed, it was so beautiful, so perfect in the way he verbalized it: 'I guess all the evidence is in, I guess I must have done it.'"

Strong evidence of a false confession, Ofshe says, is when the narrative is at odds with the known facts of the case or has been clearly fed to the suspect, however inadvertently, by the police themselves. "Sawyer was wrong about almost everything," Ofshe says, "except for several details"—like the position of the victim's body—"that were clearly introduced by Fire and Dean."

Ultimately, Ofshe's testimony helped exonerate Sawyer, whose confession was suppressed in 1989 after the groundskeeper had spent 14 months in jail awaiting trial. Shortly thereafter, Ofshe—by now increasingly sought by desperate defense attorneys—helped free Mark Nunez, Leo Bruce and Dante Parker, who, fingered by a psychiatric patient and subjected to a highly coercive interrogation, had falsely confessed to killing nine people at a Buddhist temple outside Phoenix. In Flagstaff, Ofshe was instrumental in winning the 1988 acquittal of George Abney, a graduate student with a history of depression, who had admitted to the ritualistic murder of a Navajo woman. In the Phoenix case, the real murderer was eventually caught and prosecuted.

"WHAT SOME OF THE PSYCHOLOGISTS SAY IS I PUT YOU IN A ROOM, you're all emotional and at the end of five or six hours, I've fed you everything," Lieut. Ralph M. Lacer is saying in his Oakland police office, several miles from Ofshe's home. "Well, if I was on the jury, I'd be rolling my eyes saying: 'Who is the dumb [expletive] who thinks this is gonna go over?'"

Fiftyish, ruddy and blond, the bespectacled Lacer was one of the interrogating officers in the high-profile case of Bradley Page, a handsome Berkeley student who had admitted—falsely, so Page and his attorneys maintained—to murdering his girlfriend, Roberta (BiBi) Lee, in a fit of anger in 1984. After two trials, the second of which Ofshe consulted on, Page was convicted of manslaughter. (He was released, after serving part of a six-year sentence, in February.)

Only part of the Page interrogation was recorded. From 11:50 A.M. to 1:10 P.M. on Dec. 10, 1984, Lacer and his partner, Sgt. Jerry Harris, taped Page as he gave them a firm, lucid account of his movements during the time since Lee had disappeared a month before—none of which included bludgeoning her to death. Then the detectives shut off the machine until 7:07 P.M., by which time Page was highly emotional, confessing to murder, albeit in vague, halting language peppered with "might haves," "would haves" and other subjunctive phrases that left Ofshe highly suspicious. Lacer freely acknowledges that Page's admission of guilt, made in the absence of hard evidence, was the heart and soul of the case against him. "If we hadn't gotten the confession," Lacer says, "Brad would've walked."

I raise Ofshe's argument, that taping interrogations in full might resolve any ambiguities.

"First of all, a tape is inhibiting," Lacer counters. "It's hard to get at the truth. And say we go for 10 hours—we have 10 hours of tape that maybe boil down to 15 or 20 minutes of you saying, 'Yes, I killed Johnny Jones.' You bet the public defender's going to have the jury listen to all 10 hours of that tape and by that time the jury won't remember what it's all about."

According to Lacer, the craft of interrogation is learned through experience. "Every day when you stop someone on the street, you're interrogating them," he says. "'Where do you live? Where you headed to?' We definitely try to establish rapport—basically, I want to get you to talk to me. But when we bring a suspect in, we keep the room bare, a table and two or three chairs, a locked door."

I glance around, aware for the first time that the interview is unfolding in the ideal interrogation setting. I ask Lacer what would happen if a person being questioned invokes his constitutional right of silence or, if he is not under arrest, his right to simply walk out the door.

"Well, that would be the end of the situation," he says. "But many times it won't happen, and here's why: I see you've got a wedding ring on, Rich. Well, say Mrs. Rich ends up dead in the house. We call you down and you say, 'I don't think I want to talk to you guys, I'm out of here.' Well, the thing is, your in-laws find out that you took that route and they know right away who killed your wife.

"Now most of the time, the suspect will set up barriers. Like you got your legs crossed—that's kind of a psychological barrier. And I lean forward, violate your personal space, get closer and closer and pretty soon we're nose to nose." As Lacer edges toward me, his eyes, though still genial, bear into mine.

"Now remember, I'm just talking, not yelling or bullying," he says. "It's not going to help matters if I suddenly say '[Expletive], that's a [expletive] black sweater you have on—I threw away the last black sweater I had like that!' " You can maybe bully a little bit verbally by saying: 'Rich, that last story was [expletive]. Let's not even go into that again.' " Lacer's eyes turn caustic through his aviator glasses.

"Now as far as yelling," he says, chummy again, "about the only time we do it here in Oakland is if someone's talking over you or if they're going off on a tangent, and I'd say, 'Hey Rich, let's get back to the *subject!*' " His voice slices through the claustrophobia of the room—a ferocity all the more unnerving because it booms from Lacer's amiable shell.

"We've been in a room together for a while, Rich," he says, chuckling. "Do you feel like confessing to anything?"

"LACER RATIONALIZES THAT SOMEONE LIKE BRADLEY PAGE—OR YOU AND I—cannot be made to confess," Ofshe says on the day after my encounter with the Oakland lieutenant. "Because it is in many ways one of the worst professional error you can make—like a physician amputating the wrong arm."

Prevention, he adds, is surprisingly simple: "Above all, no confession ought be accepted unless it has been corroborated with clear-cut and powerful evidence. And you must never instigate a high-pressure, accusatory interrogation unless you have a good and sound reason to do it."

Another safeguard, Ofshe reiterates, is to record interrogations. Early last year, the professor helped win a significant victory in the same Clearwater courthouse where the Sawyer case was heard. Relying substantially on Ofshe's testimony, Judge Claire K. Luten formed a forceful opinion that he confession of Francis Dupont, an alcoholic drifter who had admitted to murdering a friend, was psychologically coerced. Moreover, Luten ruled that the failure to tape the interrogation of Dupont was in direct violation of due process.

"I'd be content to devote myself to that issue until I am too old to work on it," Ofshe says.

In a sense, this is Ofshe's moment, for never has the nation been more attuned to what happens in a courtroom. Yet for the plain citizen—the juror—he is also a problematic figure, a bearded academic speaking in tones of unassailable authority about social psychology, a discipline that resounds with squishy inexactitude. Ofshe's theories about false confession, however well researched, risk being perceived as just another set of legal loopholes. And his "one innocent man or woman" might well be shrugged off—probably not worth the trouble and surely not worth the risk.

For which reason Ofshe emphasizes the most basic preventive to false confession: if you find yourself being questioned about a crime you know you did not commit, resist at all costs the impulse to be helpful, no matter how charming or forbidding the interrogator might be.

"I tell my classes," Ofshe says, "that if they ever find themselves in that situation, remember the four magic words of the criminal justice system: 'I want a lawyer.' "

Unit Selections

Key Points to Consider

❖ What do you think of the argument that spending time on the Internet can interfere with "normal" social life and thus have a negative effect on a person's feelings? What would be the strongest evidence for such a proposition? What complicating factors would have to be taken into consideration when testing this idea?

❖ What do you think of the evolutionary psychologists' explanation for some of the differences between men and women in the area of sexual behavior? What is their strongest evidence? Their weakest evidence? Can their findings be explained in any other way?

❖ Using the John Gottman selection on various marriage styles, can you think of any romantic couples that you know who fit into each type? If not, why not? Do the couples you know show signs of more than one type? Do they exhibit a different style entirely? Explain your answer.

 **Links**   **www.dushkin.com/online/**

These sites are annotated on pages 4 and 5.

A young man stands on a narrow suspension bridge that stretches over a river 230 feet below. The bridge is only 5 feet wide, over 400 feet long, and it constantly swings and sways in the wind. Even for someone without a fear of heights, crossing this bridge while looking at the river far below is definitely an arousing experience. In fact, a considerable number of the people who visit this popular tourist spot every year find themselves unable to cross the bridge at all. While standing on the bridge, the young man is approached by an attractive young woman who asks him to participate in a psychology research project she is working on—all he has to do is write a brief imaginative story in response to a picture she gives him. He does so, and when he is finished, the experimenter gives him her phone number in case he wants to learn more about the experiment.

A few miles away, another young man stands on another bridge—but this one is not scary at all. It is solidly built, does not sway and wobble, and stands only 10 feet above a peaceful stream. The same attractive woman approaches this man with the same request, and, again she gives him her phone number when the experiment ends. Who do you think is more likely to call the young woman later? When this experiment was actually carried out, the results were clear—men on the arousing bridge were much more likely than men on the safe bridge to call the female experimenter later on. Not only that, but the stories the men on the arousing bridge wrote were noticeably different; they contained significantly more references to sex. In short, the men on the arousing bridge apparently reacted in a very different way to the young woman—they experienced a greater sense of physical attraction to her, and acted on that attraction later on by calling her up. Even though men on the sturdy bridge met the same young woman, they did not experience the same physical attraction.

This experiment is just one example of some of the work done by psychologists who study social relationships. This area of social psychology turns out to be a very broad one indeed, and a wide variety of topics fall under its umbrella. One research question, for example, that has attracted a lot of attention is this: What are the factors that influence the initial attraction (both romantic and nonromantic) that we feel for another person? Considerable research indicates that being similar to the other person is important, as is the sheer physical attractiveness of that other. Living or working in close proximity to other people also increases the likelihood of attraction to them.

Other researchers have tackled issues such as identifying the processes that are important for maintaining friendships over time. The level of self-disclosure in the relationship seems to be important, as does the general feeling by both participants that what they are receiving from the relationship is roughly equivalent to what their partner is receiving; that is, issues of fairness seem to play a crucial role. Still, other investigators have concerned themselves with the question of long-term romantic relationships: which factors lead to initial romantic attraction; which factors contribute to long-term satisfaction; and, how do couples deal with conflict and disagreements in long-term relationships?

The selections in this unit are divided into two subsections, the first of which addresses a very modern topic—the effect of the Internet on social life and social feelings. The first selection, "Isolation Increases with Internet Use," describes a recent study that received wide attention when it found that people who spend more time online reported greater levels of depression and loneliness. One possible explanation for such a finding is that Internet use might interfere with our usual "in person" social contact. The second selection, "Sad and Lonely in Cyberspace?" examines this same research from a more skeptical point of view and considers some of its possible limitations.

The second subsection focuses exclusively on romantic relationships. In "The Biology of Beauty," Geoffrey Cowley summarizes the evolutionary perspective on physical attractiveness: what makes men attractive to women, and women attractive to men. The evolutionary view is that physical features serve as indicators of physical and reproductive fitness to potential mates, and that certain features are therefore universal indicators of attractiveness. In "Infidelity and the Science of Cheating," Sharon Begley presents the evolutionary perspective on jealousy, which attempts to explain a common finding: that men are typically more upset by a mate's sexual infidelity, while women are more upset by a mate's emotional infidelity. In the final article, "Marriage Styles: the Good, the Bad, and the Volatile," noted psychologist John Gottman describes three distinct styles of marriage characterized by very different levels of emotion and conflict. Surprisingly, Gottman's research suggests that all three styles can be very successful, as long as the overall positivity in the relationship considerably outweighs the negativity.

Isolation increases with Internet use

The Internet connects us with people we might otherwise never meet—and may be leaving us lonelier than ever.

By Scott Sleek
Monitor staff

A clergyman discovered the professional benefits of the Internet when he joined an online discussion group with colleagues in his denomination. There, he got advice on subjects for sermons and effective ways to deal with congregants.

But the clergyman also noticed that he was spending less time talking with his wife, whose verbal moral support had once been just as beneficial as—perhaps even more than—the advice he received from his online peers.

Psychologist Robert Kraut, PhD, of Carnegie Mellon University's Human–Computer Interaction Institute, points to the case of the clergyman—whom he talked to as part of his research on computer use—as an example of the paradoxical role that the Internet has come to play in our lives.

The technology that has allowed people to keep in closer touch with distant family members and friends, to find information quickly and to develop friendships with people from around the world, is also replacing vital day-to-day human interactions. A computer monitor can't give you a hug or laugh at your jokes. And some psychologists worry that the Internet's widening popularity will lead to further isolation among a population that, although gravitating toward virtual communities in cyber-space, seems to have lost a genuine sense of belonging and connection.

In fact, Kraut and his colleagues, in a study to be released this month in *American Psychologist,* report that greater use of the Internet leads to shrinking social support and happiness, and increases in depression and loneliness. The study is the first to look specifically at the impact that Internet use has on general emotional well-being.

And the findings were unexpected, Kraut says, given that most people use the Internet for chat lines and e-mail, not just to isolate themselves in mounds of electronic information.

"We were surprised to find that what is a social technology, unlike the television, has kind of antisocial consequences," Kraut says.

Learning from mistakes

The Internet could change the lives of Americans as much as the telephone in the early 20th century or the television in the 1950s and 60s, Kraut contends. Numerous research and marketing firms have pegged the number of American households using the Internet at anywhere from 60 million to 70 million. People use it for everything from making plane reservations to downloading games to e-mailing relatives. And some spend many hours on multi-user domains, or MUDS, where they assume fictional identities in role-playing games.

But studies are showing the social prices of online living. Psychologists have already widely publicized their findings about people who are addicted to the Internet.

Kraut and his co-researchers are perhaps the first to show how the Internet affects people who log on regularly, but don't appear to be addicted to cyberspace. They studied 169 individuals from 93 diverse households in Pittsburgh during their first two years online. They recorded each participant's Internet use by employing custom-designed logging programs. And using self-report measures, they assessed each participant's level of social involvement and psychological well-being before they went online, and again a year or two later.

They found a direct correlation between participants' level of Internet use and their reports of social activity and happiness. As their use of the Internet increased, the participants reported a decrease in the amount of social support they felt and in the number of social activities they were involved in. They also reported being more depressed and lonely.

Psychologist Viktor Brenner, PhD, of Marquette University, has also found some troubling effects of Internet use. In a study reported last year in *Psychological Reports* (Vol. 80, No. 3, pp. 879–882), Brenner posted an Internet usage survey as a World Wide Web page. (The web page is no longer active.) Most of the 563 valid responses came from males who averaged 34 years of age, completed 15 years of education and used the Internet about 19 hours a week. Most reported instances of Internet use interfering with other aspects of their lives, including taking up time that they would have used for other activities. A few reported serious consequences from their time spent online, such as getting in trouble with an employer or becoming socially isolated from people other than Internet friends.

From *APA Monitor*, September 1998, pp. 1, 30-31. © 1998 by the American Psychological Association. Reprinted by permission.

A poor substitute

Psychologists have yet to pinpoint the reasons Internet use can hamper psychological well-being, but they have plenty of theories. Many users, caught in the allure of connecting with a global array of people with similar interests, seem to be substituting weak online friendships for their stronger real-life relationships, says Sara Kiesler, PhD, one of Kraut's colleagues in the Carnegie Mellon study.

In their research, Kraut, Kiesler and their peers found several examples of people who developed seemingly valuable friendships online:

• A woman exchanged mittens with a stranger she met on a knitting listserv.

• A woman met a couple in Canada, whom she later visited during her summer vacation.

• A teen-ager met his prom date online.

But national survey data show only 22 percent of people who had been using the Internet for two or more years had ever made a new friend on the Internet, the researchers note. And those friendships tend to be of low quality.

"You don't have to deal with unpleasantness, because if you don't like somebody's behavior, you can just log off," says Kiesler. "In real life, relationships aren't always easy. Yet dealing with some of those hard parts is good for us. It helps us keep connected with people.

"Also, the kinds of people you meet online don't really know you," she adds. "If you need surgery, or you have something wrong in your family, they're not around—they're not there for you."

Avoiding the same mistakes

Like many technologies, the Internet has lulled people with its novelty and convenience, which will create a sense of dependency and some troubling social consequences, says Allen Kanner, PhD, a Berkeley, Calif., psychologist who teaches ecopsychology and other courses at the Wright Institute and other graduate schools throughout the Bay Area. Kanner said he's glad somebody is looking at the Internet's impact, noting that behaviorists produced minimal data on the social effects of the television, the phone or the car until those technologies were heavily embedded into our lives.

"The car allowed people to travel far greater distances," he notes, "but it also created suburbs and highways all over the place. So the positive advantages also caused huge social changes, such as traffic jams, pollution and people moving further away from each other.

"We're so excited about the advantages [of technology] that we quickly dismiss what actually is happening," Kanner adds. "As psychologists, we could ask some very good questions about what's the difference between talking on the phone and talking face to face. We've assumed there is none."

But others warn against overemphasizing the negative aspects of technology. Like any technology, the World Wide Web can lead to good or bad behaviors, says John Grohol, PsyD, creator of Mental Health Net (www.cmhc.com/), a massive index of mental health-related web sites, online mailing lists and newsgroups. And he believes it provides some vital societal benefits, such as the large number of online self-help groups that exist today. Those are especially important in small communities that aren't large enough to sustain a support group, he adds.

"If you lived out in rural Montana or Kansas, you'd have a hard time finding a panic disorder support group," he says. "This allows those people to get connected, to share advice."

Another example of the Internet's social utility is a public electronic network (PEN) set up in Santa Monica, Calif., to facilitate grassroots organizing. The system, set up in 1989 in public buildings, allowed scores of residents—including homeless citizens—to access the network. Some users formed an action group to identify local issues that needed attention and to develop civic projects. One of the group's biggest accomplishments was developing a service center for job-seeking homeless people. Psychologist Michele Andrisin Wittig, PhD, of California State University, Northridge, and Joseph Schmitz, of the University of Tulsa's faculty of communication, surveyed participants in the network and reported their findings in the *Journal of Social Issues* (Vol. 52, No. 1, pp. 53–69).

"Our respondents told us that PEN helped foster links among diverse others," they write. "They reported enhanced capability to interact with others who differ in socioeconomic status and power. Thus, they formed more diverse social networks that centered on common interests, but transcended economic or geographical bounds."

The right balance

Many psychologists say behavioral research should demonstrate ways to find a healthy balance between time spent online and time spent talking with family and friends in person. In fact, people could integrate their online and in-person lives by, say, calling or getting together with friends they've met online, suggests John Suler, PhD, who studies online behavior as a psychology professor at Rider University in Lawrenceville, N.J.

Kraut says he's trying to incorporate that balance in his own community. He's proposing that his local school and synagogue create electronic communication forums for students so they can use to discuss homework assignments, make plans for social gatherings or even receive online tutoring. Kraut has also limited the amount of time his teen-age son spends online.

But he's also seeing the ways the Internet can enhance family connections. "Every member of our family spends time online," he says. "And when we are, we can't be doing things with each other. But we also keep up with our son in college. Even though he's distant, when he needed to know how to cook something, we could give the directions electronically."

SAD AND LONELY IN CYBERSPACE?

Why the new Net-depression study is something to get bummed about.

BY SCOTT ROSENBERG

"Sad, Lonely World Discovered in Cyberspace": The front-page headline in Sunday's New York Times conjured an image of intrepid explorers trekking to the edge of a precipice to win a precious glimpse of some remote tribe. It's a romantic, attention-getting picture, which is no doubt what attracted Times editors to the wording. But—as so often is the case with media portraits of Net culture—the truth is far more mundane.

The accompanying article reports the results of a study of about 160 people in Pittsburgh conducted by a team of social scientists from Carnegie Mellon University. The researchers found people who'd never been online before, put computers in their homes, tracked their Net use and then used psychological questionnaires to discover how their online sojourns affected their psychological well-being. The project—called HomeNet—found some small but, its creators insist, statistically significant connection between hours spent online and participants' reported feelings of loneliness and depression.

In other words: *The Net bums you out!*

Unlike the notorious "cyberporn" study that emerged from Carnegie Mellon in 1995 only to have its trustworthiness and methodology blasted to bits by online critics, the HomeNet study—which will appear this week in the American Psychologist (there's a draft online at the HomeNet site)—isn't riddled with gaping holes, massive fallacies and crafty distortions. But before we all conclude that the Internet is hazardous to our mental health, it's worth pondering some of the many questions about the HomeNet study that

weren't raised in the initial Times coverage—and that don't seem to be getting heard as that article echoes through the mediasphere thanks to *CNN*, *AP*, the *BBC* and others.

First of all, the statistically significant changes the researchers report are quite small—like a 1 percent increase on the depression scale for people who spend an hour a week online. (We're not talking about clinical-level, fire-up-the-Prozac style depression here.) The study attempts to find subtle gradations on the basis of the kind of "How are you feeling today on a scale of one to five?" quizzes that psychologists like to use to measure people's moods—and anyone who's ever taken one of those tests knows it's hardly an exact science. The researchers only tested people twice, at the start and the end of the two-year study—which doesn't provide a very wide set of data points to offset the impact of other factors (time of year, state of the economy, random personal crises). Teenagers, unsurprisingly, tended to spend more time online and also show a greater rate of loneliness and depression—and that could easily account for the correlation the researchers found between increased Net use and dampened moods.

Beyond these statistical issues, there's a deeper problem with the study's basic setup. The researchers chose to limit their subjects to people who hadn't been online before, because they wanted to perform a "before and after" kind of study that would help them isolate the specific effect of Net use on individual psyches. So the participants in the study weren't got free computers and Internet access so they could be studied.

It's tough to know exactly what direction that would skew the study toward—but easy to see that there's an unnatural premise at the heart of the research. One obvious problem is that the researchers have no idea whether their subjects got bummed out because of what they encountered on the Net, or simply because they wound up sitting in front of a computer monitor rather than working in their gardens or playing ball. Is the increase in "loneliness and depression" caused by the Internet itself or simply by computer use, regardless of whether the modem's on? The study can't say.

By far the biggest flaw in the HomeNet research, however, is the way it lumps all Internet usage into one big heap. Using the Net to organize a charity drive or a political campaign is a different experience from using it to stare at pornography (as if anyone would do the latter with a bunch of psychologists watching). Building your own Web site is different from pounding on a search engine hunting down some obscure fact. There is no uniform "Internet experience," and you can't draw conclusions about how time on the Net affects people's psyches until you know what people are doing with that time.

The researchers have suggested one explanation for their results: In spending more time on the Net, people are trading the "strong" social bonds of face-to-face friendships and relationships for the "weak" ties of the disembodied online realm—and that may ultimately leave them feeling more isolated. There's some good sense in that observation. But the "weakness" of online ties is a relative matter: The report also notes that going online may help broaden the social support network for people who live in more isolated locales than, say, Pittsburgh.

Much of the utopian rhetoric about online community emerged from spaces like the *Well* and *Echo*—communities that have geographical centers (the Well in the Bay Area, Echo in New York) and that don't permit anonymity. The long-term denizens of such communities will snort with derision at the idea that the friendships and relationships they've built there are any less "real" or valuable than those they've built offline. (My own critique of the HomeNet study draws from the spirited discussions of it this week on the Well.)

But such happy experiences can't easily be duplicated in forums and online environments that have rapidly shifting populations, easy access to anonymity and no geographical center of gravity. Without those characteristics that knit an online space into the fabric of offline life, the online "community" can readily descend into flame-throwing anarchy and alienating mind games. Depressing? You bet.

As the Internet grows, we will be faced with a complex choice between two visions of the new communications medium: Is it going to evolve into the vast postmodern playground of shifting identity that scholars like *Sherry Turkle* have mapped—a no-place where everyone can be whatever they want, and nobody means anything to anyone else? Or is it going to emerge as an extension of our real-world lives, overcoming barriers of time and distance but not obliterating our feelings of identity, connection and responsibility toward one another?

The HomeNet researchers say they're moving forward with follow-up studies. Here's a tip for them: Don't give headline writers an excuse to translate minute percentage deviations in a tiny, unscientific sample population into exciting discoveries of whole "worlds" of emotional distress. Don't just tally the hours people spend on the Net, but track where they go and what they do with their time. Look at the differences between people who frequent anonymous chat rooms and those who join real communities. Then, and only then, ask them if they're happy.

Looking good is a universal human obsession. How do we perceive physical beauty, and why do we place so much stock in it? Scientists are now taking those questions seriously, and gaining surprising insights.

THE BIOLOGY OF BEAUTY

By Geoffrey Cowley

WHEN IT COMES TO CHOOSING a mate, a female penguin knows better than to fall for the first creep who pulls up and honks. She holds out for the fittest suitor available—which in Antarctica means one chubby enough to spend several weeks sitting on newly hatched eggs without starving to death. The Asian jungle bird *Gallus gallus* is just as choosy. Males in that species sport gaily colored head combs and feathers, which lose their luster if the bird is invaded by parasites. By favoring males with bright ornaments, a hen improves her odds of securing a mate (and bearing offspring) with strong resistance to disease. For female scor-

pion flies, beauty is less about size or color than about symmetry. Females favor suitors who have well-matched wings—and with good reason. Studies show they're the most adept at killing prey and at defending their catch from competitors. There's no reason to think that any of these creatures understands its motivations, but there's a clear pattern to their preferences. "Throughout the animal world," says University of New Mexico ecologist Randy Thornhill, "attractiveness certifies biological quality."

Is our corner of the animal world different? That looks count in human affairs is beyond dispute. Studies have shown that people considered attractive fare better with

parents and teachers, make more friends and more money, and have better sex with more (and more beautiful) partners. Every year, 400,000 Americans, including 48,000 men, flock to cosmetic surgeons. In other lands, people bedeck themselves with scars, lip plugs or bright feathers. "Every culture is a 'beauty culture'," says Nancy Etcoff, a neuroscientist who is studying human attraction at the MIT Media Lab and writing a book on the subject. "I defy anyone to point to a society, any time in history or any place in the world, that wasn't preoccupied with beauty." The high-minded may dismiss our preening and ogling as distractions from things that matter, but the stakes can be enor-

 From *Newsweek*, June 3, 1996, pp. 61–66.

Beauty isn't all that matters in life; most of us manage to attract mates and bear offspring despite our physical imperfections. And the qualities we find alluring say nothing about people's moral worth. Our weakness for 'biological quality' is the cause of endless pain and injustice.

mous. "Judging beauty involves looking at another person," says University of Texas psychologist Devendra Singh, "and figuring out whether you want your children to carry that person's genes."

It's widely assumed that ideals of beauty vary from era to era and from culture to culture. But a harvest of new research is confounding that idea. Studies have established that people everywhere—regardless of race, class or age—share a sense of what's attractive. And though no one knows just how our minds translate the sight of a face or a body into rapture, new studies suggest that we judge each other by rules we're not even aware of. We may consciously admire Kate Moss's legs or Arnold's biceps, but we're also viscerally attuned to small variations in the size and symmetry of facial bones and the placement of weight on the body.

This isn't to say that our preferences are purely innate—or that beauty is all that matters in life. Most of us manage to find jobs, attract mates and bear offspring despite our physical imperfections. Nor should anyone assume that the new beauty research justifies the biases it illuminates. Our beautylust is often better suited to the Stone Age than to the Information Age; the qualities we find alluring may be powerful emblems of health, fertility and resistance to disease, but they say nothing about people's moral worth. The human weakness for what Thornhill calls "biological quality" causes no end of pain and injustice. Unfortunately, that doesn't make it any less real.

N O ONE SUGGESTS THAT POINTS OF attraction never vary. Rolls of fat can signal high status in a poor society or low status in a rich one, and lip plugs go over better in the Kalahari than they do in Kansas. But local fashions seem to rest on a bedrock of shared preferences. You don't have to be Italian to find Michelangelo's David better looking than, say, Alfonse D'Amato. When British researchers asked women from England, China and India to rate pictures of Greek men, the women responded as if working from the same crib sheet. And when researchers at the University of Louisville showed a diverse collection of faces to whites, Asians and Latinos from 13 coun-

tries, the subjects' ethnic background scarcely affected their preferences.

To a skeptic, those findings suggest only that Western movies and magazines have overrun the world. But scientists have found at least one group that hasn't been exposed to this bias. In a series of groundbreaking experiments, psychologist Judith Langlois of the University of Texas, Austin, has shown that even infants share a sense of what's attractive. In the late '80s, Langlois started placing 3- and 6-month-old babies in front of a screen and showing them pairs of facial photographs. Each pair included one considered attractive by adult judges and one considered unattractive. In the first study, she found that the infants gazed significantly longer at "attractive" white female faces than at "unattractive" ones. Since then, she has repeated the drill using white male faces, black female faces, even the faces of other babies, and the same pattern always emerges. "These kids don't read Vogue or watch TV," Langlois says. "They haven't been touched by the media. Yet they make the same judgments as adults."

What, then, is beauty made of? What are the innate rules we follow in sizing each other up? We're obviously wired to find robust health a prettier sight than infirmity. "All animals are attracted to other animals that are healthy, that are clean by their standards and that show signs of competence," says Rutgers University anthropologist Helen Fisher. As far as anyone knows, there isn't a village on earth where skin lesions, head lice and rotting teeth count as beauty aids. But the rules get subtler than that. Like scorpion flies, we love symmetry. And though we generally favor average features over unusual ones, the people we find extremely beautiful share certain exceptional qualities.

W HEN RANDY THORNHILL started measuring the wings of Japanese scorpion flies six years ago, he wasn't much concerned with the orgasms and infidelities of college students. But sometimes one thing leads to another. Biologists have long used bilateral symmetry—the extent to which a creature's right and left sides match—to gauge what's known as developmental stability. Given ideal growing conditions,

paired features such as wings, ears, eyes and feet would come out matching perfectly. But pollution, disease and other hazards can disrupt development. As a result, the least resilient individuals tend to be the most lopsided. In chronicling the scorpion flies' daily struggles, Thornhill found that the bugs with the most symmetrical wings fared best in the competition for food and mates. To his amazement, females preferred symmetrical males even when they were hidden from view; evidently, their smells are more attractive. And when researchers started noting similar trends in other species, Thornhill turned his attention to our own.

Working with psychologist Steven Gangestad, he set about measuring the body symmetry of hundreds of college-age men and women. By adding up right-left disparities in seven measurements—the breadth of the feet, ankles, hands, wrists, and elbows, as well as the breadth and length of the ears—the researchers scored each subject's overall body asymmetry. Then they had the person fill out a confidential questionnaire covering everything from temperament to sexual behavior, and set about looking for connections. They weren't disappointed. In a 1994 study, they found that the most symmetrical males had started having sex three to four years earlier than their most lopsided brethren. For both men and women, greater symmetry predicted a larger number of past sex partners.

That was just the beginning. From what they knew about other species, Thornhill and Gangestad predicted that women would be more sexually responsive to symmetrical men, and that men would exploit that advantage. To date, their findings support both suspicions. Last year they surveyed 86 couples and found that women with highly symmetrical partners were more than twice as likely to climax during intercourse (an event that may foster conception by ushering sperm into the uterus) than those with low-symmetry partners. And in separate surveys, Gangestad and Thornhill have found that, compared with regular Joes, extremely symmetrical men are less attentive to their partners and more likely to cheat on them. Women showed no such tendency.

It's hard to imagine that we even notice the differences between people's elbows, let alone stake our love lives on them. No one carries calipers into a singles bar. So why do these measurements predict so much? Because, says Thornhill, people with symmetrical elbows tend to have "a whole suite of attractive features." His findings suggest that besides having attractive (and symmetrical) faces, men with symmetrical bodies are typically larger, more muscular and more athletic than their peers, and more dominant in personality. In a forthcoming study, researchers at the University of Michigan find evidence that facial symmetry is also associated with health. In analyzing diaries kept by 100 students over a two-month period, they found that the least symmetrical had the most physical complaints, from insomnia to nasal congestion, and reported more anger, jealousy and withdrawal. In light of all Thornhill and Gangestad's findings, you can hardly blame them.

IF WE DID GO COURTING WITH calipers, symmetry isn't all we would measure. As we study each other in the street, the office or the gym, our beauty radars pick up a range of signals. Oddly enough, one of the qualities shared by attractive people is their averageness. Researchers discovered more than a century ago that if they superimposed photographs of several faces, the resulting composite was usually better looking than any of the images that went into it. Scientists can now average faces digitally, and it's still one of the surest ways to make them more attractive. From an evolutionary perspective, a preference for extreme normality makes sense. As Langlois has written, "Individuals with average population characteristics should be less likely to carry harmful genetic mutations."

So far, so good. But here's the catch: while we may find average faces attractive, the faces we find most beautiful are not average. As New Mexico State University psychologist Victor Johnston has shown, they're extreme. To track people's preferences, Johnston uses a computer program called FacePrints. Turn it on, and it generates 30 facial images, all male or all female, which you rate on a 1–9 beauty scale. The program then "breeds" the top-rated face with one of the others to create two digital offspring, which replace the lowest-rated faces in the pool. By rating round after round of new faces, you create an ever more beautiful population. The game ends when you award some visage

a perfect 10. (If you have access to the World Wide Web, you can take part in a collective face-breeding experiment by visiting http://www.psych.nmsu.edu/~vic/faceprints/.)

For Johnston, the real fun starts after the judging is finished. By collecting people's ideal faces and comparing them to average faces, he can measure the distance between fantasy and reality. As a rule, he finds that an ideal female has a higher forehead than an average one, as well as fuller lips, a shorter jaw and a smaller chin and nose. Indeed, the ideal 25-year-old woman, as configured by participants in a 1993 study, had a 14-year-old's abundant lips and an 11-year-old's delicate jaw. Because her lower

BODY LANGUAGE

When men are asked to rank figures with various weights and waist-hip ratios (0.7 to 1.0), they favor a pronounced hourglass shape. The highest-ranked figures are N7, N8 and U7 (in that order). The lowest ranked is O10.

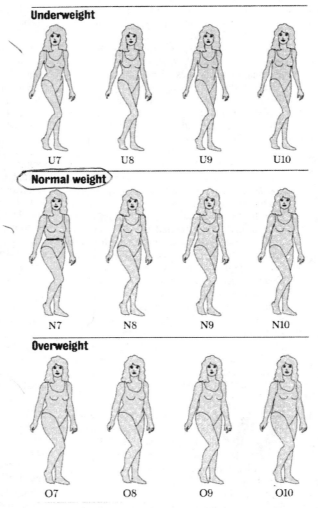

THE ORDER CHOSEN: (1) N7, (2) N8, (3) U7, (4) U8, (5) N9, (6) N10, (7) O7, (8), U9, (9) O8, (10) U10, (11) O9, (12) O10 SOURCE: DEVENDRA SINGH, UNIVERSITY OF TEXAS AT AUSTIN

face was so small, she also had relatively prominent eyes and cheekbones.

The participants in that study were all college kids from New Mexico, but researchers have since shown that British and Japanese students express the same bias. And if there are lingering doubts about the depth of that bias, Johnston's latest findings should dispel them. In a forthcoming study, he reports that male volunteers not only consciously prefer women with small lower faces but show marked rises in brain activity when looking at pictures of them. And though Johnston has yet to publish specs on the ideal male, his unpublished findings suggest that a big jaw, a strong chin and an imposing brow are as prized in a man's face as their opposites are in a woman's.

Few of us ever develop the heart-melting proportions of a FacePrints fantasy. And if it's any consolation, beauty is not an all-or-nothing proposition. Madonna became a sex symbol despite her strong nose, and Melanie Griffith's strong jaw hasn't kept her out of the movies. Still, special things have a way of happening to people who approximate the ideal. We pay them huge fees to stand on windblown bluffs and stare into the distance. And past studies have found that square-jawed males not only start having sex earlier than their peers but attain higher rank in the military.

None of this surprises evolutionary psychologists. They note that the facial features we obsess over are precisely the ones that diverge in males and females during puberty, as floods of sex hormones wash us into adulthood. And they reason that hormonal abundance would have been a good clue to mate value in the hunter-gatherer world where our preferences evolved. The tiny jaw that men favor in women is essentially a monument to estrogen—and, obliquely, to fertility. No one claims that jaws reveal a woman's odds of getting pregnant. But like breasts, they imply that she could.

Likewise, the heavy lower face that women favor in men is a visible record of the surge in androgens (testosterone and other male sex hormones) that turns small boys into 200-pound spear-throwers. An oversized jaw is biologically expensive, for the androgens required to produce it tend to compromise the immune system. But from a female's perspective, that should make jaw size all the more revealing. Evolutionists think of androgen-based features as "honest advertisements" of disease resistance. If a male can afford them without falling sick, the thinking goes, he must have a superior immune system in the first place.

No one has tracked the immune responses of men with different jawlines to see if these predictions bear out (Thornhill has proposed a study that would involve comparing volunteers' responses to a vaccine). Nor is it clear whether penis size figures into these equations. Despite what everyone thinks he knows on the subject, scientists haven't determined that women have consistent preferences one way or the other.

O UR FACES ARE SIGNAtures, but when it comes to raw sex appeal, a nice chin is no match for a perfectly sculpted torso—especially from a man's perspective. Studies from around the world have found that while both sexes value appearance, men place more stock in it than women. And if there are social reasons for that imbalance, there are also biological ones. Just about any male over 14 can produce sperm, but a woman's ability to bear children depends on her age and hormone levels. Female fertility declines by two thirds between the ages of 20 and 44, and it's spent by 54. So while the both sexes may eyeball potential partners, says Donald Symons, an anthropologist at the University of California in Santa Barbara, "a larger proportion of a woman's mate value can be detected from visual cues." Mounting evidence suggests

FACIAL FANTASIES

As a rule, average faces are more attractive than unusual ones. But when people are asked to develop ideal faces on a computer, they tend to exaggerate certain qualities.

Average proportions
This computer-generated face has the dimensions typical of Caucasian 20-year-olds.

Ideal proportions
Most visions of the perfect female face have small jaws and abnormally lush lips.

SOURCE: VICTOR JOHNSTON, NEW MEXICO STATE UNIVERSITY

the 80,000 calories needed to sustain a pregnancy, and the curves they create provide a gauge of reproductive potential. "You have to get very close to see the details of a woman's face," says Devendra Singh, the University of Texas psychologist. "But you can see the shape of her body from 500 feet, and it says more about mate value."

Almost anything that interferes with fertility—obesity, malnutrition, pregnancy, menopause—changes a woman's shape.

a slight increase in waist size relative to hip size can signal reproductive problems. Among 500 women who were attempting in vitro fertilization, the odds of conceiving during any given cycle declined by 30 percent with every 10 percent increase in WHR. In other words, a woman with a WHR of .9 was nearly a third less likely to get pregnant than one with a WHR of .8, regardless of her age or weight. From an evolutionary perspective, it's hard to imagine men not responding to such a revealing signal. And as Singh has shown repeatedly, they do.

Defining a universal standard of body beauty once seemed a fool's dream; common sense said that if spindly Twiggy and Rubens's girthy Three Graces could all excite admiration, then nearly anyone could. But if our ideals of size change from one time and place to the next, our taste in shapes is amazingly stable. A low waist-hip ratio is one of the few features that a long, lean Barbie doll shares with a plump, primitive fertility icon. And Singh's findings suggest the fashion won't change any time soon. In one study, he compiled the measurements of Playboy centerfolds and Miss America winners from 1923 to 1990. Their bodies got measurably leaner over the decades, yet their waist-hip ratios stayed within the narrow range of .68 to .72. (Even Twiggy was no tube; at the peak of her fame in the 1960s, the British model had a WHR of .73.)

The same pattern holds when Singh generates line drawings of different female figures and asks male volunteers to rank them

Even infants spend more time gazing at pictures of 'attractive' faces than at 'unattractive' ones. 'These kids don't read Vogue or watch TV, yet they make the same judgments as adults,' says psychologist Judith Langlois.

there is no better cue than the relative contours of her waist and hips.

Before puberty and after menopause, females have essentially the same waistlines as males. But during puberty, while boys are amassing the bone and muscle of paleolithic hunters, a typical girl gains nearly 35 pounds of so-called reproductive fat around the hips and thighs. Those pounds contain roughly

Healthy, fertile women typically have waist-hip ratios of .6 to .8, meaning their waists are 60 to 80 percent the size of their hips, whatever their actual weight. To take one familiar example, a 36-25-36 figure would have a WHR of .7. Many women outside this range are healthy and capable of having children, of course. But as researchers in the Netherlands discovered in a 1993 study, even

for attractiveness, sexiness, health and fertility. He has surveyed men of various backgrounds, nationalities and ages. And whether the judges are 8-year-olds or 85-year-olds, their runaway favorite is a figure of average weight with a .7 WHR. Small wonder that when women were liberated from corsets and bustles, they took up girdles, wide belts and other waist-reducing contraptions. Last year alone, American women's outlays for shape-enhancing garments topped a half-billion dollars.

To SOME CRITICS, THE SEARCH FOR A biology of beauty looks like a thinly veiled political program. "It's the fantasy life of American men being translated into genetics," says poet and social critic Katha Pollitt. "You can look at any feature of modern life and make up a story about why it's genetic." In truth, says Northwestern University anthropologist Micaela di Leonardo, attraction is a complicated social phenomenon, not just a hard-wired response. If attraction were governed by the dictates of baby-making, she says, the men of ancient Greece wouldn't have found young boys so alluring, and gay couples wouldn't crowd modern sidewalks. "People make decisions about sexual and marital partners inside complex networks of friends and relatives," she says. "Human beings cannot be reduced to DNA packets."

Homosexuality is hard to explain as a biological adaptation. So is stamp collecting. But no one claims that human beings are mindless automatons, blindly striving to replicate our genes. We pursue countless passions that have no direct bearing on survival. If we're sometimes attracted to people who can't help us reproduce, that doesn't mean human preferences lack any coherent design. A radio used as a doorstop is still a radio. The beauty mavens' mission—and that of evolutionary psychology in general—is not to explain everything people do but to unmask our biases and make sense of them. "Our minds have evolved to generate pleasurable experiences in response to some things while ignoring other things," says Johnston. "That's why sugar tastes sweet, and that's why we find some people more attractive than others."

The new beauty research does have troubling implications. First, it suggests that we're designed to care about looks, even though looks aren't earned and reveal nothing about character. As writer Ken Siman observes in his new book, "The Beauty Trip," "the kind [of beauty] that inspires awe, lust, and increased jeans sales cannot be evenly distributed. In a society where everything is supposed to be within reach, this is painful to face." From acne to birth defects, we wear our imperfections as thorns, for we know the world sees them and takes note.

A second implication is that sexual stereotypes are not strictly artificial. At some level, it seems, women are designed to favor dominant males over meek ones, and men are designed to value women for youthful qualities that time quickly steals. Given the slow pace of evolutionary change, our innate preferences aren't likely to fade in the foreseeable future. And if they exist for what were once good biological reasons, that doesn't make them any less nettlesome. "Men often forgo their health, their safety, their spare time and their family life in order to get rank," says Helen Fisher, the Rutgers anthropologist, "because unconsciously, they know that rank wins women." And all too often, those who can trade cynically on their rank do.

But do we have to indulge every appetite that natural selection has preserved in us? Of course not. "I don't know any scientist who seriously thinks you can look to nature for moral guidance," says Thornhill. Even the fashion magazines would provide a better compass.

With KAREN SPRINGEN

SOCIETY: YOU MUST REMEMBER THIS, A KISS IS BUT A KISS

Infidelity and the Science of Cheating

Why do men find sexual infidelity by their mates so distressing? Why do women find emotional infidelity so threatening? The new view blames it all on our genetic inheritance, a faddish intellectual trend that is likely to gain momentum in the coming years.

BY SHARON BEGLEY

Think of a committed romantic relationship that you have now, or that you had in the past. Now imagine that your spouse, or significant other, becomes interested in someone else. What would distress you more:

• Discovering that he or she has formed a deep emotional attachment to the other, confiding in that person and seeking comfort there rather than from you?

• Discovering that your partner is enjoying daily passionate sex with the other person, trying positions rarely seen outside the Kamasutra?

While this makes for an interesting party game—though we don't advise trying it around the family Christmas table—the question has a more serious purpose. Researchers have been using such "forced choice" experiments to probe one of the more controversial questions in psychology: why do more men than women say sexual betrayal is more upsetting, while more women than men find emotional infidelity more disturbing? Psychologist David Buss of the University of Texas, Austin, first reported this gender gap in 1992. Since then other researchers have repeatedly found the same pattern. But when it comes to explaining *why* men and women differ, the battle rages.

The year now ending brought claims that genes inherited from our parents make us risk takers or neurotic, happy or

Why do men
prefer women in short skirts? At the dawn of humanity women in long skirts tripped, squashing their babies.

sad. In the new year, watch out for ever more studies on how genes passed down from Neanderthal days make us what we are. "There is tremendous interest in evolutionary perspectives in psychology," says John Kihlstrom of Yale University, editor of the journal Psychological Science. And not just among scientists. In 1996, magazine articles waxed scholarly on how evolution explains, for instance, Dick Morris's extramarital escapades. Basically, his DNA made him do it.

The debate shapes up like this. Evolutionary psychologists argue that sex differences in jealousy are a legacy of humankind's past, a biological imperative that no amount of reason, no veneer of civilization, can entirely quash. In other words, genes for traits that characterized the earliest humans shape how we think, feel and act, even if we are doing that thinking, feeling and acting in cities rather than in caves. In particular, men fly into a rage over adultery because to do so is hardwired into their genes (not to mention their jeans). The reason is that a man can never be altogether sure of paternity. If, at the dawn of humanity, a man's partner slept around, he could have wound up inadvertently supporting the child of a rival; he would also have had fewer chances of impregnating her himself. That would have given him a poor chance of transmitting his genes to the next generation. Or, put another way, only men who carried the gene that made them livid over a spouse's roaming managed to leave descendants. Says UT's Buss, "Any man who didn't [do all he could to keep his wife from straying sexually] is not our ancestor."

FOR A WOMAN, THE STAKES WERE DIFFERENT. IF HER partner sired another's child, his infidelity could have been over in minutes. (OK, seconds.) But if he became emotionally involved with another woman, he might have abandoned wife No. 1. That would have made it harder for her to raise children. So women are evolutionarily programmed to become more distressed at emotional infidelity than sexual infidelity.

The journal Psychological Science recently devoted a special section to the controversy. Leading off: a study by Buss, working with colleagues from Germany and the Netherlands, in which 200 German and 207 Dutch adults were asked the standard "which is more upsetting" question. As usual, more men than women in both cultures said that sexual infidelity bothered them more than emotional infidelity. "This sex difference is quite solid," says Buss. "It's been replicated by our critics and in crosscultural studies, giving exactly the results that the evolutionary theory predicts."

Critics of the evolutionary paradigm say it is dangerous to call the jealousy gender gap a product of our genes. "This theory holds profound implications for legal and social policy," says psychologist David DeSteno of Ohio State University. "Men could get away with murder [of a sexually unfaithful spouse] by attributing it to their biology and saying they had no control over themselves." What's more, he argues, the theory is wrong. First, if there are genes for jealousy, they can apparently be influenced by culture. Although in every country more men than women were indeed more upset by sexual infidelity than the emotional variety, the differences between the sexes varied widely. Three times as many American men than women said that sexual treachery upset them more; only 50 percent more German men than women said that. The Dutch fell in between. So the society in which one lives can change beliefs, and thus make the gender gap larger or smaller.

More problematic for evolutionary psychology is another repeated finding. Yes, more men than women find sexual infidelity more disturbing. Something like 45 percent of men and 10 percent of women, or 30 percent of men and 8 percent of women (the numbers depend, says Buss, on how the question is worded), were more upset by the idea of sexual betrayal. But look more closely at the numbers for men. If 45, or 30,

percent say that sexual betrayal disturbs them more, that means that most (55 percent, 70 percent) are *not* disturbed more by it. Yet evolutionary theory predicts that, even though men should not be indifferent to emotional infidelity, they should care more about the sexual kind.

Scientists who have been skeptical about the "my genes made me think it" theory have a different explanation for the jealousy gender gap. What triggers jealousy depends not on ancient genes, they argue, but on how you think the opposite gender connects love to sex and sex to love. Or, as psychologists Christine Harris and Nicholas Chistenfeld of the University of California, San Diego, propose, "reasonable differences between the sexes in how they interpret evidence of infidelity" explain the gender gap. In other words, a man thinks that women have sex only when they are in love; if he learns that a woman has had sex with another man, he assumes that she loves him, too. Thus sexual infidelity means emotional infidelity as well. But men believe also that women can be emotionally intimate with another man without leaping into bed with him. A woman's emotional infidelity, then, implies nothing beyond that. By this reasoning, men see sexual betrayal as what Peter Salovey of Yale University and OSU's DeSteno call a "double shot" of infidelity. Sexual infidelity is therefore more threatening than mere emotional infidelity.

A woman, on the other hand, notices that men can have sex without love. Thus a man's sexual betrayal does not necessarily mean that he has fallen in love with someone else. So adultery bothers her less than it does men. But a woman also notices that men do not form emotional attachments easily. When they do, it's a real threat to the relationship. Says DeSteno, "Whichever type of infidelity represents a double shot would bother someone more."

Now scientists are designing experiments to show whether the mind's ability to reason, rather than genes, can explain the jealousy gender gap. The UCSD team asked 137 undergraduates the "which distresses you more" question. As expected, more men than women picked sexual infidelity as more upsetting. But the researchers also found differences in men's and women's beliefs. Women thought that, for men, love implies sex more often than sex implies love. And men said that, for women, sex implies love about as strongly as love implies sex. This difference in assessments of the opposite sex, argues the UCSD psychologists, explains all the gender gap in jealousy. Of course a woman is more bothered by a man's emotional infidelity than by sexual betrayal: a man in love is a man having sex, they figure, but a man having sex is not necessarily a man in love. Now, there's a shock.

OTHER EXPERIMENTS UNDERMINE AS WELL THE "MY genes made me think it" argument. DeSteno and Salovey asked 114 undergraduates, and then 141 adults ages 17 to 70, how likely it is that someone of the opposite sex who is in love will soon be having sex, and how likely that someone of the opposite sex who is having sex is or will be in love. Anyone, man or woman, who believed that love is more likely to mean sex than sex is to mean love was more upset by emotional infidelity than by sexual infidelity. And anyone, man or woman, who believed that someone having sex is someone in love found sexual infidelity more upsetting. These data, says DeSteno, "argue against the evolutionary interpretation. Which infidelity upsets you more seems related to [gender] only because [gender] is correlated with beliefs about whether sex implies love and love implies sex."

Evolutionary psychologists don't buy it. Buss points to studies showing that a woman is at greatest risk of being battered, and even murdered, by her partner when he suspects her of sexual infidelity. "Men's sexual jealousy is an extremely powerful emotion. It makes them go berserk," says Buss. "The 'rational' arguments don't square with [the fact that] jealousy feels 'beyond rationality.' This vague implication that culture and socialization [cause sex differences] is very old-social-science stuff that sophisticated people don't argue anymore.... Sometimes I feel that I am amidst members of the Flat Earth Society."

For all the brickbats being hurled, there is some common ground between the opposing camps. Buss and colleagues believe that jealousy, like other emotions sculpted by evolution, is "sensitive to sociocultural conditions." And those who scoff at evolutionary psychology agree that, as DeSteno says, "of course evolution plays a role in human behavior." The real fight centers on whether that role is paramount and direct, or whether biology is so dwarfed by culture and human reason that it adds little to our understanding of behavior. Spinning stories of how Neanderthal genes make us think and act the way we do undeniably makes for a lively parlor game. (Example: men prefer women in short skirts because they learned, millennia ago on the savanna, that women in long skirts tended to trip a lot and squash their babies.) And it is one that will be played often in 1997. If there is a lesson here, it may be this: be wary of single-bullet theories advanced so brilliantly that their dazzle gets in the way of their content.

MARRIAGE STYLES: THE GOOD, THE BAD, AND THE VOLATILE

John Gottman, Ph.D., with Nan Silver

Late at night, countless TV sets around the nation still tune in to watch Ralph and Alice go at it on reruns of *The Honeymooners*. His take-no-prisoners attacks and her smart-alecky comebacks have reduced generations of Americans to belly laughs. There's something about the marital explosions that detonate in their sparse Brooklyn living room that so many of us find endearing and entertaining.

You probably know of at least one couple like the Cramdens. These high-decibel twosomes often entertain their unfortunate neighbors with ear-shattering discussions about whether to buy solid or chunk-style tuna, or put 60- or 75-watt bulbs above the medicine cabinet. Most psychologists would probably call such frequent verbal sniping dysfunctional, even pathological. For years, marriage counselors have tried to steer couples away from this sort of bickering, convinced that it poisons a marriage.

It's certainly true that few people would aspire to a union fraught with so much tension and strife—but here's the surprise: there are couples whose fights are as deafening as the Honeymooners' yet who have long-lasting, happy marriages. If you had made that claim to me before I began my research I would have found it unlikely. But after years of tracking married couples of all sorts I have discovered that what makes a relationship work, or fall apart, is far from obvious. Some of our traditional notions of marital stability may be misguided. To see this for yourself, try your hand at predicting which of the following three newly married couples I studied remained happily married some four years later.

Couple Number One

Bert and Betty Oliver, both thirty, met at a friend's wedding. For a year they sustained a long-distance romance complete with frequent plane trips and multipage phone bills. Eventually Betty moved from Cincinnati to Chicago to be with Bert and they married six months later. Bert works long, grueling hours as manager of a printing plant, a circumstance that puts some stress on their marriage. Both said they came from families where the parents weren't very communicative or intimate. Bert and Betty were determined to learn from their parents' mistake and made communication a priority in their relationship. Although they squabbled occasionally, they usually addressed their differences before the anger boiled over. Rather than shouting matches, they dealt with disagreements by having "conferences" in which each person aired his or her perspective. They tried to be understanding of each other's point of view and usually were able to arrive at a compromise. Married only two years when first interviewed, Betty expressed delight that she had been able to find that elusive creature: "a truly nice man." Bert still considered himself lucky that someone as lovely as Betty was interested in him.

Couple Number Two

Max Connell, forty, and Anita Gallo, twenty-five, were also married about two years when first interviewed. Max, a carpenter, met Anita on the job—he was doing repairs at a home where she was working as a nanny. In the beginning, Max was concerned that Anita would consider him too old, but she said his age was one of the things that initially attracted her. What immediately caught Max's eye was Anita's expressiveness—whatever she was feeling, she let him know. "If I try to put something off that's bothering me for maybe two days, there will be a major explosion," Anita explained. "Instead, I have to deal with it right away." Both admitted that they quarreled far more than the average couple. Their engagement was marked by so many turf wars that twice they came close to calling off the wedding. Even after marrying, they tended to interrupt each other and defend their own viewpoint rather than listen to what their partner was expressing. Eventually, however, they would reach some sort of accord. Despite their frequent tension, they seemed to take much delight in each other. They spent far more of their time together laughing, joking, and being physically affectionate than they did squabbling. Both considered passion and independence crucial factors in their lives together. They acknowledged that they had their problems, but like Bert and Betty, considered themselves happily married.

COUPLE NUMBER THREE

The Nelsons, Joe, twenty-nine, and Sheila, twenty-seven, seemed as closely paired as matching bookends. Both grew up in the suburbs of St. Louis, went to private schools, considered church-going a major focus of their lives, and were devoted to horseback riding. They said they thought alike about most everything and felt an "instant comfort" from the start. The Nelsons spent a good deal of time apart—he in his basement workshop and she in her sewing room where she devoted herself to cross-stitching. Still, they enjoyed each other's company and fought very rarely. "Not that we always agree," Sheila explained, "but we're not into conflict." When tension did arise, both considered a solo jogging session around the local country club more helpful in soothing the waters than talking things out or arguing. Asked about their major areas of tension, they gave a short list of relatively trivial concerns such as Sheila's tardiness or Joe's lack of interest in weekend chores when a Cardinals game was on TV. Sheila also mentioned as if in passing that Joe wanted to have sex far more frequently than she did, a situation that remained unresolved. In all, Joe and Sheila were proud of how well they got along. They knew that in some marriages opposites attract—"We have friends that are like that and it does work," said Sheila. "But that's not for us," Joe added.

If you guessed that couple number one, Betty and Bert Oliver, were still happily married four years later, you are right. If you guessed the same for couple number two, Anita and Max, or number three, the Nelsons, you are right again and again. If you thought only Bert and Betty were going to make it, then you're probably a clinical psychologist or have read plenty of books and articles on what makes a marriage work. Marriages like theirs, which emphasize communication and compromise, have

long been held up as the ideal. Yet, after tracking the fate of so many couples over the years, I have had to reject the notion that there is only one type of successful marriage. Rather, I believe that marriages settle into one of five different styles over time. While two of these types do lead to marital dissolution, there are three very different styles that are quite stable. Bert and Betty, Anita and Max, and Joe and Sheila are examples of these three successful marital adaptations. In other words, each represents a very specific kind of marriage that our research has linked to long term stability and happiness. The closer a marriage comes to settling into one of these three adaptations, the better its chances for permanency seem to be.

One important way we identify what type of marriage a couple has is by how they fight. Although there are other dimensions that are telling about a union, the intensity of argument seems to bring out a marriage's true colors. To classify a marriage, we look at the frequency of fights, the facial expressions and physiological responses (such as pulse rate and amount of sweating) of both partners during the confrontation, as well as what they say to each other and their tone of voice. Using these observations as our guideposts, we have named the three types of stable marriages based on their style of combat: validating, volatile, or avoidant. . . .

THE MAGIC RATIO: ACCENTUATE THE POSITIVE; DON'T ELIMINATE THE NEGATIVE

By now you may be wondering how these three very different types of marriages can be equally successful, or how couples with such clear difficulties, differences, or apparent inadequacies can stay happily together. The answer is that happiness isn't found in a particular style of fighting or making up. Rather, our research suggests that what really separates contented couples from those in deep marital misery is a healthy balance between their positive and negative feelings and actions toward each other. For example, I mentioned that volatile couples stick together by *balancing* their frequent arguments with a lot of love and passion. But by balance I do not mean a fifty-fifty equilibrium. As part of our research we carefully charted the amount of time couples spent fighting versus interacting positively—touching, smiling, paying compliments, laughing, etc. Across the board we found there was a very specific ratio that exists between the amount of positivity and negativity in a stable marriage, whether it is marked by validation, volatility, or conflict avoidance.

That magic ratio is *5 to 1*. In other words, as long as there is five times as much positive feeling and interaction between husband and wife as there is negative, we found the marriage was likely to be stable. It was based on this ratio that we were able to predict whether couples were likely to divorce: in very unhappy couples, there tended to be more negative than positive interaction.

One way to think of a stable couple is as a stereo system in which five times as much power is emitted from the positive loudspeaker as from the negative one. No matter what the particular couple's volume level, the balance between their positive and negative speakers remains roughly the same. High-volume volatile couples may yell and scream a lot, but they spend five times as much of their marriage being loving and making up. Validators have a moderate amount of tension and an immoderate level of fun, loving, and warmth. Quieter, avoidant couples may not display as much passion as the other types, but they display far less criticism and contempt as well—the ratio is still 5 to 1.

The three successful styles of marriage are equally successful adaptations that allow very different kinds of couples to maintain this crucial ratio over time. In other words, these three styles may be universal ways of preserving this important balance (or rather, *imbalance* in favor of the positive scale). Whether a couple settles into a validating, volatile, or avoidant marriage may depend on their particular temperaments, backgrounds, and personalities.

You can think of the 5-to-1 ratio as akin to the pH of soil, the balance between acidity and alkalinity that is crucial to fertility. Your marriage needs much more positivity than negativity to nourish your love. Without it, your relationship is in danger of withering and dying, just like a fragile vine that is planted in soil that is too acidic, too sandy, or too dry. In that 5-to-1 ratio, positivity acts as a nutrient, nurturing the affection and joy that are crucial if your love is to weather the rough spots.

While I found that this magic ratio of 5-to-1 held across all three stable types, the picture was very different for couples who were heading for a breakup: they showed slightly more negative than positive acts. This difference in the two ratios meant that in their moment-to-moment interactions husbands and wives in each of the three stable kinds of marriages were balancing their negativity with a whopping amount of positivity, whereas those couples who were heading for divorce were doing far too little on the positive side to compensate for the growing negativity between them. For those in the low-key avoidant marriages, less positivity is needed, because less negativity is expressed. But for those in the passionate, high-volatility matches, a very high level of positivity is demanded to make up for all the negativity in the air.

What were the negative emotions? You will read all about them in this book, particularly criticism and contempt, defensiveness and withdrawal, loneliness and isolation. But the list does not include anger! When I started the research I assumed, like most researchers and clinicians, that anger was destructive if there was "too much" of it. But when I looked at what predicted divorce or separation, I found that anger only has negative effects in marriage if it is expressed along with criticism or contempt, or if it is defensive.

What exactly were these stable couples doing with each other to maintain a positive balance for their negative emotions? For one thing, by and large—even in the volatile couples—they were far less negative than the couples who eventually split up. When they brought up disagreements, they were less extreme in expressing feelings like anger or frustration. They complained and got angry, to be sure, but they were less critical of their spouse, less defensive, less contemptuous, and they were engaged—not disapproving—listeners. Even the men in conflict-avoiding marriages, who were not very engaged as listeners, were very positive when it became their turn to speak; their withdrawal as listeners was not the sullen type that leads to being a defensive speaker.

What was even more striking was the many ways, large and small, that stable couples showed their positivity. It translates into a useful list of ways to put more weight on the positive side of the equation in your marriage. For example:

Show interest. Be actively interested in what your partner is saying. Your wife, for example, complains about an employee who is irresponsible and makes her miss her bus. You say, with feeling and energy, "He really did that? I can't believe he came late again and you had to stay and miss your bus!" But interest can be signaled more subtly, simply by showing you are truly listening and involved—timely "uh-huhs," nods, and looking your spouse in the eye while she talks.

Be affectionate. You can show affection in low-key, subtle ways simply through quiet acts of tenderness: touching or holding hands while you watch TV, intertwining your feet while you read the Sunday paper together. Such physical affection has a contented, dreamy quality, like sitting in front of the fire and enjoying its warmth together. There need be nothing said. More actively, little things you say or do can remind your partner of your affection: a reminiscence of a happy time together, of an expression of solidarity ("This is our problem, not just yours; we're in this together"), doing something thoughtful—or simply offering to do it. Affection is implicit any time the two of you are having a really good time together. And, of course, there are the most obvious expressions of affection, voicing your feelings of love, or romantic passion.

Show you care. Small acts of thoughtfulness are a powerful way to boost the positivity in your marriage. Some examples: You are shopping and you pass a florist; you buy your wife some flowers she'd like. Or you're in the grocery store and you think of getting your husband's favorite ice cream. Or you just take a few minutes during your busy day and think about what your partner is facing today; for example, "Right now she is about to run a meeting about staff conflicts and she is real worried about how it will go because of that domineering person on her staff." And you call up to check in, wish her well, see how things are going.

Be appreciative. You put positive energy into the marriage simply through appreciating it—thinking about and remembering positive moments from your past, thinking fondly about your partner, and so on. Stoking these positive memories and thoughts is a counterbalance to those moments when you may get carried away by negativity and find it hard to recall anything good about your marriage. Agreeing with your partner's ideas, suggestions, or solutions is another form of appreciation. And every time you let your partner know that you realize you've got a good thing—say, by giving a compliment or expressing pride in your partner—you strengthen the bond between you.

Show your concern. Whenever your partner tells you about something distressing or troubling, express your concern. Be supportive when your partner is blue or worried: "Your job is really getting you down and I'm bothered by that. Let's talk it over." Apologies help; say your partner was upset by something you said, and has turned on you with hurt and anger—it makes a big difference if you're able to say, "I'm really sorry that what I said hurt your feelings" instead of becoming defensive about it and trying to justify your remark.

Be empathic. Empathy, showing your partner an emotional resonance, is a potent form of affection. You can show that you really understand and feel what your partner is feeling just through an expression on your face that matches your partner's. But empathy can't be faked. If you say, "I know how you feel," without it really being true, your partner will sense that false emotional note. More empathic is saying something that shows understanding like, "Oh, that really hurt when she said that, didn't it?"

Be accepting. Even if your partner is saying something you don't agree with, let your partner know what he or she is saying makes sense and is important—that you respect it. This acceptance can be tacit, such as assenting with a "yeah" while your partner is talking, which shows you are listening, want to hear more, and that what's being said makes some sense to you; it also shows that you accept the feelings being expressed. Summarizing your partner's point of view during a spat is another form of acceptance, even if you still disagree.

Joke around. Playful teasing, wittiness, silliness, and just having an uproarious time together is especially nourishing. If you, like most couples, have private jokes that only you share, such joking is a way not only to have fun but is also a statement of the intimate and exclusive bond between you. But if your spouse does not find your teasing, hostile, or sarcastic jokes funny, beware: that is an act of belligerence, not humor.

Share your joy. When you're feeling delighted, excited, or just having a really good time, let your partner know it.

Of course, you probably do much or most of this spontaneously. But it may be helpful to remember that these are the marks that keep your marriage on the positive side of that 5-to-1 ratio. And while all of this comes naturally when things are good between you, an intentional effort during rocky periods can help you get back to a more positive balance.

Like the Second Law of Thermodynamics, which says that in closed energy systems things tend to run down and get less orderly, the same seems to be true of closed relationships like marriages. My guess is that if you do nothing to make things get better in your marriage but do not do anything wrong, the marriage will still tend to get worse over time. To maintain a balanced emotional ecology you need to make an effort—think about your spouse during the day, think about how to make a good thing even better, and act.

BASIC MARITAL NUTRIENTS: LOVE AND RESPECT

In our study of long-term marriages we recruited couples from a wide range of backgrounds who had been married twenty to forty years to the same partner. Despite the wide differences in occupations, lifestyles, and the details of their day-to-day lives, I sense a remarkable similarity in the tone of their conversations. No matter what style of marriage they have adopted, their discussions, for the most part, are carried along by a strong undercurrent of two basic ingredients: love and respect.

These are the direct opposite of—and antidote for—contempt, perhaps the most corrosive force in marriage. But all the ways partners show each other love and respect also ensure that the positive-to-negative ratio of a marriage will be heavily tilted to the positive side.

The abundance of love and respect in these long-term marriages is evident everywhere. Watching the tapes, I see a great deal of affection exchanged through gestures, eye contact, and facial expressions. During the silent "rest periods" between each of Mike and Dorothy's conversations, for example, we spy Dorothy catching Mike's eye and flirting with him in what appears to be some secret sign language. Later on, he brags shamelessly to the interviewer about Dorothy's talent at crafts and gardening. This is a common occurrence among partners from these long-term marriages. Many jump at the chance to tell the interviewer about their partner's skills and achievements. They also express genuine interest in the details of each other's lives. When conflicts arise, each gives consideration to the other's point of view.

One couple who met as peace activists in Berkeley in the 1960s, for example, appear to get a big kick out of their heated debate over free speech, censorship, and civil liberties. They've been hashing out the same issues for more than two decades, gaining esteem in one another's eyes as their arguments grow sharper. Later on, this same couple reflects aloud on how proud they are of their children, and how nice it is just to feel each other's toes under the covers.

Such masters of marital harmony express lots of empathy and sympathy for one another. When illness strikes one partner, the other is there with just the right amount of nurturing and support. They also offer one another refuge from the tedium and indignities of daily life. They're likely to say things like, "I'm really sorry that the computer ate your sales report," or, "Your boss obviously underestimates your hidden talent."

What about your marriage? Do you and your spouse take the opportunity to show your love and respect on a regular basis? How are these feelings expressed in your relationship? Here is a quick test to help you to identify your strengths and weaknesses.

SELF-TEST: IS THERE ENOUGH LOVE AND RESPECT IN YOUR MARRIAGE?

Answer "yes" or "no" to each of the following statements, depending on whether you mostly agree or disagree. As before, take the test on behalf of your partner also, if necessary.

1. My spouse seeks out my opinions.
YOU: Yes No YOUR PARTNER: Yes No

2. My spouse cares about my feelings.
YOU: Yes No YOUR PARTNER: Yes No

3. I don't feel ignored very often.
YOU: Yes No YOUR PARTNER: Yes No

4. We touch each other a lot.
YOU: Yes No YOUR PARTNER: Yes No

5. We listen to each other.
YOU: Yes No YOUR PARTNER: Yes No

6. We respect each other's ideas.
YOU: Yes No YOUR PARTNER: Yes No

7. We are affectionate toward one another.
YOU: Yes No YOUR PARTNER: Yes No

8. I feel that my partner takes good care of me.
YOU: Yes No YOUR PARTNER: Yes No

9. What I say counts.
YOU: Yes No YOUR PARTNER: Yes No

10. I am important in our decisions.
YOU: Yes No YOUR PARTNER: Yes No

11. There's lots of love in our marriage.
YOU: Yes No YOUR PARTNER: Yes No

12. We are genuinely interested in one another.
YOU: Yes No YOUR PARTNER: Yes No

13. I just love spending time with my partner.
YOU: Yes No YOUR PARTNER: Yes No

14. We are very good friends.
YOU: Yes No YOUR PARTNER: Yes No

15. Even during rough times, we can be empathetic.
YOU: Yes No YOUR PARTNER: Yes No

16. My spouse is considerate of my viewpoint.
YOU: Yes No YOUR PARTNER: Yes No

17. My spouse finds me physically attractive.
YOU: Yes No YOUR PARTNER: Yes No

18. My partner expresses warmth toward me.
YOU: Yes No YOUR PARTNER: Yes No

19. I feel included in my partner's life.
YOU: Yes No YOUR PARTNER: Yes No

20. My spouse admires me.
YOU: Yes No YOUR PARTNER: Yes No

Scoring: If you checked "yes" to fewer than seven items, then it is likely you are not feeling adequately loved and respected in your marriage. You need to be far more active and creative in adding affection to your relationship.

THE ECOLOGY OF MARRIAGE

The balance between negativity and positivity seems to be the key dynamic in what amounts to the emotional ecology of every marriage. Like the atmosphere or oceans, the health of an intimate relationship is an ecosystem of sorts, one where there are crucial rates of emotional exchange. If these rates are in balance, love thrives; when they get too far out of balance, then the love between a couple can start to wither and die, like an endangered species starved of its basic nutrients.

There seems to be some kind of thermostat operating in healthy marriages that regulates the balance between positivity and negativity, preserving a sound emotional ecology. It's as if, for example, when partners in a stable marriage get contemptuous, they correct it with lots of positivity—not necessarily right away, but sometime soon.

The balance also implies a strange thing, something you, like me, may find hard to believe at first: that certain kinds of *negativity* may actually have some *positive* function in marriages. For example, some degree of negativity may help keep sexual passion in a marriage. Many couples have experienced the aphrodisiacal effect of a good fight—once it's time to make up. Perhaps for such couples certain kinds of negativity act like fuel that reignites desire. Its role in a healthy marriage may be to spur a cycle of closeness and distance that can renew love and affection. "Off" times allow couples to become reacquainted periodically and heighten their love. Too much of it, of course, can consume a marriage forever.

A friend once told me a story of a fight he had with his wife in which she felt that he had ignored her when they had house guests. She was very upset, but she would not discuss her feelings. For the first time in years she refused to talk to him. He was very distressed by all this, but gradually he accepted it and they both became silent, angry, recriminating, and sullen. Although they stayed distantly polite, this distance grew and grew over time. They still slept in the same bed but they avoided touching each other.

One day he saw his wife dressing as they prepared to go out together to a special concert. The evening had been planned months in advance, the tickets to the concert were very expensive, and neither of them had any intention of not going. As he watched his wife dress for the evening and comb her long hair he was struck by her beauty in a way he hadn't experienced in years. He was hypnotized by her shining hair, and he fell in love with the look of pride and dignity she held in her aloofness from him.

As the evening proceeded they found that they both enjoyed the concert a great deal and they forgot themselves a little bit. Their hands met and the touch was as electric as when they had first become lovers. They looked deeply into one another's eyes and kissed. That night they made passionate love. Afterward they held each other, and in the morning everything was all right. It was better than all right—something had been renewed. My friend and I wondered if the fight was really about anything real at all, or if it was part of a dance of distance and closeness in a marriage that in some way serves to renew the courtship, or, at least, the attraction.

One of the first things to go in a marriage is politeness. In some ways this simply reflects increasing comfort. But it leads to taking one another for granted, and it can lead to rudeness. The difference between the conversation of spouses and people who are strangers is that the married couples are far less polite to each other than to the strangers. When paired with a stranger, even newlyweds accepted the other person's opinions more readily, disagreed less, and were more polite than they were with their partners. In a marriage there are delicate balances operating, and negativity and conflict may sometimes serve positive functions of renewal.

One intriguing question is why negativity is necessary at all for a marriage to survive. Why don't stable marriages have a positive-to-negative ratio that is more like 100 to 1? Wouldn't marriages work best if there were *no* disagreements? Our research suggests that in the short run this may be true. But for a marriage to have real staying power, couples need to air their differences, whether they resolve them in a volatile, validating, or minimizing style. For example, we found that couples who fought were less satisfied with their marriages than those who described their interactions as peaceful. But when we checked on these couples three years later, we found the situation had reversed. Those who did *not* fight earlier on were less likely to have maintained stable marriages than those who were more confrontational. The originally "happy" couples were more likely to be on the trajectory toward divorce, or even be divorced, than the others. In other words, what may lead to temporary misery in a marriage—disagreement and anger— may be healthy for it in the long run. Rather than being destructive, occasional anger can be a resource that helps the marriage improve over time.

Such findings have led to my belief that in the ecology of marriage a certain amount of negativity is required for the union to thrive. In the wild, it is usual for species to have a predator that keeps its population in check and ensures the survival of the fittest. Antelopes, for example, are naturally preyed upon by lions. If there are too many lions in the environs, the antelope population will dwindle dangerously. Not enough lions and the antelope population becomes too large, causing it to die off from lack of food. Predators also play a clean-up role, weeding out the weakest members of a population so that the strongest ones, those most likely to spawn healthy offspring, are most likely to survive.

I think that in the marital ecosystem negativity is the predator. In a sense, it is the lion that preys on the positive interactions between husband and wife. Too much negativity and the marriage becomes doomed. But too little can be destructive as well. In the ecology of marriage, some degree of negative interaction keeps the union strong. A certain amount of conflict is necessary to help couples weed out actions and ways of dealing with each other that can harm the marriage in the long run. Even avoidant couples do air their conflicts—they just have an avoidant way of resolving them. I don't believe their marriages would be stable if they didn't talk over their complaints at all.

It's important to keep in mind that negativity comes in many different guises. A marriage can be harmed by too much of it or certain types of it. Namely, when negative energy includes great stubbornness, contempt, defensiveness, or withdrawal from interaction, the results on the marriage can be devastating. And when a couple fails to find the equilibrium of a stable marital style, then they are vulnerable to having those corrosive, negative forces eat away at their marriage. . . .

Unit 6

Key Points to Consider

❖ What kind of evidence supports the view that both prejudiced and nonprejudiced people are familiar with negative racial stereotypes? Do you agree that nonprejudiced people must deliberately and consciously attempt to substitute tolerant values for their own unconscious stereotyped beliefs? Does this research suggest any possible solutions to the problem of prejudice in society?

❖ Not all discrimination is blatant. What subtle forms of discrimination can you identify in today's society toward women, minorities, or any other group? Is any form of discrimination ever justified? Why, or why not?

❖ Besides men and women, what other social groups are depicted in the media in ways that might perpetuate stereotypes? Racial groups? Occupations? Different age groups? How powerful do you think such depictions are? What are all the ways (positive and negative) that stereotypes can affect the individual who is being stereotyped?

 **Links**

www.dushkin.com/online/

These sites are annotated on pages 4 and 5.

In colonial America, relatively few people were allowed to vote. Women could not. Blacks could not. Even white men, if they lacked property, could not. It took many years, the Civil War, and the passage of constitutional amendments for this particular form of discrimination to eventually pass from the scene. Even so, many would argue today that discrimination against women, minorities, and those at the lower end of the economic spectrum continues, although usually in less obvious forms. The tendency for humans to make negative judgments about others on the basis of their membership in some social group, and then to act on those judgments, is a powerful one.

As the title implies, this unit covers three distinct but related topics: prejudice, discrimination, and stereotyping. *Prejudice* refers to the negative attitude that is directed toward some people simply because they are members of some particular social group. Thus, the feelings of distaste that one might experience when encountering a member of some minority group would be an example of prejudice. In such a case, the prejudiced feelings would also probably influence the way in which our hypothetical person evaluated and judged everything that the minority group member did. In contrast, *discrimination* refers to a negative action directed toward the members of some particular social group. That is, while prejudice refers only to negative feelings, discrimination crosses the line into actual behavior. Thus, yelling a racial slur, or failing to hire someone because of her religion, would be examples of discrimination. As you might imagine, however, those who hold prejudiced attitudes are generally more likely to engage in discriminatory behavior as well. The third concept, *stereotyping*, is more cognitive in tone than the other two. Stereotyping refers to the tendency that people have to see all members of a specific social group as being alike—that is, to not recognize the differences that exist and to exaggerate the similarities. Thus, stereotypes per se are distinct from the negative feelings and negative behavior that characterize prejudice and discrimination.

The first subsection in this unit considers the topic of prejudice, and both articles are concerned with a recent and highly influential approach to studying prejudice. In "Where Bias Begins: The Truth about Stereotypes," Annie Murphy Paul reports on research suggesting that everyone—prejudiced and nonprejudiced alike—is aware of racial stereotypes and has that knowledge automatically activated by encountering a member of that race. What distinguishes prejudiced and nonprejudiced people is what comes next; prejudiced people largely accept those stereotypes and act on them, while nonprejudiced people consciously inhibit these initial responses and substitute other, more tolerant values. In the second selection, "Breaking the Prejudice Habit," psychologist Patricia Devine takes this argument a bit further and describes some of her own research that supports the idea that nonprejudiced people often find themselves wrestling with conflicting impulses: their immediate prejudiced reaction and their conscious rejection of that response.

The second subsection tackles the issue of discrimination. In "Sex, Schemas, and Success: What's Keeping Women Back?" Virginia Valian asks whether gender discrepancies in salary and status are the result of overt discrimination. Her conclusion is that such discrepancies need not result from any overt acts of discrimination, but may result from the more subtle effects of stereotyping and cognitive biases. The second selection, "Is Feedback to Minorities Positively Biased?" examines the flip side of discrimination—the possibility that under some circumstances members of minority groups might be given misleadingly positive feedback in order to avoid the tension that might result if more accurate feedback were given.

The third subsection consists of two articles that address stereotyping. The first, "Minorities' Performance Is Hampered by Stereotypes" describes some research by Claude Steele that indicates that the very existence of a negative stereotype about some group can hinder that group's performance. The article also describes some interventions that successfully counteract such "stereotype threat." The second selection, "Huck Finn vs. The 'Superpredators,'" examines the language and imagery used in the mass media to describe the violent acts of white and minority children and teenagers. According to this article, negative stereotypes about the aggressiveness of African American and Latino youth lead them to be described in more negative terms than whites even when their actions are very similar.

Prejudice, Discrimination, and Stereotyping

WHERE BIAS BEGINS:
THE TRUTH ABOUT STEREOTYPES

Psychologists once believed that only bigoted people used stereotypes. Now the study of unconscious bias is revealing the unsettling truth: We all use stereotypes, all the time, without knowing it. We have met the enemy of equality, and the enemy is us.

By Annie Murphy Paul

Mahzarin Banaji doesn't fit anybody's idea of a racist. A psychology professor at Yale University, she studies stereotypes for a living. And as a woman and a member of a minority ethnic group, she has felt firsthand the sting of discrimination. Yet when she took one of her own tests of unconscious bias, "I showed very strong prejudices," she says. "It was truly a disconcerting experience." And an illuminating one. When Banaji was in graduate school in the early 1980s, theories about stereotypes were concerned only with their explicit expression: outright and unabashed racism, sexism, anti-Semitism. But in the years since, a new approach to stereotypes has shattered that simple notion. The bias Banaji and her colleagues are studying is something far more subtle, and more insidious: what's known as automatic or implicit stereotyping, which, they find, we do all the time without knowing it. Though out-and-out bigotry may be on the decline, says Banaji, "if anything, stereotyping is a bigger problem than we ever imagined."

Previously researchers who studied stereotyping had simply asked people to record their feelings about minority groups and had used their answers as an index of their attitudes. Psychologists now understand that these conscious replies are only half the story. How progressive a person seems to be on the surface bears little or no relation to how prejudiced he or she is on an unconscious level—so that a bleeding-heart liberal might harbor just as many biases as a neo-Nazi skinhead.

As surprising as these findings are, they confirmed the hunches of many students of human behavior. "Twenty years ago, we hypothesized that there were people who said they were not prejudiced but who really did have unconscious negative stereotypes and beliefs," says psychologist Jack Dovidio, Ph.D., of Colgate University. "It was like theorizing about the existence of a virus, and then one day seeing it under a microscope."

The test that exposed Banaji's hidden biases—and that this writer took as well, with equally dismaying results—is typical of the ones used by automatic stereotype researchers. It presents the subject with a series of positive or negative adjectives, each paired with a characteristically "white" or "black" name. As the name and word appear together on a computer screen, the person taking the test presses a key, indicating whether the word is good or bad. Meanwhile, the computer records the speed of each response.

A glance at subjects' response times reveals a startling phenomenon: Most people who participate in the experiment—even some African-Americans—respond more quickly when a positive word is paired with a white name or a negative word with a black name. Because our minds are more accustomed to making these associations, says Banaji, they process them more rapidly. Though the words and names aren't subliminal, they are presented so quickly that a subject's ability to make deliberate choices is diminished—allowing his or her underlying assumptions to show through. The same technique can be used to measure stereotypes about many different social groups, such as homosexuals, women, and the elderly.

THE UNCONSCIOUS COMES INTO FOCUS

From these tiny differences in reaction speed—a matter of a few hundred milliseconds—the study of automatic stereotyping was born. Its immediate ancestor was the cognitive revolution of the 1970s, an explosion of psychological research into the way people think. After decades dominated by the study of observable behavior, scientists wanted a closer look at the more mysterious operation of the human brain. And the development of computers—which enabled scientists to display information

LIKE THE CULTURE, OUR MINDS ARE SPLIT ON THE SUBJECTS OF RACE, GENDER, SEXUAL ORIENTATION.

very quickly and to measure minute discrepancies in reaction time—permitted a peek into the unconscious.

At the same time, the study of cognition was also illuminating the nature of stereotypes themselves. Research done after World War II—mostly by European émigrés struggling to understand how the Holocaust had happened—concluded that stereotypes were used only by a particular type of person: rigid, repressed, authoritarian. Borrowing from the psychoanalytic perspective then in vogue, these theorists suggested that biased behavior emerged out of internal conflicts caused by inadequate parenting.

The cognitive approach refused to let the rest of us off the hook. It made the simple but profound point that we all use categories—of people, places, things—to make sense of the world around us. "Our ability to categorize and evaluate is an important part of human intelligence," says Banaji. "Without it, we couldn't survive." But stereotypes are too much of a good thing. In the course of stereotyping, a useful category—say women—becomes freighted with additional associations, usually negative. "Stereotypes are categories that have gone too far," says John Bargh, Ph.D., of New York University. "When we use stereotypes, we take in the gender, the age, the color of the skin of the person before us, and our minds respond with messages that say hostile, stupid, slow, weak. Those qualities aren't out there in the environment. They don't reflect reality."

Bargh thinks that stereotypes may emerge from what social psychologists call in-group/out-group dynamics. Humans, like other species, need to feel that they are part of a group, and as villages, clans, and other traditional groupings have broken down, our identities have attached themselves to more ambiguous classifications, such as race and class. We want to feel good about the group we belong to—and one way of doing so is to denigrate all those who aren't in it. And while we tend to see members of our own group as individuals, we view those in out-groups as an undifferentiated—stereotyped—mass. The categories we use have changed, but it seems that stereotyping itself is bred in the bone.

Though a small minority of scientists argues that stereotypes are usually accurate and can be relied upon without reservations, most disagree—and vehemently. "Even if there is a kernel of truth in the stereotype, you're still applying a generalization about a group to an individual, which is always incorrect," says Bargh. Accuracy aside, some believe that the use of stereotypes is simply unjust. "In a democratic society people should be judged as individuals and not as members of a group," Banaji argues. "Stereotyping flies in the face of that ideal."

PREDISPOSED TO PREJUDICE

The problem, as Banaji's own research shows, is that people can't seem to help it. A recent experiment provides a good illustration. Banaji and her colleague, Anthony Greenwald, Ph.D., showed people a list of names—some famous, some not. The next day the subjects returned to the lab and were shown a second list, which mixed names from the first list with new ones. Asked to identify which were famous, they picked out the Margaret Meads and the Miles Davises—but they also chose some of the names on the first list, which retained a lingering familiarity that they mistook for fame. (Psychologists call this the "famous overnight-effect.") By a margin of two-to-one, these suddenly "famous" people were male.

Participants weren't aware that they were preferring male names to female names, Banaji stresses. They were simply drawing on an unconscious stereotype of men as more important and influential than women. Something similar happened when she showed subjects a list of people who might be criminals: without knowing they were doing so, participants picked out an overwhelming number of African-American names. Banaji calls this kind of stereotyping *implicit,* because people know they are making a judgment—but just aren't aware of the basis upon which they are making it.

Even further below awareness is something that psychologists call automatic processing, in which stereotypes are triggered by the slightest interaction or encounter. An experiment conducted by Bargh required a group of white participants to perform a tedious computer task. While performing the task, some of the participants were subliminally exposed to pictures of African-Americans with neutral expressions. When the subjects were then asked to do the task over again, the ones who had been exposed to the faces reacted with more hostility to the request—because, Bargh believes, they were responding in kind to the hostility which is part of the African-American stereotype. Bargh calls this the "immediate hostile reaction," which he believes can have a real effect on race relations. When African-Americans accurately perceive the hostile expressions that their white counterparts are unaware of, they may respond with hostility of their own—thereby perpetuating the stereotype.

Of course, we aren't completely under the sway of our unconscious. Scientists think that the automatic activation of a stereotype is immediately followed by a conscious check on unacceptable thoughts—at least in people who think that they are not prejudiced. This internal censor successfully restrains overtly biased responses. But there's still the danger of leakage, which often shows up in non-verbal behavior: our expressions, our stance, how far away we stand, how much eye contact we make.

The gap between what we say and what we do can lead African-Americans and whites to come away with very different impressions of the same encounter, says Jack Dovidio. "If I'm a white person talking to an African-American, I'm probably monitoring my conscious beliefs very carefully and making sure everything I say agrees with all the positive things I want to express," he says. "And I usually believe I'm pretty successful because I hear the right words coming out of my mouth." The listener who is paying attention to non-verbal behavior, however, may be getting quite the opposite message. An African-American student of Dovidio's recently told him that when she was growing up, her mother had taught her to observe how white people moved to gauge their true feelings toward blacks. "Her mother was a very astute ama-

THE CATEGORIES WE USE HAVE CHANGED, BUT STEREOTYPING ITSELF SEEMS TO BE BRED IN THE BONE.

WE HAVE TO CHANGE HOW WE THINK WE CAN INFLUENCE PEOPLE'S BEHAVIORS. IT WOULD BE NAIVE TO THINK THAT EXHORTATION IS ENOUGH.

teur psychologist—and about 20 years ahead of me," he remarks.

WHERE DOES BIAS BEGIN?

So where exactly do these stealth stereotypes come from? Though automatic-stereotype researchers often refer to the unconscious, they don't mean the Freudian notion of a seething mass of thoughts and desires, only some of which are deemed presentable enough to be admitted to the conscious mind. In fact, the cognitive model holds that information flows in exactly the opposite direction: connections made often enough in the conscious mind eventually become unconscious. Says Bargh: "If conscious choice and decision making are not needed, they go away. Ideas recede from consciousness into the unconscious over time."

Much of what enters our consciousness, of course, comes from the culture around us. And like the culture, it seems that our minds are split on the subjects of race, gender, class, sexual orientation. "We not only mirror the ambivalence we see in society, but also mirror it in precisely the same way," says Dovidio. Our society talks out loud about justice, equality, and egalitarianism, and most Americans accept these values as their own. At the same time, such equality exists only as an ideal, and that fact is not lost on our unconscious. Images of women as sex objects, footage of African-American criminals on the six o'clock news,—"this is knowledge we cannot escape," explains Banaji. "We didn't choose to know it, but it still affects our behavior."

We learn the subtext of our culture's messages early. By five years of age, says Margo Monteith, Ph.D., many children have definite and entrenched stereotypes about blacks, women, and other social groups. Adds Monteith, professor of psychology at the University of Kentucky: "Children don't have a choice about accepting or rejecting these conceptions, since they're acquired well before they have the cognitive abilities or experiences to form their own beliefs." And no matter how progressive the parents, they must compete with all the forces that would promote and perpetuate these stereotypes: peer pressure, mass media, the actual balance of power in society. In fact, prejudice may be as much a result as a cause of this imbalance. We

create stereotypes—African-Americans are lazy, women are emotional—to explain why things are the way they are. As Dovidio notes, "Stereotypes don't have to be true to serve a purpose."

WHY CAN'T WE ALL GET ALONG?

The idea of unconscious bias does clear up some nettlesome contradictions. "It accounts for a lot of people's ambivalence toward others who are different, a lot of their inconsistencies in behavior," says Dovidio. "It helps explain how good people can do bad things." But it also prompts some uncomfortable realizations. Because our conscious and unconscious beliefs may be very different—and because behavior often follows the lead of the latter—"good intentions aren't enough," as John Bargh puts it. In fact, he believes that they count for very little. "I don't think free will exists," he says, bluntly—because what feels like the exercise of free will may be only the application of unconscious assumptions.

Not only may we be unable to control our biased responses, we may not even be aware that we have them. "We have to rely on our memories and our awareness of what we're doing to have a connection to reality," says Bargh. "But when it comes to automatic processing, those cues can be deceptive." Likewise, we can't always be sure how biased others are. "We all have this belief that the important thing about prejudice is the external expression of it," says Banaji. "That's going to be hard to give up."

One thing is certain: We can't claim that we've eradicated prejudice just because its outright expression has waned. What's more, the strategies that were so effective in reducing that sort of bias won't work on unconscious beliefs. "What this research is saying is that we are going to have to change dramatically the way we think we can influence people's behaviors," says Banaji. "It would be naive to think that exhortation is enough." Exhortation, education, political protest—all of these hammer away at our conscious beliefs while leaving the bedrock below untouched. Banaji notes, however, that one traditional remedy for discrimination—affirmative action—may still be effective since it bypasses our unconsciously compromised judgment.

But some stereotype researchers think that the solution to automatic stereotyping lies in the process itself. Through practice, they say people can weaken the mental links that connect minorities to negative stereotypes and strengthen the ones that connect them to positive conscious beliefs. Margo Monteith explains how it might work. "Suppose you're at a party and someone tells a racist joke—and you laugh," she says. "Then you realize that you shouldn't have laughed at the joke. You feel guilty and become focused on your thought processes. Also, all sorts of cues become associated with laughing at the racist joke: the person who told the joke, the act of telling jokes, being at a party drinking." The next time you encounter these cues, "a warning signal of sorts should go off—'wait, didn't you mess up in this situation before?'—and your responses will be slowed and executed with greater restraint."

That slight pause in the processing of a stereotype gives conscious, unprejudiced beliefs a chance to take over. With time, the tendency to prevent automatic stereotyping may itself become automatic. Monteith's research suggests that, given enough motivation, people may be able to teach themselves to inhibit prejudice so well that even their tests of implicit bias come clean.

The success of this process of "deautomatization" comes with a few caveats, however. First, even its proponents concede that it works only for people disturbed by the discrepancy between their conscious and unconscious beliefs, since unapologetic racists or sexists have no motivation to change. Second, some studies have shown that attempts to suppress stereotypes may actually cause them to return later, stronger than ever. And finally, the results that Monteith and other researchers have achieved in the laboratory may not stick in the real world, where people must struggle to maintain their commitment to equality under less-than-ideal conditions.

Challenging though that task might be, it is not as daunting as the alternative researchers suggest: changing society itself. Bargh, who likens de-automatization to closing the barn door once the horses have escaped, says that "it's clear that the way to get rid of stereotypes is by the roots, by where they come from in the first place." The study of culture may someday tell us where the seeds of prejudice originated; for now the study of the unconscious shows us just how deeply they're planted.

Breaking the Prejudice Habit

Patricia G. Devine, PhD,
University of Wisconsin, Madison

Patricia G. Devine, PhD, is Professor of Psychology at the University of Wisconsin, Madison. Before becoming Professor, she was a Visiting Fellow at Yale University and an Associate Professor at Wisconsin.

Dr. Devine received the Gordon Allport Intergroup Relations Prize from the Society for the Psychological Study of Social Issues in 1990 and the APA Distinguished Scientific Award for Early Career Contribution to Psychology in 1994. She is the author or coauthor of several journal articles and is the coeditor of *Social Cognition: Impact on Social Psychology* (Academic Press, 1994). Her research interests include prejudice and intergroup relations, stereotyping, dissonance, and resistance to persuasion. Dr. Devine received her PhD in Social Psychology from Ohio State University in 1986.

Legal scholars, politicians, legislators, social scientists, and lay people alike have puzzled over the paradox of racism in a nation founded on the fundamental principle of human equality. Legislators responded with landmark legal decisions (e.g., Supreme Court ruling on school desegregation and the Civil Rights laws) that made overt discrimination based on race illegal. In the wake of the legislative changes, social scientists examined the extent to which shifts in whites' attitudes kept pace with the legal changes. The literature, however, reveals conflicting findings. Whereas overt expressions of prejudice on surveys declined (i.e., verbal reports), more subtle indicators (i.e., nonverbal measures) continue to reveal prejudice even among those who say they renounced prejudice. A central challenge presented to contemporary prejudice researchers is to explain the disparity between verbal reports and the more subtle measures.

Some reject the optimistic conclusion suggested by survey research and argue that prejudice in America is not declining; it is only changing form— becoming more subtle and disguised. By this argument, most (if not all) Americans are assumed to be racist, with only the *type* of racism differing between people. Such conclusions are based on the belief that *any* response that results in differential treatment between groups is taken as evidence of prejudice. However, this definition fails to consider *intent* or motive and is based on the assumption that nonthoughtful (e.g., nonverbal) responses are, by definition, more trustworthy than thoughtful responses. Indeed, nonverbal measures are assumed to be good indicators of prejudice precisely because they do not typically involve careful thought and people do not control them in the same way that they can control their verbally reported attitudes.

Rather than dismiss either response as necessarily untrustworthy, my colleagues and I have tried to understand the origin of both thoughtful and nonthoughtful responses. By directly addressing the disparity between thoughtful and nonthoughtful responses, our approach offers a more optimistic analysis regarding prospects for prejudice reduction than the extant formulations. To foreshadow, our program of research has been devoted to understanding (a) how and why those who truly renounce prejudice may continue to experience prejudice-like thoughts and feelings and (b) the nature of the rather formidable challenges and obstacles that must be overcome before one can succeed in reducing the disparity between thoughtful and nonthoughtful responses.

Automatic and Controlled Processes in Prejudice

The distinction between automatic and controlled cognitive processes has been central to our analysis in prejudice reduction. Automatic processes occur unintentionally, spontaneously, and unconsciously. We have evidence that both low- and high-prejudiced people are vulnerable to automatic stereotype activation. Once the stereotype is well learned, its influence is hard to avoid because it so easily comes to mind. Controlled processes, in contrast, are under the intentional control of the individual. An important aspect of such processes is that their initiation and use requires time

From *Psychological Science Agenda*, January/February 1996, pp. 10–11. © 1996 by the American Psychological Association.
Reprinted by permission.

and sufficient cognitive *capacity*. Non-prejudiced responses require inhibiting the spontaneously activated stereotypes and deliberately activating personal beliefs to serve as the basis for responses. Without sufficient time or cognitive capacity, responses may well be stereotype-based and, therefore, appear prejudiced.

The important implication of the automatic/controlled process distinction is that if one looks only at nonthoughtful, automatic responses, one may well conclude that all white Americans are prejudiced. We have found important differences between low- and high-prejudiced people based on the personal beliefs that each hold, despite similar knowledge of and vulnerability to the activation of cultural stereotypes. Furthermore, low-prejudiced people have established and internalized nonprejudiced personal standards for how to treat members of stereotyped groups. When given sufficient time, low-prejudiced people censor responses based on the stereotype and, instead, respond based on their beliefs. High-prejudiced people, in contrast, do not reject the stereotype and are not personally motivated to overcome its effect on their behavior.

A strength of this approach is that it delineates the role of both thoughtful and nonthoughtful processes in response to stereotyped group members. Eliminating prejudice requires overcoming a lifetime of socialization experiences, which, unfortunately, promote prejudice. We have likened reducing prejudice to the breaking of a habit in that people must first make a decision to eliminate the habit and then *learn* to inhibit the habitual (prejudiced) responses. Thus, the change from being prejudiced to nonprejudiced is not viewed as an all or none event, but as a process during which the low-prejudiced person is especially vulnerable to conflict between his or her enduring negative responses and endorsed nonprejudiced beliefs. For those who renounce prejudice, overcoming the "prejudice habit" presents a formidable task that is likely to entail a great deal of internal conflict over a protracted period of time.

Prejudice With and Without Compunction

In subsequent work, we examined the nature and consequences of the internal conflict associated with prejudice reduction. Specifically, we have focused on the challenges faced by those individuals who have internalized nonprejudiced personal standards and are trying to control their prejudiced responses, but sometimes fail. We have shown that people high and low in prejudice (as assessed by a self-report technique) have qualitatively different affective reactions to the conflict between their verbal reports concerning how they *should* respond in situations involving contact with members of stereotyped groups and how they say they actually *would* respond. Low-prejudiced people, for example, believe that they should not feel uncomfortable sitting next to an African American on a bus. High-prejudiced people disagree, indicating that it's acceptable to feel uncomfortable in this situation. When actual responses violate personal standards, low-prejudiced people experience guilt or "prejudice with compunction," but high-prejudiced individuals do not. For low-prejudiced people, the coexistence of such conflicting reactions threatens their nonprejudiced self-concepts. Moreover, these guilt feelings play a functional role in helping people to "break the prejudice habit." That is, violations combined with guilt have been shown to help low-prejudiced people to use controlled processes to inhibit the prejudiced responses and to replace them with responses that are based on their personal beliefs.

Interpersonal Dynamics of Intergroup Contact

Until recently, our research has focused rather exclusively on the nature of internal conflict associated with prejudice reduction efforts. However, many of the challenges associated with prejudice reduction are played out in the interpersonal arena, and we believe it's important to explore the relevance of our work to issues of intergroup tension. Thus, one of our current lines of research is devoted to exploring the nature of the challenges created by the intergroup contact when people's standards are "put on the line."

In interpersonal intergroup contact situations, we have found that although low-prejudiced people are highly motivated to respond without prejudice, there are few guidelines for "how to do the intergroup thing well." As a result, many experience doubt and uncertainty about how to express their nonprejudiced attitudes in intergroup situations. Thus, for low-prejudiced people, their high motivation to respond without prejudice may actually interfere with their efforts to convey accurately their nonprejudiced intentions. Under these circumstances, they become socially anxious; this anxiety disrupts the typically smooth and coordinated aspects of social interaction. Their interaction styles become awkward and strained, resulting in nonverbal behaviors such as decreased eye contact and awkward speech patterns. These are exactly the types of subtle responses that have typically been interpreted as signs of prejudice or antipathy. Indeed, it is not possible to distinguish between the type of tension that arises out of antipathy toward the group or social anxiety based on these signs alone.

We argue that it may be important to acknowledge that there are qualitatively distinct forms of intergroup tension experienced by majority group members, which are systematically related to their self-reported level of prejudice. For some, the tension can arise out of antipathy, as was always thought in the prejudice literature, but for others, the tension arises out of anxiety over trying to do the intergroup thing well. Functionally then, we have different starting points for trying to reduce intergroup tension. Strategies for attempting to reduce intergroup tension differ when the problem is conceived as one of improving skills rather than one of changing negative attitudes.

Conclusion

To sum up, although it is not easy and clearly requires effort, time, and practice, prejudice appears to be a habit that can be broken. In contrast to the prevailing, pessimistic opinion that little progress is being made toward the alleviation of prejudice, our program of research suggests that many people appear to be embroiled in the difficult or arduous process of overcoming their prejudices. During this process, low-prejudiced people are confronted with rather formidable challenges from within, as people battle their spontaneous reactions, and from the interpersonal settings in which people's standards are put on the line. We are sanguine that by developing a realistic analysis of the practical challenges faced by those who renounce prejudice, we may be able to identify strategies that may facilitate their prejudice reduction efforts.

It is important to recognize that we are not claiming to have solved the problem of intergroup prejudice, nor are we suggesting that prejudice has disappeared. The past several years have witnessed a disturbing increase in the incidence of hate crimes against minorities. And a sizable proportion of white Americans continue to embrace old-fashioned forms of bigotry. Nevertheless, we hope that by developing an understanding of the challenges associated with breaking the prejudice habit, we may gain insight into the reasons low-prejudiced people establish and internalize nonprejudiced standards. Armed with this knowledge, we may be able to encourage high-prejudiced people to renounce prejudice. And when they do, we will be in a better position to understand their challenges and, perhaps, to assist them in their efforts.

Sex, Schemas, and Success

What's Keeping Women Back?

BY VIRGINIA VALIAN

men 72% tenured in 1995–96 women 48% tenured in 1995–96

THE TERM *GLASS CEILING* HAS BECOME POPULAR AS A way of referring to women's lack of representation at the top levels of organizations. The term suggests that invisible factors—as much as or more so than overt discrimination—keep women from rising to the top. It also suggests that those hidden factors will probably not simply disappear with time. And it implies, moreover, that women's performance is at least equal to that of their male peers, for a ceiling keeps people down despite their competence.

Although disputes about the implications of the glass ceiling continue, solid data from social and cognitive psychology, sociology, and economics show that men and women receive unequal returns for equal investments. More important, the evidence reveals the perceptions and practices that create and maintain inequality. To move forward, we must understand how our cognitive processes unconsciously distort our judgments about men and women and thereby

Virginia Valian is professor of psychology at the City University of New York's Hunter College and professor of psychology and linguistics at CUNY's Graduate Center. This article is based on her most recent book, Why So Slow? The Advancement of Women *(MIT Press, 1998). References to the studies in this article appear in* Why So Slow?

perpetuate the inequities that we have long been try-ing to overcome. Such an understanding will allow us to determine remedies for the present impasse, ranging from affirmative action to better methods for evaluating job applicants and employees.

> In academia men and women now start out with equal salaries, but they do not progress at the same pace.

Salary Discrepancies

DISCREPANCIES BETWEEN MEN'S AND WOMEN'S SALA-ries occur both in the business world and in aca-demia. In 1991 economists Mary Lou Egan and Marc Bendick conducted a survey of U.S. profes-sionals working in occupations with an interna-tional focus. The males and females in the study resembled one another in many ways, such as years of work experience, range of specialties, and hours worked each week. But factors that bene-fited men did not help women to the same degree. Women's achievements and qualifications ap-peared to be worth less than men's.

For example, a bachelor's degree contributed $28,000 to a man's annual salary but only $9,000 to a woman's. And not constraining one's career for one's spouse added $21,900 to men's yearly income but only $1,700 to women's. Some factors that added to men's salaries subtracted from women's. Having lived outside the United States added $9,200 a year for men but subtracted $7,700 for women. Speaking a language other than English added $2,600 for men but cost women $5,100. Of the seventeen factors Egan and Bendick examined, fourteen helped men more than women.

This study is typical of others in the literature. Women tend to benefit less from their qualifications than men do. In many cases, women's human capi-tal—their training, years of job experience, and so on—is less than men's. But even when men and women are equal in human capital, or when their differences are statistically equalized, men get more from their investments than women do.

Men's advantage above and beyond their greater human capital is often termed discrimina-

tion. Those who argue that the residual unex-plained disparity between men and women is evi-dence of discrimination have been criticized for incorrectly assuming that all relevant factors have been measured and that the single variable of dis-crimination accounts for the remaining unex-plained differences. Thus, the criticism continues, discrimination could appear to be taking place only because of a failure to specify all the relevant sex differences.

Others have made the opposite criticism, argu-ing that some economic studies have erred by in-cluding variables that may themselves be the consequence of discrimination. For example, lesser work skills may be the result of less oppor-tunity to acquire skills. While both criticisms point out potential pitfalls, the studies to date ap-pear neither to overlook major factors contribut-ing to disparity nor systematically to under- or overestimate discrimination.

In academia men and women now start out with equal salaries, but they do not progress at the same pace. Data from the National Science Foundation (NSF) for 1993 showed that full-time academic male and female scientists were close to parity in their salaries one to two years after they received their Ph.D.'s. But three to eight years af-ter completing the Ph.D., women earned 92 per-cent of men's salaries, and at nine to thirteen years afterward, women earned only 90 percent of their male counterparts' salaries (NSF, unpublished data). Similar data hold for male and female hu-manists.

In medicine, as well, the pattern is early parity followed by a gap. Income data for 1990 for phy-sicians under forty-five with two to five years of experience showed equal earnings (once human capital differences were controlled for). But for physicians with six to nine years of experience, women earned 96 percent as much as men. The story is the same in field after field; initial salaries are now close to equal for similarly trained young men and women. But disparities develop quickly.

Rank and Tenure

AS WITH SALARY, SO WITH RANK AND TENURE IN academia. Male and female faculty members begin on a close to equal footing but become unequal over time. In 1995, for example, about 12 percent of men and women humanists five years or fewer beyond receipt of the Ph.D. had tenure; 3 percent of the men were full professors compared with 2 percent of the women. But six to fifteen years after completion of the Ph.D., 65 percent of male humanists had tenure, while only 51 percent of women humanities professors did; 21 percent of the men were full professors, compared with 10 percent of the women.

Data for scientists are thinner, but a detailed study of highly qualified scientists conducted at Harvard by Gerhard Sonnert and Gerald Holton found that women were less successful at moving through the ranks than men. For example,

> # People tend to underestimate women and overestimate men in ways ranging from height to professional ability.

women who had earned their degrees in the physical sciences, math, or engineering after 1978 were almost a full rank behind their male peers between 1987 and 1990, the years of the study; women in the social sciences were more than three-fourths of a rank behind. That lower rate held even after controlling for productivity and other variables. Women, unlike men, traded off rank for institutional prestige. For women, the more prestigious their institution, the lower their rank; for men there was no such relationship.

Data from the AAUP and other sources show no reduction in tenure disparity in recent decades. In 1976–77, 64 percent of male professors had tenure, while 44 percent of female professors did. In 1995–96, 72 percent of men were tenured, but only 48 percent of women were. In other words, the tenure gap was 20 percentage points in 1976–77 and 24 percentage points in 1995–96. (The persistence of the gap is not attributable to increasing percentages of women in assistant-professor positions.)

Gender Schemas

AS THESE DATA REVEAL, WOMEN RISE TOO SLOWLY through the professions, and their credentials appear to be worth less than men's. To understand why that is so, I developed an explanation that relies on two key concepts: gender schemas and the accumulation of advantage. Our unarticulated beliefs about men and women—gender schemas—make it harder for women (and easier for men) to accumulate advantage and rise to the top.

Schemas are hypotheses that we use to interpret social events. A schema resembles a stereotype, but is more inclusive and neutral. Gender schemas are hypotheses that we all share, men and women alike, about what it means to be male or female. Schemas assign different psychological traits to males and females. We see boys and men as capable of independent action, as agents; they are task-oriented and instrumental. We see girls and women as nurturant, communal, and expressive. In brief, men act; women feel and express their feelings.

Women have more trouble than men in reaching the top because our gender schemas skew our perceptions and evaluations, causing us to overrate men and underrate women. Experimental and theoretical work in social and cognitive psychology and sociology supports this thesis. People are not perceived as people but as males or females. Once gender schemas are invoked, they work to the disadvantage of women and the advantage of men by directing and skewing perception.

Laboratory experiments that control for variables that might affect people's judgments have illustrated how gender schemas operate. The findings from such experiments complement the statistical data offered in the preceding paragraphs. Despite their artificiality, the experiments allow us to isolate the factors that account for the lag in women's achievements.

Take, for example, a laboratory study conducted by New York University psychologist Madeline Heilman that asked different groups of students in an M.B.A. program to evaluate a female applicant for a managerial job. The number of other women candidates in a pool of eight people varied for each group of student evaluators. For one group, the female applicant was the only woman; for others, she was one of two women, one of three, one of four, or one of eight.

Composition of Pool

WHEN WOMEN MADE UP 25 PERCENT OR LESS OF THE applicant pool, the female candidate was evaluated more negatively than when women made up 37.5 percent or more of the pool. Being in a small minority made a female applicant appear less qualified and less worth hiring. Even more interesting were the assessments of the woman's personality. When women made up 25 percent or less of the applicant pool, the student judges perceived the female applicant as more stereotypically feminine—unambitious, emotional, indecisive, and soft—than when women accounted for 37.5 percent or more of the pool.

Such skewed perceptions pervade every evaluation of men and women. Even for objective characteristics such as height, people do not perceive males and females accurately. In a compelling laboratory experiment by University of Kansas psychologist Monica Biernat and her colleagues, college students were shown photographs of other students and were asked to estimate their height in feet and inches. The photos always contained a reference item, such as a desk or a doorway, so that height could be accurately estimated.

The experimenters matched the photographs so that for every photograph of a man of a given height, there was a woman of the same height. Here, then, was an easily visible characteristic to be measured in "objective" units. One might have expected accurate evaluations. But the evaluators' knowledge that men are on average taller than women affected their judgment. When exposed to a sample contrary to the general rule, they perceived the women as shorter and the men as taller than they really were. In this experiment, as is typical, there were no differences in how male and female observers perceived others.

This experiment and others suggest that if someone has a schema about sex differences, that schema affects the person's judgments. Observers perceive individuals who diverge from schemas in light of their own gender hypotheses. If the schema is accurate, as it is for height differences, that will exacerbate errors made about individuals. Evaluators tend not to question their judgment, because it is supported by a real overall difference.

The implication of schemas for judgments of professional competence are clear. Evaluators may be faced with men and women who are matched on the qualities relevant to success. The evaluators may sincerely believe that they are judging the candidates objectively. Yet they are likely to overestimate the men's qualifications and underestimate the women's because of schemas that represent men as more capable than women.

Take, for example, data from a study of postdoctoral fellowships awarded by the Swedish Medical Research Council in 1995. Women made up 46 percent of the applicant pool but only 20 percent of the winners, because panels of senior scientists rated women as inferior to men in scientific competence. A subsequent analysis used an "impact" index to rate the candidates' productivity and the prestige of the journals in which they published. This analysis showed that women with a hundred or more impact points had been rated by the original panels as equal in scientific competence to men with twenty points. The evaluators no doubt considered themselves to be objective and impartial judges of scientific merit. But as these and other findings on gender schemas suggest, people tend to underestimate women and overestimate men in ways ranging from height to professional ability whenever they have antecedent beliefs about sex differences even when those beliefs are unarticulated.

No Credit for Leadership

GENDER SCHEMAS NOT ONLY MAKE IT DIFFICULT FOR women to be evaluated accurately; they also make it difficult for women to reap the benefits of their achievements and be recognized as leaders. Consider a study in which college students viewed slides of five people seated around a table working together on a project. The students were asked to identify the leader of the group. In same-sex groups, the man or woman sitting at the head of the table was always selected as the leader. In mixed-sex groups, a man at the table's head was reliably picked out as the leader. But if a woman sat at the head, she was not always labeled as the leader; a man seated elsewhere was chosen as the leader about as often. As in other studies, there were no differences in the perceptions of female and male participants.

Failing to label a woman seated at the head of a table as a leader may have no discriminatory impetus behind it. But a woman leader is nevertheless prone to lose out compared with a man

> Mountains *are* molehills, piled one on top of the other.

in the same position, because she is less likely to receive the automatic deference that marks of leadership confer on men. As a result, the woman is objectively hurt even if observers intend no hurt. She has to work harder to be seen as a leader.

A real-life example from a prestigious university, circa 1990, shows gender schemas in action. A new female faculty member in a science department at a prestigious university has a conference with her department chair about what courses she will teach. She is eager to teach a large introductory lecture course. The chair refuses, saying that the students will not accept a woman in that format. The woman presses a bit, saying she thinks she can do it and would like to try. The chair doesn't want to take a chance and instead gives the lecture course to a new male faculty member.

We can ask two questions about his decision: why does he make it and how does it affect the woman's future? The chair makes that decision because gender schemas influence how he perceives and evaluates the scientist. He sees her not just as a scientist but as a female scientist. As such, she is probably unable to handle a large group of people. She lacks the authority a male automatically has by virtue of his sex.

We might be tempted to dismiss the incident. We might be tempted to tell the woman not to make a mountain out of a molehill. But the woman ends up teaching a laboratory course that requires much more work, giving her less time for research and publishing and putting her at a disadvantage relative to her male colleague who teaches the lecture course. She also has had a small failure she didn't deserve, giving her a small psychological disadvantage, because she has something to worry about that her male colleague does not.

Accumulation of Advantage

ALTHOUGH A SINGLE COURSE ASSIGNMENT IS A small thing, small things add up. Success is largely the accumulation of advantage, the parlaying of small gains into larger ones. Mountains *are* molehills, piled one on top of the other.

A computer simulation demonstrates how the accumulation of advantage and disadvantage can work. Psychologist Richard Martell and his colleagues at Teachers College of Columbia University created a model eight-level hierarchical institution, staffed initially by equal numbers of men and women. Their model assumed that over time a certain percentage of incumbents would be promoted from one level to the next. It also assumed a tiny bias in favor of promoting men, a bias accounting for only 1 percent of the variability in promotion. The researchers ran the simulation through a series of promotions. After many runs, the highest level in the institution was 65 percent male. In the long run, a molehill of bias creates a mountain of disadvantage.

Our gender schemas cause us systematically to overrate men and underrate women. Our doing so culminates in lower salaries and slower rates of promotion for women. Knowing how these gender schemas work can help us understand why women in fields such as international business gain less advantage from their credentials than their male colleagues do. When men learn another language and live outside the United States, they are seen as preparing for their careers, engaging in those activities not because they enjoy them but because they expect an economic return. Women, in contrast, are perceived as choosing such activities for pleasure. Men accumulate advantage more easily than women because men are seen as more professional than women.

One School's Success Story

FORTUNATELY, THE SITUATION IS NOT HOPELESS. WE can improve women's status in different ways, institutionally and personally. The Johns Hopkins University School of Medicine has shown what can be done to address the problem of lower salaries and slower promotion rates for women.

In 1990 the university's Department of Medicine had only four women associate professors. A task force found that women were put up for promotion later than their male peers, both because evaluators failed to identify qualified women and because women did not realize what was required for promotion. Each female faculty member (and later, each male faculty member) began to receive annual evaluations that gave her explicit information about her progress. The women also obtained concrete information in monthly meetings on how to develop their careers and how to handle different problems that would arise. On top of that, senior faculty members learned how to mentor their junior colleagues, so that disparities in treatment between junior men and women could be eliminated.

The monthly meetings and mentoring addressed serious problems in the department's treatment of junior faculty members. Mentors gave junior men more guidance and help than they gave junior women. For example, mentors invited junior men to serve as chairs at conferences six times as often as they invited junior women to do so. The junior men thus received more public exposure than their female colleagues.

Within five years, the program was a success. By 1995, with no change in the criteria for promotion, the department had twenty-six women associate professors. More subtle aspects of the women's experience also improved. In 1990, 38 percent of the women said that the institution welcomed them, while 74 percent of the men said so. In 1993, 53 percent of the women felt welcome—a dramatic improvement within a short period of time, albeit one that fell short of equity. The Johns Hopkins experience demonstrates that institutions willing to dedicate resources to improving the status of their female employees can do so.

Affirmative Action

AFFIRMATIVE ACTION IS ANOTHER INSTITUTIONAL TOOL that can counteract the effects of gender schemas. Designed to guarantee representation of women and minorities in the work force according to their numbers and qualifications, affirmative action policies implicitly acknowledge the social and psychological realities that I have just described. Affirmative action recognizes that gender-blind policies are impossible to implement because there are no gender-blind evaluators.

Affirmative action procedures acknowledge that people are not hired simply on the basis of their qualifications. Those who have an unfair advantage because of their membership in a particular group receive preferential treatment according to characteristics irrelevant to the jobs they seek. Those irrelevant characteristics have prevented women and minorities from getting their fair share of good jobs.

> Affirmative action helps to counteract the continuing, if unwitting, overvaluation of white males.

Although affirmative action has been misperceived as making employers hire a woman or minority candidate over a more qualified white man, it in fact ensures the hiring of female and minority candidates who are more qualified than their white male competitors. It also gives hiring preference to female or minority candidates who are as qualified as white male applicants. The goal is a work force in which no group is overrepresented.

The misunderstanding about affirmative action stems in part from our belief that hiring procedures are meritocratic and that the best person gets the job. Even though we all have ample evidence that the "best person" (if such a notion can be sensibly defined) does not always get the job, we cling to the idea of a "just world" in which the deserving are rewarded and the unrewarded are undeserving. We rely on principles of meritocracy and fair play to justify decisions that we make about others. Our explicit commitment to equality makes it difficult for us to perceive the extent to which we make unfair, nonmeritocratic

evaluations and decisions based on gender and race schemas.

Those schemas are themselves the other source of our misconceptions about affirmative action. From the outset, nonwhite, nonmale job candidates are perceived as having fewer qualifications than white male applicants. Such persons, it is assumed, need affirmative action to get a job. In reality, however, affirmative action helps to counteract the continuing, if unwitting, overvaluation of white males.

Better Reasoning

BESIDES IMPLEMENTING INSTITUTIONAL REFORMS TO eliminate the inequities that gender schemas encourage, people can learn to reason better. The findings of cognitive psychology can help us avoid mistakes in judging other people. Even without the influence of schemas, evaluators are prone to errors in reasoning. They tend to give too much weight to extreme examples, ignore information about how frequently different events occur, and overestimate the value of their personal experience. Social schemas intensify those errors.

A common error is the failure to appreciate covariation, the phenomenon in which two factors vary together. For example, University of British Columbia psychologist Mark Schaller and his colleagues asked college students to assess the leadership potential of men and women in a fictitious company in which most executives were men and most office workers women. Within each group, the same percentages of men and women showed leadership ability. In this example, leadership ability and status within the company covaried. The covariation misled the male student judges, who erroneously inferred that the male workers had more leadership ability than the females. Those students saw only that, overall, more men than women showed high leadership ability; they neglected the fact that most executives were men. Follow-up studies demonstrated that students were less likely to make such gender errors after receiving training in the logic of covariation. People can be trained to reason in a way that will minimize the effects of gender schemas.

A similar reasoning error is the blocking of relevant hypotheses. If people have a hypothesis that explains a regularity, they tend not to entertain other valid hypotheses. That is, they often fail to perceive causes that might contribute to a person's performance if a prior hypothesis—such as a gender schema—independently predicts that performance.

An experiment by University of Utah psychologist David Sanbonmatsu and colleagues demonstrated how blocking works. Participants in the experiment learned a number of facts about fictitious students who had taken a welding course. Many of the facts were irrelevant to the students' success or failure, but one piece of information—about course load—was important. Students with a light course load passed, and those with a heavy course load failed. Participants also received information about the students' gender. One group learned that all the passing students were male and all the failing students were female. Another group learned that half the students who passed were male, and half the students who failed were male. Participants were asked to evaluate why some students had passed and others had failed.

The experimenters reasoned that participants would expect males to be more likely than females to pass a welding course. If the gender information supported such an expectation, they thought, the participants would not notice the other characteristic that predicted performance, namely course load. The division of success and failure along gender lines would block students from seeing that gender covaried with course load. In contrast, participants given information that did not support expectations based on gender schemas would tend to see that course load explained the students' performance. The results verified the predictions.

The welding experiment has obvious implications for judgments about women in professional settings. People who see a woman fail at a task they expect her to fail at because of the influence of gender schemas will probably not perceive other possible causes of her failure. They will attribute her failure to her sex instead of looking for other reasons, even if those other reasons actually caused her failure. They may even feel that a search for other causes is a search for excuses.

Evaluators can learn how to correct for blocking in the same way that they can learn to understand covariation. Once trained to reduce errors in their reasoning, these people may then be able to mitigate the effects of gender schemas in their own judgments. Understanding that their own gender-based expectations may affect their assessment of other people, these evaluators will thus judge others more fairly and accurately.

On balance, there is some reason for optimism. Although women's advancement is too slow, although gender schemas operate covertly and bias evaluations, although small examples of bias add up, and although people's reasoning is often flawed, we can understand how these processes work and do something about them. Relying on our knowledge of how schemas work and how advantage accumulates, we can make institutions genuinely fair.

Is Feedback to Minorities Positively Biased?

By Kent D. Harber, American Institutes for Research

Kent D. Harber is a research scientist at American Institutes for Research, a not-for-profit social science research institute. He received his doctorate in social psychology from Stanford University in 1995 and then completed postdoctoral training in health behavior at the Washington University School of Medicine. His research interests include minority education, social support and coping, and time perspective. He is particularly interested in the social dynamics of subjectively risky communication.

Dr. Harber conducted the research described in this article while at the University of Michigan, where he was a visiting doctoral student. The Society for the Psychological Study of Social Issues (SPSSI) awarded this work first prize in its 1996 Social Issue Dissertation competition. A portion of this research has been published in the *Journal of Personality and Social Psychology* (March, 1998).

Giving performance feedback is often a tricky business. In large part this is because feedback delivery involves two social goals that are often in conflict. The primary purpose of feedback is to supply accurate information about performance. But feedback cannot only be veridical. It must also be sensitive to and respectful of a person's dignity, and be protective of his or her self esteem and morale. For these reasons, satisfying both the informational and interpersonal requirements of feedback—particularly negative feedback—can be difficult.

The inherent challenges of supplying feedback may become even more complicated when feedback suppliers are white and feedback recipients are minorities. Our society's lingering legacy of racial discrimination can undermine the mutual trust that is essential for feedback exchanges. Whites, aware of the suspicions minorities may have regarding their underlying attitudes, can become uncertain and awkward in their encounters with members of other ethnic groups. As a result, whites' interactions with minorities can be shaped by ef-

forts to avoid intergroup tension. However, such efforts may run counter to performance feedback, which often involves necessary criticism.

One way that whites may negotiate this dilemma is by muting criticism and amplifying praise when giving feedback to a minority person. My research explores whether whites do, in fact, place this kind of positive bias on their feedback to minorities.

Demonstrations of the Feedback Bias

In my studies white participants were asked to review an essay they believed had been volunteered by a fellow student who sought to benefit from peer feedback. The essay was intentionally riddled with grammatical errors and content flaws. The following excerpt is representative of the overall quality of the composition.

> Similarly, the big oil spills got peoples attention until they go away, then they seem to forget. Whose thought about the Exxon Valdez spill in Alaska? . . . Finally not too long ago the Ozone Hole was discovered and also global warming—raising the Earth's temperature.

Participants learned about the race of the fictive writer by reviewing a demographics survey that the writer had supposedly completed. The fictive writer's survey answers were identical across conditions except for one item concerning campus affiliations. For participants assigned to the "black writer" condition, this item read "Black Students' Union," while for participants in the "white writer" condition this item was left blank. After reviewing this bogus profile on the fictive writer, the participants critiqued the essay.

The purpose of these ruses was to reproduce the kind of dilemma in which the feedback bias is likely to occur. Participants were asked to take a critical stance towards another student's academic work (a task

that many students find uncomfortable), to review material in which some degree of criticism was nearly unavoidable, and to relay their criticisms back to the writer. Recall that effective feedback involves a delicate balance between candor and sensitivity. If the mores of intergroup discourse inhibit hostile communication, then this balance should have been positively skewed among participants who believed that they were giving feedback to a black fellow student.

Indeed, that is what I found. Participants in the "black writer" condition supplied more positive comments and fewer

> *Participants in the "black writer" condition supplid more positive comments and fewer negative comments than did participants in the "white writer" condition.*

negative comments than did participants in the "white writer" condition. Participants in the "white writer" condition could be quite harsh in their comments, as for example the participant who wrote to the fictive white writer, "When I read college work this bad I just want to lay my head down on the table and cry." Participants in the "black writer" condition were never so negative. They could, however, send paradoxical messages, such as "Great essay! Just fix the organization and grammar, and develop the argument, and it'll be fine!"

Participants also were given 7-point rating sheets to use in indicating how much added work they thought the essay required. These scales called for a more explicit, summative evaluation of essay quality. As with the written comments, the fictive black writer was more favorably evaluated than was the fictive white writer.

What Accounts for the Feedback Bias?

Beyond showing that whites place a positive bias on their feedback to minorities, I also wanted to get some indication of why the bias might occur. My hypothesis is that this positive bias reflects social motives, stemming from whites' interracial concerns. However, there are potential cognitive explanations for the feedback bias that do not invoke social motives at all. For example, the bias might arise because many whites hold blacks to a lower standard of writing competence, leading to an automatic handicapping, of sorts, when reviewing a black person's written work. Or it could be that whites have particularly high expectations of fellow whites, leading them to be especially harsh when evaluating blatantly substandard work composed by a white writer. There is a sizable body of social cognitive research consistent with these alternative explanations.

Kent Harber

One clue as to whether the feedback bias arises out of social motives or out of relatively automatic cognitive processes is to see if it is equally likely to occur in circumstances of higher versus low social risk. If the bias is insensitive to these conditions, then the cognitive case is stronger, because the bias is less likely a response to interpersonal considerations. On the other hand, if the bias is selective for conditions of high social risk, then social motives are more strongly indicated.

As it turns out, writing composition tasks naturally provide the conditions for assessing the role of social risk in feedback delivery. The criteria for reviewing writing are generally of two kinds; evaluation of writing mechanics (e.g., spelling and grammar) and assessment of writing content (e.g., ideas and reasoning). Evaluating mechanics poses relatively little social risk to feedback suppliers. This is because there are objective standards, such as dictionaries and style manuals, which justify criticisms and thereby shield feedback suppliers from the appearance of prejudice. In contrast, there are typically no such established standards for evaluating content. Moreover, the content of what a person writes reflects more closely on sensitive personal attributes, such as their quality of thought. For these reasons, feedback suppliers may experience greater subjective risk when criticizing the content rather than the mechanics of another person's writing.

If the positive feedback bias is driven by social motives, then the bias should be especially pronounced in feedback related to essay content. Results from the initial feedback study, and a replication of it, revealed this predicted pattern. The more favorable essay comments and ratings supplied by participants in the "black writer" condition were nearly all related to essay content. There was virtually no difference between "black writer" and "white writer" conditions in the evaluation of essay mechanics. The rating sheet, which asked for separate ratings of content and mechanics, showed the same pattern. These results are not conclusive evidence that the feedback bias arises out of social motives. However, they are consistent with the social motives approach, and they are not readily explained by the social cognitive research on race based evaluation biases.

To further test the social motive explanation I conducted a subsequent study (unpublished) that examined how recipient demeanor and race interactively affect feedback. After reviewing the substandard essay, participants conferred with either a black or a white research confederate who posed as the essay writer. In this face to face encounter, confederates responded in either a friendly or unfriendly manner. I expected participants in the "unfriendly black writer" condition to interpret confederate un-

Inflated praise and insufficient criticism may . . . deprive minorities of conditions in which they are most likely to excel.

friendliness as a sign that they, the participants, had committed an interracial trespass. Consequently, I predicted that these participants would provide more positive feedback, as a way to repair this inferred intergroup breach. This prediction was confirmed. The "unfriendly" black confederate received verbal feedback that was more positive compared to confederates in any of the other three conditions.[1]

Social Implications of the Positive Feedback Bias

There is a growing consensus that minority students selectively benefit from academic settings in which they are challenged. Inflated praise and insufficient criticism may undermine this challenge, and thereby deprive minorities of conditions in which they are most likely to excel. A positive feedback bias might also send minority students down a primrose path of inflated expectations, leading to disappointment and confusion. Repeated exposure to the bias may lead to cynicism regarding positive feedback from whites, causing minorities to dismiss genuine praise as an expression of intergroup politeness, or as a sign of lowered expectations. Cumulatively, these effects might exacerbate the problem of intergroup distrust, as minorities come to regard both criticism and encouragement from whites as tainted by racial attitudes.

Unanswered Questions Regarding the Feedback Bias

Important questions regarding interracial feedback remain unanswered. Does the bias arise between other racial and ethnic groups, and in situations where minority group members are feedback suppliers and majority group members are feedback recipients? How is interracial feedback affected when the performance being reviewed is of superior, rather than sub average, quality? To what degree does the bias occur among those who routinely supply feedback, such as teachers, supervisors, and physicians? How might the bias be affected when outcomes have important consequences, such as affecting the recipient's academic standing or job status? Answers to these questions are needed to more fully gauge the extent and nature of the feedback bias.

Conclusion

Interracial feedback may be especially complicated because it involves intertwining sets of vulnerabilities. Feedback suppliers may worry about appearing prejudiced; recipients may worry about being under valued. Both parties, aware of their own and each other's concerns, may be diverted from the forthright give and take that characterizes productive feedback. Yet such frank interchanges are often necessary to advance achievement. It may therefore be important to identify and create the feedback conditions where both minorities and whites expect to be taken at face value.

1. *Although participants behaved as predicted, I have no information that directly links their feedback to how they interpreted confederates' response styles.*

Minorities' performance is hampered by stereotypes

Women and ethnic minorities may fall short of their potential when they feel judged based on negative stereotypes.

By Tori DeAngelis

Monitor Staff

What makes a woman who is gifted in math or science drop out of graduate school, or an African-American who had intended to get a doctoral degree leave college in his sophomore year?

According to current theories, the reasons range from sociocultural to genetic—from the effects of poverty to faulty genes.

Through studies on women and minorities, Stanford University professor Claude Steele, PhD, has inserted a fresh viewpoint into the discussion. In a Master Lecture at APA's 1996 Annual Convention, Steel presented a social psychology theory on minority performance that demonstrates an interface between social events and one's internal interpretation of those events.

Stereotype threat

The theory holds that a source of achievement problems for women in math and blacks more generally in school is what he calls "stereotype threat." For women, the stereotype is that they have limited ability in math and science compared to men; for blacks, it's that they're short on academic ability compared to whites. The fear of being judged by and perhaps conforming to the negative stereotype causes them to effectively "freeze up" and perform worse in the area than they otherwise would.

While stereotype threats affect everyone, they gain more power when they threaten a domain one is heavily invested in, according to Steele. The stereotype that women can never reach the heights of math performance that men can, for example, poses a strong threat to women who heavily identify with the math field. Because the stereotype for women holds that they are *limited* and not *lacking* in math ability, the threat is particularly unnerving because a woman never knows when she'll hit her peak performance, he added.

The theory also accounts for efforts to distance one's self from stereotype threats. If people decide they're not heavily invested in a domain—sometimes because the stereotype threat is too great—they may disavow a domain entirely. Steele believes this is the process by which many African-American youngsters leave school early, and why many women avoid quantitative fields.

Testing the theory

Steel's first experiments to test the theory, done with Steven Spencer, PhD, looked at top-level female math students at the University of Michigan. Here, the team examined the possibility that women for whom math

> **"The findings show that something as minimal as getting rid of stereotype threat can have a dramatic effect on minority students' grades."**
>
> *Claude Steele, PhD*
> *Stanford University*

performance is extremely important will be negatively affected by the stereotype that women don't perform as well as men in *high-level* math skills.

The team had male and female math students with equally strong academic records take a math test far above their knowledge level. (The participants weren't told anything about possible stereotypes because Steele believes that the stereotype will activate automatically.) A control group took an English test, where the stereotype for women didn't apply. If the women did worse than men on the difficult math test, Steele reasoned, it would be a first step in showing that a stereotype can adversely affect performance. (The finding, however, could also show that women simply perform worse on difficult math tests than men, he noted.)

In fact, the women's test scores were four times lower than men on the math test; they performed equally well on the English text.

The next experiments tested whether women would perform better on an easy math exam compared to a difficult one, to continue to test the notion that it is the higher-level math areas that pose a stereotype challenge to women. As expected, the women did better than the men on the easy test, but much worse on the harder exam.

Until this point in his studies, an outside observer wouldn't find the data surprising, Steele noted: Similar findings have been used to support the contention that genes influence performance and ability, he said.

So for the next set of studies, Steele looked at whether stereotype threat, not ability, affects performance. Again, ace math students took a difficult math test, but this time the women were told they were taking a test on which men and women are known to perform equally well.

"The women's performances went up rather dramatically," Steele said. The results suggest that stereotype threat is to blame, because the equal-performance factor was the only variable to change.

Studies on blacks

Steele and colleague Joshua Aaronson, PhD, have found similar results studying the academic ability of African-Americans. Here, they tested the stereotype that blacks have less academic ability than whites: Steele's theory holds that bright African-American college students in particular would be highly threatened by that stereotype.

In one study, black and white students received a difficult verbal text. Participants in one condition were told the test diagnosed verbal ability; in the other, they were told that the test was a problem-solving procedure. As posited, the blacks did worse in the ability condition, but performed as well as whites in the problem-solving condition.

Steele also examined whether race-based stereotypes interfered with blacks' performance. Again using both ability and "problem-solving" conditions, Steele gave white and African-American students an 80-item, word-completion task. The task has test-takers fill in a third word after two initial words, writing down whatever word comes to mind that is related to the first two words. Ten items could be completed using words based on race issues or stereotypes: "Face" and "rice," for instance, could be completed with "race," while "late" and "lace" could be finished with "lazy."

Black students in the ability group ended items with race-based words much more often than any other participants, indicating that for African-Americans, merely sitting down to take a difficult ability test is enough to activate racial stereotypes in their thinking.

In related studies, blacks in the "ability" condition reported less of a preference for items associated with African-American culture, such as basketball and hip-hop music.

These data highlight the situational nature of stereotype threat, he believes. Past researchers have interpreted minority people's efforts to distance themselves from their group as proof that they internalize negative stereotypes. "But this evidence suggests that distancing is a more situational tactic to avoid being seen stereotypically," he said.

Interventions

For the last five years, Steele has been testing his theory in the field, to see if removing stereotype threats might help African-American students improve their academic performance and integrate more fully into campus life.

He has set up a dormitory-based program at the University of Michigan that is the antithesis of so-called "remedial" programs for ethnic minorities. He recruits a group of students representing the racial and ethnic mix on campus to live in a dorm together and take part in the program during their freshman year.

All of the students join in a workshop that challenges their academic abilities and pushes them to go beyond the curriculum. The purpose is to challenge the stereotype that minorities need extra academic help.

All participants also meet informally each week to discuss the value of diversity and communication. The meeting encourages them to air thoughts and feelings about personal, social and political events. Steele believes the set-up "tells minority students and women they have a legitimate point of view." It also helps to defeat academic-ability stereotypes for blacks, for example, by showing them they're not the only ones to panic over midterms.

The program is helping to close the gap between black students' achievement test scores and their grades, Steele said. As his theory predicts, black students with higher grades and better academic performance benefit the most: They're most likely to be affected by stereotype threats because they're most invested in the academic domain.

For students who enter the program with weaker achievement test scores, the paradigm has been less effective, he admitted. "The findings show that something as minimal as getting rid of stereotype threat can have a dramatic effect on minority students' grades," Steele said. "But for students from any group who aren't well-prepared, more attention may be needed."

Huck Finn vs. the 'superpredators'

■ The media create vastly different images of young white and minority killers, many analysts say. The white teens are often depicted as too small, too smart or too innocent-looking to have committed their acts.

By ZACHARY R. DOWDY
Boston Globe

Boston juvenile public defender Bill Talley was irked as he read and watched the news of six fatal schoolyard shootings in eight months by white youths in American hamlets.

In news reports in the nation's top newspapers and magazines, including *Washington Post*, the *New York Times, Boston Globe, Chicago Tribune, Los Angeles Times* and *Newsweek*, Kip Kinkel, 15, accused of killing his parents and two classmates in a gun rampage in Oregon last month, was "skinny," "slight," "diminutive" or "freckle-faced" with an "innocent" look.

Other white school assailants received the same treatment.

Luke Woodham, convicted two weeks ago in Mississippi of killing two students, was described by print and broadcast reporters as "the chubby, poor kid at Pearl High School who always seemed to get picked on," a "nerd" and "intelligent but isolated."

Michael Carneal, who allegedly killed three students in West Paducah, Ky., was described as "thin" and "a solid B student." Mitchell Johnson and Andrew Golden, who allegedly killed four girls and a teacher in Jonesboro, Ark.,

After Kip Kinkel, 15, allegedly killed his parents and two classmates he was described in newspapers and magazines as "skinny," "slight," "diminutive," and "freckle-faced."

were "little boys." Andrew Wurst, who allegedly killed a teacher in Edinboro, Pa., was a "shy and quirky eighth-grader with an offbeat sense of humor."

Jacob Davis, who allegedly killed a student in Fayetteville, Tenn., was "among the brightest and most promising that Lincoln County High School had to offer."

These descriptions, Talley says, contrast markedly with those used in reports on young African-American and Latino killers in big cities.

"No one's calling" these white youth "maggots or animals," said Talley, who defends many African and Latino youth in court. "Not that this (Kinkel) coverage is bad, but the question is: Why isn't the same type of language used when there are black and Latino defendants?"

Roxbury District Court Judge Milton Wright also saw sharp differences from his courtroom in Boston. For example, a story on the Kinkel shooting in *Newsweek* began this way: "With his shy smile and slight build, 15-year-old Kip Kinkel has an innocent look that is part Huck Finn and part Alfred E. Neuman—boyish and quintessentially American."

"Quintessentially American?" Wright said. "That always means white."

Several media analysts agree.

"Never is an African-American kid or a Latino kid described as an all-American kid," said Darnell Hawkins, a professor of African-American studies and sociology at the University of Illinois at Chicago.

Analysts say the references are symptomatic of how the news media create vastly different images for young white criminals and youths of color.

These observers say the huge coverage of the school shootings, which violate a place considered safe and almost sacred, is appropriate. But they say the media often dress up violent white youths even when they were known for violent or cultish behavior. Analysts say such coverage widens the racial divide by depicting young black and Latino

Media Studies

Though there are no race-based studies on word descriptions of youthful criminals, several studies have shown how the media stereotypes black and white people.

■ Professor Robert Entman of North Carolina State University found in a 1994 study of Chicago television news that blacks suspected of violent crime were shown twice as much in the physical grasp of police as whites suspected of violent crime. He also found that white people, in a city that is half black, were portrayed as Good Samaritans 13 times more often than black people.

■ In a 1997 study, Gilliam found that viewers of television news often thought criminals were black or Latino even when broadcasts showed no faces and made no mention of race.

■ In a 1997 study of 214 hours of local television news in California, by the Berkeley Media studies Group, 55 percent of stories on youths involved violence, though less than 1 percent of youths are arrested for violent crimes. Black and Latino youths were more than twice as likely as white teenagers to be interviewed for stories on violence.

tion for the Advancement of Colored People, recently told the National Press Club: "If this were black kids doing this, you'd see op-ed pieces . . . talking about a pathology of violence loose in the community, about some dangerous elements being unleased, about the breakdown in family values."

When violent crime in urban communities reached alarming peaks, a 1992 *Washington Post* article referred to it as "the pathology of random violence that is decimating black youth across the country." A 1991 article in the *Atlantic Monthly* said, "The emergence of predominantly black underclass neighborhoods rife with the worse symptoms of social pathology has proved to be one of the most disturbing developments in the United States."

Many news stories since then have discussed whether black teenage killers are "superpredators." News accounts of young black murder suspects culled from a Nexis-Lexis search of youth killing often describe them in court as "blank-faced," "dazed" or "showing no emotion." Unlike the more human terms given the white school killers, young black suspects often are not described physically at all. Often, the first description of them is whether the boys were in a gang.

District Attorney Ralph Martin of Boston said many young black suspects are "seemingly sweet of countenance, and lacking in obvious bravado." But Martin said he rarely sees black youths described that way when their names make the newspapers.

The Rev. Ray Hammond, a chairman of the Ten-Point Coalition, known nationally for its work against juvenile crime, said the media do not "relate to Raheem," choosing a synonym for black youth. "To them, he's from another culture, another world . . . someone who slides down an inevitable path, one from which he cannot be saved."

Still, others said race is not a factor in the differing coverage.

Dan Polsby, a Northwestern University Law School professor who comments on the media, *Washington Post* columnist James Glassman, and Bill Kovach, a director of the Neiman Foundation at Harvard University, said the school shooting have a special shock value because the crimes brutally revealed *rural* adolescent angst.

Though there are no race-based studies on word descriptions of youthful criminals, several studies have shown how the media stereotypes black and white people.

■ Professor Robert Entman of North Carolina State University found in a 1994 study of Chicago television news that blacks suspected of violent crime were shown twice as much in the physical grasp of police as whites suspected of violent crime. He also found that white people, in a city that is half black, were portrayed as good Samaritans 13 times more often than black people.

■ In a 1997 study, Gilliam found that viewers of television news often thought criminals were black or Latino even when broadcasts showed no faces and made no mention of race.

■ In a 1997 study of 214 hours of local television news in California, by the Berkeley Media Studies Group, 55 percent of stories on youths involved violence, though less than 1 percent of youths are arrested for violent crimes. Black and Latino youths were more than twice as likely as white teenagers to be interviewed for stories on violence.

"That's in contrast to Caucasian kids in news stories, who appear in a variety of roles," said Lori Dorfman, co-director of the Berkeley Media Studies Group.

The result, Gilliam said, is that the image of a white teenager killer often does not register in the newsroom. Gilliam thinks that even when young minority suspects have no record of trouble, they are still described in less sympathetic terms. And she perceives another key difference:

killers as inhuman while making their white counterparts seem too small, too smart or too innocent-looking to have committed their acts.

"This is thinly veiled racial coding," said Franklin Gilliam, a political scientist at the University of California at Los Angeles. "They might have said this is a normal kid, but to say he's Huck Finn is a little much."

In commenting on the coverage of the schoolyard attacks, Julian Bond, chairman of the National Associa-

"If my predisposition is that white kids are good, and one goes bad, I don't blame all whites or all kids. But an act by a black kid is perceived as having implications for the entire group."

Entman and Daniel Romer of the University of Pennsylvania say the media need to examine how they describe young people. Using Huck Finn or the *Mad* magazine mascot to describe violent white youth is questionable, they say, since there are no lovable black rascal icons seared into the nation's consciousness. "A black kid wouldn't get that kind of language," Romer said.

Gilliam said reporters also should avoid racial coding. In a national Nexis-Lexis search of news stories, no school shootings were associated with any "pathology." Despite the horror of their crimes, no story linked Kinkel, Woodham, Carneal, Johnson, Golden, Wurst or Davis with the term "superpredator."

Professor Robert Entman of North Carolina State University found in a 1994 study of Chicago television news that blacks suspected of violent crime were shown twice as much in the physical grasp of police as whites suspected of violent crime.

In his National Press Club speech, Bond said it is time that America recognized factors behind youth violence that cut across race and class. "It seems to me there's kind of a pathology out there, some kind of love of guns, a gun culture out there that's dangerous and insidious," Bond said.

People like Hammond, of the Ten-Point Coalition, are waiting to see if the coverage will result in the Kip Kinkels and Luke Woodhams being seen as individual problems that white America can separate itself from, or if those incidents ring a national alarm over how too many teenagers of all colors use guns to solve their problems.

"It will be interesting to see where it goes from here," Hammond said. "Black kids have long been canaries in the coal mine, but no one wanted to look down where the black canaries were. We were invisible. Now that the canaries are visible, and next door, they are not so easy to ignore."

Unit Selections

Key Points to Consider

❖ In your opinion, what is the likely effect on aggressive behavior of owning a gun? On what do you base your opinion? How would you respond to someone with the opposite view? How could you resolve this conflict?

❖ What do you think of the argument that something about the culture of the South makes violent actions more likely to occur? Do you see any relevance between the issues dealt with in the first article and the hypothesis about violence and honor in the South? Explain.

❖ What do you think is the relationship between self-esteem and aggressive behavior? How and why would one's feelings about the self affect whether or not aggressive behavior occurs?

 **Links** ## www.dushkin.com/online/

These sites are annotated on pages 4 and 5.

The evidence that human beings are capable of great violence is all around us—all you have to do is read a newspaper or watch the evening news. Every day, people are shot, stabbed, beaten, or otherwise treated in a violent manner by friends, family, or strangers. People are attacked for the color of their skin, their political ideas, their membership in a rival gang, or just because they were in the wrong place at the wrong time. Nations war against other nations, and in civil conflicts nations war against themselves. Faced with millions and millions of victims, it is hard to disagree with the conclusion that the capacity for aggression is fundamental to human nature.

Of course, it may depend on what you mean by aggression. As it turns out, coming up with one clear definition of aggression has been very difficult. For example, does aggression require a clear intention to harm? That is, must I intend to hurt you in order for my behavior to be called aggressive? Must aggression be physical in nature, or can my verbal attacks on you also be labeled aggressive? Does aggression have to be directed toward a human being? What about violence toward animals, or even inanimate objects, such as when I become angry during a round of golf and bend my putter around a tree? Even after decades of research on this topic, social psychologists still disagree on what exactly defines an aggressive act.

Although social psychology does not completely ignore the role of biological factors in aggression, its usual focus is on identifying the environmental factors that influence aggressive behavior. One approach to understanding a form of aggression known as hostile aggression (aggression carried out for its own sake) has been to identify situational factors that cause unpleasant emotional states, which might then cause aggressive actions. For example, the failure to reach an important goal might lead to the unpleasant feeling of frustration, and these feelings can then trigger aggression. Hot and uncomfortable environments might also contribute to unpleasant emotional states, and thus contribute to heightened aggression.

In contrast to hostile aggression, which is carried out for its own sake, instrumental aggression is carried out in order to attain some other goal or objective. This form of aggression is often explained in terms of social learning theory, which holds that people can learn to carry out aggressive actions when they observe others doing so, and when those others are rewarded for their actions. Thus, this theory contends that people frequently learn to use aggression as a tool for getting something they want. One place where such behaviors can be learned, of course, is the mass media, and many studies (and congressional hearings) have been carried out to determine the role of television and other media in teaching violence to children.

The first selection in this section, "Gunslinging in America," examines the difficulty of answering what appears to be a simple question: Does having a

gun in the household increase or decrease the likelihood of gun-related aggression? While the presence of a gun might be thought to act as a cognitive cue for aggression (i.e., the weapons effect), interpreting the research results is difficult. The second selection, "Violence and Honor in the Southern United States," examines a fascinating phenomenon—the fact that ever since homicide records have been kept, the murder rate in the South has been substantially higher than in any other region. This article considers the possibility that something about the historic cultural norms in the South is responsible for such high levels of homicide.

The next three articles examine the same basic question from different vantage points. In the first, "The American Way of Blame," Martin Seligman sets forth the issue of self-esteem's relationship to aggression in young adults. Then, in "Aggression and Self-Esteem," Ervin Staub argues that self-esteem is probably not a good predictor of aggression because of a variety of complicating factors. In the third article, "Low Self-Esteem Does Not Cause Aggression," Roy Baumeister argues more strongly that low self-esteem really has no connection at all to heightened aggression, although certain individuals with high self-esteem might indeed show such a connection.

In the final article, "Anatomy of a Violent Relationship," researchers Neil Jacobson and John Gottman describe some of the results of their investigations of conflict among violent couples. Among other interesting findings, they report that male abusers can be seen as falling into one of two groups: the emotionally explosive "Pit Bulls" and the colder, more deliberately abusive "Cobras."

GUNSLINGING IN AMERICA

Does a gun make you safer or increase your likelihood of violent death? A slew of recent studies have claimed to answer this question once and for all. But all they may actually prove is how difficult it is to say anything about violence and human behavior. **By Fred Guterl**

SAM WALKER WAS NOT YOUR AVERage american gun owner. For one thing, he had no interest whatsoever in hunting. And whereas the average gun owner owns at least three guns, Walker owned only one, a .38-caliber revolver, which friends persuaded him to buy for the sole purpose of protecting himself and his family in their suburban Houston home. Walker didn't even particularly like guns. He still hadn't gotten around to acquainting himself with his new weapon when his burglar alarm went off one weekday morning last December. Notified by his security company of the intrusion, Walker rushed home from work, quietly entered the house, took the gun out from the spot where he had left it for safekeeping, and, hearing a noise, moved stealthily up the stairs and opened a closet door. He saw a movement, a figure, and in a split second fired. The smoothly oiled gun worked perfectly, and Walker's aim was true. A body fell to the floor. It was his 16-year-old daughter. She had cut school that day and had

hidden in the closet to avoid her father. It wound up costing her her life.

If Walker's tragic story argues against the benefits to be gained by gun ownership, consider an incident that happened a month later, across the country in New York City. One weekday morning in January, in front of a Brooklyn government building in broad daylight, Eric Immesberger stopped to give a man directions. Suddenly a second man came out from behind a pillar and knocked Immesberger to the ground. The two men then demanded his wallet and started beating him. Now, it just so happens that Immesberger is an investigator for the Brooklyn district attorney, and, more to the point, he was armed with a 9-millimeter semiautomatic handgun. He managed to pull his weapon and shoot one of the robbers in the chest. The other fled. Immesberger was later treated at a hospital for a broken nose.

Which case better represents the reality of owning a gun? It depends, of course, on whom you ask. But one point is indisputable: murder is committed

more frequently in the United States than just about anywhere else in the developed world, and guns are its chief instrument. For African American males between the ages of 14 and 25, guns are the leading cause of death. And despite the recent downward blip in the numbers, crimes in the United States are far more likely to lead to death than they are in any other developed country. Every two and a half years, guns kill as many Americans as died in the Vietnam War. The litany of statistics is as deadening as it is depressing. Although few people would argue that cleansing the population of all guns wouldn't go a long way to trimming the firearms fatality rate, the country's 230 million guns, shielded by the Second Amendment, seem likely to remain in circulation for a long time.

Lacking a consensus on gun control, lawmakers have in recent years at least tried to put fewer guns in the hands of criminals and more in the hands of law-abiding citizens. The Brady Bill, for instance, seeks to curtail the proliferation of handguns, the weapons of choice for both crime and self-defense, by imposing background checks and a waiting period on new purchases. At the same time, the states are passing laws making it easy for residents to carry concealed handguns. But is arming the citizenry a good way to offset the risk of crime?

In the last decade researchers have focused unprecedented attention on the problem, and authors of some of the more dramatic studies have managed to amass impressively large stacks of press clippings. But science has not been especially helpful here. So far, nobody has been able to marshal convincing evidence for either side of the debate. "The first point that's obvious in any scientific reading of the field is the extreme paucity of data," says Franklin Zimring, a professor of law at the University of California at Berkeley. "What we have is critically flawed—on both sides." Indeed, the scientific literature on the subject seems to teach very little, except for the tedious fact that it is difficult to say anything rigorously scientific about human behavior—particularly aggression.

WHAT'S OBVIOUS BY NOW TO most scientists is that assessing the risk of owning a gun is nothing like assessing the risk of smoking cigarettes was 30 or 40 years ago. Back then medical researchers convinced themselves quickly of the cause-and-effect relationship between cigarettes and cancer. Although they had no direct, mechanistic proof, the epidemiological evidence proved the case far beyond any reasonable doubt. With guns, such a link has proved elusive, to say the least. Researchers think that about half of American households possess guns, they're fairly sure that about two-thirds of these households have handguns, and they believe the proportion of handguns, within the total number of guns of all types, is rising. Their reasoning rests partly on the assumption that most guns bought these days are intended for self-defense; because of their small size, handguns are the overwhelming choice for this purpose. They also assume that the relative number of handguns owned will be reflected in the relative number of firearms deaths caused by handguns—about 60 percent.

Given the magnitude of the violence and the prevalence of the weapons, it is surprising that science has come to the issue of risk only recently. Criminologists have spent several decades exploring the impact of guns on crime and the behavior of criminals, but they have neglected the question of individual risk. When the medical profession got interested in guns in the early 1980s, it made them a public health issue, looking at the risk to the public at large. Emergency room doctors see the associated hazards every day, in the children who die or are wounded by playing with guns, in the successful and unsuccessful teenage suicides, and in countless other gun-related accidents such as Walker's, in which the gun itself functions properly in only a narrow mechanical sense and the risk is more clearly seen in retrospect. And this public health perspective spurred renewed interest in studies that test to what degree the presence of guns increases the likelihood of death to their owners. But this approach, of course, focused on gun ownership as a societal issue; it did not assume the point of view of the individual. Doing so would have treated a gun as a consumer product, like a power drill or a lawn mower or a food processor, that carries with it a certain risk of accidental injury or death that must be weighed against its benefits.

Many of these public health studies attracted a great deal of publicity because they seemed to settle the question of risk once and for all. Arthur Kellermann, an emergency room doctor, is perhaps the most prolific and visible of the medical researchers who have tried to quantify the risk of owning a gun. Although he is a southerner who was raised with guns and who likes target shooting, he has nonetheless become a major source of bumper-sticker statistics for gun-control advocates. He insists that he has proved not only that a gun is a poor deterrent to residential crime but that having one actually increases the chance that somebody in your home will be shot and killed. In particular, his studies conclude that gun-owning households, when compared with gunless ones, are almost three times as likely to be the scene of a homicide and almost five times as likely to be the scene of a suicide. "If having a gun in the home was a good deterrent," Kellermann says, "then we should have seen few guns in the homes of murder victims. But we found the opposite."

Kellermann's work has drawn fire from researchers who suspect that his passion for the issue has blinded him to ambiguities in his data. "Kellermann has decided that guns are bad, and he's out to prove it," says Yale sociologist Albert Reiss. Although in general criminologists don't object to Kellermann's research methods, they part company in their interpretation of his results. His evidence, say critics, is so riddled with uncertainties as to preclude any definitive interpretation.

UPON CLOSE INSPECTION, KELLERmann's results are much more modest than his dramatic conclusions would indicate. He chose to study guns in the home not only because lots of people buy them for self-defense and keep them in a drawer beside their beds but also because *home* is a well-defined place that simplifies the task of collecting data. Police homicide records specifically include the location of each incident and the weapon used, and it was a straightforward matter for Kellermann to follow up each case by interviewing surviving family members and friends. The problem was in coming up with a suitable control group against which to draw comparisons. Ideally, you want to pair each victim with a control that differs from the victim only in that one was shot and the other wasn't. Kellermann devised a clever methodology for doing so. For each victim, he randomly selected one neighbor after another until he found someone who was the same age, sex, and race. Eventually he assembled "matched pairs" for 388 homicide victims.

When he compared the victims with the control group, however, he found that many more factors differentiated the two groups than their victim status. It turned out that the households in which homicides took place were more likely to contain a family member who abused alcohol or drugs and had a history of domestic violence—these factors contributed to the likelihood of homicide independent of the existence of guns. Kellermann took pains to compensate for these other factors using standard statistical techniques of epidemiology. In essence, he tried to estimate how much each factor, such as alcohol abuse, might have influenced the homicide rate among victims in his study, and then he adjusted his figures accordingly.

What neither Kellermann nor his critics can know for certain is whether this

THE RESULTS OF ONE SURVEY, TO FIND OUT HOW OFTEN GUNS ARE USED IN SELF-DEFENSE, DEPICT THE COUNTRY'S GUN OWNERS AS HOLDING BACK A TIDAL WAVE OF VIOLENCE AND CRIME.

statistical juggling actually uncovers any underlying trends or whether something else is going on that Kellermann hasn't accounted for. Kellermann himself admits the possibility of some kind of "psychological confounding"—that some intangible factor such as aggression, rather than merely the presence of guns, is influencing the results. Critics also point out that the victims in Kellermann's study may have gotten guns because they felt themselves to be threatened in some way, which means they might have suffered higher homicide rates even if they hadn't bothered to arm themselves. "Kellermann has shown that homicide victims are more likely to keep a gun at home, but criminologists have known that for years," says Gary Kleck, of Florida State University in Tallahassee.

Kellermann's even more dramatic figures on suicide in the home are especially problematic, mainly because Kellermann relies on the numbers without offering an explanation. "There's no theory to account for his conclusion," says Zimring. Suicide is also thought to be prone to substitution—that is, although guns are the preferred instrument of suicide in the United States, a person bent on suicide can easily find a substitute if need be. Since Kellermann's study focuses on suicides in the home, it doesn't account for the victim, who lacking a gun, decides instead to jump off a bridge.

Regardless of their personal feelings on guns, criminologists, who tend to look at violence through the lens of police statistics and surveys, are usually more open than doctors to the possibility that a gun can now and then deter a crime. Trouble is, social scientists are poorly equipped to measure events that do not occur—crimes that are averted because the would-be victim had a gun. As a result, criminologists have resorted to surveys to get at this phenomenon. Most recently, Kleck conducted a survey

to find out how often gun owners actually use their guns in self-defense. His controversial results depict the country's gun owners as holding back a tidal wave of violence and crime. He estimates that 2.5 million times each year, somebody somewhere in America uses a gun in self-defense. This figure has become a mantra of the National Rifle Association (with whom Kleck has no affiliation).

Most other criminologists are critical of Kleck's methods, and almost all of them are incredulous at the results. A big complaint is that he leaves it to his survey respondents to define a "defensive gun use," so he may have captured incidents that most people would consider trivial. "An awful lot of what some people would call self-defense is, like, somebody asks you for a quarter and you tell them to get lost, but as you walk away you keep your hand on your gun," says Philip Cook, a Duke University economist. In addition, many incidents that people report as self-defense may in fact be assault, in which the respondent takes a more active role than he admits. "In many instances, we may only be talking to one side of an argument," says Zimring.

What this criticism comes down to is that Kleck, like Kellermann and all the other researchers in this field, is guilty of failing to explain what happens when people carry guns, and how possessing one affects their interactions with criminals. As Reiss puts it, "We know very little about how motivation enters into an action." Zimring likens efforts to understand the deterrent effect of guns to "dancing with clouds." Kleck himself admits that "the better the research, the more it tends to support the null hypothesis—that gun ownership and control laws have no net effect on violence."

Even when a seemingly perfect opportunity for a real-life experiment presents itself, as it did recently to criminologist David McDowall, the null hypothesis is often all that a criminologist is left with.

Several years ago, Florida, Mississippi, and Oregon adopted "shall issue" laws requiring the states to issue a license to almost anybody who wants to carry a concealed handgun. McDowall saw that the effect of these laws would give him a laboratory in which to test the arms-race hypothesis: he could find out whether criminals, knowing their victims are more likely to be armed with handguns, are more likely to use guns themselves. He could also find out whether citizens, when armed, can deter crime.

After the new laws were passed, permits to carry concealed handguns rose enormously—in Florida the number of licenses soared from 17,000 before the law was passed in 1987 to 141,000 seven years later. After studying five cities, McDowall found that the rate of firearms homicides increased overall by 26 percent. Although this would seem to support the arms-race hypothesis, the results were inconsistent. Whereas McDowall had expected the effects of the liberalized laws to be greatest in Miami, the biggest city in the study and the one with the highest crime rate, the rise in homicides there was too small to be statistically significant. However, McDowall believes his evidence is strong enough to show that armed citizens do not decrease the number of firearms-related deaths.

D ESPITE THE FRUSTRATING LACK of clarity, researchers are universally optimistic that, with time and the accretion of data, insight into the mechanism of violence will come, and with it, a greater consensus on the real risks of guns. For the time being, however, there will remain very little one researcher can say about risk that another researcher cannot refute. Most favor restricting the availability of guns by mandating background checks and waiting periods, which serve to some degree to keep guns out of the hands of "hotheads" and criminals. There is also a consensus that higher homicide rates have everything to do with the preponderance of guns—an obvious inference when considering, say, crime statistics of London and New York. These two cities have similar crime rates, but the homicide rate from burglaries and robberies in gun-rich New York is vastly higher—54 times higher in 1992, according to Zimring. "America doesn't have a crime problem," he says, "it has a lethal violence problem. It's that thin layer of lethal crime that Americans are afraid of."

Given that purging guns from the population is problematic, would the world be safer if each law-abiding citizen carried a gun? Alessandro Veralli hesitates before answering this question. For most of his adult life, he has carried a concealed handgun almost everywhere he goes, whether it's out to the movies with his wife or to the local hardware store on a Saturday afternoon. Yet Veralli, a Master Firearms Instructor for the New York City Police Department and an NRA life member, admits that as a civilian he has had very little opportunity to use his gun. If he ever found himself a customer at a liquor store that was being held up, in most cases his training and common sense would tell him to lie low rather than start a shootout. If he was out with his wife and a thief demanded his wallet, he would probably hand it over. "In a robbery, there's not much you can do except maybe shoot at the guy as he's walking away," he says. "But what if he shoots back? I'd be putting my wife in danger, and for what?" He carries a gun for the hypothetical extreme case when having it might mean the difference between life and death. "Personally I'd hate to get into a bad situation and think that I might have been able to do something if I had had a gun," he says.

But should other citizens carry guns? "I'm tempted to say yes," he says, but then he demurs. "Maybe it makes sense in other parts of the country where they have more space. New York, though, is too crowded. There's something about all these people being confined in a small space. People can fly off the handle over little things. I don't think I'd want to see each and every one of them carrying a gun."

Violence and Honor in the Southern United States

Richard E. Nisbett

Dov Cohen

THE U.S. SOUTH HAS LONG BEEN viewed as a place of romance, leisure, and gentility. Southerners have been credited with warmth, expressiveness, spontaneity, close family ties, a love of music and sport, and an appreciation for the things that make life worth living—from cuisine to love.

But there has also been the claim that there is a darker strain to southern life. For several centuries, the southern United States has been regarded as more violent than the northern part of the country.[1] This belief has been shared by foreign visitors, northerners, and southerners with experience outside the South. Duels, feuds, bushwhackings, and lynchings are more frequently reported in the correspondence, autobiographies, and newspapers of the South than of the North from the eighteenth century on.[2] The rates of homicide in some areas of the South in the nineteenth century make the inner city of today look almost like a sanctuary. According to one accounting, in the plateau region of the Cumberland Mountains between 1865 and 1915, the homicide rate was 130 per 100,000[3]—more than ten times today's national homicide rate and twice as high as that of our most violent cities.

Excerpted from *Culture of Honor: The Psychology of Violence in the South.* © 1996 by Westview Press Inc. Reprinted by permission of Westview Press, a member of Perseus Books, L.L.C. All rights reserved.

Not only homicide but also a penchant for violence in many other forms are alleged to characterize the South. The autobiographies of southerners of the eighteenth and nineteenth centuries often included accounts of severe beatings of children by parents and others.[4] And southern pastimes and games often involved violence that is as shocking to us today as it was at the time to northerners. In one game called "purring," for example, two opponents grasped each other firmly by the shoulders and began kicking each other in the shins at the starting signal. The loser was the man who released his grip first.[5] Even more horrifying to modern (and to contemporaneous northern) sensibilities was a favorite sport of frontiersmen called fighting "with no holds barred," which meant that weapons were banned but nothing else was. Contestants could and did seek to maim their opponents.[6] Thus gouged-out eyes and bitten-off body parts were common outcomes of such fights.

Cases of southern violence often reflect a concern with blows to reputation or status—with "violation of personal honor"—and the tacit belief that violence is an appropriate response to such an affront. The journalist Hodding Carter has written that in the 1930s he served on a jury in Louisiana that was hearing a case concerning a man who lived next to a gas station where the hangers-on had been teasing him for some time. One day he opened fire with a shotgun, injuring two of the men and killing an innocent bystander. When Carter proposed a verdict of guilty, the other eleven jurors protested: "He ain't guilty. *He wouldn't of been much of a man if he hadn't shot them fellows."* [7] A historian has written of the same period that it was impossible to obtain a conviction for murder in some parts of the South if the defendant had been insulted and had issued a warning that the insult had to be retracted.[8] And until the mid-1970s, Texas law held that if a man found his wife and her lover in a "compromising position" and killed them, there was no crime—only a "justifiable homicide."[9]

The young men of the South were prepared for these violent activities by a socialization process designed to make them physically courageous and ferocious in defense of their reputations: "From an early age small boys were taught to think much of their own honor, and to be active in its defense. Honor in this society meant a pride of manhood in masculine courage, physical strength and warrior virtue. Male children were trained to defend their honor without a moment's hesitation."[9]

Even very young children were encouraged to be aggressive, learning that "they were supposed to grab for things, fight on the carpet to entertain parents, clatter their toys about, defy parental commands, and even set upon likely visitors in friendly roughhouse."[10] Children themselves rigor-

ously enforced the code of honor. A boy who dodged a stone rather than allow himself to be hit and then respond in kind ran the risk of being ostracized by his fellows.[11]

The southerners' "expertise" in violence is reflected in their reputed success as soldiers.[12] Southerners have been alleged, at least since Tocqueville's commentary on America, to be more proficient in the arts of war than northerners and to take greater pride in their military prowess. Twentieth-century scholars have documented the southern enthusiasm for wars, their overrepresentation in the national military establishment, and their fondness for military content in preparatory schools and colleges.[13]

Explanations for Southern Violence

There are many "Souths"—the Cavalier South of seventeenth- and eighteenth-century Virginia, founded by the inheritors of the medieval knightly tradition of horsemanship and skill in battle; the mountain South, originating in eastern Appalachia and moving southward and westward decade by decade; the plantation South, based on growing cotton; and the western South, based on the herding of cattle in dry plains and hills that could sustain no other form of agriculture. Of the explanations that we will cite for southern violence, certain ones apply plausibly to some of these regions but less plausibly to others.

Four major explanations have been offered for the southern tendency to prefer violence: the higher temperature of the South and consequently the quicker tempers of southerners, the tradition of slavery, the greater poverty of the South, and the putative "culture of honor" of the South. We argue that the role of "honor" is independent of, and probably greater than, any role played by the other three.

Temperature. It has been suggested that at least a part of the violence of the South can be accounted for by the characteristically higher temperatures of the South.[14] It is indeed possible to show that variation in temperature in a locality is associated with the number of violent crimes there,[15] and we will examine the role played by temperature in the most dramatic form of violence, namely homicide.

Slavery. Slavery has long been held responsible for the violence of the South.[16] Abigail Adams was of the opinion that whites inflicted on themselves the same sort of violent treatment that they accorded their slaves.[17] Thomas Jefferson concurred, in his *Notes on Virginia,* as did many other thoughtful southerners. John Dickinson, an eighteenth-century revolutionary from the eastern shore of Maryland, believed that the institution of slavery led to southern "pride, selfishness, peevishness, violence."[18] Toc-

queville also believed that slavery was responsible for the South's violence, but he emphasized, rather than the "contagion" from treatment of the slaves, the idleness encouraged by slavery:

> As [the Kentuckian] lives in an idle independence, his tastes are those of an idle man . . . and the energy which his neighbor devotes to gain turns with him to a passionate love of field sports and military exercises; he delights in violent bodily exertion, he is familiar with the use of arms, and is accustomed from a very early age to expose his life in single combat.[19]

At several points in this book we will assess the evidence for and against both aspects of slavery as explanations for southern violence.

Poverty. A third explanation for the greater violence of the South has to do with poverty. The South is poorer than any other region of the country and always has been; in each region of the country and in every sort of population unit, from rural county to large city, poverty is associated with higher homicide rates.

A variant of the economic explanation focuses not on absolute income or wealth but rather on disparities in income. Some argue that inequality in wealth breeds violence. We will attempt to assess the role of poverty and inequality in the violence of the South both in rates of homicide and in preference for violence as a means of conflict resolution.

Violence and the Culture of Honor

We believe that the most important explanation for southern violence is that much of the South has differed from the North in a very important economic respect and that this has carried with it profound cultural consequences. Thus the southern preference for violence stems from the fact that much of the South was a lawless, frontier region settled by people whose economy was originally based on herding. As we shall see, herding societies are typically characterized by having "cultures of honor" in which a threat to property or reputation is dealt with by violence.

Virtue, Strength, and Violence

Cultures of honor have been independently invented by many of the world's societies. These cultures vary in many respects but have one element in common: The individual is prepared to protect his reputation—for probity or strength or both—by resort to violence. Such cultures seem to be particularly likely to develop where (1) the individual is

155

at economic risk from his fellows and (2) the state is weak or nonexistent and thus cannot prevent or punish theft of property. And those two conditions normally occur together: Herding, for example, is the main viable form of agriculture in remote areas, far from government enforcement mechanisms.

Some cultures of honor emphasize the individual's personal honesty and integrity in the sense that honor is usually meant today. That has always been one of the major meanings of the concept. Dr. Samuel Johnson, the eighteenth-century compiler of the first English dictionary, defined honor as "nobility of soul, magnanimity, and a scorn of meanness." This is "honour which derives from virtuous conduct."[20] Honor defined in those terms is prized by virtually all societies; the culture of honor, however, differs from other cultures in that its members are prepared to fight or even to kill to defend their reputations as honorable men.

The culture of honor also differs from others in an even more important respect. In addition to valuing honor defined as virtuous conduct, it values—often far more—honor defined as respect of the sort "which situates an individual socially and determines his right to precedence."[21] Honor in this sense is based not on good character but on a man's strength and power to enforce his will on others. Again, almost all societies value honor defined as precedence or status. The culture of honor differs from other cultures in that violence will be used to attain and protect this kind of honor. Honor, as we use the term in this book, is well captured by ethnographer David Mandelbaum's characterization of the Arabic and Persian word for honor—*izzat*. "It is a word often heard in men's talk, particularly when the talk is about conflict, rivalry, and struggle. It crops up as a kind of final explanation for motivation, whether for acts of aggression or beneficence."[22]

A key aspect of the culture of honor is the importance placed on the insult and the necessity to respond to it. An insult implies that the target is weak enough to be bullied. Since a reputation for strength is of the essence in the culture of honor, the individual who insults someone must be forced to retract; if the instigator refuses, he must be punished—with violence or even death. A particularly important kind of insult is one directed at female members of a man's family.

In the Old South, as in the ancient world, "son of a bitch" or any similar epithet was a most damaging blow to male pride.... To attack his wife, mother, or sister was to assault the man himself. Outsider violence against family dependents, particularly females, was a breach not to be ignored without risk of ignominy. An impotence to deal with such wrongs carried all the weight of shame that archaic society could muster.[23]

Herding Economies and the Culture of Honor

The absence of the state makes it possible for an individual to commit violence with impunity, but it is not a sufficient condition for creating a culture that relies on violence to settle disputes. Hunting-gathering societies appear to have relatively low levels of violence, even though their members are not usually subjects of any state.[24] And farmers, even when they live in societies where the state is weak, typically are not overly concerned with their reputation for strength nor are they willing to defend it with violence.[25]

Herding and Vulnerability to Loss. There is one type of economy, however, that tends to be associated worldwide with concerns about honor and readiness to commit violence to conserve it. That is the economy based on herding of animals.[26] Together with some anthropologists, we believe that herding societies have cultures of honor for reasons having to do with the economic precariousness of herdsmen.[27] Herdsmen constantly face the possibility of loss of their entire wealth—through loss of their herds. Thus a stance of aggressiveness and willingness to kill or commit mayhem is useful in announcing their determination to protect their animals at all costs.

Herding and Sensitivity to Insults. Herdsmen adopt a stance of extreme vigilance toward any action that might imply that they are incapable of defending their property. Early in his career, in fact, the herdsman in some cultures may deliberately pick fights to show his toughness. As the ethnographer J. K. Campbell wrote of Mediterranean herding culture:

The critical moment in the development of the young shepherd's reputation is his first quarrel. Quarrels are necessarily public. They may occur in the coffee shop, the village square, or most frequently on a grazing boundary where a curse or a stone aimed at one of his straying sheep by another shepherd is an insult which inevitably requires a violent response.[28]

Herding and the Uses of Warfare

People who herd animals usually live in places such as mountains, semideserts, and steppes, where because of the ecology, crop farming is inadequate to provide for basic food needs. They have little surplus and sometimes experience genuine want. Thus they are often tempted to take the herds of other groups. As a consequence, "theft and raiding are endemic to pastoral peoples."[29] Or, as one herdsman of the Middle East put it, "Raids are our agriculture."[30] Thus skill at warfare is valuable to a herdsman in a way that it is not to a hunter-gatherer or a farmer. It is no accident that it is the herding peoples of Europe who have been reputed to be the best soldiers over the centuries, that "to the Scots, as to the Swiss, Swedes, Albanians, Prussians and other people of Europe's margins and infertile uplands, war has been something of a national industry."[31]

In addition to the "marginal" northern Europeans, many if not most Mediterranean groups—including the traditional cultures of such peoples as the Andalusians of southern Spain, the Corsicans, Sardinians, Druze, Bedouins, Kabyle of Algeria, and Sarakatsani of Greece—are characterized as holding to a version of the culture of honor.[32] These groups all have economies that are greatly dependent on herding. Many other traditional societies of Africa[33] and the steppes of Eurasia and North America[34] also have (or had) herding economies and cultures of honor.

There are some interesting natural experiments that show that people who occupy the same general region but differ in occupation also differ in their predilections toward toughness, violence, and warfare. Anthropologist Robert Edgerton studied two neighboring tribes in East Africa, each of which included a group of herders and a group of farmers. Edgerton reported that in both tribes, the pastoralists exhibited "a syndrome that can best be described as *machismo*," whereas farmers manifested "the insistent need to get along with . . . neighbors."[35]

In North America, the Navajo and the Zuni also inhabit similar ecological niches, but the Navajo are herders and the Zuni are farmers. The Navajo are reputed to be great warriors (right up to the present—they served in large numbers and with distinction in World War II). The Zuni are more peaceable and have not been noted as warriors at any time in their history.[36]

An even better natural experiment came with the introduction of the horse to the American Indians of the Plains. Prior to the arrival of the horse, the tribes of the Plains had been relatively peaceful; after its introduction, many tribes began to behave like herders everywhere. They reckoned their wealth in terms of the number of horses they owned, they staged raids on their neighbors, and they began to glorify warfare.[37]

Herding and the Weakness of the State

Since herding usually takes place in regions where geography and low population density conspire against the ability of law enforcement officials to reach their targets, defense against enemies is left up to the individual and the small community in which he lives.

For many people in such circumstances, the prevailing form of law is the feud—with the threat of deadly consequences for family members as the primary means of maintaining order. Hence it should be no surprise that the feuding societies of the world are preponderantly herding societies.[38]

The Scotch-Irish and the Herding Economy in Europe and America

What has the reputed violence of the U.S. South to do with the culture of honor as it might be evidenced by a Greek shepherd, an East African warrior, or a Navajo? In our view, a great deal.

The northern United States was settled by farmers—Puritans, Quakers, Dutch, and Germans. These people were cooperative, like farmers everywhere, and modern in their orientation toward society. They emphasized education and quickly built a civilization that included artisans, tradespeople, businesspeople, and professionals of all sorts.

In contrast, the South was settled primarily by people from the fringes of Britain—the so-called Scotch-Irish.[39] These people had always been herders because the regions where they lived—Ireland, Scotland, Wales—were not in general suitable for more-intensive forms of agriculture.[40]

The Celts and Their Descendants

The Scottish and the Irish were descendants of the Celts, who had kept cattle and pigs since prehistoric times and had never practiced large-scale agriculture.[41] Like other herding peoples, the Celts reckoned their wealth in terms of animals, not land, and were accustomed to intertribal warfare and cattle raiding.[42] The Romans feared the Celts because of their ferocity (though the Romans were not impressed with the Celts' organizational abilities). Over centuries of war, including Julius Caesar's famous battles with the Gauls, the Celts were driven into Britain. Subsequent wars—with Vikings, Danes, Angles, Saxons, and other Germanic peoples—drove them to the least hospitable fringe areas. The battles really never ceased, however, especially along the Scottish frontier with England and between the Scottish and Irish in Ulster.

One cannot know how relevant the distant past of this culture is. But it may be worth noting that the Celtic peoples did not develop the characteristics of farmers until their emigration to America.[43] They did not undergo the transformation common elsewhere in Europe from serf to peasant to bourgeois farmer. When they engaged in agriculture at all, it was generally of the horticultural or slash-and-burn variety in which

a field was cultivated for three or four years and then left to lie fallow for a decade or more.[44] Such a method is the most efficient one when, as is true in most of the range of the Celtic peoples, the soil is unproductive. An important characteristic of this method of farming is that it does not encourage permanence on the land. Periodic movement was common,[45] a fact to bear in mind when one contemplates the behavior of the Scotch-Irish after they came to America.

The Scotch-Irish in the U.S. South and West

The immigration of the Scotch-Irish to North America began in the late seventeenth century and was completed by the early nineteenth century. The group was composed largely of Ulster Scots, Irish, and both lowland and highland Scots.[46] The impoverished, deeply Roman Catholic Irish who came later in the nineteenth century, as well as the Presbyterian, often highly educated Scots, were culturally very different from these earlier immigrants, who were both more secular and more inclined to violence as a means of settling disputes.[47]

Their new land, if anything, served to reinforce the herding economy practiced by the Scotch-Irish immigrants.[48] With its mountains and wide-open spaces, America, especially the Appalachians and the South, was ideally suited to the herding life and to horticulture.[49] The Scotch-Irish tended to seek out relatively unproductive lands to homestead, but even when they found themselves on highly productive land, they tended to farm in low-efficiency, horticultural fashion rather than in the more efficient agrarian manner that involves clearing the land of stumps, rotating crops, and making the sort of improvements that would have made movement away from the land hard to contemplate.[50]

The geography and low population density probably served to increase culture-of-honor tendencies in another respect as well: Because of the remoteness and ruggedness of the frontier, the law was as weak in America as it had been in Britain: "In the absence of any strong sense of order as unity, hierarchy, or social peace, backsettlers shared an idea of order as a system of retributive justice. The prevailing principle was *lex talionis,* the rule of retaliation."[51] Or, as a North Carolina proverb stated, "Every man should be sheriff on his own hearth."

The southerner, thus, was of herding origin, and herding remained a chief basis of the economy in the South for many decades. Not until the invention of the cotton gin in the early nineteenth century would there be a viable economic competitor to herding. The cotton gin made possible the plantation South. But by the early nineteenth century, the characteristic cultural forms of the Celtic

herding economy were well established, and at no time in the nineteenth century did southern folkways even in the farming South converge on those of the North.[52]

When we refer to "the South" in this book, we always mean to include the states of the deep South as well as the mountain states of Tennessee, Kentucky, and West Virginia; but many of our generalizations hold, often with equal force, to the West. The herding economy moved with the Scotch-Irish to the West—that is, to Texas and Oklahoma and the mostly southern portions of the mountain West that were settled by southerners. Again, the herding economy was basic because of the ecology. Thus, it should not be surprising that the westerner, like the southerner, shared the common characteristics of herding peoples everywhere: He used violence to protect his herd and his property; he was hypersensitive to insult because of its implications for his strength and ability to defend himself; he was skilled in the arts of combat; and he was careful to train his children, especially boys, to be capable of violence when needed.

Though we have relied on the findings of the ethnographer and historian, their methods are limited in their capacity to address these issues. Even the best-considered assertions by scholars can be challenged as mistaken subjective interpretations by other scholars. Moreover, quantitative social scientists themselves have presented conflicting evidence. Some maintain, on the basis of one type of data or another, collected by one method or another, that there is no culture of honor, no greater violence, and no attitudinal network supportive of violence existing in the South today—if there ever was. . . .

Notes

1. Gastil, 1989, p. 1473.
2. Fischer, 1989; Redfield, 1880, cited in Gastil, 1989, p. 1473.
3. Caudill, 1962, p. 46.
4. Fischer, 1989, p. 689.
5. McWhiney, 1988, p. 154.
6. Gorn, 1985, p. 20.
7. Carter, 1950, p. 50, emphasis in original.
8. Brearley, 1934.
9. Fischer, 1989, p. 690.
10. Wyatt-Brown, 1982, p. 138.
11. McWhiney, 1988, p. 203.
12. Napier, 1989.
13. May, 1989, p. 1108.
14. Anderson, 1989.
15. Anderson, 1989; Cotton, 1986; Reifman, Larrick, and Fein, 1991; Rotton and Frey, 1985.
16. Gastil, 1971.
17. Ammerman, 1989, p. 660.
18. Quoted in Wyatt-Brown, 1982, p. 153.
19. Tocqueville, [1835] 1969, p. 379.

20. Johnson, 1839.
21. Pitt-Rivers, 1965, p. 36.
22. Mandelbaum, 1988, p. 20.
23. Wyatt-Brown, 1982, p. 53.
24. Farb, [1968] 1978; O'Kelley and Carney, 1986.
25. Edgerton, 1971; Farb, [1968] 1978, pp. 121–122.
26. Edgerton, 1971, pp. 16–17; Farb, [1968] 1978, pp. 9–10; Galaty, 1991, p. 188; Lowie, 1954; Peristiany, 1965, p. 14.
27. See, for example, O'Kelley and Carney, 1986, pp. 65–81.
28. Campbell, 1965, p. 148.
29. O'Kelley and Carney, 1986, p. 65.
30. Black-Michaud, 1975, p. 199.

31. Keegan, 1944, p. 167.
32. Black-Michaud, 1975; Gilmore, 1990; Peristiany, 1965; Fisek, 1983.
33. Galaty and Bonte, 1991.
34. Lowie, 1954; Farb, [1968] 1978.
35. Edgerton, 1971, pp. 18, 297.
36. Farb, [1968] 1978, pp. 258–259.
37. Farb, [1968] 1978, p. 9–10; Lowie, 1954.
38. Black-Michaud, 1975.
39. Fischer, 1989; McWhiney, 1988; Wyatt-Brown, 1982, p. 38.
40. Blethen and Wood, 1983, p. 7.
41. Chadwick, 1970, p. 25; McWhiney, 1988, p. xxiv.

42. Corcoran, 1970, p. 25; Chadwick, 1970, p. 37.
43. Cunliffe, 1979, p. 198.
44. Blethen and Wood, 1983, p. 20.
45. McWhiney, 1988, p. 9.
46. Fischer, 1989, pp. 613–634; McWhiney, 1988, p. xli.
47. McWhiney, 1988, esp. pp. xxxvii and xli.
48. McWhiney, 1988, pp. xli ff; Wyatt-Brown, 1982, p. 36.
49. Fitzpatrick, 1989, p. 71.
50. Blethen and Wood, 1983, p. 20.
51. Fischer, 1989, p. 765.
52. Fischer, 1989.

The American way of blame*

By Martin E. P. Seligman
APA President

In the last year there has been a cascade of multiple murders in school by American boys. In the 1950s there were none.

What changed, and do these changes give us some clues about how to end this nightmare?

The outer world of boys has, of course, changed, but their inner world has changed as well—in an astonishing and dismaying way. The outer changes are better known, but they bear repeating: easy access to guns, contagion fostered by the media and the waning of parental supervision.

The psychological changes are even more frightening. Traditional American child-rearing in individual responsibility has been replaced by a self-esteem movement. This movement tells parents and educators that their first duty is to make kids feel good about themselves. Kids are taught mantras like 'I am special,' and they believe them. Low self-esteem is seen as the cause of teen-age pregnancy, depression, suicide, drug abuse and violence, and so teaching self-esteem is supposed to be a vaccine.

A recipe for violence

Unfortunately it turns out that hit men, genocidal maniacs, gang leaders and violent kids often have high self-esteem, not low self-esteem. A recipe for their violence is a mean streak combined with an unwarranted sense of self-worth. When such a boy comes across a girl or parents or schoolmates who communicate to him that he is not all that worthy, he lashes out.

To top it off, our kids are imbued with victimology, which today has become the American way of blame. It is too routine for adults and their kids to explain all their problems as victimization. When a boy in trouble sees himself as a victim, this festers into seething anger. With easy availability of guns, it can explode as murder.

The tabloid reporting of mass murder feeds into this state of the child's mind and so is contagious. Murder is reported on the front page and leads the nightly news in gory color and audible sobbing. The airing of the shattered emotions of the victims' families and friends is only marginally newsworthy, yet it goes on for days, and has a galvanizing effect on the potential copycat.

All this occurs against a background of kids watching several hours of TV daily with about one murder per hour. When killing becomes routine entertainment, the inhibitions against killing melt. For the child who feels victimized by other kids and his parents and his schoolteachers, being able to fantasize so concretely about wreaking this vengeance is empowering and delicious. These outer and inner changes suggest a short-term stop gap and long-term solution. Every secondary school should consider installing metal detectors right away. When a weapon is found on any student, the right move is not just to expel, but to talk. A psychologist may be able to see the difference between a schoolyard bully and a potential killer.

What's required to stop it

In the long run, we need much more than metal detectors. There are more competent experts than I am to spell out how to limit access to guns, how to change the reporting of mass murder and how to persuade parents to spend more time with their kids. What I believe needs changing is the way kids think about their troubles. Baseless self-esteem is easily shattered by the usual setbacks of growing up; when, in a boy with a mean streak, it combines with blaming parents, peers and the schools—blaming anyone but himself—it can become violent. We need to teach our children warranted self-esteem and realistic optimism—based on the skills of doing well in the world, on doing well with others and on personal responsibility. These research-based programs improve the ways that all kids think about their troubles, manage emotions, solve problems and communicate with others. But when it comes to aggression, counseling—which focuses only on the child—has limits. Programs involving the family and the school do much better. Whole communities suffer the consequences of schoolyard violence, and whole communities are required to stop it.

---

*See also articles 34 and 35 in this *Annual Editions: Social Psychology.*

Aggression and self-esteem

By Ervin Staub, PhD
University of Massachusetts at Amherst

The following opinion piece is in response to "The American way of blame,"* the July "Presidents column" by Martin E. P. Seligman. To read that column, visit www.apa.org/monitor/jul98/pc.html.

The traditional view of the relationship between self-esteem and aggression has been that low self-esteem gives rise to aggression. In his column, Martin E. P. Seligman proposed that it is high self-esteem that is related to aggression. There is increasing information on this issue and challenging the traditional view has been valuable. I will offer some considerations, however, to suggest that this relationship is quite complex and, as yet, far from clear. I will focus on children, because one purpose of Seligman's column was to question the value of programs that promote high-self-esteem in children.

Dan Olweus found that bullies do not have low self-esteem. John Coie and Kenneth Dodge, in reviewing research on aggression in children, reported that aggressive boys do not have low self-concepts and tend to blame others rather than themselves for "negative outcomes."

Several avenues may lead children, specifically boys, to become aggressive. Some boys are effective in getting what they want through aggression. It is possible that they have become aggressive through parental permissiveness, which is related to aggression, and possibly parental encouragement to be tough and aggressive.

More common are boys who are ineffectual aggressors, who in addition to being aggressive are angry, argumentative and disruptive. They tend to be rejected by peers but are unaware of this. Not knowing that they are rejected makes it difficult for them to improve their peer relations. Over time, they become more aggressive and less effective in conventional realms, such as school.

It seems likely that the origins of these boys' aggression is harsh, punitive parenting, the most researched avenue to aggressiveness. Its results include poor social skills, deficiency in academic work and poor performance in school. Aggressive boys see other people as hostile, especially to themselves. They respond to hostility they perceive or imagine by aggressive actions, which creates hostility to them.

On the face of it, it does not make good psychological sense that these children (and adults) would have high self-esteem. It is possible that some aggressive boys do have low self-esteem. Earlier research suggested such a relationship and in a dissertation I supervised, Andrew Theiss found that in college students low self-esteem was associated with greater self-reported agression in response to provocation. Other aggressive boys are defensive and fulfill the need for seeing themselves in a good light by having a "compensatory" self-esteem. Aggressive boys blaming others for negative outcomes, which is consistent with the Freudian view of projection of one's own problemamatic characteristics into others, supports the notion of some kind of defensive process. Since self-report and even inference from observation are far from foolproof, they may fake a high self-esteem.

But perhaps the answer lies not simply in level of self-esteem, but what self-esteem is based on. Children and youth will strive to gain a positive image of themselves. Many boys who become aggressive don't have the socially valued means to gain such a positive image: competence and good performance in school, good relations with peers. They organize their self-esteem, therefore, around strength, power, physical superiority over others. Their early experiences as victims, the models of aggression around them, and the culture's focus on male strength and superiority all facilitate this. It is how self-esteem is constituted, what self-esteem is based on, that may matter.

But the self-esteem of aggressive boys appears to be very vulnerable, fragile. Its maintenance requires specific circumstances and behaviors on their part. This again raises the question whether we can consider it a genuinely positive self-esteem. It is also maintained in ways that creates continuous trouble for them.

Their inadequacy in realms that tend to be the socially valued sources of esteem may continue to frustrate them. Because they have not gotten enough respect in their lives, respect becomes especially important. They try to gain identity and self-respect by congregating with other kids like themselves, whether in the classroom or as members of gangs. Gang culture, which focuses on respect and on

boosting the self-esteem of members, helps to elevate their self-esteem. It is worth noting, however, that frequently self-esteem, whether high or low, may have no causal relationship to aggression. Instead, mistrust, perceptions of others' bad intentions and the feelings these generate and other factors have causal influence.

Would programs that attempt to directly raise the self-esteem of the kind of boys I focused on reduce or increase their aggressiveness? It would increase it if they come to feel more entitled and then in turn frustrated. It would reduce it if they come feel respected and cared about without having to show strength and power. Research on resilience shows the importance of children's connection to caring adults-teachers, counselors or friends of the family.

Neither self-esteem, nor established patterns of aggression can truly be changed without experiences that a.) make the world seem safer—partly by connection to caring, benevolent people—and b.) create greater self-awareness and awareness of other people and help aggressive children learn to effectively fulfill their needs and goals in constructive ways.

---

*Editor's Note: See article 33 of this *Annual Editions: Social Psychology;* also see article 35.

Ervin Staub, professor of psychology at the University of Massachusetts at Amherst, has studied helping and altruism, youth violence, and the origins and prevention of genocide and ethnopolitical conflict.

COUNTERPOINT

Low self-esteem does not cause aggression

By Roy F. Baumeister, PhD
Case Western Reserve University

Martin E. P. Seligman and Ervin Staub* have offered different views about the relation of self-esteem to aggression. I would like to offer my own hard-won views about this issue. I have devoted much of my career to studying self-esteem, partly because I shared the optimistic hope that it would hold the key to solving many social and individual problems in modern society, including aggression. Regrettably, the data have convinced me that those hopes were largely misplaced. High self-esteem helps people feel good but its ability to produce beneficial outcomes is small to negligible.

Seligman is correct to attack the view that low self-esteem causes aggression. In my own work, an extensive literature review (*Psychological Review*, 1996) and laboratory experiments (*Journal of Personality and Social Psychology*, 1998) have contradicted it More generally, people with low self-esteem tend to be shy, modest, self-effacing, reluctant to take risks, unsure about themselves and likely to blame themselves for failure. Aggressive, violent people are not like that.

On the contrary, we have found that aggressive people have very favorable views of themselves. But, as Staub suggests, the relationship is complex. High self-esteem is a heterogeneous category that contains violent and nonviolent, nonaggressive people. The aggressive subset of people with high self-esteem is narcissistic: They regard themselves as superior to others, think they deserve special treatment and privileges, and are emotionally invested in being admired by others. They turn aggressive toward anyone who questions their inflated opinions of themselves.

What about hidden low self-esteem? Staub suggests that some people act confident but secretly suffer from self-loathing, and that aggression could derive from that low self-esteem. There are two arguments against this view. First, several researchers (including Olweus on bullies) have failed to find the hidden self- loathing behind the narcissistic or egotistical front. They conclude that aggressors do not typically have low self-esteem.

Second, the view is ultimately illogical. Suppose someone were able to show that aggressors have egotistical surface veneers but secret, hidden low self-esteem. What would the cause of aggression be? We know that overt low self-esteem doesn't cause violence. Hence the crucial factor would be the fact of being hidden. But that means to shift attention away from the low self-esteem itself and on to what is hiding it—which returns us to the narcissistic, egotistical veneer. Moreover, the therapeutic intervention to prevent violence would then focus not on altering the low self-esteem but on making it overt instead of hidden, because overt low self-esteem is nonviolent.

Staub is right to say we must consider what self-esteem is based on— but that line of thought leads back to supporting Seligman's call to dismantle the school self-esteem movement. All too often, this movement takes the form of uncritical self-celebration as an entitlement of being a human being, instead of applauding hard-earned achievements. Awarding trophies to all contestants or "socially promoting" students who haven't learned the material is not conducive to well-founded self-esteem. In fact, these practices may cultivate inflated views of self and entitlements, which

 From *APA Monitor*, January 1999.

constitute the dangerous form of high self-esteem. I see nothing wrong with praising a child (or adult) for an outstanding or brilliant performance. I see plenty wrong with praising everyone even when the actual achievements are mediocre.

Can anyone benefit from self-esteem boosting, in school or therapy? Sure. Some people genuinely fail to recognize their abilities and achievements and might short-change themselves. But these are a small minority. Many research findings show that most Americans already hold inflated opinions of themselves.

My profound disappointment with the benefits of self-esteem has been partly offset by discovering something else that does seem to work. Self-control, as in being able to regulate one's emotions, impulses, performance patterns and thoughts, has plenty of positive payoff, for the individual and society. Self-control problems are central to most problems in our society: teen pregnancy, drug abuse, violence, school failure, unsafe sex, alcohol abuse, money problems and debt, eating disorders, ill health, and more. My conclusion, therefore, echoes Seligman's call to discontinue schools' self-esteem programs. Instead of dismantling them altogether, though, I suggest we focus them on instilling the capacity to control, discipline and regulate oneself. Ironically, in the long run, that approach will even probably do better for self-esteem. Self-control permits the individual to discipline the self to achieve goals and to fulfill social and personal obligations. That creates a stronger basis for self-esteem than indiscriminate flattery.

---

*Editor's Note: See also articles 33 and 34 of this *Annual Editions: Social Psychology* for the articles by Martin E. P. Seligman and Erwin Staub.

Roy F. Baumeister holds the E.B. Smith Professorship in the Liberal Arts at Case Western Reserve University. His recent books include "Evil: Inside Human Violence and Cruelty" (Freeman, 1997), "Losing Control: How and Why People Fail at Self-Regulation" (Academic, 1994) and "Self-Esteem: the Puzzle of Low Self-Regard" (Plenum, 1993).

ANATOMY OF A

Violent

RELATIONSHIP

By Neil S. Jacobson, Ph.D., and John M. Gottman, Ph.D.

Each year at least 1.6 million
U.S. women are beaten by their husbands

Yet we know surprisingly little about why so many men erupt into violence, and why they feel such a need to control their women with brutal behavior.

Here, two leading marriage researchers plunge into the red-hot core of domestic abuse—observing violent couples in the heat of conflict—and surface with some startling answers.

Don was having a miserable day. There were rumors of layoffs at work, and his supervisor had been on his case for coming in late. Not only was he sick of not getting credit for doing his work well, he was sure he was about to get caught in some kind of vise he could not control. Now Don was test-driving the car he had asked his wife, Martha, to pick up from the garage. As he listened to his car's motor, he knew instantly that she had been hoodwinked. That damn rattle was still there when he drove up hills! By the time he pulled into their driveway, he was so mad that he almost hit Martha's car.

"What is it with you?" Don railed as he walked into the house. "Couldn't you tell that the damn car still wasn't running right?"

Martha, who was cooking dinner, responded calmly. "Is something wrong with the car? It sounded fine to me."

"Couldn't you tell you'd been had by the garage mechanics? Are you really that stupid?" he continued.

Martha started defending herself. "Wait a minute. I may know nothing about cars, but I resent being called 'stupid.'"

From *Psychology Today*, March/April 1998, pp. 60–65, 81, 84. Excerpted from *When Men Batter Women: New Insights into Ending Abusive Relationships*. Reprinted with the permission of Simon & Schuster. © 1998 by Neil Jacobson and John Gottman.

Don continued railing against the mechanics and against Martha for not standing up to them. He was beginning to see red, and he warned her to shut up.

But Martha didn't shut up. "If you're such a big man, why didn't you stand up to the mechanics the last time they gypped you?"

Don punched Martha in the face—hard. It was not the first punch of their marriage. But she deserved it, he told himself as he continued to hit her and yell at her. All he had wanted, he said, was a little empathy about his problems—and here she was siding with the enemy. Only a small part of him, a dim whisper in his brain, wanted to beg her forgiveness, and by the next day he would manage to squelch even that dim light of remorse.

How does a marital argument like this, one that seems to start out in near-ordinary frustration, escalate so quickly into violence? This question had come up time and again in our work as creators of couples-therapy techniques and in our two decades as social scientists studying marriage. We knew that the existing studies of the dynamics of battering didn't provide

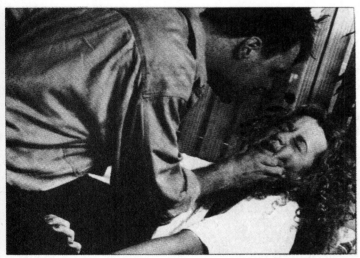

Esbin-Anderson/The Image Works

adequate answers, because they relied on after-the-fact reports by batterers and their victims, reports which are often biased and easily distorted. Particularly with battering, abundant psychological research shows that people are simply not reliable observers of their own or their intimate partner's behavior. So we decided to do something that no one had ever done before—directly observe the arguments of violent couples ourselves.

Using a simple public service announcement asking for couples experiencing marital conflict, we were able to obtain a sample of 63 battering couples, as well as a control group of couples who were equally dissatisfied with their marriage but had no history of violence. All these volunteers agreed to come into the laboratory, have electrodes hooked up to their bodies to record heart rate

and other vital signs, and be videotaped in the midst of arguments. (We also provided important safeguards, including exit interviews to ensure the woman's safety, and referrals to battered women's shelters.)

As you'll see, in the eight years of this study we made a number of myth-shattering discoveries:

- Batterers share a common profile: they are unpredictable, unable to be influenced by their wives, and impossible to prevent from battering once an argument has begun.
- Battered women are neither passive nor submissive; sometimes they are as angry as the batterers. But women almost never batter men.
- Batterers can be classified into two distinct types, men whose temper slowly simmers until it suddenly erupts into violence, and those who strike out immediately. This difference has important implications for women leaving abusive relationships.
- Emotional abuse plays a vital role in battering, undermining a woman's confidence.
- Domestic violence can decrease on its own—but it almost never stops.
- Battered women do leave at high rates, despite the increased danger they face when leaving the relationship.

Battering's Beginnings

Battering is physical aggression with a purpose: to control, intimidate, and subjugate another human being. It is always accompanied by emotional abuse, often involves injury, and virtually always causes fear in the battered woman. In our study, battering couples had at least two episodes of kicking or hitting with a fist, or at least one incident of potentially lethal violence, such as strangling.

Can women ever be batterers? In our study, we found that some battered women defend themselves, and hit or push as often as their husbands do. Some people claim that there is a huge underground movement of battered husbands. However, statistics on violent women do not take into account the impact and function of the violence. According to research conducted by Dina Vivian, Ph.D., at the State University of New York at Stonybrook, women are much more likely to be injured and in need of medical care than men, and much more likely to be killed by their husbands than the reverse. Women are the ones who are beaten up. These injuries help to sustain the fear, which is the force that provides battering with its power.

What about couples who periodically have arguments that escalate into pushing and shoving, but not beyond? We discovered large numbers of these couples, and we found that the husbands almost never become batterers.

While it is important to know about this low-level violence, we were concerned with the dynamics of severely violent couples.

Arguments under The Microscope

Through our research, we were able to reconstruct hundreds of violent arguments. Although we knew we would not directly observe violence between our subjects, we could observe their nonviolent arguments in the laboratory, ask them about these encounters, then judge their accounts of violent arguments by the accuracy of these reports.

When we put violent arguments under a microscope this way, we discovered a number of familiar themes. One of the most startling was our inability to predict when batterers would cross over into violence. While emotional abuse often preceded physical abuse, it was such a common occurrence in the relationship that it did not serve as an accurate warning sign. Further, there was no way for the battered woman to control when emotional abuse would turn into physical abuse. Martha could have shut up when Don told her to. But would this have stopped Don from hitting her? We have discovered that once an episode starts, there is nothing that the woman can do to affect its course.

Despite this inability, the women in our study did not become passive or submissive. Even when the batterers reacted to everyday requests with emotional abuse, the women typically responded calmly and assertively. We found that they wanted to inject as much normalcy into their lives as possible, and they didn't want to give up on their dream of the family life that they wanted.

However, in all the videotapes we made, never did we hear a batterer say anything like, "That's a good point," or "I never thought of that,"—comments that most married men (and women) say all the time during an argument. Instead, we observed that batterers became more aggressive when their wives asserted themselves. When Martha challenged him, we saw that Don responded violently in an attempt to maintain his dominance, no matter what the costs.

Another way that batterer's arguments diverged from those of nonviolent couples—perhaps the key difference—is that nonviolent couples have what we call "a withdrawal ritual," where at some point the escalation process stops or reverses itself. Some couples take breaks, other couples compromise, still others do both. In battering couples, the women are typically quite willing to stop at a point where they start to sense danger, but once the husbands are "activated," violence follows. Although the violence is unpredictable, we were able to identify certain warning signs. When belligerence and contempt during an argument were combined with attempts to squelch, control, or dominate a wife's behavior, that was

a sign that a batterer was close to crossing the line. Don's contemptuous way of asking Martha whether she was "really that stupid," and his attempt to dominate her by telling her to shut up, demonstrate a classic prelude to battering.

Surprisingly, both in the lab and at home, battered women expressed as much belligerence and contempt as their husbands did. Like most people, battered women get angry when they are insulted and degraded. We saw much effort on the part of the women to contain their anger, but it tended to leak out anyway. Nevertheless, their initial responses—like Martha's retort to Don about not standing up to the mechanics—could hardly be considered provocations to violence.

The Slow Burn: "Pit Bulls"

Men like Don metabolize anger in a kind of slow burn: it gradually increases but never lets up. We call them "Pit Bulls" because they grow more and more aggressive until they finally attack. These men, we have found, constitute about 80 percent of batterers.

Pit Bulls have unrelenting contempt for women, and yet are extremely dependent on them. This creates a unique dynamic in their behavior. In many unhappy marriages, when one partner (usually the woman) requests change, the other one (usually the man) resists change, and eventually the woman's requests become demands, and the man's avoidance becomes withdrawal. But Pit Bulls often both demand and withdraw. We can see this in the incessant demands that Don made of Martha. Everything she did (including getting the car fixed) was wrong because nothing she did was quite enough for Don. Martha had to watch every move she made, give up her friends and family, account for all of her time, avoid Don's jealousy, and try to satisfy what he called his "simple need for a little empathy." Yet even as she walked on eggshells, she was attacked for being a "stupid bitch." Don blamed Martha for his own neediness, and punished her for it almost every day they were together.

Through this scrutiny and these constant demands, Pit Bulls establish control. Control is important to these men because they genuinely feel that they will be abandoned if they do not maintain constant vigilance over their wives. One particularly sinister form of control they use is known as "gaslighting." This technique—which gets its name from the film *Gaslight*, in which Charles Boyer convinces Ingrid Bergman she is going insane—involves a systematic denial of the wife's experience of reality. For example, when one of our subjects slapped his wife in front of a neighbor, he denied that he had done it, telling her that this kind of behavior was inconsistent with his personality, and that her accusations of abuse came from

Can Batterers JUST STOP?

"Why do women stay?" That question haunts anybody who has observed domestic violence. But a far more practical question is, How can the men be stopped? Maryland psychologist Steven Stosny, Ph.D., has developed a remarkable and effective treatment program for battering men. Even a year after treatment, an astonishing 86 percent have ended the physical abuse, and 73 percent have stopped the verbal and emotional abuse. The national dropout rate for battering programs is one out of two; Stosny's is only one out of four.

Treating batterers is something that most therapists shy away from. How did you get into it?

I became interested in spouse and child abuse at the age of two. I grew up in a violent family, where we had police and ambulances coming to the door. It took a while for me to get up the courage to get into this field, and when I started a group with severe batterers, I wanted to learn how they got that way, to learn how to prevent abuse. I was surprised when they stopped being abusive.

So how do you approach batterers?

Our program is based on the idea that most batterers can't sustain attachment, and because of this, they become flooded with feelings of guilt, shame, and abandonment, which they regulate with aggression. We teach them a five-step technique called HEALS. First, we start with the concept of *Heal*. Our clients learn that blame is powerless, but compassion is true power, and has the ability to heal. Next, you *Explain* to yourself the core hurt that anger is masking: feeling unimportant, disregarded, guilty, devalued, rejected, powerless, and unlovable. All abusive behavior is motivated by these core hurts. Then you *Apply* self-compassion. Let's say your wife calls you a brainless twit, and you feel she doesn't love you. You want to punish her for reminding you that you're unlovable. We teach men to replace this core feeling with self-compassion. "She feels unloving, but she still loves me. My instinct might be to call her a filthy slut, but she said what she said because she's hurt and feeling bad." Then you move into a feeling of *Love*, for yourself and your wife. And finally, you solve the problem by presenting your true position without blaming or attacking the other person: you say, "I care about you, but I have a problem with your calling me a brainless twit." You are healing your core hurt through love rather than anger.

So you're saying the batterer is really trying to heal his hurt core, and he can do it with compassion instead of abuse. Still, how can someone used to physical aggression learn to be so rational?

We call it teaching Mr. Hyde to remember what Dr. Jekyll learned. These men have to learn emotional regulation and the rewards of change based on compassion. We ask them to remember an incident that made them angry, to feel the anger again, and follow the steps of HEALS 12 times a day for four weeks. It almost works like a vaccination. You feel the core hurt for five seconds at a time when you practice, and you develop an immunity to it.

Why is your dropout rate so low?

It's a 12-week program, and if they don't do their homework, they go to jail. We have surprisingly little resistance. I also say "If you don't feel much better about yourself, we'll give you your money back. You'll like yourself better when you're compassionate." I've treated over 1200 abusers in my career, and even the antisocial ones—no matter how justified they felt at the time—never felt proud of hurting someone they loved. Our group is about becoming proud.

Does this work even for the true sociopaths, the ones Jacobson and Gottman call Cobras?

These people are not afraid of the criminal justice system and they don't usually come to treatment. Most people in treatment are different. They're the dependent personalities who only hurt ones they love, and who get over-involved in the relationship. If sociopaths and people with antisocial personality disorders do come into treatment, they don't learn compassion. But they do learn to use emotional regulation techniques to keep from getting upset. Some of them use this as another form of superiority—you're going to get hysterical and I'm not—but it's better than beating up their wives in front of the children. It's a form of harm reduction.

Why does this work better than traditional treatment?

Most treatment programs focus on how men's domination causes domestic violence. We say that the real gender variable is that culture doesn't teach men to regulate their negative emotions, or sustain trust, compassion, and love. Numerous studies have shown that. We socialize girls and women to have an emotional vocabulary, and this has nothing to do with education level. We look into the eyes of little girls and reward them when they cry or express other emotions, but when a little boy expresses emotions, we call him a sissy. Boys are taught to keep vulnerable emotions submerged, and don't develop an emotional vocabulary.

And if you can't tell sadness from loneliness from disappointment from rejection from being devalued, the bad feelings get overloaded easily. The strongest emotion is anger.

What about the women? Do you counsel them at all?

We put the safety of the victim first. We say, "We're sure you're not going to be abused any more, but it's very unlikely you'll have a good relationship with your abuser." We tell the women that there's more to life than not being abused. And we have a higher separation rate than the average. While 75 percent of women and children in shelters go back to their husbands, out of 379 couples to go through our program so far, 46 percent of them have left their spouses.

How do you treat substance abusers?

We conduct our treatment simultaneously with substance abuse treatment. Even though this hurts our treatment outcomes—98 percent of our recidivism is from alcohol and drugs—it's important because the nervous system bounce makes a person more irritable when coming off a drug, and I prefer they have some skills first.

Roland Maiuro, Ph.D., of the University of Washington, has been conducting a controlled study using the antidepressant Paxil to treat abusers. Maiuro found that abusers has consistently low serotonin levels, which were perhaps rendered even lower by their negative patterns of behavior. Have you seen Prozac-like drugs work with batterers?

I always tell abusers to try antidepressants. Anything that increases serotonin will reduce shame. And shame causes anger and aggression. I'll bet money that when studies like Maiuro's come out, we will see a significant reduction in violence. The problem is getting them to take it.

They'll take any illicit drug, but they won't take Prozac. But Prozac and HEALS will work best. It may even get the sociopaths.

How can we prevent domestic violence from happening in the first place?

If you treat it in the early stages you can prevent murders from happening. But you can't do this with a gender war. Community meetings against domestic violence have one or two men, and few minorities. Saying you're against domestic violence scares off people, and attracts the ones who really believe in the battle of the sexes. By demonizing the batterer, it makes him more isolated.

But if we make community organization about being for the creation of safe and secure families, they will have a much broader appeal.

her own disturbed mind. Although her face still hurt from the slap, she thought to herself that maybe she had made it all up. The neighbor, a friend of the husband's, went along and said he didn't see anything.

This technique of denying the woman's reality can be so effective that, when used in combination with methods to isolate the woman from other people, it causes battered women to doubt their own sanity. This is the ultimate form of abuse: to gain control of the victim's mind.

Lightning Strikes: "Cobras"

When Don and Martha started arguing, Don's heart rate would go up, he would sweat, and he'd exhibit other signs of emotional arousal. Most people show this response. However, we were astonished to find that as some batterers become more verbally aggressive, there is a decrease in heart rate. Like the cobra who becomes still and focused before striking its victim at over 100 miles an hour, these men calm themselves internally and focus their attention while striking swiftly at their wives with vicious verbal aggression.

When we separated these calm batterers from those who became internally aroused, we found other profound differences between the two groups. These "Cobras"—who constituted about 20 percent of our sample—were more likely to have used or threatened to use a knife or a gun on their wives, and were more severely violent than the other batterers. Only three percent of Pit Bulls had a history of extramarital violence, while 44 percent of Cobras did. And while about 33 percent of Pit Bills qualified for a diagnosis of "antisocial personality disorder"—which includes a long history of impulsive criminal behavior, childhood episodes of lying, stealing, fire setting, and cruelty to animals—fully 90 percent of the Cobras met the criteria. Finally, even though both groups abused alcohol at high rates, Cobras were more likely to be dependent on illegal drugs, such as cocaine and heroin, and were much less emotionally attached to their wives.

George was a typical Cobra. In the year prior to entering our research project, George had threatened to kill Vicky numerous times. One night several weeks before coming to see us, George came home late after he'd been out drinking and found Vicky and their two year-old daughter Christi sharing a pizza. Vicky was angry with him for missing dinner, and ignored him when he arrived. Her silence angered him, and he shouted, "You got a problem?" When she remained silent, he slammed his fist into the pizza, knocked her off the chair, dragged her across the room by her hair, held her down, and spat pizza in her face. He then beat her up, yelling, "You've ruined my life!"

The contrast between this incident and the altercation between Don and Martha over the car shows how Cobras are far more emotionally aggressive towards their wives at the start of their arguments than Pit Bulls. While Don became increasingly heated and less controlled over the course of the argument, George escalated the situation extremely rapidly, using both physical and verbal abuse in the service of control, intimidation, and subjugation. He was in Vicky's face twice as fast as she ever expected. This quick response is typical of the way Cobras control their wives—a tactic which they use because it often quiets the partner quickly and with minimal effort.

Another main difference between Cobras and Pit Bulls is that Cobras come from more chaotic family backgrounds. In our study, 78 percent of the Cobras came from violent families, compared to 51 percent of Pit Bulls. (In the population at large, 20 to 25 percent of children grow up in violent homes.) George's childhood was a classic example. He was beaten and neglected by both parents, and sexually abused by his prostitute mother's male customers. Like other Cobras, he came from a background that seriously crushed the implicit trust that every child has in his or her parents. This horrible childhood background, we believe, had somehow led the Cobras to vow to themselves that no one would ever control them again.

MEN CAN CHANGE

An astonishing 54 percent of our male volunteers showed decreases in violence during the second of two follow-up years. In fact, some men no longer met our standards for being included in our violent group. But

> **Batterers subscribe to an "honor code" that makes them unable to accept any influence—no matter how gentle—from women.**

this decrease in violence may be misleading. Once control is established over a woman through battering, perhaps it can be maintained by continued emotional abuse with intermittent battering used as a terrifying reminder of what is possible in the marriage. Cobras' violence was so severe that it may have been easier for them than for the Pit Bulls to maintain control through emotional abuse alone. Still, only seven percent of batterers in our study stopped their violence altogether in the two-year follow-up period.

We did observe several examples of husbands stopping the violence when it was unsuccessful in controlling their wives. George stopped beating Vicky as soon as she responded to his bullying with anger of her own.

WHEN WOMEN WON'T LEAVE

Three years after our two-year follow-up, we recontacted many of the battered women and their husbands. Despite the greater incidence of mental illness, drug addiction, emotional abuse, and severe violence in Cobra relationships, the typical pattern among the Cobra couples was for the wives to be committed to the marriages. While almost half of Pit Bull marriages dissolved within two years, by the five-year follow-up point, only 25 percent of women married to Cobras had left them; these women not only recognized the danger of trying to leave them, but often were quite attached to them.

Why would a woman be attached to a man as dangerous as George? Surprisingly, Vicky—like 80 percent of women married to Cobras—tested normal on our personality scales. However, she described her childhood as a "war zone" where her father would one day be absent and disengaged, and then suddenly become physically abusive toward Vicky's mother and all of the kids. She ran away from home to find a better life. And when she became pregnant by George, she tried to build her dream life. With her dashing new husband, she would finally have the home she had always wanted.

But when Vicky realized her dream of a normal, non-abusive relationship would never come to pass with George, she made the decision to leave. With Vicky and other battered women, "giving up the dream" was a pivotal step in shifting from fear to contempt and a determination to leave. Battered women need to be helped to "give up the dream" sooner, and this process should occur in conjunction with a careful safety plan and the support of an experienced helper.

Once Vicky implemented her safety plan, which included restraining orders against George and notifying his employer, the Navy, she found that George lost interest in her and went on to new pursuits. We found that Cobras will not pursue women who leave them unless it is easy and causes them little hassle to do so. But there are exceptions, and this is where help from an expert is essential.

Pit Bulls are the opposite of Cobras: easier to leave in the short run, but harder to leave in the long run. When Martha left Don and called it a trial separation, Don had little problem with it. But when she continued the separation for more than a month, he began to abuse and stalk her.

After three years of this, Martha consistently and forcefully asserted her rights. She divorced him. She hung up on him. She ended a definitive conversation with a "F___ you!" and refused to talk to him. Don might have killed her at this time. Pit Bulls have a great capacity to minimize, deny, or distort reality, and they can often justify to themselves stalking, continued abuse, and at times even murder. But Martha got lucky. Don began to leave her alone when it was clear that she would no longer be responsive to his threats. By that time, she had decided that even death was preferable to being under Don's spell.

EMERGING FROM HELL

We began this study with the goal of learning about the relationship between batterers and battered women, and we learned a great deal. We expected to focus on the men, especially when we came upon the distinction between Pit Bulls and Cobras. But during our exit interviews, we found the women in our study to be resourceful and courageous, and over time we began to realize that our work was also about the heroic struggle of battered women. These women start with a dream and truly descend into hell, and for a period of time seem stuck there. But they do not give up. They continue to struggle. Our main cause for optimism is that many of them emerge from hell and live to love again.

Unit 8

Key Points to Consider

❖ What kind of motivations lead people to volunteer their time and energy to help others? Would you call these motivations "egoistic" or "altruistic"? What factors seem to be especially important in determining whether people continue their volunteering or not? How do the results of the research in "The Effects of 'Mandatory Volunteerism' on Intentions to Volunteer" relate to this issue of people's motivation for helping?

❖ Do you agree with Robert Levine's findings regarding the relationship between city size and helpfulness? Why do you think that citizens of smaller towns were more helpful? Would similar results have been obtained if the helping opportunity was a true emergency, as in the bystander intervention research?

 **Links** www.dushkin.com/online/

These sites are annotated on pages 4 and 5.

Early in the semester, you volunteer to participate in a psychology experiment being conducted at your school. When you arrive at the appointed time and place you are greeted by the experimenter, who explains that the research project requires you to complete a series of questionnaires measuring different aspects of your personality. The experimenter gives you the questionnaires and then returns to his office for the 30 minutes it will take you to complete them. After 5 minutes or so, you hear a loud crash in the hallway, and then you hear what sounds like a person groaning softly. What do you do?

Most of us have a very clear idea about what we would do—we would leave the room, look for the person who apparently fell, and try to help him or her. And sure enough, when research like this is conducted, that is what happens . . . some of the time. When students are alone in the room when the crash occurs, they are quite likely to help, just as we might expect. When several students are in the room together, however, they are less likely to help; in fact, the more people in the room, the less helping occurs. Thus, there is something about being in a group of people that makes us less likely to respond to the needs of another during an emergency. Strange.

Strange it may be, but research like this is one example of the kind of work that is done by social psychologists who study helping behavior. This particular kind of experiment is an attempt to understand a phenomenon known as "bystander intervention"—when bystanders actively get involved during an emergency to try to help the victim. Research has consistently demonstrated that having a large number of bystanders can actually reduce the amount of aid that is given, in part because each person takes less and less responsibility for helping the victim.

Other approaches to helping have tried to uncover the different kinds of motivations that lead people to help. Some people seem to help, for example, because they have a strong sense of obligation to care for others who are in need; this sense of obligation is often created early in life. Sometimes people help in order to reduce the level of arousing distress they feel when they see a victim; thus, helping the other person actually serves to help oneself as well. Helping that also provides a benefit to the helper is usually termed "egoistic" helping. There is also evidence that sometimes people help simply for the goal of easing another's burden, and they are not doing so to achieve personal gain. Helping of this kind is usually referred to as "altruistic" helping, because its ultimate goal is to benefit another.

In the first selection in this unit, "Volunteerism and Society's Response to the HIV Epidemic," psychologists Mark Snyder and Allen Omoto focus on a particular form of helping: volunteerism. Each year millions of people donate their time and energy to their communities in some way, and in this selection

the authors consider the various motives that can lead people to volunteer, and the motives that can lead them to continue volunteering over the long haul.

"Cities with Heart" approaches the question of helping in an interesting way: by surreptitiously studying the helping behavior of people living in 36 different U.S. cities to see if they differed in their willingness to help a stranger. In general, people in the largest cities helped the least, and this article considers some of the possible reasons for this, including stress levels and feelings of community.

In "Cause of Death: Uncertain(ty)," Robert Cialdini discusses the theory mentioned at the beginning of this overview—the bystander intervention model. He describes the model itself, what led to its initial formulation, and how it has been tested. He also provides some very specific, practical advice about how to ensure that you can get help during an emergency.

Finally, in "The Effects of 'Mandatory Volunteerism' on Intentions to Volunteer," the authors examine a fairly recent phenomenon: schools requiring students to perform a certain amount of volunteer work as part of their studies. Their research suggests the interesting conclusion that at least some of the time such mandatory helping actually reduces the likelihood that the students will offer such help in the future.

Volunteerism and Society's Response to the HIV Epidemic

Mark Snyder and Allen M. Omoto

Mark Snyder is Professor of Psychology at the University of Minnesota. **Allen M. Omoto** is Assistant Professor of Psychology at the University of Kansas. Address correspondence to Mark Snyder, Department of Psychology, University of Minnesota, 75 East River Road, Minneapolis, MN 55455-0344, or Allen M. Omoto, Department of Psychology, 426 Fraser Hall, University of Kansas, Lawrence, KS 66045-2160.

In 1981, the Centers for Disease Control reported the first case of what would come to be known as AIDS. Now, barely a decade later, there are over 200,000 confirmed cases of AIDS in the United States and an estimated 1.5 million Americans infected with HIV (the virus that causes AIDS). The World Health Organization projects that, by the year 2000, 30 to 40 million adults and children worldwide will have been infected with HIV, and most of them are expected to develop AIDS.[1] Clearly, with neither a vaccine nor a cure in sight, the full impact of AIDS, as devastating and profound as the epidemic has been, has yet to be felt, and will surely touch all of our lives.

Society has responded to the HIV epidemic on a number of fronts, including at least three for which the skills and expertise of psychologists, as scientists and practitioners, can be tapped: (a) providing psychological services for persons living with AIDS (PWAs), (b) developing behavior change campaigns to reduce the likelihood of HIV transmission, and (c) implementing public education programs to address matters of prejudice and discrimination associated with AIDS and PWAs.[2] In our research, we are examining a remarkable social phenomenon born of the HIV epidemic—AIDS volunteerism and its implications for each of these fronts.

A critical component of society's response has been the development of community-based grass-roots organizations of volunteers involved in caring for PWAs and in educating the public about HIV, AIDS, and PWAs. Volunteers fill many roles; some provide emotional and social support as "buddies" to PWAs, whereas others help PWAs with their household chores or transportation needs. Volunteers also staff information, counseling, and referral hotlines; make educational presentations; raise funds; and engage in social, legal, and political advocacy. In the United States, AIDS volunteer programs have emerged in every state, in cities large and small, and in rural areas as well. AIDS volunteerism is a compelling testimonial to human kindness and to the power of communities of "ordinary people" to unite and organize in response to extraordinary events.[3]

As remarkable as AIDS volunteerism is, it actually is part of a pervasive social phenomenon in American society. A recent Gallup Poll estimated that, in 1989, 98.4 million American adults engaged in some form of volunteerism, with 25.6 million giving 5 or more hours per week to volunteer work—volunteer services worth some $170 billion.[4] In addition to working on HIV-related issues, volunteers provide companionship to the elderly, health care to the sick, tutoring to the illiterate, counseling to the troubled, food to the hungry, and shelter to the homeless.

Although the study of helping has long been a mainstay of research in the psychological sciences, volunteerism is a form of prosocial action about which there is little systematic literature.[5] Volunteerism is, however, marked by several distinctive features. Volunteers typically seek out their opportunities to help, often deliberate long and hard about the form and the extent of their involvements, and may carefully consider how different volunteer opportunities fit with their own needs, goals, and motivations. Many forms of volunteerism also entail commitments to ongoing helping relationships that have considerable duration and require sizable personal costs in time, energy, and expense.

We view AIDS volunteerism not only as an intriguing social phenomenon, but also as paradigmatic of sustained and potentially costly helping behavior. In one survey,[6] we found that AIDS volunteers overwhelmingly had actively sought out their volunteer opportunities (over 80% indicated that they had approached their AIDS organizations on their own initiative). Moreover, their involvement represented a substantial and recurring time commitment (on average, 4 hr per week) that extended over a considerable length of time (1½ years on average, and often spanning several years). Finally, these volunteers were giving of themselves in trying and stressful circumstances (spending time with PWAs and confronting the tragic realities of serious illness and death) and doing so at some personal cost (with many reporting feeling stigmatized as a result of their AIDS work).

THREE STAGES OF THE VOLUNTEER PROCESS

In our research, we are seeking to understand the social and psychological aspects of volunteerism. Our research is grounded in a three-stage conceptual model of the *volunteer process,* a model that specifies psychological and behavioral features associated with each stage and speaks to activity at three levels of analysis: the individual volunteer, the organizational context, and the broader social system.[7]

The first stage of the volunteer process involves *antecedents* of volunteerism and addresses the questions "who volunteers?" and "why do they volunteer?" In the case of AIDS, considerations at the antecedents stage focus on the attitudes, values, and motivations that dispose people to serve as AIDS volunteers, as well as the needs and

From *Current Directions in Psychological Science,* August 1992, pp. 113–116. © 1992 by the American Psychological Society. Reprinted by permission of Blackwell Publishers.

goals that AIDS volunteer work may fulfill for individuals.

The second stage concerns *experiences* of volunteers and the dynamics of the helping relationships that develop between volunteers and the people with whom they work. In the specific case of AIDS, it is important to recognize that these relationships are carried out against the stressful backdrop of chronic illness and even death. Of additional concern are the effects of AIDS volunteers on the general treatment and coping processes of PWAs, as well as changes that occur in volunteers themselves.

The third stage focuses on *consequences* of volunteerism and is concerned with how volunteer work affects volunteers, members of their social networks, and society at large. For AIDS volunteers, it is possible that their work has not only beneficial effects on personal attitudes, knowledge, and behaviors, but also negative consequences of stigmatization and social censure. When it comes to societal issues, moreover, AIDS volunteerism may possess the potential for encouraging social change as volunteers transmit their new attitudes and behavior to their friends and associates and, by extension, to the broader social system.

BASIC RESEARCH AND PRACTICAL PROBLEMS

In our research, we are engaged in a coordinated program of cross-sectional and longitudinal field studies coupled with experiments conducted in the laboratory and sampling from diverse populations of volunteers and nonvolunteers. Thus, we have conducted a national survey of currently active AIDS volunteers, querying them about their motivations for volunteering, their experiences, and the consequences of their involvement in AIDS volunteerism, thereby generating cross-sectional data relevant to the three stages of the volunteer process. In an extended longitudinal study, we are also tracking new volunteers over the course of their service providing emotional support and living assistance to PWAs; in this long-term study, we are examining the same people at all stages of the volunteer process. Finally, we are conducting laboratory experiments and field intervention studies, each relevant to one or more stages of the volunteer process.

At each stage of our conceptual model, relevant psychological theories and the evidence of basic research are helping us to frame research questions, the answers to which, we hope, will have implications for addressing practical issues related to volunteerism, as well as

for building bridges between basic research and practical application. To illustrate the ways in which our research builds these bridges, let us examine two important practical matters that are rooted in different stages of the volunteer process and the theoretically informed answers to them derived from our program of research. Specifically, we examine issues of volunteer recruitment and retention.

The Recruitment of Volunteers

Recruitment is one of the key concerns at the antecedents stage. There are many formidable barriers that can keep prospective volunteers from getting involved; in the case of AIDS, not only are there limits of time and energy but also, for many people, fear of AIDS and death and concerns about stigmatization. What, then, motivates people to volunteer to staff an AIDS hotline or to be buddies for PWAs?

Guided by a functionally oriented theory of motivation (which proposes that apparently similar acts of volunteerism may reflect markedly different underlying motivations), we have been examining the motivations of AIDS volunteers. We have utilized exploratory and confirmatory factor analytic techniques in developing and validating a self-report inventory to assess five primary motivations for AIDS volunteerism, each one reliably measured by five different items.[8] The first set of motivations involves personal *values* (e.g., "because of my humanitarian obligation to help others"). The second set invokes considerations related to *understanding* (e.g., "to learn about how people cope with AIDS"). The third set taps *community concern* and reflects people's sense of obligation to or concern about a community or social grouping (e.g., "because of my concern and worry about the gay community"). The fourth set concerns *personal development* and centers on issues of personal growth (e.g., "to challenge myself and test my skills"). The fifth category assesses *esteem enhancement* and includes considerations about current voids or deficits in one's life (e.g., "to feel better about myself").[9]

The development of this motivational inventory has made possible a more thorough analysis of the psychology of AIDS volunteerism. This work has revealed that, despite what appears to be a commonality of purpose in being a volunteer, there is striking individual-to-individual variability in the motivations that are most and least important. An appreciation of different motivations, moreover, has great practical import for volunteer recruitment. Because vol-

unteering serves different psychological functions for different people, volunteer organizations would be well advised to tailor their recruitment messages to particular motivations of selected sets of potential volunteers. In recruiting volunteers who would be motivated by esteem enhancement, for instance, recruitment appeals could stress how AIDS volunteerism provides many opportunities for people to work through personal fears, anxieties, and doubts rather than, say, stressing humanitarian obligations and images of kindness (which could be used to appeal to prospective volunteers motivated by value-based concerns).

The Retention of Volunteers

Why do some volunteers continue to donate their time and services, and why do others stop? A persistent frustration in volunteer programs is the high rate of attrition (i.e., dropout) of volunteers. As difficult as it may be to recruit volunteers, it is sometimes even more difficult to ensure their continued service. Considerations of the experiences and consequences stages of the process may shed light on matters of attrition and longevity of service because the experiences associated with volunteer work and the consequences that result from it likely influence volunteers' effectiveness, their satisfaction, and the length of time they ultimately remain active. To examine some of these possibilities, we recontacted one set of AIDS volunteers a year after they had told us about their work. At that time, approximately one half of the original sample was still active with their AIDS organizations, and we proceeded to ask both quitters and stayers about their experiences as volunteers and the consequences of their work.[8]

We found no differences between the quitters and stayers in reported satisfaction with their service and commitment to the purposes of their AIDS organizations. Where quitters and stayers differed, however, was in their perceptions of the costs of their volunteer work. Despite having engaged in satisfying and rewarding volunteer work, quitters more than stayers said they felt that volunteering had taken up too much time and—an important point—caused them to feel embarrassed, uncomfortable, or stigmatized. The negative consequences and not the rewards of the work, then, distinguished quitters from volunteers who continued to serve.

Bringing our analysis full circle, we also found that initial motivations for volunteering were related to attrition and length of service. To the extent that people espoused esteem enhancement or personal development reasons for their work (rather than community concern, values, or understanding), they were likely to still be active volunteers at our 1-year follow-up; moreover, esteem enhancement and understanding motivations proved valuable as predictors of the total length of service of these volunteers. Thus, volunteer attrition seemed not to be associated with the relatively "self-less" or other-focused motivations, as one might expect, but with more "selfish" desires of feeling good about oneself and acquiring knowledge and skills. Good, and perhaps romanticized, intentions related to humanitarian concern simply may not be strong enough to sustain volunteers faced with the tough realities and personal costs of working with PWAs. Therefore, volunteer organizations, in combating attrition, may want to remind volunteers of the personal rewards of their work rather than underscoring how volunteer efforts benefit clients and society. Similarly, volunteers may be better prepared for their work by having the potential costs of volunteerism made explicit to them at the outset; in this way, volunteers could be "prepared for the worst" and thereby "inoculated" against the negative impact of the personal costs of their service.

CONCLUSIONS

To conclude, let us explicitly address a recurring theme in our research—the relation between basic research and practical problems. Our research is simultaneously basic and applied. As much as it informs applied concerns with the current and potential roles of volunteerism in society's response to AIDS, our work also speaks directly to theoretical concerns about the nature of helping relationships and, more generally, the dynamics of individual and collective action in response to societal needs. With a dual focus on applied and theoretical concerns, our program of research embodies the essential components of *action research,* in which basic and applied research mutually inform and enrich one another and, under optimal circumstances, basic research is advanced and effective social action is undertaken.[10]

It is said that a society is judged by how it responds in times of need. Clearly, the age of AIDS is a time of the greatest need. The HIV epidemic represents not only a medical crisis, but also a broader set of challenges to individuals and to society. Among these challenges are those to researchers in the social and behavioral sciences. By all accounts, the number of AIDS cases will only increase in the years ahead, and, as medical advances extend the life expectancy of

PWAs, more and more people will be living with AIDS and living *longer* with AIDS. As the HIV epidemic continues and intensifies, so too will the importance of contributions of theory-based research relevant to all facets of AIDS. Ultimately, when the history of the HIV epidemic is written, we hope that the psychological sciences will have proven themselves integral to society's collective response to AIDS.

Acknowledgments—This research and the preparation of this manuscript have been supported by grants from the American Foundation for AIDS Research (No. 000741-5 and 000961-7) and from the National Institute of Mental Health (No. 1 RO1 MH47673) to Mark Snyder and Allen M. Omoto. We thank the volunteers and staff of the Minnesota AIDS Project (Minneapolis, MN) and the Good Samaritan Project (Kansas City, MO) for their cooperation and participation in this research.

Notes

1. AIDS spreading faster than thought, *The Kansas City Star*, p. A-3 (February 12, 1992).

2. G.M. Herek and E.K. Glunt, An epidemic of stigma: Public reaction to AIDS, *American Psychologist, 43,* 886–891 (1988); S.F. Morin, AIDS: The challenge to psychology, *American Psychologist, 43,* 838–842 (1988).

3. P.S. Arno, The nonprofit sector's response to the AIDS epidemic: Community-based services in San Francisco, *American Journal of Public Health, 76,* 1325–1330 (1988); S.M. Chambré, The volunteer response to the AIDS epidemic in New York City: Implications for research on voluntarism, *Nonprofit and Voluntary Sector Quarterly, 20,* 267–287 (1991); J.A. Dumont, Volunteer visitors for patients with AIDS, *The Journal of Volunteer Administration, 8,* 3–8 (1989); P.M. Kayal, Gay AIDS voluntarism as political activity, *Nonprofit and Voluntary Sector Quarterly, 20,* 289–331 (1991); S.C. Ouellette Kobasa, AIDS and volunteer associations: Perspectives on social and individual change, *The Milbank Quarterly, 68* (S2), 280–294 (1990); D. Lopez and G.S. Getzel, Strategies for volunteers caring for persons with AIDS, *Social Casework, 68,* 47–53 (1987).

4. Independent Sector, *Giving and Volunteering in the United States* (Gallup Organization for Independent Sector, Washington, DC, 1990).

5. For perspectives on the literature on volunteerism, see S.M. Chambré, Kindling

points of light: Volunteering as public policy, *Nonprofit and Voluntary Sector Quarterly, 18,* 249–268 (1989); E.G. Clary and M. Snyder, A functional analysis of altruism and prosocial behavior: The case of volunteerism, *Review of Personality and Social Psychology, 12,* 119–148 (1991); J. Van Til, *Mapping the Third Sector: Voluntarism in a Changing Social Economy* (Foundation Center, New York, 1988).

6. A.M. Omoto, M. Snyder, and J.P. Berghuis, The psychology of volunteerism: A conceptual analysis and a program of action research, in *The Social Psychology of HIV Infection,* J.B. Pryor and G.D. Reeder, Eds. (Erlbaum, Hillsdale, NJ, 1992).

7. A.M. Omoto and M. Snyder, Basic research in action: Volunteerism and society's response to AIDS, *Personality and Social Psychology Bulletin, 16,* 152–165 (1990); Omoto, Snyder, and Berghuis, note 6.

8. M. Snyder and A.M. Omoto, Who helps and why? The psychology of AIDS volunteerism, in *Helping and Being Helped: Naturalistic Studies,* S. Spacapan and S. Oskamp, Eds. (Sage, Newbury Park, CA, 1991); M. Snyder and A.M. Omoto, AIDS volunteers: Who volunteers and why do they volunteer? in *Leadership and Management,* V.A. Hodgkinson and R.D. Sumariwalla, Eds. (Independent Sector, Washington, DC, 1991).

9. Similar sets of motivations have also emerged from other attempts to measure the motives of AIDS volunteers. See, e.g., M.J. Williams, Gay men as "buddies" to persons living with AIDS and ARC, *Smith College Studies in Social Work, 59,* 38–52 (1988); L.M. Wong, S.C. Ouellette Kobasa, J.B. Cassel, and L.P. Platt, *A new scale identifies 6 motives for AIDS volunteers,* poster presented at the annual meeting of the American Psychological Society, Washington DC (June 1991). On the motivations served by volunteerism in general, see E.G. Clary, M. Snyder, and R.D. Ridge, Volunteers' motivations: A functional strategy for the recruitment, placement, and retention of volunteers, *Nonprofit Management and Leadership* (in press).

10. K. Lewin, *Field Theory in Social Science* (Harper, New York, 1951; original work published 1944); Omoto and Snyder, note 7.

Recommended Reading

Omoto, A.M., Snyder, M., and Berghuis, J.P. (1992). The psychology of volunteerism: A conceptual analysis and a program of action research. In *The Social Psychology of HIV Infection,* J.B. Pryor and G. D. Reeder, Eds. (Erlbaum, Hillsdale, NJ).

Snyder, M., and Omoto, A.M. (1991). Who helps and why? The psychology of AIDS volunteerism. In *Helping and Being Helped: Naturalistic Studies,* S. Spacapan and S. Oskamp, Eds. (Sage, Newbury Park, CA).

Cities *With* Heart

SUMMARY **Researchers dropped pens, feigned injuries, and begged for change in 36 cities to find out where people are most helpful to strangers. Rochester, New York, is the kindest city surveyed, while New York City ranks last. The unkindest cities are likely to be polluted and have high population density. The kindest cities have a tradition of helping: Rochester also finished first in a similar survey taken 53 years ago.**

by Robert V. Levine

Thomas Wolfe once wrote that city people "have no manners, no courtesy, no consideration for the rights of others, and no humanity." Here in post-Rodney King America, most of us would agree that urban residents see more than their share of human nature's nastier side. Ample evidence demonstrates that the rates of crime and violence rise with population density.

But what of the benevolent side of city people? While growing up in New York City, I was taught that big cities simply have more of everything, both good and bad. Of course, there were more criminals. But I was assured that beneath the seemingly harsh exteriors, you would find as many compassionate hearts as in any small town.

Over the past two years, my research group—students Todd Martinez, Gary Brase, Kerry Sorenson, and other volunteers—spent much of their summer vacations traveling nationwide conducting these experiments. We compared the fre-

Robert V. Levine is professor and chair of the psychology department at California State University, Fresno.

quency of helpful acts in various places to answer two basic questions. First, how does overall helping compare from one city and region to another? Second, which characteristics of communities best predict how helpful residents are toward strangers?

WHERE DO PEOPLE HELP?

The team conducted six different experiments in 36 cities of various sizes in all four regions of the country:

Dropped a Pen. Walking at a moderate pace, the researcher approached a solitary pedestrian passing in the opposite direction. When 15 to 20 feet away, the researcher reached into his pocket, "accidentally" dropped his pen behind him, and continued walking. Helping was scored on a five-point scale, ranging from no help offered to picking up the pen and running back to hand it to the researcher.

Helping a Blind Person Across the Street. Researchers dressed in dark glasses and carrying white canes acted the role of blind persons needing help crossing the street. Just before the light

turned green, they stepped up to the corner, held out their cane, and waited for help. A trial was terminated after 60 seconds or when the light turned red, whichever came first. Helping was measured on a two-point scale: helped

> **Researchers dressed in dark glasses and carried white canes to act the role of blind persons.**

or did not help.

A Hurt Leg. Walking with a heavy limp and wearing a large, clearly visible leg brace, researchers "accidentally" dropped and then unsuccessfully struggled to reach down for a pile of magazines as they came within 20 feet of a passing pedestrian. Helping was scored on a three-point scale ranging from no help to picking up the magazines and asking to be of further assistance.

Change for a Quarter. With a quarter in full view, researchers approached

Reprinted with permission from *American Demographics*, October 1993, pp. 46–50. © 1993 by American Demographics, Inc., Ithaca, NY.

Helping Behavior

Disregard for strangers seems to increase with population density and environmental stress.

(36 cities ranked by overall score for helping behavior, and population density rank, environmental stress rank, and pace of life rank)

	overall helping rank	lowest population density	least environmental stress	fastest pace of life
1	Rochester, NY	Bakersfield, CA	East Lansing, MI	Boston, MA
2	East Lansing, MI	Fresno, CA	Indianapolis, IN	Buffalo, NY
3	Nashville, TN	Santa Barbara, CA	Worcester, MA	New York, NY
4	Memphis, TN	Shreveport, LA	Atlanta, GA	Salt Lake City, UT
5	Houston, TX	Chattanooga, TN	Buffalo, NY	Columbus, OH
6	Chattanooga, TN	Knoxville, TN	Memphis, TN	Worcester, MA
7	Knoxville, TN	Nashville, TN	San Francisco, CA	Providence, RI
8	Canton, OH	East Lansing, MI	Shreveport, LA	Springfield, MA
9	Kansas City, MO	Sacramento, CA	Springfield, MA	Rochester, NY
10	Indianapolis, IN	Kansas City, MO	Boston, MA	Kansas City, MO
11	St. Louis, MO	Rochester, NY	Kansas City, MO	St. Louis, MO
12	Louisville, KY	Columbus, OH	Nashville, TN	Houston, TX
13	Columbus, OH	Canton, OH	Providence, RI	Paterson, NJ
14	Detroit, MI	Indianapolis, IN	Rochester, NY	Bakersfield, CA
15	Santa Barbara, CA	Louisville, KY	Chicago, IL	Atlanta, GA
16	Dallas, TX	Memphis, TN	Louisville, KY	Detroit, MI
17	Worcester, MA	St. Louis, MO	Paterson, NJ	Youngstown, OH
18	Springfield, MA	Worcester, MA	Chattanooga, TN	Indianapolis, IN
19	San Diego, CA	Youngstown, OH	Columbus, OH	Chicago, IL
20	San Jose, CA	Springfield, MA	Dallas, TX	Philadelphia, PA
21	Atlanta, GA	Atlanta, GA	Knoxville, TN	Louisville, KY
22	Bakersfield, CA	Dallas, TX	Salt Lake City, UT	Canton, OH
23	Buffalo, NY	San Diego, CA	Detroit, MI	Knoxville, TN
24	Salt Lake City, UT	Houston, TX	Houston, TX	San Francisco, CA
25	Boston, MA	Salt Lake City, UT	Los Angeles, CA	Chattanooga, TN
26	Shreveport, LA	Buffalo, NY	Philadelphia, PA	Dallas, TX
27	Providence, RI	Providence, RI	San Jose, CA	Nashville, TN
28	Philadelphia, PA	Detroit, MI	Bakersfield, CA	San Diego, CA
29	Youngstown, OH	San Jose, CA	Fresno, CA	East Lansing, MI
30	Chicago, IL	Philadelphia, PA	New York, NY	Fresno, CA
31	San Francisco, CA	Boston, MA	Sacramento, CA	Memphis, TN
32	Sacramento, CA	San Francisco, CA	San Diego, CA	San Jose, CA
33	Fresno, CA	Los Angeles, CA	St. Louis, MO	Shreveport, LA
34	Los Angeles, CA	Paterson, NJ	Santa Barbara, CA*	Sacramento, CA
35	Paterson, NJ	Chicago, IL	Canton, OH*	Los Angeles, CA
36	New York, NY	New York, NY	Youngstown, OH*	Santa Barbara, CA*

Note: See Behind the Numbers for explanation of overall helping score. Boxes denote ties.
* data no available   Source: Environmental stress rank is based on Zero Population Growth.
Environmental Stress Index. 1991; and author's research.

pedestrians passing in the opposite direction and asked politely if they could make change. Responses were scored on a four-point scale ranging from totally ignoring the request to stopping to check for change.

Lost Letter. A neat handwritten note reading, "I found this next to your car," was placed on a stamped envelope addressed to the researcher's home. The envelope was then left on the windshield of a randomly selected car parked at a meter in a main shopping area. The response rate was measured by the share of letters that later arrived because people were helpful enough to mail them.

United Way Contributions. As a general measure of charitable contributions, we looked at 1990 per capita contributions to United Way campaigns in each city.

The researchers conducted the experiments in downtown areas on clear summer days during primary business hours, targeting a relatively equal number of able-bodied men and women pedestrians. They conducted 379 trials of the blind-person episode; approached approximately 700 people in each of the dropped-pen, hurt-leg, and asking-for-change episodes; and left a total of 1,032 "lost" letters.

NEW YORK, NEW YORK

New York State is home to both the most and least helpful of the 36 cities. Rochester ranks first, closely followed by a group of small and medium-sized cities in the South and Midwest. New York City ranks last.

Generally speaking, the study did not find much difference from city to city. At the extremes, however, the differences are dramatic. In the dropped-pen situation, a stranger would have lost more than three times as many pens in Chicago as in Springfield, Massachusetts. Nearly 80 percent of passersby checked their pockets for change in first-place Louisville, compared with 11 percent in last-place Paterson, New Jersey. Fresno came in dead last on two measures, returning only half (53 percent) as many letters as did San Diego (100 percent). Also, Fresno's per capita contribution to United Way is less than one-tenth that of front-runner Rochester.

Why are people so much less helpful in some places than in others? Studies have shown that urban dwellers are

Towns With Pity

Rochester places first in only one measure of helping behavior, but it ranks first overall.

(36 cities ranked by overall score for helping behavior, and ranks for individual tests of helping behavior, 1992)

	overall helping rank	dropped pen	hurt leg	make change	blind person	lost letter	United Way
1	Rochester, NY	Springfield, MA	Chattanooga, TN	Louisville, KY	Kansas City, MO	San Diego, CA	Rochester, NY
2	East Lansing, MI	Santa Barbara, CA	Fresno, CA	Houston, TX	Knoxville, TN	Detroit, MI	Chattanooga, TN
3	Nashville, TN	East Lansing, MI	Nashville, TN	Knoxville, TN	Rochester, NY	East Lansing, MI	Columbus, OH
4	Memphis, TN	Louisville, KY	Sacramento, CA	Canton, OH	Bakersfield, CA	Indianapolis, IN	Indianapolis, IN
5	Houston, TX	San Francisco, CA	Shreveport, LA	Detroit, MI	Dallas, TX	Worcester, MA	St. Louis, MO
6	Chattanooga, TN	Memphis, TN	Memphis, TN	East Lansing, MI	Nashville, TN	Knoxville, TN	Kansas City, MO
7	Knoxville, TN	Dallas, TX	San Diego, CA	Boston, MA	Chicago, IL	Canton, OH	Philadelphia, PA
8	Canton, OH	Houston, TX	Providence, RI	Nashville, TN	Columbus, OH	Columbus, OH	Dallas, TX
9	Kansas City, MO	Salt Lake City, UT	San Jose, CA	Worcester, MA	East Lansing, MI	San Francisco, CA	Nashville, TN
10	Indianapolis, IN	Bakersfield, CA	Canton, OH	Santa Barbara, CA	Indianapolis, IN	San Jose, CA	Boston, MA
11	St. Louis, MO	Detroit, MI	Kansas City, MO	Buffalo, NY	St. Louis, MO	Chattanooga, TN	Springfield, MA
12	Louisville, KY	Canton, OH	Atlanta, GA	Kansas City, MO	Memphis, TN	Rochester, NY	Canton, OH
13	Columbus, OH	Knoxville, TN	Houston, TX	Rochester, NY	Buffalo, NY	Salt Lake City, UT	Atlanta, GA
14	Detroit, MI	Nashville, TN	Paterson, NJ	San Jose, CA	Houston, TX	St. Louis, MO	Worcester, MA
15	Santa Barbara, CA	St. Louis, MO	St. Louis, MO	Indianapolis, IN	Atlanta, GA	Los Angeles, CA	Louisville, KY
16	Dallas, TX	Indianapolis, IN	Bakersfield, CA	Chattanooga, TN	New York, NY	Louisville, KY	Memphis, TN
17	Worcester, MA	San Diego, CA	Youngstown, OH	Memphis, TN	Santa Barbara, CA	Memphis, TN	Buffalo, NY
18	Springfield, MA	Worcester, MA	Rochester, NY	Bakersfield, CA	Louisville, KY	Santa Barbara, CA	Detroit, MI
19	San Diego, CA	Atlanta, GA	Santa Barbara, CA	Salt Lake City, UT	Canton, OH	Youngstown, OH	Houston, TX
20	San Jose, CA	Rochester, NY	Detroit, MI	Columbus, OH	Philadelphia, PA	Houston, TX	Knoxville, TN
21	Atlanta, GA	Fresno, CA	East Lansing, MI	Springfield, IL	Shreveport, LA	Sacramento, CA	San Jose, CA
22	Bakersfield, CA	Paterson, NJ	Salt Lake City, UT	St. Louis, MO	Providence, RI	Buffalo, NY	East Lansing, MI
23	Buffalo, NY	Kansas City MO	Dallas, TX	Fresno, CA	Detroit, MI	Dallas, TX	Chicago, IL
24	Salt Lake City, UT	Los Angeles, CA	Springfield, IL	Shreveport, LA	Los Angeles, CA	Kansas City, MO	San Francisco, CA
25	Boston, MA	Sacramento, CA	Boston, MA	Youngstown, OH	San Jose, CA	Nashville, TN	Providence, RI
26	Shreveport, LA	Shreveport, LA	Worcester, MA	Dallas, TX	Worcester, MA	New York, NY	Santa Barbara, CA
27	Providence, RI	Chattanooga, TN	Chicago, IL	Los Angeles, CA	Chattanooga, TN	Springfield, IL	Youngstown, OH
28	Philadelphia, PA	Columbus, OH	Indianapolis, IN	Philadelphia, PA	San Francisco, CA	Philadelphia, PA	San Diego, CA
29	Youngstown, OH	Boston, MA	Columbus, OH	Atlanta, GA	Youngstown, OH	Chicago, IL	New York, NY
30	Chicago, IL	Philadelphia, PA	Knoxville, TN	San Diego, CA	Boston, MA	Providence, RI	Los Angeles, CA
31	San Francisco, CA	Providence, RI	Buffalo, NY	Chicago, IL	Fresno, CA	Atlanta, GA	Sacramento, CA
32	Sacramento, CA	San Jose, CA	Louisville, KY	Providence, RI	Paterson, NJ	Boston, MA	Salt Lake City, UT
33	Fresno, CA	Youngstown, OH	Philadelphia, PA	San Francisco, CA	Sacramento, CA	Paterson, NJ	Shreveport, LA
34	Los Angeles, CA	Buffalo, NY	San Francisco, CA	Sacramento, CA	San Diego, CA	Shreveport, LA	Paterson, NJ
35	Paterson, NJ	New York, NY	New York, NY	New York, NY	Springfield, MA	Bakersfield, CA	Bakersfield, CA
36	New York, NY	Chicago, IL	Los Angeles, CA	Paterson, NJ	Salt Lake City, UT	Fresno, CA	Fresno, CA

Note: See text for explanation of individual helping tests. See Behind the Numbers for explanation of overall helping score.
Source: 1999 per capita contributions to the United Way campaigns in each city; and author's research.

more likely than rural people to do each other harm. Our results indicate that they are also less likely to do them good. This unwillingness to help increases with the degree of "cityness." In other words, density drives strangers apart.

"Cities give not the human senses room enough," wrote Ralph Waldo Emerson. Urban theorists have long argued that crowding brings out our worst nature, and these data support that notion. Places with lower population den-

> **Nearly 80 percent offered to make change in Louisville, Kentucky; only 11 percent did in Paterson, New Jersey.**

sities are far more likely to offer help, particularly in situations that call for face-to-face, spontaneous responses such as a dropped pen, a hurt leg, or the need for change. Research shows that squeezing many people into a small space leads to feelings of alienation, anonymity, and social isolation. At the same time, feelings of guilt, shame, and social commitment tend to decline. Ultimately, people feel less responsible for their behavior toward others—especially strangers.

Population density has direct psychological effects on people. It also leads to stressful effects on people. It also leads to stressful conditions that can take a toll on helping behavior. For example, people are less helpful in cities that have higher costs of living. These high costs are, in turn, related to population density, because the laws of supply and demand drive up the prices of land and other resources when they are limited.

High concentrations of people also produce stress on the environment. We compared our findings with Zero Population Growth's Environmental Stress Index, which rates the environmental quality of cities. As predicted, people were less helpful in environmentally stressed-out cities.

Stressful situations and their consequent behaviors ultimately sustain one another. Violent crime results from

stressful conditions but is itself a source of urban stress. Ultimately, inaction becomes the norm. Big cities see more of the worst and less of the best of human nature.

One characteristic that does not affect helping behavior is the general pace of life. In a previous study of the same cities, we looked at four indicators of the pace of life: walking speed, work speed, speaking speed, and clock and watch accuracy. Since helping people essentially demands a sacrifice of time, people who live in cities where time is at a premium would presumably be less helpful.

Yet there is no consistent relationship between a city's pace of life and its helpfulness. Some cities fit the expected pattern. New York, for example, has the third-fastest pace of life and is the least helpful place. But Rochester has the ninth-fastest pace, and its people are most helpful. Laid-back Los Angeles, the slowest city, is also one of the least helpful, ranking 34th.

Todd Martinez, who gathered data in both New York City and (pre-Rodney King situation) Los Angeles, was acutely aware of the differences between the two cities. "I hated doing L.A. People looked at me but just didn't seem to want to bother," he says. "For a few trials, I was acting the hurt-leg episode on a narrow sidewalk with just enough space for a person to squeeze by. After I dropped my magazines, one man walked up very close to me, checked out the situation, and then side-stepped around me without a word.

"Los Angeles was the only city that I worked where I found myself getting frustrated and angry when people didn't help. In New York, for some reason, I never took it personally. People looked like they were too busy to help. It was as if they saw me, but didn't really notice me or anything else around them."

To real-life strangers in need, of course, thoughts are less important than actions. The bottom line is that a stranger's prospects are just as bleak in New York as in Los Angeles. People either find the time to help or they don't.

ROCHESTER'S SECOND WIN

More than 50 years ago, sociologist Robert Angell combined a series of statistics from the 1940 census to assess the 'moral integration' of 43 U.S. cities. Angell measured the degree to which

citizens were willing to sacrifice their own private interests for the public good ("Welfare Effort Index") and the frequency with which people violated one another's person and property ("Crime Index"). Angell's methods are not comparable with the current study, but to our astonishment, Rochester also ranked number one on Angell's moral integration index in 1940.

Harry Reis, a psychology professor at the University of Rochester who grew up in New York City, is "not the least bit surprised" by the performance of his adopted home. "I like to describe Rochester as a nice place to live—in both the best and the mildest sense of the word," he says. "It's very traditional and not always very innovative. But it's a town where the social fabric hasn't deteriorated as much as in other places. Unlike New York City, people here don't laugh when you speak of ideals like 'family values.' They take their norms of social responsibility seriously."

Even when people do help in New York City, their altruism sometimes takes a hard edge. On the lost-letter measure, many of the envelopes we received from people had been opened. In almost all cases, the finder had resealed the envelope or mailed the letter in a new one. Sometimes they even attached

> **While growing up in New York city, I was taught by loving, caring people to ignore the cries of strangers.**

notes, usually apologizing for opening the letter. Only from New York City, however, did we receive an envelope with its entire side ripped and left open. On the back of the letter, the "helper" had scribbled, in Spanish, a very nasty accusation about the researcher's mother. Below that, he or she added in straightforward English: "F— you." It is fascinating to imagine this angry New Yorker, perhaps cursing while walking to the mailbox, yet feeling compelled by the norm of social responsibility to assist a stranger. Ironically, this rudely returned letter added to New York's helpfulness score.

While growing up in New York City, I was taught by loving, caring people to ignore the cries of strangers. I learned to walk around people stretched unconscious on sidewalks, because I was told that they just need to "sleep it off." I learned to ignore screams from fighting couples: "they don't want your help." And I was warned to disregard the ramblings of mentally disturbed street people because "you never know how they'll react." The ultimate message: "Don't get involved."

Do our data prove that urbanites are less caring people? Perhaps not. For one thing, no comparable data from small towns exist to show that people there are more helpful than are urbanites. Furthermore, city dwellers we talked with claimed over and over that they care deeply about the needs of strangers, but that the realities of city living prohibit them from reaching out. Many are simply afraid to make contact with strangers. Some are concerned that others might not want unsolicited help. They claim that the stranger might be afraid of outside contact or, in some cases, that it would be patronizing or insulting to offer them help. People speak with nostalgia about the past, when they thought nothing of picking up hitchhikers or arranging a square meal for a hungry stranger. Many express frustration—even anger—that life today deprives them of the satisfaction of feeling like good Samaritans.

To some degree, these may be the rationalizations of unwilling helpers trying to preserve a benevolent self-image. But the evidence, in fact, indicates that helping is affected less by people's inherent nature than by the environment. Studies reveal that seemingly minor changes in a situation can drastically affect helping behavior. In particular, the size of the place where one was raised has less to do with how helpful one is than does the size of one's current home. In other words, small-town natives and urbanites are both less likely to offer help in urban areas.

The future of urban helping may not be as bleak as it seems. Just as the environment can inhibit helping behavior, researchers are currently exploring ways to modify the environment to encourage it. Experiments have found that increasing the level of personal responsibility people feel in a situation increases the likelihood they will help. It also helps to make people feel guilty when they don't help others.

A little more than a century ago, John Habberton wrote: "Nowhere in the world are there more charitable hearts with plenty of money behind them than in large cities, yet nowhere else is there more suffering." The current status of helping activity in our cities is dismal. But helping, like language and other human skills, is a learned behavior.

Research indicates that children who are exposed to altruistic models on television tend to follow suit. Just think how much good it could do them to see positive role models in real life.

Behind the Numbers Three large, medium, and smaller cities were sampled in each of the four census-defined regions of the U.S. (Northeast, North Central, South, and West). Travel distance within each region was a factor in selection of cities. The data for the five experiments were collected in two or more locations, in downtown areas during main business hours, on clear days during the summer months of 1990 and 1991. For the three measures that required approaching pedestrians, only individuals walking alone were selected. Children apparently under 17 years old, handicapped, very old people, and people with heavy packages were excluded. For the purposes of analysis, each of the 36 cities was treated as a single subject. For each city, the six measures of helping were converted to standardized scores, to which the value "10" was added to eliminate negative values. These adjusted standardized scores were then averaged to produce the overall helping score.

CAUSE OF DEATH: UNCERTAIN(TY)

By Robert B. Cialdini

All the weapons of influence discussed in this book* work better under some conditions than under others. If we are to defend ourselves adequately against any such weapon, it is vital that we know its optimal operating conditions in order to recognize when we are most vulnerable to its influence. We have already had a hint of one time when the principle of social proof worked best—with the Chicago believers. It was a sense of shaken confidence that triggered their craving for converts. In general, *when we are unsure of ourselves, when the situation is unclear or ambiguous, when uncertainty reigns, we are most likely to look to and accept the actions of others as correct* (Tesser, Campbell, & Mickler, 1983).

In the process of examining the reactions of other people to resolve our uncertainty, however, we are likely to overlook a subtle, but important fact: Those people are probably examining the social evidence, too. Especially in an ambiguous situation, the tendency for everyone to be looking to see what everyone else is doing can lead to a fascinating phenomenon called pluralistic ignorance. A thorough understanding of the pluralistic ignorance phenomenon helps explain a regular occurrence in our country that has been termed both a riddle and a national disgrace: the failure of entire groups of bystanders to aid victims in agonizing need of help.

The classic example of such bystander inaction and the one that has produced the most debate in journalistic, political, and scientific circles began as an ordinary homicide case in New York City's borough of Queens. A woman in her late twenties, Catherine Genovese, was killed in a late-night attack on her street as she returned from work. Murder is never an act to be passed off lightly, but in a city the size and tenor of New York, the Genovese incident warranted no more

space than a fraction of a column in the *New York Times*. Catherine Genovese's story would have died with her on that day in March 1964 if it hadn't been for a mistake.

The metropolitan editor of the *Times*, A. M. Rosenthal, happened to be having lunch with the city police commissioner a week later. Rosenthal asked the commissioner about a different Queens-based homicide and the commissioner, thinking he was being questioned about the Genovese case, revealed something staggering that had been uncovered by the police investigation. It was something that left everyone who heard it, the commissioner included, aghast and grasping for explanations. Catherine Genovese had not experienced a quick, muffled death. It had been a long, loud, tortured, *public* event. Her assailant had chased and attacked her in the street three times over a period of 35 minutes before his knife finally silenced her cries for help. Incredibly, 38 of her neighbors watched from the safety of their apartment windows without so much as lifting a finger to call the police.

Rosenthal, a former Pulitzer Prize-winning reporter, knew a story when he heard one. On the day of his lunch with the commissioner, he assigned a reporter to investigate the "bystander angle" of the Genovese incident. Within a week, the *Times* published a long, front-page article that was to create a swirl of controversy and speculation. The initial paragraphs of that report provided the tone and focus of the story:

> For more than half an hour 38 respectable, law-abiding citizens in Queens watched a killer stalk and stab a woman in three separate attacks in Kew Gardens.
>
> Twice the sound of their voices and the sudden glow of their bedroom lights interrupted him and frightened him off. Each time he returned, sought her out, and

*From *Influence: Science and Practice*, 3/e, edited by Robert B. Cialdini, chapter 4, pp. 106–114. © 1993 by HarperCollins College Publishers. Reprinted by permission of Addison Wesley Educational Publishers, Inc.

stabbed her again. Not one person telephoned the police during the assault; one witness called after the woman was dead.

That was two weeks ago today. But Assistant Chief Inspector Frederick M. Lussen, in charge of the borough's detectives and a veteran of 25 years of homicide investigations, is still shocked.

He can give a matter-of-fact recitation of many murders. But the Kew Gardens slaying baffles him—not because it is a murder; but because "good people" failed to call the police. (Ganzberg, 1964)

As with Assistant Chief Inspector Lussen, shock and bafflement were the standard reactions of almost everyone who learned the story's details. The shock struck first, leaving the police, the newspeople, and the reading public stunned. The bafflement followed quickly. How could 38 "good people" fail to act under those circumstances? No one could understand it. Even the murder witnesses themselves were bewildered. "I don't know," they answered one after another. "I just don't know." A few offered weak reasons for their inaction. For example, two or three people explained that they were "afraid" or "did not want to get involved." These reasons, however, do not stand up to close scrutiny: A simple anonymous call to the police could have saved Catherine Genovese without threatening the witnesses' future safety or free time. No, it wasn't the observers' fear or reluctance to complicate their lives that explained their lack of action; something else was going on there that even they could not fathom.

Confusion, though, does not make for good news copy. So the press as well as the other media—several papers, TV stations, and magazines that were pursuing follow-up stories—emphasized the only explanation available at the time: The witnesses, no different from the rest of us, hadn't cared enough to get involved. Americans were becoming a nation of selfish, insensitive people. The rigors of modern life, especially city life, were hardening them. They were becoming "The Cold Society," unfeeling and indifferent to the plight of their fellow citizens.

In support of this interpretation, news stories began appearing regularly in which various kinds of public apathy were detailed. Also supporting such an interpretation were the remarks of a range of armchair social commentators, who, as a breed, seem never to admit to bafflement when speaking to the press. They, too, saw the Genovese case as having large-scale social significance. All used the word apathy, which, it is interesting to note, had been in the headline of the *Time[s]*'s front-page story, although they accounted for the apathy differently. One attributed it to the effects of TV violence, another to repressed aggressiveness, but most implicated the "depersonalization" of urban life with its "megalopolitan societies" and its "alienation of the individual from the group." Even Rosenthal, the newsman who first broke the story and who ultimately made it the subject of a book, subscribed to the city-caused apathy theory.

Nobody can say why the 38 did not lift the phone while Miss Genovese was being attacked, since they cannot say themselves. It can be assumed, however, that their apathy was indeed one of the big-city variety. It is almost a matter of psychological survival, if one is surrounded and pressed by millions of people, to prevent them from constantly impinging on you, and the only way to do this is to ignore them as often as possible. Indifference to one's neighbor and his troubles is a conditioned reflex in life in New York as it is in other big cities. (A. M. Rosenthal, 1964)

As the Genovese story grew—aside from Rosenthal's book, it became the focus of numerous newspaper and magazine pieces, several television news documentaries, and an off-Broadway play—it attracted the professional attention of a pair of New York-based psychology professors, Bibb Latané and John Darley. They examined the reports of the Genovese incident and, on the basis of their knowledge of social psychology, hit on what had seemed like the most unlikely explanation of all—the fact that 38 witnesses were present. Previous accounts of the story had invariably emphasized that no action was taken, even *though* 38 individuals had looked on. Latané and Darley suggested that no one had helped precisely because there were so many observers.

The psychologists speculated that, for at least two reasons, a bystander to an emergency will be unlikely to help when there are a number of other bystanders present. The first reason is fairly straightforward. *With several potential helpers around, the personal responsibility of each individual is reduced:* "Perhaps someone else will give or call for aid, perhaps someone else already has." So with everyone thinking that someone else will help or has helped, no one does. The second reason is the more psychologically intriguing one; it is founded on the principle of social proof and involves the pluralistic ignorance effect. Very often an emergency is not obviously an emergency. Is the man lying in the alley a heart-attack victim or a drunk sleeping one off? Is the commotion next door an assault requiring the police or an especially loud marital spat where intervention would be inappropriate and unwelcome? What is going on? In times of such uncertainty, the natural tendency is to look around at the actions of others for clues. We can learn, from the way the other witnesses are reacting, whether the event is or is not an emergency.

What is easy to forget, though, is that everybody else observing the event is likely to be looking for social evidence, too. Because we all prefer to appear poised and unflustered among others, we are likely to search for that evidence placidly, with brief, camouflaged glances at those around us. Therefore everyone is likely to see everyone else looking unruffled and failing to act. As a result, and by the principle of social proof, the event will be roundly interpreted as a nonemergency. This, according to Latané and Darley (1968b) is the state of pluralistic ignorance "in which each person decided that since nobody is concerned, nothing is wrong. Meanwhile, the danger may be mounting to the point where a single individual, uninfluenced by the seeming calm of others, *would* react."[1]

A Scientific Approach

The fascinating upshot of Latané and Darley's reasoning is that, for an emergency victim, the idea of "safety in numbers" may often be completely wrong. It might be that someone in need of emergency aid would have a better chance of survival if a single bystander, rather than a crowd, were present. To test this unusual thesis, Darley, Latané, their students, and colleagues performed a systematic and impressive program of research that produced a clear set of findings (for a review, see Latané & Nida, 1981). Their basic procedure was to stage emergency events that were observed by a single individual or by a group of people. They then recorded the number of times the emergency victim received help under those circumstances. In their first experiment (Darley & Latané, 1968), a New York college student who appeared to be having an epileptic seizure received help 85 percent of the time when there was a single bystander present but only 31 percent of time with five bystanders present. With almost all the single bystanders helping, it becomes difficult to argue that ours is "The Cold Society" where no one cares for suffering others. Obviously it was something about the presence of other bystanders that reduced helping to shameful levels.

Other studies have examined the importance of social proof in causing widespread witness "apathy." They have done so by planting within a group of witnesses to a possible emergency people who are rehearsed to act as if no emergency were occurring. For instance, in another New York-based experiment (Latané & Darley, 1968a), 75 percent of lone individuals who observed smoke seeping from under a door reported the leak; however, when similar leaks were observed by three-person groups, the smoke was reported only 38 percent of the time. The smallest number of bystanders took action, though, when the three-person groups included two individuals who had been coached to ignore the smoke; under those conditions, the leaks were reported only 10

percent of time. In a similar study conducted in Toronto (A. S. Ross, 1971), single bystanders provided emergency aid 90 percent of the time, whereas such aid occurred in only 16 percent of the cases when a bystander was in the presence of two passive bystanders.

After more than a decade of such research, social scientists now have a good idea of when bystanders will offer emergency aid. First, and contrary to the view that we have become a society of callous, uncaring people, once witnesses are convinced that an emergency situation exists, aid is very likely. Under these conditions, the number of bystanders who either intervene themselves or summon help is quite comforting. For example, in four separate experiments done in Florida (R. D. Clark & Word, 1972, 1974), accident scenes involving a maintenance man were staged. When it was clear that the man was hurt and required assistance, he was helped 100 percent of the time in two of the experiments. In the other two experiments, where helping involved contact with potentially dangerous electric wires, the victim still received bystander aid in 90 percent of the instances. In addition, these extremely high levels of assistance occurred whether the witnesses observed the event singly or in groups.

The situation becomes very different when, as in many cases, bystanders cannot be sure that the event they are witnessing is an emergency. Then a victim is much more likely to be helped by a lone bystander than by a group, especially if the people in the group are strangers to one another (Latané & Rodin, 1969). It seems that the pluralistic ignorance effect is strongest among strangers: Because we like to look graceful and sophisticated in public and because we are unfamiliar with the reactions of those we do not know, we are unlikely to give off or correctly read expressions of concern when in a group of strangers. Therefore, a possible emergency is viewed as a nonemergency and a victim suffers.

A close look at this set of research findings reveals an enlightening pattern. All the conditions that decrease an emergency victim's chances for bystander aid exist normally and innocently in the city, in contrast to rural areas:

1. Cities are more clamorous, distracting, rapidly changing places where it is difficult to be certain of the nature of the events one encounters.
2. Urban environments are more populous; consequently, people are more likely to be with others when witnessing a potential emergency situation.
3. City dwellers know a much smaller percentage of fellow residents than do people who live in small towns; therefore, city dwellers are more likely to find themselves in a group of strangers when observing an emergency.

These three natural characteristics of urban environments—their confusion, their populousness, and their low levels of acquaintanceship—fit in very well with the

---

[1]The potentially tragic consequences of the pluralistic ignorance phenomenon are starkly illustrated in a UPI news release from Chicago:

A university coed was beaten and strangled in daylight hours near one of the most popular tourist attractions in the city, police said Saturday.

The nude body of Lee Alexis Wilson, 23, was found Friday in dense shubbery alongside the wall of the Art Institute by a 12-year-old boy playing in the bushes.

Police theorized she may have been sitting or standing by a fountain in the Art Institute's south plaza when she was attacked. The assailant apparently then dragged her into the bushes. She apparently was sexually assaulted, police said.

Police said thousands of persons must have passed the site and one man told them he heard a scream about 2 P.M. but did not investigate because no one else seemed to be paying attention.

factors shown by research to decrease bystander aid. Without ever having to resort to such sinister concepts as "urban depersonalization" and "megalopolitan alienation," then, we can explain why so many instances of bystander inaction occur in our cities.

Devictiming Yourself

Explaining the dangers of modern urban life in less ominous terms does not dispel them. Furthermore, as the world's populations move increasingly to the cities—half of all humanity will be city dwellers within a decade (Newland, 1980)—there will be a growing need to reduce those dangers. Fortunately, our newfound understanding of the bystander "apathy" process offers real hope. Armed with this scientific knowledge, an emergency victim can increase enormously the chances of receiving aid from others. The key is the realization that groups of bystanders fail to help because the bystanders are unsure rather than unkind. They don't help because they are unsure an emergency actually exists and whether they are responsible for taking action. When they are sure of their responsibilities for intervening in a clear emergency, people are exceedingly responsive!

Once it is understood that the enemy is the simple state of uncertainty, it becomes possible for emergency victims to reduce this uncertainty, thereby protecting themselves. Imagine, for example, you are spending a summer afternoon at a music concert in a park. As the concert ends and people begin leaving, you notice a slight numbness in one arm but dismiss it as nothing to be alarmed about. Yet, while moving with the crowd to the distant parking areas, you feel the numbness spreading down to your hand and up one side of your face. Feeling disoriented, you decide to sit against a tree for a moment to rest. Soon you realize that something is drastically wrong. Sitting down has not helped; in fact, the control and coordination of your muscles has worsened, and you are starting to have difficulty moving your mouth and tongue to speak. You try to get up but can't. A terrifying thought rushes to mind: "Oh, God, I'm having a stroke!" Groups of people are passing by and most are paying no attention. The few who notice the odd way you are slumped against the tree or the strange look on your face check the social evidence around them and, seeing that no one else is reacting with concern, walk on convinced that nothing is wrong.

Were you to find yourself in such a predicament, what could you do to overcome the odds against receiving help? Because your physical abilities would be deteriorating, time would be crucial. If, before you could summon aid, you lost your speech or mobility or consciousness, your chances for assistance and for recovery would plunge drastically. It would be essential to try to request help quickly. What would be the most effective form of that request? Moans, groans, or outcries probably

would not do. They might bring you some attention, but they would not provide enough information to assure passersby that a true emergency existed.

If mere outcries are unlikely to produce help from the passing crowd, perhaps you should be more specific. Indeed, you need to do more than try to gain attention; you should call out clearly your need for assistance. You must not allow bystanders to define your situation as a nonemergency. Use the word "Help" to show your need for emergency aid, and don't worry about being wrong. Embarrassment is a villain to be crushed. If you think you are having a stroke, you cannot afford to be worried about the possibility of overestimating your problem. The difference is that between a moment of embarrassment and possible death or lifelong paralysis.

Even a resounding call for help is not your most effective tactic. Although it may reduce bystanders' doubts that a real emergency exists, it will not remove several other important uncertainties within each onlooker's mind: What kind of aid is required? Should I be the one to provide the aid, or should someone more qualified do it? Has someone else already gone to get professional help, or is it my responsibility? While the bystanders stand gawking at you and grappling with these questions, time vital to your survival could be slipping away.

Clearly, then, as a victim you must do more than alert bystanders to your need for emergency assistance; you must also remove their uncertainties about how that assistance should be provided and who should provide it. What would be the most efficient and reliable way to do so?

Many Are Called But Only One Should Be Chosen

Based on the research findings we have seen, my advice would be to isolate one individual from the crowd: Stare, speak, and point directly at that person and no one else: "You, sir; in the blue jacket, I need help. Call an ambulance." With that one utterance you would dispel all the uncertainties that might prevent or delay help. With that one statement you will have put the man in the blue jacket in the role of "rescuer." He should now understand that emergency aid is needed; he should understand that he, not someone else, is responsible for providing the aid; and, finally, he should understand exactly how to provide it. All the scientific evidence indicates that the result should be quick, effective assistance.

In general, then, your best strategy when in need of emergency help is to reduce the uncertainties of those around you concerning your condition and their responsibilities. Be as precise as possible about your need for aid. Do not allow bystanders to come to their own conclusions because, especially in a crowd, the principle of social proof and the consequent pluralistic ignorance effect might well cause them to view your situation as a nonemergency. Of all the techniques in this book designed to produce compliance with a request, this one is the most important to remember. After all, the failure of your request for emergency aid could mean your life.

Not long ago, I received some firsthand evidence proving this point. I was involved in a rather serious automobile collision. Both I and the other driver were plainly hurt: He was slumped, unconscious, over his steering wheel while I managed to stagger, bloody, from behind mine. The accident had occurred in the center of an intersection in full view of several individuals stopped in their cars at the traffic light. As I knelt in the road beside my car door; trying to clear my head, the light changed. The waiting cars began to roll slowly through the intersection; their drivers gawked but did not stop.

I remember thinking, "Oh no, it's happening just like the research says. They're all passing by!" I consider it fortunate that, as a social psychologist, I knew enough about the bystander studies to have that particular thought. By thinking of my predicament in terms of the research findings, I knew exactly what to do. Pulling myself up so I could be seen clearly, I pointed at the driver of one car: "Call the police." To a second and a third driver, pointing directly each time: "Pull over, we need help." The responses of these people were instantaneous. They summoned a police car and ambulance immediately, they used their handkerchiefs to blot the blood from my face, they put a jacket under my head, they volunteered to serve as witnesses to the accident, and one person even offered to ride with me to the hospital.

Not only was this help rapid and solicitous, it was infectious. After drivers entering the intersection from the other direction saw cars stopping for me, they stopped and began tending to the other victim. The principle of social proof was working for us now. The trick had been to get the ball rolling in the direction of aid. Once that was accomplished, I was able to relax and let the bystanders' genuine concern and social proof's natural momentum do the rest.

THE EFFECTS OF "MANDATORY VOLUNTEERISM" ON INTENTIONS TO VOLUNTEER

Arthur A. Stukas,[1] Mark Snyder,[2] and E. Gil Clary[3]

[1]Univeristy of Northern Colorado, [2]University of Minnesota, and [3]College of St. Catherine

Abstract—*With the widespread emergence of required community-service programs comes a new opportunity to examine the effects of requirements on future behavioral intentions. To investigate the consequences of such "mandatory volunteerism" programs, we followed students who were required to volunteer in order to graduate from college. Results demonstrated that stronger perceptions of external control eliminated an otherwise positive relation between prior volunteer experience and future intentions to volunteer. A second study experimentally compared mandates and choices to serve and included a premeasured assessment of whether students felt external control was necessary to get them to volunteer. After being required or choosing to serve, students reported their future intentions. Students who initially felt it unlikely that they would freely volunteer had significantly lower intentions after being required to serve than after being given a choice. Those who initially felt more likely to freely volunteer were relatively unaffected by a mandate to serve as compared with a choice. Theoretical and practical implications for understanding the effects of requirements and constraints on intentions and behavior are discussed.*

For decades now, psychologists have sought to understand the factors that lead people to help others in need (see Krebs & Miller, 1985). Initial work focused on helping in emergencies or other short-term "spontaneous helping" situations in which a potential helper is faced with an unexpected need for help, calling for an immediate decision to act, and an opportunity to provide one and only one relatively brief act of help (e.g., Latané & Darley, 1970). More recently, students of helping behavior have increasingly come to recognize that, to gain a fuller understanding of who helps and why, they must also study helping that is planned and sustained over time (e.g., Clary, Snyder, Ridge, et al., 1998; Cnaan & Goldberg-Glen, 1991; Omoto & Snyder, 1995; Smith, 1994; Snyder & Omoto, 1992). The prototypical example of planned, sustained helping is volunteerism. Every year, millions of people volunteer their time and effort to act as tutors for children and adults, companions for the lonely, and health care providers for the sick; in 1995 alone, an estimated 23 million American adults spent at least 5 hr each week in volunteer service (Independent Sector, 1996).

However, even though many people do volunteer, many do not (51% of 1995 survey respondents had not volunteered in the past 12 months; Independent Sector, 1996). Indeed, society has recognized that extra effort may be necessary to inspire its members to help, and consequently the United States has created federal programs such as the Peace Corps and VISTA. Recently, the call to volunteer has become even louder as those in need of help see public supports eliminated. To promote citizen participation, various institutions have started to use their authority to require, as opposed to "inspire," individuals to engage in community service. In particular, many educational institutions have sought to increase levels of "volunteer" activity by requiring community service of their students (Keith, 1994). Moreover, governments have gone so far as to establish community-service requirements as conditions of graduation from high school (e.g., the State of Maryland; Sobus, 1995).

In addition to directly enhancing the welfare of the community, an implicit, if not always explicit, goal of these "mandatory volunteerism" programs is to increase levels of future volunteerism, thereby ensuring a continuing pool of volunteers from which the community can draw in times of need (Sobus, 1995). Many service-learning proponents believe that requiring students to volunteer will accomplish this goal by promoting the personal, social, and civic development of students and the internalization of prosocial values that lead to intentions to volunteer (Giles & Eyler, 1994; Sobus, 1995). However, mandating volunteerism with such aims in mind raises the question of whether behavior performed under external pressure actually leads to internalization of prosocial values and future behavioral intentions (e.g., Deci & Ryan, 1985, 1987).

Indeed, it can be argued that requirements to volunteer may reduce interest in volunteer activities by altering individuals' perceptions of why they help. If mandated students begin to perceive that they help only when required or rewarded, then their intentions to freely engage in volunteer service in the future may be reduced (e.g., Batson, Coke, Jasnoski, & Hanson, 1978; Clary, Snyder, & Stukas, 1998; Kunda & Schwartz,

Address correspondence to Arthur A. Stukas, Department of Psychology, McKee 0014, University of Northern Colorado, Greeley, CO 80639; e-mail: aastuka@bentley.unco.edu.

From *Psychological Science*, January 1999, pp. 59–64. © 1999 by the American Psychological Association. Reprinted by permission of Blackwell Publishers.

1983). In keeping with this theory, Piliavin and Callero (1991) reported that blood donors who gave blood for the first time under coercion expressed lesser intentions to continue donating in the future than those who were not coerced. Requirements (and other coercive techniques) may also engender psychological reactance (Brehm & Brehm, 1981); limiting an individual's freedom to act may lead to desires to reestablish that freedom, which can be accomplished by derogating the forced activity and by refusing to perform it once the mandate has been lifted.

Most theories about the undermining of interest in an activity suggest that this effect may be strongest for individuals with initial interest in the activity (e.g., Lepper, Greene, & Nisbett, 1973). One important indicator of interest in volunteering is previous involvement in volunteer activities, and we expect that experienced individuals may be most likely to suffer from required service programs; in other words, predictions of an inhibiting effect presuppose that individuals possess established behavioral intentions and habits that can be inhibited by a requirement. Given that a principal defining characteristic of volunteerism is its sustained nature, it is not unreasonable to expect that prior volunteer experience may play a pivotal role in determining how people respond to mandatory volunteerism programs. Certainly, under ordinary circumstances, prior experience is an influential determinant of later intentions. For example, Charng, Piliavin, and Callero (1988) have shown that continued experience as a blood donor can lead to the role of blood donor becoming a central part of the self-concept and donating becoming habitual and routine. We do not doubt that the same process occurs for other types of volunteerism. However, when requirements to serve are placed on experienced volunteers, their intentions to continue to engage in voluntary action may be short-circuited.

Although an inhibiting effect can be theorized to occur for those persons with established histories of volunteer action, we suggest that prior experience itself may not be the sole predictor of the consequences of mandatory volunteerism. Indeed, survey research indicates that many students have a positive attitude toward instituting community-service requirements at their schools (e.g., Independent Sector, 1992), and may not feel particularly "forced" into volunteerism because they are already advocates of such service-learning programs. Other students, however, have a less positive attitude and may feel that these programs are unnecessary and that they will volunteer when and if they have the time and inclination; these students might feel forced to serve.

Given students' varied reactions to mandatory volunteerism, we hypothesized that the effects of prior experience on intentions to volunteer following required service are moderated by perceptions of the external control being exerted by the requirements. Feeling forced to volunteer may weaken the positive relation between past experience and future intentions. Thus, in a study testing this hypothesis, we predicted that when individuals perceived lower levels of external control, their prior experience and future intentions would be positively related; that is, as prior experience increased, so too would intentions to volunteer in the future. However, we expected that when individuals perceived higher levels of external control,

prior experience and future intentions would be unrelated or perhaps even negatively related; in other words, as prior experience increased, future intentions would remain relatively constant or perhaps even decrease. This pattern of results would demonstrate that under high levels of perceived external control, individuals with the most prior experience (who would otherwise have the highest future intentions) suffer the greatest inhibiting effect on their intentions to volunteer.

STUDY 1

In 1993, the University of St. Thomas in St. Paul, Minnesota, incorporated a new graduation requirement into its undergraduate business program: All students were required to engage in 40 hr of community service. A noncredit, tuition-free course, coordinated by a business faculty member, was designed to track students' fulfillment of the requirement and to help them choose an appropriate service opportunity (e.g., being a companion to an elderly person or a tutor to an illiterate child). The introduction of this requirement provided us with a "real world" laboratory in which we could follow students, all of whom were required to volunteer, over the course of their service and examine the factors that affected their intentions to volunteer subsequently.

Method

Participants

A total of 371 business majors (192 men and 179 women) who were required to enroll in the service-learning course (Business 200, or B200) completed initial and follow-up surveys as a component of the course.[1] Data were collected from six separate classes between the fall of 1993 and the spring of 1995.

Procedure

Participants completed surveys, administered during the first and last class meetings of B200, which marked the beginning and end of their mandated service performed over the course of 12 weeks. The initial survey included measures of prior volunteer experience and the extent to which participants felt they were engaging in service only because they were required, as well as other measures. The follow-up survey included among its items measures of future intentions to volunteer.

---

1. The 371 participants came from a pool of 612 business majors who were enrolled in B200 during the time period of this study. Thirty-six of these students did not attend the orientation session and thus did not complete the initial survey. Of those students who completed the initial survey, 64.4% also completed the follow-up survey. The 35.6% of students who did not complete the final survey had been excused by the instructor from the final session of the course, when the final survey was administered, and failed to return a mailed follow-up survey. On average, these students were significantly older, were more likely to be male, and had more of their time set aside for a paid job than students who completed the final survey. For an additional 39 students, data for one or more of the variables included in our analyses were missing; these students were included only in those analyses for which it was appropriate.

Thus, to assess just how much participants felt they were performing their community service because of the mandate, we developed a two-item measure ($r = .46$, $p < .01$) for use in the pretest: "I am participating in B200 only because it is required of me" and "Even if I weren't in the B200 program, I would be volunteering" (reverse coded). The combined scale ranged from 2 to 14 (with higher scores indicating greater perceptions of external control[2]) and had a mean of 8.3 and a standard deviation of 3.4.

At the end of the program, participants were asked to indicate the likelihood (on a 7-point scale; 1 = *extremely unlikely*, 7 = *extremely likely*) that they would volunteer at several points in the future. Our behavioral-intentions index was an average of responses to six items: "I will work at the same site next semester," "I will volunteer somewhere else next semester," "I will be a volunteer 1 year from now," "I will be a volunteer 3 years from now," "I will be a volunteer 5 years from now," and "I will be a volunteer 10 years from now." The internal consistency (alpha) of this index was .82.

Results

We predicted that for students who perceived lower levels of external control, prior volunteer experience would be an influential and positive determinant of later intentions to continue their work in the future; by contrast, students who felt higher levels of external control would demonstrate a much weaker relation between experience and intentions, mostly because experienced volunteers would have comparatively lower intentions. We employed hierarchical regression to investigate this hypothesis.

Specifically, the strategy used to test such moderated effects involved entering the *past experience* factor (estimated total number of months volunteered in one's lifetime; $M = 12$ months, $SD = 18$ months[3]) on the first step of the regression analysis and then entering the *external control* factor on the second step and the *interaction* term (a multiplicative product of the first two scores) on the third step. Moderation was indicated by a significant increase in the r^2 value from Step 2 to Step 3 (Baron & Kenny, 1986).

The results of this analysis demonstrated that past experience had a main effect on intentions: Students with more experience were more likely to intend to volunteer in the future at the program's end than were students who began with less experience, $r^2 = .036$, $F(1, 330) = 12.28$, $p < .001$. There was also a main effect of perceptions of external control on intentions (after experience had already been entered into the equation); students who felt more external control upon starting

B200 were less likely to intend to volunteer at its finish, r^2 improvement = .177, $F(1, 329) = 74.10$, $p < .001$.

Our primary hypothesis, however, was that the effects of experience on students' intentions would be moderated by perceptions of external control, and, indeed, we found a statistically significant interaction of experience and external control, r^2 improvement = 0.21, $F(1, 328) = 8.86$, $p < .01$. When students perceived the service-learning program to be more controlling of their behavior, the positive relation between past volunteer experience and future intentions was weakened; thus, students who had the greatest past experience and who also felt controlled did not have the highest future intentions—instead, their intentions were undermined by the requirement. For those students who did not feel controlled, past experience was positively correlated with future intentions (i.e., students with the most experience were most likely to intend to volunteer in the future). To provide a graphic representation of this analysis, we plotted regression lines for three levels of external control: the mean, 1 standard deviation above the mean, and 1 standard deviation below the mean (as recommended by Cohen & Cohen, 1983, p. 323) (see Fig. 1).

As is apparent from this graph, students with lower levels of perceived external control (plotted at external control = 4.9) demonstrated a positive relation between prior experience and future intentions (the upwardly sloping regression line). Students at higher levels of perceived external control (external control = 11.7) demonstrated a slightly negative relation between prior experience and future intentions (the downwardly sloping regression line). For students at the mean of the external-control scale (external control = 8.3), prior experience and future intentions were essentially unrelated (the middle regression line, which is almost flat).

Discussion

The findings of this field study demonstrated that in the context of a mandatory volunteerism program, behavioral intentions to engage in volunteer work in the future were positively related to past histories of volunteerism—but only for students who did not feel that the program had overly controlled their behavior. These results support the findings of earlier research demonstrating that external constraints to act, in the form of requirements or rewards, may reduce interest in an activity (e.g., Batson et al., 1978; Kunda & Schwartz, 1983). This research has consistently shown that such decrements in interest result most strongly for individuals with prior interest in an activity. Indeed, in our study, when external constraints were perceived to be controlling, an inhibiting effect was strongest for participants with greater prior experience as volunteers—individuals for whom such an inhibiting effect was possible.

Conducting this research with students in an actual mandatory volunteerism program gives us confidence that we have assessed reactions to requirements as they exist in actual educational environments. Yet investigating these effects in the field with actual required volunteers also meant that we were unable to conduct a true experiment; all participants were ex-

---

2. Correlates of perceptions of external control were investigated. Higher perceptions of control were significantly associated with fewer months of prior experience ($r = -.13$) age ($r = .11$), and the motivations measured by our (Clary, Snyder, Ridge, et al., 1998) Volunteer Functions Inventory (rs from $-.15$ to $-.50$). A significant gender difference in perceptions of control indicated that men had higher perceptions of control ($M = 8.87$) than women ($M = 7.45$), $t(330) = -3.87$, $p < .000$.

3. Six individuals with outlying scores on the experience variable (more than 6 years of prior experience) had their scores altered to 73 months, as recommended by Tabachnick and Fidell (1996, p. 69).}

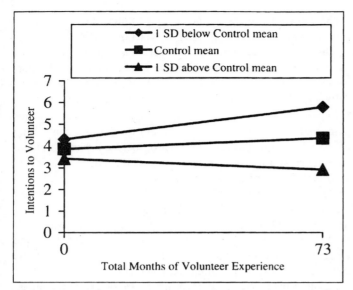

Fig. 1. Future intentions to volunteer regressed on prior volunteer experience at three levels of perceived external control.

posed to the same mandatory volunteerism program, and we could not randomly assign students to conditions and compare those who had been mandated to volunteer with those who had been assigned to choose to volunteer. However, the students entered the program with sufficient variability in their assessments of whether they would be volunteering regardless of the requirement, and our statistical analysis of the moderating effects of perceptions of control allowed us to make comparisons that are functionally similar to those that would be available from an experimental manipulation of mandated and freely chosen volunteerism.[4] Nevertheless, with our second study, we did conduct an experimental examination in which participants were randomly assigned to be required or freely allowed to volunteer; in this way, we could more conclusively demonstrate whether or not future intentions to volunteer were inhibited by requirements to serve.

STUDY 2

In Study 2, we used experimental methods in the laboratory to explicitly compare two routes to volunteerism, requirements and free choices. One possible outcome of an explicit comparison of the effects of required and more freely chosen service is that future intentions will be much higher after volunteer activity is freely chosen than after volunteer activity is required. That is, if service is not required but instead "induced" with an eye toward maintaining students' perceptions of self-determination, students may be less likely to demonstrate the ill effects of feeling controlled.

Given the results of our first study, it seemed likely, however, that individuals' reactions to a manipulation of mandated versus freely chosen volunteerism might depend on their initial

feelings about whether external control would be necessary to get them to volunteer. That is, we thought those who would freely volunteer (without a requirement) might not be differentially affected by being mandated or given a choice; they might be unlikely to have their intentions undermined by a requirement. Those who initially felt that a requirement would be necessary to get them to volunteer might feel more externally controlled by a mandate than a choice; consequently, they could have their intentions undermined by a requirement but not a free choice.

Therefore, in this second study, we examined not only the situational effects of mandates and choices to volunteer, but also whether such effects were moderated by preexisting person-centered judgments about externally controlled volunteerism. In a pretest, long before students were invited to the laboratory, we measured their perceptions about whether they would volunteer freely or only if controlled.[5] Our prediction was that students who thought a high degree of external control would be necessary to get them to volunteer would have much lower intentions to volunteer after being required to serve than after being given a choice; we also expected that students who thought they were likely to volunteer freely (i.e., who thought little external control would be necessary to get them to volunteer) would have higher intentions to volunteer and that their intentions would be relatively unaffected by being mandated to serve (as compared with freely choosing to do so).

Method

Participants

Sixty-three University of Minnesota psychology undergraduates (35 men and 28 women) participated in the study for extra credit.

Procedure

At the start of the semester, participants completed measures related to their inclinations to volunteer freely. Specifically, they responded on 7-point scales to the following questions: "To what extent do you believe that you would only volunteer if it were required of you?" and "To what extent do you believe that when you volunteer it will be because you freely choose to do so?" (reverse coded). Answers to these two items were correlated at $r = .31$ and were averaged into a scale with higher scores indicating greater preexisting perceptions of external control.

Several weeks later, we recruited participants by telephone for a study of "leisure time activities." Upon arrival at the laboratory, they were told that the specific activities under consideration were entertainment (watching music videos) and volunteerism (reading textbooks for the blind). It was emphasized that this volunteer activity was common on campus and

---

4. This examination of the moderating effect of external control on the relation between past experience and prospectively measured future intentions involved predicting a higher order interaction between variables. Such predictions, in some ways, also reduce the threats to internal validity in our nonexperimental design (Cook & Campbell, 1979).

5. Because the effects of control existed even for participants lowest in experience in our first study, we chose not to reexamine the effects of experience in Study 2 and focused instead on subjectively perceived and objectively manipulated control.

that students had the opportunity to continue reading for the blind in the future if they so desired; thus, this was a true volunteer position. All participants were told that the protocol was to allow them to choose the activity they wanted to perform, to perform the activity for 30 min, and then to complete a questionnaire about their attitudes toward the activity.

However, we randomly assigned half of the participants to be told next that because of a scarcity of individuals in the volunteerism condition, they would be forced to read for the blind (mandate condition); we persuaded the other half to choose volunteerism through an induced-compliance technique (i.e., we told them that they did not have to select reading for the blind but it would really help if they did; all students agreed to volunteer in this choice condition). We then taught participants to read a textbook into a tape recorder, and they did so for 15 min.

Afterward, they completed dependent measures. As a manipulation check, students responded to several items designed to examine whether they felt controlled by our choice and mandate conditions.[6] Specifically, they responded to the following two items on 7-point scales: "To what extent did you freely choose to engage in today's task?" and "To what extent do you believe that you read to the blind today only because it was required of you?" (reverse scored). These two items were averaged to form a scale with higher scores indicating greater perceptions of free choice. Participants in the choice condition ($M = 4.72$) were more likely to feel that they had freely chosen to read to the blind than participants in the mandate condition ($M = 3.58$), $t(61) = 3.08$, $p < .01$.

Participants also responded to the following seven items designed to assess their intentions to volunteer: "How likely is it that you will engage in some form of volunteer work this quarter?" " . . .next quarter?" " . . .next summer?" " . . .in the next year?" "How likely is it that you will be a volunteer 3 years from now?" " . . . 5 years from now?" and " . . . 10 years from now?" These items were averaged to form a scale with high scores indicating greater future intentions to volunteer; this scale had excellent internal consistency (alpha = .88).

Results

To investigate whether preexisting perceptions of external control moderated how the conditions of choice and mandate influenced future intentions to volunteer, we performed a median split on the external-control scale. We then performed a planned contrast to examine our hypothesis that individuals with greater perceptions of external control (i.e., those who were not prepared to volunteer freely) would respond differentially to the choice and mandate conditions, whereas individuals with lower perceptions of external control (i.e., those who were prepared to volunteer freely) would be relatively unaffected by the manipulation, as suggested by the results of Study 1. Thus, this contrast compared students who had high

perceptions of external control and were forced to read to the blind (−3), students who had high perceptions of external control and chose to read to the blind (−1), students who had low perceptions of external control and were forced to read to the blind (+2), and students who had low perceptions of external control and chose volunteerism (+2).

This planned comparison was significant, $t(53) = 2.88$, $p < .01$: Mean intention to volunteer in the future was 4.04 for the high-external-control/mandate group, 4.99 for the high-external-control/choice group, 5.03 for the low-external-control/mandate group, and 5.49 for the low-external-control/choice group (Fig. 2). As expected, individuals who had higher perceived external control had lower intentions to volunteer in the future after being required than after being led to freely choose to volunteer. Individuals who had lower perceived external control (who had higher intentions overall) were relatively unaffected by the mandate versus choice conditions.[7]

Discussion

The results of this experiment demonstrated not only that participants had different initial perceptions of whether it would take control to get them to volunteer or whether they would do so freely, but also that those who had different initial perceptions responded differently to mandates to serve and choices to serve. That is, participants who were more inclined against freely volunteering subsequently reported greater future intentions to volunteer when they completed service that was chosen rather than mandated. In contrast, mandates and choices seem not to have differentially affected participants who were initially inclined toward volunteering freely; regardless of the context under which their service was initiated, these individuals reported greater future intentions to volunteer than did those who were initially less likely to volunteer freely.

These results confirm the hypothesis, suggested by Study 1, that required volunteerism is more likely to reduce the intentions of those who perceive that they are being controlled than those who perceive themselves as volunteering freely. That is, compared with conditions of free choice, mandatory volunteerism does have a greater negative impact—but only on those individuals who feel less inclined to volunteer of their own free will.

GENERAL DISCUSSION

Taken together, the field study and the laboratory experiment presented here suggest that whereas earlier laboratory research found that intentions to help (in more short-term or spontaneous helping situations) were undermined by external inducements (Batson et al., 1978; Kunda & Schwartz, 1983), there may actually be important boundary conditions to this effect.

---

6. Six individuals whose scores on these items were outliers within their particular condition were eliminated from further analyses after the t test checking the manipulation.

7. Although it may appear that our significant contrast value is largely attributable to a main effect of perceived external control, we also performed a contrast that explicitly compared individuals with high perceived external control under conditions of mandate and choice (contrast: −1, 1, 0, 0). This contrast was also significant, $t(53) = 2.03$, $p < .05$.

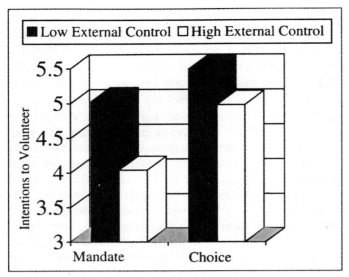

Fig. 2. Future intentions to volunteer after mandated and chosen volunteer activity as a function of perceived external control.

In our first study, we found that a required program undermined the relationship between past experience and future intentions only for those individuals who felt more externally controlled by the program. Students' subjective perceptions of how much a requirement controlled their behavior were a strong moderator of their reactions to the program (e.g., Deci & Ryan, 1987), and stronger perceptions of external control had greater inhibiting effects on those students with the most prior volunteer experience (e.g., Lepper et al., 1973). In our second study, individuals' preexisting feelings about whether they would freely choose to volunteer or not moderated whether a requirement to volunteer (as compared with a choice) affected future intentions to volunteer. This finding, that readiness to volunteer moderated the effects of requirements and choices to volunteer, goes beyond theories about the effects of subjective perceptions of external control (e.g., Deci & Ryan, 1987) to suggest that assessments individuals provide in advance can predict whether they will be negatively affected by requirements to volunteer.

Thus, given these converging results in experimental and nonexperimental investigations conducted in the laboratory and field, it may be the case that requirements to volunteer undermine the future behavioral intentions only of those individuals who currently do not feel free to volunteer (perhaps for a variety of reasons, which may involve interest or available time and resources). That is, only those individuals who would not otherwise be volunteering (Study 1) or who feel that it would take external control to get them to volunteer (Study 2) may find their future intentions undermined by a requirement to volunteer.

Perhaps such subjective assessments are viable moderators of reactions to requirements only for activities that, like volunteering, are typically planned and chosen. Indeed, few activities so overtly suggest a conceptualization of individuals as active, purposeful, and agenda setting (Snyder & Cantor, 1998; Snyder, Clary, & Stukas, in press). Planned helpfulness, as typically construed, represents a phenomenon in which the sa-

lient (external) cues for action are less demanding than the cues in short-term or emergency intervention situations, and usually involves processes that encourage people to look inward for guidance in deciding whether to get involved in helping (e.g., Clary & Snyder, 1991; Clary, Snyder, Ridge, et al., 1998; Omoto & Snyder, 1995; Snyder & Cantor, 1998; Snyder et al., in press). When the typically planned helpfulness of volunteerism is turned into the required helpfulness of mandatory volunteerism, individual agendas may be placed at odds with the agenda of the institution establishing the requirement. Future intentions to volunteer may depend importantly on whether individuals' personal agendas are in harmony or in conflict with the agenda behind the requirement.

The two investigations presented here demonstrate how basic theoretical research can be linked to applied and practical attempts to understand real-world social issues (Snyder, 1993). By using psychological theories about the effects of external inducements to act on future behavioral intentions, not only have we been able to advance theory (by identifying important boundary conditions), but we are also positioned to suggest possible routes for reducing the negative impact of requirements to volunteer. For example, institutions that choose to impose community-service requirements may reduce inhibiting effects by giving students a sense of freedom and autonomy in meeting their requirements. Allowing participants to design the focus and specific details of their service may effectively solve this problem; students themselves may be able to come up with the most creative ways to serve within the frameworks of their existing personal agendas. With such practical and theoretical benefits, action research on volunteerism may be beneficial both to psychological science and to society.

Acknowledgments—This research was supported by grants from the Gannett Foundation and the Aspen Institute's Nonprofit Research Fund to Mark Snyder and E. Gil Clary, and by grants from the National Science Foundation and National Institute of Mental Health to Mark Snyder. This article was written while Mark Snyder held the Chaire Francqui Interuniversitaire au Titre étranger at the Université de Louvain (Louvain-la-Neuve, Belgium). We wish to acknowledge the assistance of the Business 200 program at the University of St. Thomas and its director, Jan Kormann, in making this research possible. We also thank Craig Hunter and Frank Condon, who served as research assistants for Study 2. Portions of this article were presented at the July 1996 meeting of the American Psychological Society in San Francisco and at the May 1998 meeting of the American Psychological Society in Washington, D.C.

REFERENCES

Baron, R., & Kenny, D. (1986). The moderator-mediator variable distinction in social psychological research: Conceptual, strategic, and statistical considerations. *Journal of Personality and Social Psychology, 51,* 1173–1182.

Batson, C. D., Coke, J. S., Jasnoski, M. L., & Hanson, M. (1978). Buying kindness: Effect of an extrinsic incentive for helping on perceived altruism. *Personality and Social Psychology Bulletin, 4,* 86–91.

Brehm, S. S., & Brehm, J. (1981). *Psychological reactance: A theory of freedom and control.* New York: Academic Press.

Charng, H., Piliavin, J. A., & Callero, P. L. (1988). Role identity and reasoned action in the prediction of repeated behavior. *Social Psychological Quarterly, 51,* 303–317.

Clary, E. G., & Snyder, M. (1991). A functional analysis of altruism and prosocial behavior: The case of volunteerism. In M. Clark (Ed.), *Prosocial behavior* (pp. 119–148). Newbury Park, CA: SAGE.

Clary, E. G., Snyder, M., Ridge, R. D., Copeland, J., Stukas, A. A., Haugen, J., & Miene, P. (1998). Understanding and assessing the motivations of volunteers: A functional approach. *Journal of Personality and Social Psychology, 74,* 1516–1530.

Clary, E. G., Snyder, M., & Stukas, A. A. (1998). Service-learning and psychology: Lessons from the psychology of volunteers' motivations. In R. G. Bringle & D. K. Duffy (Eds.), *With service in mind: Concepts and models for service-learning in psychology* (pp. 35–50). Washington, DC: American Association of Higher Education.

Cnaan, R. A., & Goldberg-Glen, R. S. (1991). Measuring motivation to volunteer in human services. *Journal of Applied Behavioral Science, 27,* 269–284.

Cohen, J., & Cohen, P. (1983). *Applied multiple regression/correlation analysis for the behavioral sciences* (2nd ed.). Hillsdale, NJ: Erlbaum.

Cook, T. D., & Campbell, D. T. (1979). *Quasi-experimentation: Design & analysis issues for field settings.* Boston: Houghton Mifflin.

Deci, E. L., & Ryan, R. M. (1985). *Intrinsic motivation and self-determination in human behavior.* New York: Plenum Press.

Deci, E. L., & Ryan, R. M. (1987). The support of autonomy and the control of behavior. *Journal of Personality and Social Psychology, 53,* 1024–1037.

Giles, D. E., Jr., & Eyler, J. (1994). The impact of a college community service laboratory on students' personal, social, and cognitive outcomes. *Journal of Adolescence, 17,* 327–339.

Independent Sector. (1992). *Volunteering and giving among American teenagers 12 to 17 years of age: Findings from a national survey.* Washington, DC: Author.

Independent Sector. (1996). *Giving and volunteering in the United States: Findings from a national survey, 1995.* Washington, DC: Author.

Keith, N. Z. (1994). School-based community service: Answers and some questions. *Journal of Adolescence, 17,* 311–320.

Krebs, D. L., & Miller, D. T. (1985). Altruism and aggression. In G. Lindzey & E. Aronson (Eds.), *Handbook of social psychology* (3rd ed., Vol. 2, pp. 1–71). New York: Random House.

Kunda, Z., & Schwartz, S. (1983). Undermining intrinsic moral motivation: External reward and self-presentation. *Journal of Personality and Social Psychology, 45,* 763–771.

Latané, B., & Darley, J. M. (1970). *The unresponsive bystander: Why doesn't he help?* New York: Appleton.

Lepper, M. R., Greene, D., & Nisbett, R. E. (1973). Undermining children's intrinsic interest with extrinsic reward: A test of the "overjustification" hypothesis. *Journal of Personality and Social Psychology, 28,* 129–137.

Omoto, A. M. & Snyder, M. (1995). Sustained helping without obligation: Motivation, longevity of service, and perceived attitude change among AIDS volunteers. *Journal of Personality and Social Psychology, 68,* 671–686.

Piliavin, J. A., & Callero, P. L. (1991). *Giving blood: The development of an altruistic identity.* Baltimore: Johns Hopkins University Press.

Smith, D. H. (1994). Determinants of voluntary association participation and volunteering: A literature review. *Nonprofit and Voluntary Sector Quarterly, 23,* 243–263.

Snyder, M. (1993). Basic research and practical problems: The promise of a "functional" personality and social psychology. *Personality and Social Psychology Bulletin, 19,* 251–264.

Snyder, M., & Cantor, N. (1998). Understanding personality and social behavior: A functionalist strategy. In D. Gilbert, S. Fiske, & G. Lindzey (Eds.) *The handbook of social psychology: Vol. 1* (4th ed., pp. 635–679). Boston: McGraw-Hill.

Snyder, M., Clary, E. G., & Stukas, A. A. (in press). The functional approach to volunteerism. In G. R. Maio & J. M. Olson (Eds.), *Why we evaluate: Functions of attitudes.* Hillsdale, NJ: Erlbaum.

Snyder, M. & Omoto, A.M. (1992). Who helps and why? The psychology of AIDS volunteerism. In S. Spacapan & S. Oskamp (Eds.), *Helping and being helped: Naturalistic studies* (pp. 213–239). Newbury Park, CA: SAGE.

Sobus, M. S. (1995). Mandating community service: Psychological implications of requiring prosocial behavior. *Law and Psychology Review, 19,* 153–182.

Tabachnick, B. G., & Fidell, L. S. (1996). *Using multivariate statistics* (3rd ed.). New York: Harper Collins.

(RECEIVED 11/18/97; REVISION ACCEPTED 6/30/98)

Unit Selections

Key Points to Consider

❖ What are the most important characteristics of a group experiencing groupthink? How do those characteristics ultimately influence the decisions reached by the group? Other than the Bay of Pigs and *Challenger* disasters, can you think of any well-known group decisions that might be examples of groupthink? Can you think of any examples from groups in your own life?

❖ How successful do you think problem-solving groups like those in the Herbert Kelman article will be in reducing group tensions? On what do you base your answer? Can you think of any other techniques which could be helpful?

❖ What do you think of Daniel Goleman's argument that it is *emotional* intelligence which best separates average from truly effective leaders? What does he mean by emotional intelligence? Would you agree that this is truly a form of intelligence? Why?

 **Links** ## www.dushkin.com/online/

These sites are annotated on pages 4 and 5.

In 1961 President John F. Kennedy and a group of his senior advisers held a series of secret meetings to plan a dramatic military action. The plan under consideration was an invasion of Cuba, and the goal was to overthrow the Communist regime of Fidel Castro. This was not to be a massive invasion, however, utilizing the United States' heavy superiority in numbers and technology; such a move would be too provocative. Instead, the plan called for the United States to secretly train and equip a relatively small force of anti-Castro Cubans—exiles driven from their homeland because of Castro's rise to power. This small force of about 1,400 men would begin the invasion by landing at the Bahia de Cochinos, or the Bay of Pigs. Seizing control of radio stations, they would broadcast news of Cuba's liberation and would then sweep across the country picking up support from the Cuban people until they would constitute a force so compelling that Castro could not endure.

They never had a chance. Supplies that were supposed to sustain the invaders failed to arrive; the tiny invading force was completely overwhelmed by the larger, better-trained Cuban military; and the anticipated uprising by the Cuban people never happened. Within 3 days the entire force had been captured or killed. Instead of a dramatic military success, the United States, and President Kennedy, suffered a humiliating political defeat in the eyes of the world; in fact, the phrase "Bay of Pigs" has come to signify any plan or action that comes to a disastrous end. In the aftermath of this debacle, moreover, it seemed painfully obvious that the plan was doomed from the start. The nagging question, then, was how could some of the smartest people in the country come to agree on a plan that in retrospect seemed to have no chance at all of succeeding? How could the group go so wrong?

That question is one of the many that social psychology has asked about groups, and the processes that occur when people meet in groups. In fact, a very interesting line of research into how groups can reach such bad decisions—a phenomenon known as "groupthink"—was directly inspired by the Bay of Pigs fiasco. According to this approach, highly cohesive groups frequently develop a mind-set characterized by secretiveness, overconfidence, and illusions of invulnerability; this in turn can lead them into decisions that overlook what should be obvious flaws. Other approaches to group decision making have focused on another common phenomenon: the fact that when groups have to choose a course of action, they often make a choice that is more extreme than the decision that each individual would make alone. That is, one effect of group discussion is to polarize the attitudes of the group members.

In addition to the issue of how groups make decisions, another topic of interest has been the impact that groups can have on the behavior of the individuals who make up the group. For example, it frequently happens that individuals work faster and more productively when in the presence of others than they do when they are alone—at least if the task they are working on is relatively simple, or if it is a task with which they have had a lot of practice. In contrast, on a new task, or one which is very complex, the presence of other people can hurt performance. Researchers who study this phenomenon, called social facilitation, have identified a variety of possible explanations for its occurrence.

The selections in this unit represent several different approaches to the study of group processes. The first selection, "Collective Delusions: A Skeptic's Guide," addresses a very interesting phenomenon: the temporary spread, sometimes very rapidly and extensively, of false beliefs among a population of people. Robert Bartholemew examines some of the ways in which familiar social psychological processes can combine to create such delusions.

In "Group Decision Fiascoes Continue: Space Shuttle *Challenger* and a Revised Groupthink Framework," the authors use the decision to launch the ill-fated space shuttle *Challenger* as an example of groupthink. They trace how some of the cognitive biases that characterize groupthink were present during the discussions leading up to the decision to launch.

The next two selections deal with the problem of international conflict. In "Group Processes in the Resolution of International Conflicts: Experiences From the Israeli-Palestinian Case," Herbert Kelman describes his ongoing project designed to help foster greater cooperation between Israelis and Palestinians in the Middle East. By using insights gained from social psychology, Kelman has created interactive problem-solving workshops which help foster greater understanding and cooperation between these two traditionally antagonistic groups. In "Psychology's Own Peace Corps," Annie Murphy Paul specifically examines international problems that arise from intense ethnic conflicts. It seems likely that this conflict can be understood at least partially in terms of psychological concepts such as stereotyping and the need to bolster self-concept by emphasizing ethnic identity.

The final article in this section, "What Makes a Leader?" is concerned with the characteristics which are common to effective leaders of groups. Author Daniel Goleman argues that to a considerable degree what separates the average leader from the gifted leader is "emotional intelligence." That is, while IQ and technical skills are important, most leaders possess these qualities; what distinguishes the best leaders are such characteristics as self-awareness, self-regulation, motivation, empathy, and social skill.

Group Processes

Collective Delusions: A Skeptic's Guide

Collective delusions are an important topic for skeptics to address as they have the potential to influence millions of people.

ROBERT BARTHOLOMEW

The word *delusion* is used by psychiatrists to describe a persistent pathological belief associated with serious mental disturbance, usually psychosis. Sociologists and social psychologists use the term *collective delusion,* or *mass delusion,* in a different sense, to describe the spontaneous, temporary spread of false beliefs within a given population. Excluded from this definition are mistaken beliefs that occur in an organized or ritualistic manner. This term is also a common source of confusion since it is often used as a "catchall" category to describe a variety of different behaviors under one convenient heading. There are four common types of collective delusions: immediate community threats, community flight panics, symbolic community scares, and collective wish-fulfillment. Being familiar with the processes involved in each, and recognizing their features, is the first line of defense to counteract their influence.

Mass delusions differ from prominent religious myths and popular folk beliefs in that they occur in an unorganized, spontaneous fashion, although they may become institutionalized. Examples of institutionalization include the incorporation of claims of widespread satanic-cult sacrifices into the teachings of church groups, or the formation of organizations intended to confirm the existence of alien visitors or Bigfoot.

History is replete with examples of group delusions, many of which may seem humorous to those outside the historical or cultural setting. For instance, in 1806 near Leeds, England, residents became terror-stricken, believing that the end of the world was imminent after a hen began laying eggs with the inscription "Christ is Coming." Masses thronged

Robert Bartholomew is a sociologist at James Cook University, Townsville 4811, Queensland, Australia.

From the *Skeptical Inquirer,* May/June 1997, pp. 29–33. © 1997 by the Committee for the Scientific Investigation of Claims of the Paranormal (CSICOP). Reprinted by permission.

to glimpse the miraculous bird—until it was discovered that the eggs had been inscribed with a corrosive ink and forced back into its body. This is one of many examples from Charles Mackay's classic, *Memoirs of Extraordinary Popular Delusions and the Madness of Crowds* (1852). Unfortunately, the outcomes are often more sinister: Nazism, mass suicide, moral "witch-hunts," real witch-hunts, communist infiltration scares, the Crusades, and unfounded fears about the casual transmission of AIDS, to name but a few.

While historical episodes of collective folly are legendary, modern occurrences are remarkably similar. The four broad categories to be surveyed all involve a rapid spread of false, but plausible, exaggerated beliefs that gain credibility within a particular social and cultural context. They can be positive and take the form of wish-fulfillment, but are usually negative and spread by fear. Rumors are an essential ingredient common to each category of delusion. As persons attempt to confirm or dismiss the accuracy of these unsubstantiated stories of perceived importance, everyday objects, events, and circumstances that would ordinarily receive scant attention become the subject of extraordinary scrutiny. Ambiguous agents are soon redefined according to the emerging definition of the situation, creating a self-fulfilling prophecy. Many factors contribute to the spread of episodes: the mass media, low education levels, the fallibility of human perception, cultural superstitions and stereotypes, group conformity, and reinforcing actions by authority figures, such as politicians, or institutions of social control, such as military agencies.

Immediate Community Threats

These collective delusions involve exaggerated feelings of danger within communities at large, where members of the affected population are concerned over what is believed to be an immediate personal threat. Episodes usually persist from a few weeks to several months and often recur periodically. Participants may express excitement and concern, but they don't panic and take flight. The underlying causes of fantasy creation and spread are the fallibility of human perception and the tendency for persons sharing similar beliefs in group settings to yield to the majority consensus.

An example of an immediate community threat occurred in Sweden during 1946, when there were mass sightings of imaginary rockets flying across the sky. In conjunction with rare cometary debris entering the atmosphere, rumors were circulating that remote-controlled German V-rockets, confiscated by the Soviets at the close of World War II, were being test-fired as a form of political intimidation or a prelude to an invasion. The historical and political contexts

were key factors in rendering the rumors plausible, as the episode occurred amid a long history of mistrust of the Soviets, including invasion fears, border disputes, and spy scandals, which had long preoccupied the Swedes for centuries. Public statements reinforcing the existence of the rockets were made by top Swedish military officials, politicians, scientists, police, and journalists. Convinced of their existence, many citizens began redefining cometary spray that was sporadically streaking across the sky as enemy rockets. Some even claimed to distinguish tail fins or a fuselage. Of 997 reports investigated by the Swedish military, including nearly 100 "crashes" in remote areas, not a single shred of evidence confirming their existence was found, despite the military's extreme measure of draining some lakes to search for evidence (Bartholomew 1993).

Occasionally, the feared agent is a mysterious attacker believed to be terrorizing a community. During a two-week period in 1956, nearly two dozen residents in Taipei, Taiwan, claimed to have been slashed by a man wielding a razor-blade-type object. Police later determined the episode to have been entirely psychological. In the wake of rumors, lacerations from such mundane sources as incidental paper cuts or bumping into an umbrella on a crowded bus were redefined (Jacobs 1965). Sometimes the imaginary threat is from an agent that is believed to cause illness, such as the series of phantom attacks in Mattoon, Illinois, during two weeks in 1944 involving a "mad gasser" (Johnson 1945). In Auckland, New Zealand, in 1973, fifty drums of the compound merphos were being unloaded at a wharf when it was noticed that several barrels were leaking, and a chemical-like smell permeated the air. After immediate requests for information on its toxicity, authorities were wrongly informed that it was extremely toxic, after which at least four hundred dock workers and nearby residents received treatment for a variety of psychosomatic complaints: headache, breathing difficulty, and eye irritation (McLeod 1975).

In non-Western settings, immediate community threats are closely associated with cultural traditions, as in the case of headhunting rumor-panics that have occurred for centuries in remote parts of Malaysia and Indonesia (Forth 1991; Barnes 1993). These episodes represent fears among "primitive" peoples of losing political control to a distant central government. Headhunting scares are characterized by sightings of head-takers and discoveries of their alleged paraphernalia. Just as the vast, ambiguous nighttime sky is an excellent catalyst for spawning UFO sightings, and lakes are conducive to sea-serpent reports, the thickly vegetated Southeast Asian jungle is ideal for misperceiving head-takers lurking in the myriad of foliage. Often villages are paralyzed with fear, travel is severely restricted, sentries are posted, and

schools are closed for months. Most head-hunting scares coincide with the nearby construction of a government bridge or building, during which it is widely believed that one or more human heads are required to produce a strong, enduring foundation. They are a projection of the state of tribal-state relations, reflecting "ideological warfare between the administrators and the administrated" (Drake 1989, 275).

Community Flight Panics

A second type of collective delusion is the community flight panic, where residents attempt to flee an imaginary threat. Episodes may last from a few hours to several days or weeks, subsiding when it is realized that the harmful agent did not materialize. Perhaps the best-known example is the panic that ensued in the United States on Halloween eve in 1938 following the realistic radio enactment of H. G. Wells's book *War of the Worlds* by the CBS Mercury Theater. In his book *The Invasion from Mars: A Study in the Psychology of Panic* (Cantril 1940), psychologist Hadley Cantril notes that in general, those panicking failed to exercise critical thinking, such as telephoning the police or checking other media sources. There remains a great potential for similar hoaxes to recur when they are presented with plausibility and a degree of realism for the participants. A similar broadcast in South America nearly a decade later had disastrous consequences. During 1949, in the vicinity of Quito, Ecuador, a radio play based upon the *War of the Worlds* resulted in tens of thousands of frantic residents pouring into the streets and fleeing for their lives, or preparing to defend themselves against Martian gas raids. Broadcast in Spanish, the program was highly realistic, including the name of a local community, Cotocallo, as the Martian landing site. The play included impersonations of politicians and vivid eyewitness descriptions. It was so convincing that police rushed to Cotocallo to repel the invaders. Quito was left with a skeleton police force that was unable to prevent an angry mob from burning down the building housing the radio station that broadcast the drama. Fifteen people were killed, including the event's mastermind.

Spontaneous mass flights from the city of London have occurred over the centuries in response to prophecies of its destruction by: a great flood in 1524, the Day of Judgment in 1736, and an earthquake in 1761 (Mackay 1852). One of many contemporary examples involving apocalyptic prophecies and mass panic occurred in Adelaide, Australia, in the month leading up to January 19, 1976. Many people fled the city and some even sold their homes after "psychic" John Nash predicted that an earthquake and tidal wave would strike at midday. Many of those who sold their homes or just left to the hills for the day were first generation Greeks and Italians—both Greece and Italy have a long history of devastating earthquakes, and belief in clairvoyants in those countries is generally taken very seriously (Bartholomew 1992).

Four Categories of Collective Delusions:
Immediate community threats
Community flight panics
Symbolic community scares
Collective wish-fulfillment

Symbolic Community Scares

Symbolic community scares typically endure in a waxing and waning fashion for years, encompassing entire countries and geographical regions. They involve less of an immediate concern for safety and welfare, and more of a general, long-term threat. They are primarily symbolic and rumor-driven, consisting of fear over the exaggerated erosion of traditional values. These moral panics are characterized by self-fulfilling stereotypes of ethnic minorities and deviants who are wrongfully indicted for evil deeds, having much in common with the infamous continental European witch persecutions of 1400 to 1650. In *Collective Behavior*, sociologist Erich Goode (1992) aptly summarizes these events, noting that they originated from the disintegration of the Roman Catholic Church during the late Middle Ages and early Renaissance. The feudal hierarchy was unraveling and peasants were migrating to cities. Scientific rationalism, with its secular philosophy, conflicted with church doctrine, and new religious denominations were being formed beyond the church's control. In an unconscious attempt to counteract secularism and reestablish traditional authority, the church-sponsored persecution of witches attempted to redefine moral boundaries, and church inquisitors focused on eradicating various deviants who were viewed as a threat.

Two prominent moral panics have persisted for the past decade. Scores of Western communities with predominantly Judeo-Christian traditions have experienced ongoing rumors about the existence of a network of satanic cults that kidnap and sacrifice children. These rumors coincide with the widespread perception of declining Western morality and traditional values. Under similar historical circumstances, subversion myths have appeared in which a particular alien group is believed to threaten the moral fabric of society. Common scapegoats include minority ethnic groups, Jews, Africans, communists, heretics, deviants, and the poor. Such myths flourish during periods of economic downturn and social unrest, and are characterized by dramatic, plausible rumors containing meaningful, timely morals or messages reflecting popular fears. During oral transmission, local details are substituted and a credible source is identified. Their function is primarily metaphorical. Victor (1990, 290) notes that the contemporary satanic-cult scare coincides with the disintegration of traditional family structures, which intensifies fears and the desire "to blame someone." Unlike scares involving imminent danger, subversion myths present a more generalized threat not only to people, but to a way of life (Hicks 1990, 387), as rumors and urban legends of local satanic cults function as cautionary cultural metaphors about the inability of the weakened family to protect children (Bromley 1989; Victor 1989). A similar symbolic process drives child sex-abuse panics that have appeared periodically in certain regions for decades (Cockburn 1990).

Collective Wish-Fulfillment

Mass wish-fulfillment involves processes similar to those that cause community threats and moral panics, except the object of interest is esteemed and satisfies psychological needs. Cases typically persist for a few weeks or months and recur periodically in clusters. Episodes involve a subconscious wish that is related to human mortality in conjunction with a plausible belief, fostering a collective quest for transcendence. Examples include Virgin Mary "appearances" (Yassa 1980; Persinger and Derr 1989), "moving" religious statues in Ireland (Toibin 1985), waves of claims and public discourse surrounding widespread reports of fairies in England before the twentieth century (Kirk 1812; Evans-Wentz 1909), and flying saucers worldwide since 1947 (Sheaffer 1981). These myths are supported by a spiritual void left by the ascendancy of rationalism and secular humanism. Within this context, and fostered by sensationalized documentaries, movies, and books, contemporary populations have been conditioned to scan the heavens for "UFOs," representing what Carl Jung (1959) termed "technological angels." These sightings serve as a projected Rorschach inkblot test of the collective psyche, underscoring the promise of rapid technological advancement during a period of spiritual decline.

Accounts of UFO occupants and fairies depict godlike beings capable of transcending natural laws and, thus, potentially elevating humans to their immortal realm. They reflect themes similar to those found in religion, mythology, and folklore throughout the world, camouflaged for contemporary acceptance (Bullard 1989). Transcendence and magical or supernatural powers are an underlying theme in most wish-fulfillments. Education builds resistance but does not provide immunity to what philosopher Paul Kurtz (1991) terms "the transcendental temptation." Even observations of imaginary and extinct creatures, such as Bigfoot and the Tasmanian "Tiger," respectively, once considered the sole domains of zoology, have undergone recent transformations with the emergence of a new motif among paranormal researchers that links extraterrestrial or paranormal themes with phantom animals (Clark and Coleman 1978; Healy and Cropper 1994). The existence of such animals can be viewed as an antiscientific symbol undermining secularism. Like claims of contact with UFOs or the Virgin Mary, evidence for the existence of Bigfoot and Tasmanian "Tigers" ultimately rests with eyewitness testimony, which is notoriously unreliable (Loftus 1979; Buckhout 1980; Ross et al. 1994).

A Note on Non-Western Delusions

Human gullibility is limited only by plausibility. This is especially apparent in non-Western countries where superstitions are often rampant. For example, in some cultures it is widely believed that eating certain foods or having contact with "ghosts" can cause one's sex organs to rapidly shrivel. It is a remarkable example of the power of self-delusion that men in parts of Asia continue to experience "koro" epidemics, convinced that they are the victims of a contagious disease that causes their penises to shrink. Episodes are triggered by rumors and last from a few days to several months and often affect thousands. "Victims" suffer intense anxiety, sweating, palpitations, insomnia, and often take the extreme measure of placing clamps or string onto the organ or having family members hold the penis in relays until treatment is obtained, usually from native healers. Occasionally women are affected, believing that their breasts and vagina are being pulled into their bodies. During a koro episode on the tiny island nation of Singapore in 1967, thousands of citizens were affected, both males and females, forcing the government to declare an emergency (Gwee 1968; Mun 1968). Pandemonium reigned during an outbreak in northeast India in 1982. So widespread was the panic that medical authorities took the drastic measure of touring the region with loudspeakers to reassure anxious residents and measured penises at intervals to demonstrate that no shrinkage was taking place (Chakraborty et al. 1983). Ignorance of human perceptual fallibility, combined with rumors and traditional beliefs, resulted in frantic citizens intensely scrutinizing their genitalia.

While koro may seem to represent extreme irrationality to outsiders, outbreaks differ from mass delusions in Western countries in only one significant respect—the rumor-related object. In this case, it is the sex organs and their changing size, shape, and firmness. For the mass delusion to occur, the object of scrutiny must be of perceived importance, and the rumor credible. Hence, in theory, the sole factor preventing similar Western epidemics is the absence of koro cultural traditions.

The Lure of Mass Delusions

Collective delusions possess a powerful seductive lure that continuously changes in a chameleon-like fashion to enable us to confirm our deepest fears or realize our greatest desires. Most Westerners can easily distinguish koro and headhunting scares as the products of myth and superstition. Yet, many of these same people are likely to believe in the reality of flying saucers, ghosts, or psychic phenomena. We must always be prepared to evaluate incredible claims based on the available facts and avoid making emotional judgments. The underlying themes of collective delusions remain constant. Circumstances surrounding the Adelaide earthquake panic of 1976 are virtually identical to those of the London earthquake panic of 1761. Contemporary child-molestation and satanic-cult fears resemble the persecution of various deviants and ethnic groups during the infamous medieval European witch-hunts. Today's wish-fulfillments parallel transcendent elements that have been prominent fixtures in religious movements for millennia. Only the form changes to reflect the social and cultural context.

References

Barnes, R. H. 1993. Construction sacrifice, kidnapping and head hunting rumours on Flores and elsewhere in Indonesia. *Oceania* 64: 146–158.

Bartholomew, R. 1992. A brief history of mass hysteria in Australia. *The Skeptic* (Australia) 12: 23–26.

Bartholomew, R. 1993. Redefining epidemic hysteria: An example from Sweden. *Acta Psychiatrica Scandinavica* 88: 178–182.

Bromley, D. G. 1989. Folk narratives and deviance construction: Cautionary tales as a response to structural tensions in the social order. In *Deviance and Popular Culture,* edited by C. Sanders.

Buckhout, R. 1980. Nearly 2,000 witnesses can be wrong. *Bulletin of the Psychonomic Society* 16: 307–310.

Bullard, T. E. 1989. UFO abduction reports: The supernatural kidnap narrative returns in technological guise. *Journal of American Folklore* 102: 147–170.

Cantril, H. 1940. *The Invasion from Mars: A Study in the Psychology of Panic.* Princeton: Princeton University Press.

Chakraborty, A., S. Das, and A. Mukherji. 1983. Koro epidemic in India. *Transcultural Psychiatric Research Review* 20: 150–151.

Clark, J., and L. Coleman. 1978. *Creatures of the Outer Edge.* New York: Warner.

Cockburn, A. 1990. Abused imaginings. *New Statesman and Society* 85: 19–20.

Drake, R. A. 1989. Construction sacrifice and kidnapping: Rumor panics in Borneo. *Oceania* 59: 269–278.

Evans-Wentz, W. Y. 1909. *The Fairy Faith in Celtic Countries.* Rennes, France: Oberthur.

Forth, G. 1991. Construction sacrifice and headhunting rumours in central Flores (Eastern Indonesia): A comparative note. *Oceania* 61: 257–266.

Goode, E. 1992. *Collective Behavior.* New York: Harcourt Brace Jovanovich.

Gwee, A. L. 1968. Koro: Its origin and nature as a disease entity. *Singapore Medical Journal* 9: 3.

Healy, T. and P. Cropper. 1994. *Out of the Shadow: Mystery Animals of Australia.* Ironbark: Chippendale.

Hicks, R. D. 1990. Police pursuit of satanic crime, part II: The satanic conspiracy and urban legends. Skeptical Inquirer 14: 378–389.

Jacobs, N. 1965. The phantom slasher of Taipei: Mass hysteria in a non-Western society. *Social Problems* 12: 318–328.

Johnson, D. 1945. The "phantom anesthetist" of Matoon: A field study of mass hysteria. *Journal of Abnormal Psychology* 40: 175–186.

Jung, C. 1959. *Flying Saucers: A Modern Myth of Things Seen in the Sky.* New York: Harcourt Brace and World.

Kirk, R. 1812. *The Secret Commonwealth of Elves, Fauns and Fairies.* London: Longman.

Kurtz, P. 1991. *The Transcendental Temptations: A Critique of Religion and the Paranormal.* Buffalo, N.Y.: Prometheus.

Loftus, E. 1979. *Eyewitness Testimony.* Cambridge, Mass.: Harvard University Press.

Mackay, C. 1852. *Memoirs of Extraordinary Popular Delusions and the Madness of Crowds, Volume 2,* London: Office of the National Illustrated Library.

McLeod, W. R. 1975. Merphos poisoning or mass panic? *Australian and New Zealand Journal of Psychiatry* 9: 225–229.

Mun, C. I. 1968. Epidemic koro in Singapore. *British Medical Journal* 1: 640–641.

Park, A. 1986. Tasmanian tiger: Extinct or merely elusive? *Australian Geographic* 1: 66–83.

Persinger, M., and J. Derr, 1989. Geophysical variables and behavior: LIV. Zeitoun (Egypt) apparitions of the Virgin Mary as tectonic strain-induced luminosities. *Perceptual and Motor Skills* 68: 123–128.

Ross, R., J. Read, and M. Toglia. 1994. *Adult Eyewitness Testimony: Current Trends and Developments.* Cambridge: Cambridge University Press.

Sheaffer, R. 1981. *The UFO Verdict.* Buffalo, N.Y.: Prometheus.

Toibin, C. 1985. *Moving Statues in Ireland: Seeing Is Believing.* County Laois, Erie: Pilgrim Press.

Victor, J. 1989. A rumor-panic about a dangerous satanic cult in Western New York. *New York Folklore* 15: 23–49.

Victor, J. 1990. The spread of satanic cult rumors. Skeptical Inquirer 14: 287–291.

Yassa, R. 1980. A sociopsychiatric study of an Egyptian phenomenon. *American Journal of Psychotherapy* 34: 246–251.

Group Decision Fiascoes Continue:

Space Shuttle Challenger and a Revised Groupthink Framework

Gregory Moorhead, Richard Ference and Chris P. Neck

In this article, the authors review the events surrounding the tragic decision to launch the space shuttle Challenger. Moorhead and his colleagues assert that the decision-making process demonstrates *groupthink,* a phenomenon wherein cohesive groups become so concerned with their own process that they lose sight of the true requirements of their task. The authors review the events in light of this concept, suggesting that the groupthink concept needs to be expanded to consider time pressures, which were surely present in the Challenger situation, as well as the kind of leadership patterns that exist in a group.

In 1972, a new dimension was added to our understanding of group decision making with the proposal of the groupthink hypothesis by Janis (1972). Janis coined the term "groupthink" to refer to "a mode of thinking that people engage in when they are deeply involved in a cohesive in-group, when the members' striving for unanimity override their motivation to realistically appraise alternative courses of action" (Janis, 1972, p. 8). The hypothesis was supported by his hindsight analysis of several political-military fiascoes and successes that are differentiated by the occurrence or non-occurrence of antecedent conditions, groupthink symptoms, and decision-making defects.

In a subsequent volume, Janis further explicates the theory and adds an analysis of the Watergate transcripts and various published memoirs and accounts of principals involved, concluding that the Watergate cover-up decision also was a result of groupthink (Janis, 1983). Both volumes propose prescriptions for preventing the occurrence of groupthink, many of which have appeared in popular press, in books on executive decision making, and in management textbooks. Multiple advocacy decision-making procedures have been adopted at the execu-

tive levels in many organizations, including the executive branch of the government. One would think that by 1986, 13 years after the publication of a popular book, that its prescriptions might be well ingrained in our management and decision-making styles. Unfortunately, it has not happened.

On January 28, 1986, the space shuttle Challenger was launched from Kennedy Space Center. The temperature that morning was in the mid-20's, well below the previous low temperatures at which the shuttle engines had been tested. Seventy-three seconds after launch, the Challenger exploded, killing all seven astronauts aboard, and becoming the worst disaster in space flight history. The catastrophe shocked the nation, crippled the American space program, and is destined to be remembered as the most tragic national event since the assassination of John F. Kennedy in 1963.

The Presidential Commission that investigated the accident pointed to a flawed decision-making process as a primary contributory cause. The decision was made the night before the launch in the Level I Flight Readiness Review meeting. Due to the work of the Presidential Commission, information concerning that meeting is available for analysis as a group decision possibly susceptible to groupthink.

In this paper, we report the results of our analysis of the Level I Flight Readiness Review meeting as a decision-making situation that displays evidence of groupthink. We review the antecedent conditions, the groupthink symptoms, and the possible decision-making defects, as suggested by Janis (1983). In addition, we take the next and more important step by going beyond the development of another example of groupthink to make recommendations for renewed inquiry into group decision-making processes.

THEORY AND EVIDENCE

The meeting(s) took place throughout the day and evening from 12:36 p.m. (EST), January 27, 1986 following the decision to not launch the Challenger due to high crosswinds at the launch site. Discussions continued through about 12:00 midnight (EST) via teleconferencing and Telefax systems connecting the Kennedy Space Center in Florida, Morton Thiokol (MTI) in Utah, Johnson Space Center in Houston, and the Marshall Space Flight Center. The Level I Flight Readiness Review is the highest level of review prior to launch. It comprises the highest level of management at the three space centers and at MTI, the private supplier of the solid rocket booster engines.

To briefly state the situation, the MTI engineers recommended not to launch if temperatures of the O-ring seals on the rocket were below 53 degrees Fahrenheit, which was the lowest temperature of any previous flight. Laurence B. Mulloy, manager of the Solid Rocket Booster at Marshall Space Flight Center, states:

> The bottom line of that, though, initially was that Thiokol engineering, Bob Lund, who is the Vice President and Director of Engineering, who is here today, recommended that 51-L [the Challenger] not be launched if the O-ring temperatures predicted at launch time would be lower than any previous launch, and that was 53 degrees (*Report of the Presidential Commission on the Space Shuttle Accident*, 1986, p. 91–92).

This recommendation was made at 8:45 p.m., January 27, 1986 (*Report of the Presidential Commission on the Space Shuttle Accident*, 1986). Through the ensuing discussions the decision to launch was made.

Antecedent Conditions

The three primary antecedent conditions for the development of groupthink are: a highly cohesive group, leader preference for a certain decision, and insulation of the group from qualified outside opinions. These conditions existed in this situation.

Cohesive Group. The people who made the decision to launch had worked together for many years. They were familiar with each other and had grown through the ranks of the space program. A high degree of *esprit de corps* existed between the members.

Leader Preference. Two top level managers actively promoted their pro-launch opinions in the face of opposition. The commission report states that several managers at space centers and MTI pushed for launch, regardless of the low temperatures.

Insulation from Experts. MTI engineers made their recommendations relatively early in the evening. The top level decision-making group knew of their objections but did not meet with them directly to review their data and concerns. As Roger Boisjoly, a Thiokol engineer, states in his remarks to the Presidential Commission:

> and the bottom line was that the engineering people would not recommend a launch below 53 degrees Fahrenheit.... From this point on, management formulated the points to base their decision on. There was never one comment in favor, as I have said, of launching by any engineer or other nonmanagement person.... I was not even asked to participate in giving any input to the final decision charts (*Report of the Presidential Commission on the Space Shuttle Accident, 1986*, p. 91–92).

This testimonial indicates that the top decision-making team was insulated from the engineers who possessed the expertise regarding the functioning of the equipment.

Janis identified eight symptoms of groupthink. They are presented here along with evidence from the *Report of the Presidential Commission on the Space Shuttle Accident* (1986).

Invulnerability. When groupthink occurs, most of all of the members of the decision-making group have an illusion of invulnerability that reassures them in the face of obvious dangers. This illusion leads the group to become overly optimistic and willing to take extraordinary risks. It may also cause them to ignore clear warnings of danger.

The solid rocket joint problem that destroyed Challenger was discussed often at flight readiness review meetings prior to flight. However, Commission member Richard Feynman concluded from the testimony that a mentality of overconfidence existed due to the extraordinary record of success of space flights. Every time we send one up it is successful. Involved members may seem to think that on the next one we can lower our standards or take more risks because it always works (*Time*, 1986).

The invulnerability illusion may have built up over time as a result of NASA's own spectacular history. NASA had not lost an astronaut since 1967 when a flash fire in the capsule of Apollo 1 killed three. Since that time NASA had a string of 55 successful missions. They had put a man on the moon, built and launched Skylab and the shuttle, and retrieved defective satellites from orbit. In the minds of most Americans and apparently their own, they could do no wrong.

Rationalization. Victims of groupthink collectively construct rationalizations that discount warnings and other forms of negative feedback. If these signals were taken seriously when presented, the group members would be forced to reconsider their assumptions each time they re-commit themselves to their past decisions.

In the Level I flight readiness meeting when the Challenger was given final launch approval, MTI engineers presented evidence that the joint would fail. Their argument was based on the fact that in the coldest previous launch (air temperature 30 degrees) the joint in question experienced serious erosion and that no data existed as to how the joint would perform at colder temperatures. Flight center officials put forth numerous technical rationalizations faulting MTI's analysis. One of these rationalizations was that the engineer's data were inconclusive. As Mr. Boisjoly emphasized to the Commission:

> I was asked, yes, at that point in time I was asked to quantify my concerns, and I said I couldn't. I couldn't quantify it. I had no data to quantify it, but I did say I knew that it was away from goodness in the current data base. Someone on the net commented that we had soot blow-by on SRM-22 [Flight 61-A, October, 1985] which was launched at 75 degrees. I don't remember who made the comment, but that is where the first comment came in about the disparity between my conclusion and the observed data because SRM-22 [Flight 61-A, October 1985] had blow-by at essentially a room temperature launch. I then said that SRM-15 [Flight 51-C, January, 1985] had much more blow-by indication and that it was indeed telling us that lower temperature was a factor. I was asked again for data to support my claim, and I said I have none other than what is being presented (*Report of the Presidential Commission on the Space Shuttle Accident*, 1986, p. 89).

Discussions became twisted (compared to previous meetings) and no one detected it. Under normal conditions, MTI would have to prove the shuttle boosters readiness for launch, instead they found themselves being forced to prove that the boosters were unsafe. Boisjoly's testimony supports this description of the discussion:

> This was a meeting where the determination was to launch, and it was up to us to prove beyond a shadow of a doubt that it was not safe to do so. This is in total reverse to what the position usually is in a preflight conversation or a flight readiness review. It is usually exactly the opposite of that (*Report of the Presidential Commission on the Space Shuttle Accident*, 1986, p. 93).

Morality. Group members often believe, without question, in the inherent morality of their position. They tend to ignore the ethical or moral consequences of their decision.

In the Challenger case, this point was raised by a very high level MTI manager, Allan J. McDonald, who tried to stop the launch and said that he would not want to have to defend the decision to launch. He stated to the Commission:

> I made the statement that if we're wrong and something goes wrong on this flight, I wouldn't want to have to be the person to stand up in front of board in inquiry and say that I went ahead and told them to go ahead and fly this thing outside what the motor was qualified to (*Report of the Presidential Commission on the Space Shuttle Accident*, 1986, p. 95).

Some members did not hear this statement because it occurred during a break. Three top officials who did hear it ignored it.

Stereotyped Views of Others. Victims of groupthink often have a stereotyped view of the opposition of anyone with a competing opinion. They feel that the opposition is too stupid or too weak to understand or deal effectively with the problem.

Two of the top three NASA officials responsible for the launch displayed this attitude. They felt that they completely understood the nature of the joint problem and never seriously considered the objections raised by the MTI engineers. In fact they denigrated and badgered the opposition and their information and opinions.

Pressure on Dissent. Group members often apply direct pressure to anyone who questions the validity of these arguments supporting a decision or position favored by the majority. These same two officials pressured MTI to change its position after MTI originally recommended that the launch not take place. These two officials pressured MTI personnel to prove that it was not safe to launch, rather than to prove the opposite. As mentioned earlier, this was a total reversal of normal preflight procedures. It was this pressure that top MTI management was responding to when they overruled their engineering staff and recommended launch. As the Commission report states:

> At approximately 11 p.m. Eastern Standard Time, the Thiokol/NASA teleconference resumed, the Thiokol management stating that they had reassessed the problem, that the temperature effects were a concern, but that the data was admittedly inconclusive (p. 96).

This seems to indicate the NASA's pressure on these Thiokol officials forced them to change their recommendation from delay to execution of the launch.

Self-Censorship. Group members tend to censor themselves when they have opinions or ideas that deviate from the apparent group consensus. Janis feels that this reflects each member's inclination to minimize to himself or herself the importance of his or her own doubts and counter-arguments.

The most obvious evidence of self-censorship occurred when a vice president of MTI, who had previously presented information against launch, bowed to pressure from NASA and accepted their rationalizations for launch. He then wrote these up and presented them to NASA as the reasons that MTI had changed its recommendation to launch.

Illusion of Unanimity. Group members falling victim to groupthink share an illusion of unanimity concerning judgments made by members speaking in favor of the majority view. This symptom is caused in part by the preceding one and is aided by the false assumption that any participant who remains silent is in agreement with the majority opinion. The group leader and other members support each other by playing up points of convergence in their thinking at the expense of fully exploring points of divergence that might reveal unsettling problems.

No participant from NASA ever openly agreed with or even took sides with MTI in the discussion. The silence from NASA was probably amplified by the fact that the meeting was a teleconference linking the participants at three different locations. Obviously, body language which might have been evidenced by dissenters was not visible to others who might also have held a dissenting opinion. Thus, silence meant agreement.

Mindguarding. Certain group members assume the role of guarding the minds of others in the group. They attempt to shield the group from adverse information that might destroy the majority view of the facts regarding the appropriateness of the decision.

The top management at Marshall knew that the rocket casings had been ordered redesigned to correct a flaw 5 months previous to this launch. This information and other technical details concerning the history of the joint problem was withheld at the meeting.

Decision-Making Defects

The result of the antecedent conditions and the symptoms of groupthink is a defective decision-making process. Janis discusses several defects in decision making that can result.

Few Alternatives. The group considers only a few alternatives, often only two. No initial survey of all possible alternatives occurs. The Flight Readiness Review team had a launch/no-launch decision to make. These were the only two alternatives considered. Other possible alternatives might have been to delay the launch for further testing, or to delay until the temperatures reached an appropriate level.

No Re-Examination of Alternatives. The group fails to reexamine alternatives that may have been initially discarded based on early unfavorable information. Top NASA officials spent time and effort defending and strengthening their position, rather than examining the MTI position.

Rejecting Expert Opinions. Members make little or no attempt to seek outside experts' opinions. NASA did not seek out other experts who might have some expertise in this area. They assumed that they had all the information.

Rejecting Negative Information. Members tend to focus on supportive information and ignore any data or information that might cast a negative light on their preferred alternative. MTI representatives repeatedly tried to point out errors in the rationale the NASA officials were using to justify the launch. Even after the decision was made, the argument continued until a NASA official told the MTI representative that it was no longer his concern.

No Contingency Plans. Members spend little time discussing the possible consequences of the decision and, therefore, fail to develop contingency plans. There is no documented evidence in the Rogers Commission Report of any discussion of the possible consequences of an incorrect decision.

The major categories and key elements of the groupthink hypothesis have been presented (albeit somewhat briefly) along with evidence from the discussions prior to the launching of the Challenger, as reported in the President's Commission to investigate the accident. The antecedent conditions were present in the decision-making group, even though the group was in several physical locations. The leaders had a preferred solution and engaged in behaviors designed to promote it rather than critically appraise alternatives. These behaviors were evidence of most of the symptoms leading to a defective decision-making process.

DISCUSSION

This situation provides another example of decision making in which the group fell victim to the groupthink syndrome, as have so many previous groups. It illus-

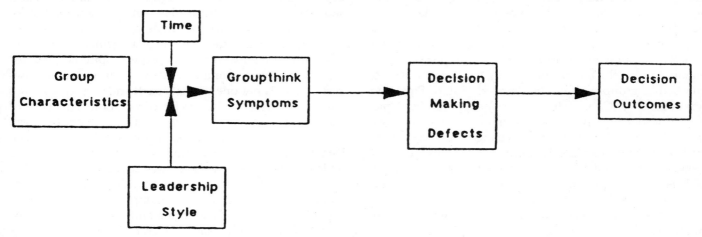

Figure 1   Revised groupthink framework

trates the situation characteristics, the symptoms of groupthink, and decision-making defects as described by Janis. This situation, however, also illustrates several other aspects of situations that are critical to the development of groupthink model. First, the element of time in influencing the development of groupthink has not received adequate attention. In the decision to launch the space shuttle Challenger, time was a crucial part of the decision-making process. The launch had been delayed once, and the window for another launch was fast closing. The leaders of the decision team were concerned about public and congressional perceptions of the entire space shuttle program and its continued funding and may have felt that further delays of the launch could seriously impact future funding. With the space window fast closing, the decision team was faced with a launch now or seriously damage the program decision. One top level manager's response to Thiokol's initial recommendation to postpone the launch indicates the presence of time pressure:

> With this LCC (Launch Commit Criteria), i.e., do not launch with a temperature greater [sic] than 53 degrees, we may not be able to launch until next April. We need to consider this carefully before we jump to any conclusions (*Report of the Presidential Commission on the Space Shuttle Accident*, 1996, p. 96).

Time pressure could have played a role in the group choosing to agree and to self-censor their comments. We propose that in certain situations when there is pressure to make a decision quickly, the elements may combine to foster the development of groupthink.

The second revision needs to be in the role of the leadership of the decision-making group. In the space shuttle Challenger incident, the leadership of the group varied from a shared type of leadership to a very clear leader in the situation. This may indicate that the leadership role needs to be clearly defined and a style that demands open disclosure of information, points of opposition, complaints, and dissension. We propose the leadership style is a crucial variable that moderates the relationship between the group characteristics and the development of the symptoms. Janis (1983) is a primary form of evidence to support the inclusion of leadership style in the enhanced model. His account of why the *same* group succumbed to groupthink in one decision (Bay of Pigs) and not in another (Cuban Missile Crisis) supports the depiction of leadership style as a moderator variable. In these decisions, the only condition that changed was the leadership style of the President. In other words, the element that seemed to distinguish why groupthink occurred in the Bay of Pigs decision and not in the Cuban Missile Crisis situation is the president's change in his behavior.

These two variables, time and leadership style, are proposed as moderators of the impact of the group characteristics on groupthink syndrome. This relationship is portrayed graphically in Fig. 1. In effect, we propose that the groupthink symptoms result from the group characteristics, as proposed by Janis, but only in the presence of the moderator variables of time and certain leadership styles.

Time, as an important element in the model, is relatively straightforward. When a decision must be made within a very short time frame, pressure on members to agree, to avoid time-consuming arguments and reports from outside experts, and to self-censor themselves may increase. These pressures inevitably cause group members to seek agreement. In Janis's original model, time was included indirectly as a function of the antecedent condition, group cohesion. Janis (1983) argued that time pressures can adversely affect decision quality in two ways. First, it affects the decision makers' mental efficiency and judgment, interfering with their ability to concentrate on complicated discussions, to absorb new information, and to use imagination to anticipate the future consequences of alternative courses of action. Second, time pressure is a source of stress that will have the effect of inducing a policy-making group to become more cohesive and more likely to engage in groupthink.

Leadership style is shown to be a moderator because of the importance it plays in either promoting or avoiding the development of the symptoms of the groupthink. The leader, even though she or he may not promote a preferred solution, may allow or even assist the group seeking agreement by not forcing the group to critically appraise all alternative courses of action. The focus of this leadership variable is on the degree to which the leader allows or promotes discussion and evaluation of alternatives. It is not a matter of simply not making known a preferred solution; the issue is one of stimulation of critical thinking among the group.

Impact on Prescriptions for Prevention

The revised model suggests that more specific prescriptions for prevention of groupthink can be made. First, group members need to be aware of the impact that a short decision time frame has on decision processes. When a decision must be made quickly, there will be more pressure to agree, i.e., discouragement of dissent, self-censorship, avoidance of expert opinion, and assumptions about unanimity. The type of leadership suggested here is not one that sits back and simply does not make known her or his preferred solution. This type of leader must be one that requires all members to speak up with concerns, questions, and new information. The leader must know what some of these concerns are and which members are likely to have serious doubts so that the people with concerns can be called upon to voice them. This type of group leadership does not simply assign the role of devil's advocate and step out of the way. This leader actually plays the role or makes sure that others do. A leader with the required style to avoid groupthink is not a laissez-faire leader or non-involved participative leader. This leader is active in directing the activities of the group but does not make known a preferred solution. The group still must develop and evaluate alternative courses of action, but under the direct influence of a strong, demanding leader who forces critical appraisal of all alternatives.

Finally, a combination of the two variables suggests that the leader needs to help members to avoid the problems created by the time element. For example, the leader may be able to alter an externally imposed time frame for the decision by negotiating an extension or even paying late fees, if necessary. If an extension is not possible, the leader may need to help the group eliminate the effects of time on the decision processes. This can be done by forcing attention to issues rather than time, encouraging dissension and confrontation, and scheduling special sessions to hear reports from outside experts that challenge prevailing views within the group.

Janis presents, in both editions of his book, several recommendations for preventing the occurrence of groupthink. These recommendations focus on the inclusion of outside experts in the decision-making process, all members taking the role of devil's advocate and critically appraising all alternative courses of action, and the leader not expressing a preferred solution. The revised groupthink framework suggests several new prescriptions that may be helpful in preventing further decision fiascoes similar to the decision to launch the space shuttle Challenger.

References

Time. Fixing NASA. June 9, 1986.

Janis, I. L. (1983). *Victims of groupthink.* Boston: Houghton Mifflin.

Janis, I. L. (1983). *Groupthink* (2nd ed., revised). Boston: Houghton Mifflin.

Report of the Presidential Commission on the Space Shuttle Accident. Washington, D.C.: July 1986.

Group Processes in the Resolution of International Conflicts

Experiences From the Israeli–Palestinian Case

Herbert C. Kelman
Harvard University

For over 20 years, politically influential Israelis and Palestinians have met in private, unofficial, academically based, problem-solving workshops designed to enable the parties to explore each other's perspective, generate joint ideas for mutually satisfactory solutions to their conflict, and transfer insights and ideas derived from their interaction into the policy process. Most of the work takes place in small groups, but the focus is on promoting change in the larger system. This article discusses 5 ways in which the workshop group serves as a vehicle for change at the macrolevel. It does so by functioning as a microcosm of the larger system, as a laboratory for producing inputs into the larger system, as a setting for direction interaction, as a coalition across conflict lines, and as a nucleus for a new relationship.

The Israeli–Palestinian conflict has long been cited as a typical case of a protracted, intractable conflict. The origins of the conflict go back to the birth of modern political Zionism at the end of the 19th century. Violence first erupted in the 1920s, and, in various forms and with varying degrees of intensity, it has pervaded the relationship between the two peoples since that time. The psychological core of the conflict has been its perception by the two sides as a zero-sum conflict around national identity and national existence, which has led over the years to mutual denial of the other's identity and systematic efforts to delegitimize the other (Kelman, 1978, 1987). Under the circumstances, the parties had been reluctant for a long time to go to the negotiation table and, indeed, to offer each other the assurances and enticements that would make negotiations safe and promising in their eyes.

Nevertheless, in response to a strong initiative from the U.S. administration, Israelis and Palestinians finally entered into a process of direct negotiations, starting with the Madrid Conference in the fall of 1991. The mere fact that the parties were negotiating represented a significant departure in the history of the conflict, but the official talks themselves, which continued in Washington, DC, for nearly two years, did not develop their own momentum and seemed to arrive at an impasse (cf. Kelman, 1992a). In the meantime, however, secret talks between representatives of Israel's Labor Party-led government (elected in June 1992) and the Palestine Liberation Organization, held in Oslo in 1993, produced a dramatic agreement that was signed by the parties on the White House lawn in September 1993. The Oslo accord took the form of an exchange of letters of mutual recognition between the official representatives of the two peoples, followed by a Declaration of Principles (DOP) that stipulated the establishment of a Palestinian authority in Gaza and Jericho as the first step in Palestinian self-rule. Despite the shortcomings of the DOP and despite the fact that the most difficult political issues were left to be resolved in the final-status negotiations, which were scheduled to begin in May 1996, the Oslo accord represents a fundamental breakthrough in the Israeli–Palestinian con-

Editor's note. Michael G. Wessells served as action editor for this article.

Author's note. This article is based on an address delivered on August 13, 1995, at the 103rd Annual Convention of the American Psychological Association in New York, on receipt of the 1995 Distinguished Group Psychologist Award from Division 49 (Group Psychology and Group Psychotherapy). The award citation read, "Involved in study, research, publication and action, he exemplifies the very best in social science. As a group psychologist, he has studied and practiced conflict resolution in real life terms, and has expanded the reach and influence of group therapeutic understanding. In making a singular contribution to Middle East peace, he models the most creative blends of academics and practice."

The action research program on which this article is based is carried out in collaboration with Nadim Rouhana of Boston College under the auspices of the Program on International Conflict Analysis and Resolution (PICAR) at the Harvard Center for International Affairs. It is supported by grants from the Nathan Cummings Foundation, the Charles R. Bronfman Foundation, the Carnegie Corporation, and the U.S. Information Agency. PICAR (Herbert C. Kelman, Director; Donna Hicks, Deputy Director) is supported by a grant from the William and Flora Hewlett Foundation.

Correspondence concerning this article should be addressed to Herbert C. Kelman, Department of Psychology, William James Hall, Harvard University, Cambridge, MA 02138. Electronic mail may be sent via Internet to hck@wjh.harvard.edu.

flict. That breakthrough derives, in my view, from the mutual recognition of the other's nationhood and each side's commitment to negotiate and make peace with the body that symbolizes and legitimates that nationhood.

It would be foolhardy to insist that the peace process set into motion by the Oslo accords is irreversible. At this writing (October 1996), the indications are that, under the current Likud-led government in Israel, the process will be slowed down but neither reversed nor entirely halted. On the other hand, slowing down the process can seriously undermine the achievement of a final peace agreement. As we have already seen, it may provoke acts of violence and counterviolence, creating an atmosphere unconducive to negotiations, and it may create new facts on the ground—such as the expansion of Israeli settlements in the West Bank—leaving no room for an agreement on the basis of territorial compromise. Although I remain optimistic about the ultimate success of the Israeli–Palestinian peace process, I am less prepared now than three years ago to predict that a peace agreement will be signed by the end of the century. But even if the current phase of the peace process were to fail, the Oslo accord has fundamentally changed the character of the conflict. What is irreversible is the fact that the unthinkable has not only been thought, but it has been acted on—the fact that the two parties have recognized each other's national identity and have, in their negotiations and interactions, acknowledged each other's legitimacy. In this sense, the Oslo accord is a breakthrough that is at least as significant as Anwar Sadat's trip to Jerusalem, which led to the Egyptian–Israeli peace agreement.

What are the forces that led to this breakthrough? On a long-term basis, the Six-Day War of 1967 created a new geopolitical and strategic situation in the Middle East, which led to the gradually evolving recognition on all sides that a historic compromise of the Palestine problem in the form of some version of a two-state solution would best serve their national interests (cf. Kelman, 1988). The powerful political obstacles to such a solution were finally overcome by short-term strategic and micropolitical considerations that can be traced to the Gulf War and the end of the Cold War. The combination of these long-term and short-term developments made negotiations necessary from the point of view of both Israeli and Palestinian interests. But a significant factor contributing to the breakthrough was the conclusion, on both sides, that negotiations were not only necessary but also possible—that they could yield an acceptable agreement without jeopardizing their national existence. This sense of possibility evolved out of interactions between the two sides that produced the individuals, the ideas, and the political atmosphere required for productive negotiations.

A variety of unofficial contacts between the two sides played a significant role in creating this sense of possibility and the climate conducive to negotiations. It is in this context that the third-party efforts in which my colleagues and I have been engaged since the early 1970s contributed to the evolving peace process (Kelman, 1995). Our work illustrates the potential contributions of social psychology and the scholar–practitioner model (Kelman 1992b) to the interdisciplinary, multifaceted task of analyzing and resolving protracted international and ethnic conflicts.

This article focuses on the ways in which the microprocess of the small-group meetings that my colleagues and I organize can serve as a vehicle for change at the macrolevel. To set the stage for this discussion, the article briefly (a) places our work in the context of the emerging field of conflict resolution, (b) describes our particular approach to conflict resolution at the international level, and (c) discusses our efforts to contribute to the Israeli–Palestinian peace process.

The Conflict Resolution Field

In the past two decades or so, the world has witnessed the development and proliferation of a variety of new approaches to conflict resolution, which together constitute a new field of theory and practice (see Kelman, 1993b). The precise boundaries of this emerging field are difficult to draw, and practitioners differ in their view of what should be included and what should be excluded.

Practitioners of conflict resolution work at different levels—ranging from the interpersonal to the international. They operate in different domains, such as the court system, public policy, labor–management relations, interethnic relations, or international diplomacy. They derive their ideas from a variety of sources, such as law, psychotherapy, management theories, group dynamics, peace research, decision theory, the study of conflict resolution in traditional societies, and theoretical models from the entire range of social science disciplines. Despite the diversity in level, domain, and intellectual origins that characterizes the work in this field, there are certain common insights and approaches to practice that run through all of its manifestations. Thus, with different degrees of emphasis, they all call for a nonadversarial framework for conflict resolution, an analytic approach, a problem-solving orientation, direct participation by the parties in conflict in jointly shaping a solution, and facilitation by a third party trained in the process of conflict resolution.

Interaction among scholar–practitioners working at different levels and in different domains is instructive and enriching and contributes significantly to the refinement of theory and technique. At the same time, it is important to keep in mind that the application of general principles requires sensitivity to the unique features of the context in which they are applied. Thus, in my own work over the years on international and intercommunal conflict, I have called attention to the need for knowledge about and experience with the particular features and issues of conflict at these levels and to the danger of direct transfer of experiences from the interpersonal and interorganizational levels to the international arena.

Interactive Problem Solving

The unofficial third-party approach to international and ethnic conflict resolution that my colleagues and I have been developing and applying derives from the pioneering efforts of Burton (1969, 1979, 1984). I have used the term *interactive problem solving* to describe the approach, which finds its fullest expression in problem-solving workshops (Kelman, 1972, 1979, 1986, 1991, 1992b, 1996; Kelman & Cohen, 1986). Within this framework, I have done some work on the Cyprus conflict, and, through the work of my students, associates, and colleagues, I have maintained an active interest in a number of other protracted identity group conflicts around the world, such as the conflicts in Northern Ireland, Sri Lanka, Rwanda–Burundi, the former Yugoslavia, and the former Soviet Union. The primary regional focus of my action research program, however, has been on the Middle East. In particular, since the early 1970s, my colleagues and I have conducted an intensive program of problem-solving workshops and related activities on the Israeli–Palestinian conflict.

Problem-solving workshops are intensive meetings between politically involved but entirely unofficial representatives of conflicting parties—for example, Israelis and Palestinians or Greek and Turkish Cypriots (see Kelman, 1993a). Workshop participants are often politically influential members of their communities. Thus, in our Israeli–Palestinian work, participants have included parliamentarians; leading figures in political parties or movements; former military officers or government officials; journalists or editors specializing in the Middle East; and academic scholars who are major analysts of the conflict for their societies and some of whom have served in advisory, official, or diplomatic positions.[1] The workshops take place under academic auspices and are facilitated by a panel of social scientists who are knowledgeable about international conflict, group process, and the Middle East region.

The discussions are completely private and confidential. There is no audience, no publicity, and no record, and one of the central ground rules specifies that statements made in the course of a workshop cannot be cited with attribution outside of the workshop setting. These and other features of the workshop are designed to enable and encourage workshop participants to engage in a type of communication that is usually not available to parties involved in an intense conflict relationship. The third party creates an atmosphere, establishes norms,

and makes occasional interventions, all conducive to free and open discussion, in which the parties address each other rather than third parties or their own constituencies and in which they listen to each other in order to understand their differing perspectives. They are encouraged to deal with the conflict analytically rather than polemically—to explore the ways in which their interaction helps to exacerbate and perpetuate the conflict, rather than to assign blame to the other side while justifying their own. This analytic discussion helps the parties penetrate each other's perspective and understand each other's concerns, needs, fears, priorities, and constraints.

Once both sets of concerns are on the table and have been understood and acknowledged, the parties are encouraged to engage in a process of joint problem solving. They are asked to work together in developing new ideas for resolving the conflict in ways that would satisfy the fundamental needs and allay the existential fears of both parties. They are then asked to explore the political and psychological constraints that stand in the way of such integrative, win–win solutions and that, in fact, have prevented the parties from moving to (or staying at) the negotiating table. Again, they are asked to engage in a process of joint problem solving, designed to generate ideas for "getting from here to there." A central feature of this process is the identification of steps of mutual reassurance—in the form of acknowledgments, symbolic gestures, or confidence-building measures—that would help reduce the parties' fears of engaging in negotiations in which the outcome is uncertain and risky. Problem-solving workshops also contribute to mutual reassurance by helping the parties develop—again, through collaborative effort—a non-threatening, deescalatory language and a shared vision of a desirable future.

Workshops have a dual purpose. First, they are designed to produce changes in the workshop participants themselves—changes in the form of more differentiated images of the enemy (see Kelman 1987), a better understanding of the other's perspective and of their own priorities, greater insight into the dynamics of the conflict, and new ideas for resolving the conflict and for overcoming the barriers to a negotiated solution. These changes at the level of individual participants are a vehicle for promoting change at the policy level. Thus, the second purpose of workshops is to maximize the likelihood that the new insights, ideas, and proposals developed in the course of the interaction are fed back into the political debate and the decision-making process in each community. One of the central tasks of the third party is to structure the workshop in such a way that new insights and ideas are likely both to be generated and to be transferred effectively to the policy process.

The composition of the workshop is crucial in this context: Great care must be taken to select participants who, on the one hand, have the interest and capacity to engage in the kind of learning process that workshops provide and, on the other hand, have the positions and

---

[1] For a description of the recruitment process, see Kelman (1992b) and Rouhana and Kelman (1992b) and Rouhana and Kelman (1994).

credibility in their own communities that enable them to influence the thinking of political leaders, political constituencies, or the general public. It should be noted that the third party's role, although essential to the success of problem-solving workshops, is strictly a facilitative role. The critical work of generating ideas and infusing them into the political process must be done by the participants themselves. A basic assumption of our approach is that solutions emerging out of the interaction between the conflicting parties are most likely to be responsive to their needs and to engender their commitment.[2]

Contributions to the Israeli–Palestinian Peace Process

Most of the Israeli–Palestinian work that my colleagues and I carried out over the years took place during the prenegotiation phase of the conflict. The primary purpose was to help create a political atmosphere that would encourage the parties to move to the negotiating table. Moreover, until 1990, the workshops that we organized were all one-time events. Although some Israelis and Palestinians, as individuals, participated in several such events, each workshop was self-contained. Because of financial, logistical, and political constraints, we were not able to bring the same group of participants together for more than one occasion.

In 1990, however, we took a major step forward in our work by organizing, for the first time, a continuing workshop (see Rouhana & Kelman, 1994). A group of highly influential Israelis and Palestinians committed themselves initially to a series of three workshop meetings over the course of a year. The first meeting took place in November 1990 and, at the end of the third meeting (in August 1991), the participants decided to continue the process.

In the meantime, external events instigated a second major new development in our work. With the convening of the Madrid Conference in the fall of 1991 and the opening of an official Israeli–Palestinian peace process, our own work moved from the prenegotiation to the negotiation phase of the conflict. We had no doubt—and the participants in the continuing workshop agreed—that there was still a great need for maintaining an unofficial process alongside of the official one. However, with the onset of official negotiations, the purpose and focus of our work had to change (Rouhana & Kelman, 1994). When negotiations are in progress, workshops can contribute to overcoming obstacles to staying at the table and negotiating productively, to creating a momentum for the negotiations, to addressing long-term issues that are not yet on the negotiating table, and to beginning

the process of peace-building that must accompany and follow the process of peacemaking.

As Nadim Rouhana and I began to formulate, along with the Israeli and Palestinian participants, the functions of the continuing workshop in the new phase of the peace process, we confronted another new development, which created both opportunities and complications. Our unofficial process was steadily moving closer to the official process. When the official negotiating teams were established, four of the six Palestinian members of the continuing workshop were appointed to key positions on them. With the Labor Party's victory in the Israeli election in 1992, several of our Israeli participants gained increasing access to the top decision makers. (In fact, eventually, one was appointed to the cabinet and another to a major diplomatic post.) These developments clearly enhanced the political relevance of the continuing workshop, but the overlap between the official and unofficial processes also created some ambiguities and role conflicts.

The meetings of the continuing workshop after the start of the official negotiations focused on the obstacles confronting the peace process at the negotiating table and on the ground but also addressed the question of the functions and composition of the continuing workshop in the new political environment. Altogether, this continuing workshop met over a three-year period. Its final session took place in August 1993, ending just a day or so before the news of the Israeli–Palestinian breakthrough that was achieved in Oslo began to emerge.

In the wake of the Oslo accord, signed in September 1993, there has been general recognition of the role that unofficial efforts have played, directly or indirectly, in laying the groundwork for the Israeli–Palestinian breakthrough. In this context, various observers—within and outside of the Middle East—have acknowledged the contributions of the activities in which my colleagues and I have been engaged over the years. In my own assessment, there are three ways in which our work, along with that of many others, has contributed (Kelman, 1995).

1. Workshops have helped to develop cadres prepared to carry out productive negotiations. Over the years, dozens of Israelis and dozens of Palestinians, many of them political influentials or preinfluentials, have participated in our workshops and related activities, including the continuing workshop in the early 1990s. Many of these individuals were involved in the discussions and negotiations that led up to the Oslo accord. Many have continued to be involved in the peace process, and some have served in the Israeli cabinet, Knesset, and foreign ministry and in leading positions in the various Palestinian political agencies.
2. The sharing of information and the formulation of new ideas in the course of our workshops have provided important substantive inputs into the ne-

---

[2] For a more detailed discussion of the workshop ground rules, the nature of the interaction between participants, and the role of the third party, see Kelman (1979), Kelman (1992b), and Rouhana and Kelman (1994).

gotiations. Through the public and private communications of workshop participants—and to some degree also through the communications of members of the third party—some of the insights and ideas on which productive negotiations could be built were injected into the two political cultures. These included shared assumptions, mutual sensitivities, and new conceptions of the process and outcome of negotiations, all of which were developed in the course of workshop interactions.

3. Workshops have fostered a political atmosphere that has made the parties open to a new relationship. Our workshops, along with various other Israeli–Palestinian meetings and projects, have done so by encouraging the development of more differentiated images of the enemy, of a deescalatory language and a new political discourse that is attentive to the other party's concerns and constraints, of a working trust that is based on the conviction that both parties have a genuine interest in a peaceful solution, and of a sense of possibility regarding the ultimate achievement of a mutually satisfactory outcome.

The Oslo agreement, of course, represented only the beginning of what has already been and will almost certainly continue to be a long and difficult process, confronting obstacles and periodic setbacks. Therefore, unofficial efforts alongside the official negotiations continue to be needed. Accordingly, when we decided to close the continuing workshop in the late fall of 1993, we immediately initiated a new project, which built on the experience and achievements of the preceding work. This new project has taken the form of a joint working group on Israeli–Palestinian relations, which held its first meeting in May 1994. The initial emphasis of the group has been on systematic exploration of the difficult political issues—including Israeli settlements, Palestinian refugees, Jerusalem, and the precise nature of Palestinian self-determination—that have been deferred to the final-status negotiations. For the first time in our work, we hope to produce and disseminate one or more joint concept papers, which will frame these issues in terms of the future relationship between the two societies that is envisaged as the long-term outcome of the final agreement.

The Role of Group Processes in Conflict Resolution

Having presented a brief description of our microlevel approach and its contribution to conflict resolution at the macrolevel, I now want to highlight the role that interaction within the small group plays in the larger process.

Most of our work takes place in the context of small groups, composed of three to six representatives of the two sides and two to four third-party facilitators. The focus of all of our efforts is on promoting change in the larger system, but direct interaction in the small-group setting can produce important inputs into the political thinking, the political debate, and the decision-making processes within the two societies and into the formal negotiations between them. Thus, changes at the individual level resulting from interaction in the small group become vehicles for change at the system level.

In the following sections, I discuss five ways in which the workshop group serves as a vehicle for change in the larger system. It does so by functioning as a microcosm of the larger system, as a laboratory for producing inputs into the larger system, as a setting for direct interaction, as a coalition across conflict lines, and as a nucleus for a new relationship. These five functions of the group are not meant to represent different theories or even different dimensions of group process. They are merely different ways of looking at the role of group processes in our intervention model. By looking at the group process from these different angles, I hope to provide a fuller and more nuanced picture of how our micro-process contributes to change at the macrolevel.

The Group as a Microcosm

The group assembled for a workshop can be viewed as a microcosm of the larger system. It is a microcosm not in the sense of a small-scale *model* that reproduces all of the forces of the larger system but in the sense of an *arena* in which the forces of the larger system may manifest themselves. We make no attempt to reproduce the larger system in our workshops. In fact, we try to create an environment that differs significantly from the one in which the conflicting parties normally interact—an environment governed by a different set of norms, in which participants are both free and obligated to speak openly, listen attentively, and treat each other as equals. Nor do we try to represent the entire political spectrum in our workshops. We look for participants who are part of the mainstream in their communities and close to the political center but who are interested in exploring the possibilities of a negotiated, mutually satisfactory solution to the conflict.

The group is a microcosm of the larger system because, despite their relative moderation, the participants share the fundamental concerns, fears, memories, and aspirations of their respective communities. As they interact with each other around the issues in conflict, they reflect their own community's perspectives, priorities, and limits of what is negotiable, not only in what they say but also in how they say it and how they act toward each other. As a result, some of the dynamics of the larger conflict are acted out in the interactions within the workshop group. Participants' interactions in the group context often reflect the nature of the relationship between their communities—their mutual distrust, their special sensitivities and vulnerabilities, their differences in power and minority—majority status—and demonstrate the self-perpetuating character of interactions among conflicting societies.

The advantage of the workshop is that it creates an atmosphere, a set of norms, and a working trust among the participants that enable them to observe and analyze these conflict dynamics at or very near the moment they occur. Such analyses are facilitated by third-party interventions in the form of process observations, which suggest possible ways in which interactions between the parties "here and now" may reflect the dynamics of the conflict between their communities (Kelman, 1979). The insights that such observations can generate are comparable to the "corrective emotional experiences" that play an important role in individual and, particularly, group psychotherapy (Alexander & French, 1946, pp. 66–68; Frank & Ascher, 1951), although our interventions are always at the intergroup rather than the interpersonal level. That is, interactions between workshop participants are relevant to our purposes only insofar as they can tell us something about the dynamics of the interaction between their communities.

In summary, the character of the workshop group as a microcosm of the larger system makes it a valuable learning experience: It provides opportunities for the participants to gain important insights into the dynamics of the conflict. I turn next to the role of the group in transmitting what is learned into the larger system.

The Group as a Laboratory

The workshop group can also be conceived as a laboratory for producing inputs into the larger system. The metaphor of the laboratory is particularly appropriate because it captures the two roles that workshops play in the macroprocess. A workshop is a specially constructed space in which the parties can engage in a process of exploration, observation, and analysis and in which they can create new products to be fed into the political debate and decision making in the two societies.

Providing a space for exploring issues in the conflict, mutual concerns, and ideas for conflict resolution is one of the key contributions of problem-solving workshops. The opportunity for joint informal exploration—playing with ideas, trying out different scenarios, obtaining a sense of the range of possible actions and of the limits for each party, and discovering potential tradeoffs—enhances the productivity of negotiations and the quality of the outcome. Such opportunities, however, are not readily available in official negotiations, in which the participants operate in representative roles, are instructed and closely monitored by their governments, are concerned about the reactions of various constituencies and third parties, and are in the business of producing binding agreements. Problem-solving workshops, by virtue of their nonbinding character, are ideally suited to fill this gap in the larger diplomatic process. The setting, the atmosphere, the ground rules, the governing norms, the agenda, and the interventions of the third party all help to make the workshop group a unique laboratory for the process of open, noncommittal exploration that does not often occur elsewhere in the system, neither in the official negotiations nor in the spontaneous interactions between the conflicting parties.

The process of exploration and joint thinking yields new products, which can be exported into the political process within and between the two communities. This is the second sense in which the laboratory metaphor captures the function of workshops. Indeed the group constitutes a workshop in the literal sense of that term: It is a specially constructed space for shaping products that are then brought back into the two communities. The sharing of perspectives, the conflict analysis, and the joint thinking encouraged in workshops enable the participants to come up with a variety of products in the form of new information, new insights, and new ideas that can advance the negotiation process: differentiated images of the other, which suggest that there is someone to talk to on the other side and something to talk about; understanding of the needs, fears, priorities, and constraints on the other side and, indeed, on one's own side; insight into the escalatory and self-perpetuating dynamics of the conflict relationship; awareness of change and the readiness for change on the other side; ideas for mutual reassurance and other ways of improving the atmosphere for negotiation; ideas for the overall shape of a mutually satisfactory solution; and ideas for redefining the conflict and reframing issues so as to make them more amenable to resolution. These products must then be exported into the political arena. It is essential, therefore, that the individuals selected as workshop participants have not only an interest in mutual exploration and learning, and skills for generating ideas and creative problem solving, but also the capacity and opportunity to utilize what they learn and to inject the workshop products into their respective communities in ways that make a political difference.

In sum, I have described the workshop group as a special space—a laboratory—in which a significant part of the work of peacemaking can be carried out. The unique contribution of the workshop to this larger process is that it provides a carefully designed environment in which constructive social interaction between the parties can take place. Let me, therefore, turn to the third image of the workshop: the group as a setting for direct interaction.

The Group as a Setting for Direct Interaction

Although international conflict and conflict resolution are societal and intersocietal processes, which cannot be reduced to the level of individual behavior, there are certain processes central to conflict resolution—such as empathy or taking the perspective of the other (which is at the heart of social interaction), learning and insight, and creative problem solving—that, of necessity, take place at the level of individuals and interactions between individuals. These psychological processes are by no means the whole of conflict resolution, but they must occur somewhere in the system if there is to be movement toward a mutually satisfactory and stable peace. Problem-solving workshops provide a setting for these processes to occur by bringing together representatives of the conflicting parties for direct interaction under conditions of confidentiality and equality and under an alternative set of norms in contrast to the norms that usually govern interactions between conflicting parties.

The context, norms, ground rules, agenda, procedures, and third-party interventions in workshops are all designed to encourage (and permit) a special kind of interaction, marked by an emphasis on addressing each other (rather than one's constituencies, third parties, or the record) and on listening to each other, an analytical focus, adherence to a "no-fault" principle, and a problem-solving orientation. This kind of interaction allows the parties to explore each other's concerns, penetrate each other's perspective, and take cognizance of each other's constraints (Kelman, 1992b). As a result, they are able to offer each other the reassurances needed for productive negotiation and mutual accommodation and to come up with solutions responsive to both sides' needs and fears.

The nature of the interaction fostered in problem-solving workshops has some continuities with a therapeutic model (Kelman, 1991). Workshop features that reflect such a model are the analytical character of the discourse, the use of here-and-now experiences as a basis for learning about the dynamics of the conflict, and the encouragement of mutual acknowledgments that have both a reassuring and a healing effect. Unlike therapy groups, however, workshops focus not on individuals and their interpersonal relations but on how their interaction may illuminate the dynamics of the conflict between their communities.

An underlying assumption of the workshop process is that products of social interaction have an emergent quality (Kelman, 1992b). In the course of direct interaction, the parties are able to observe firsthand their differing reactions to the same events and the different perspectives these reflect, the differences between the way they perceive themselves and the way the other perceives them, and the impact that their statements and actions have on each other. Out of these observations, they can jointly shape new insights and ideas that could not have been predicted from what they initially brought to the interaction. Certain kinds of solutions to the conflict can emerge only from the confrontation of assumptions, concerns, and identities during face-to-face communication.

The emergence of ideas for solution to the conflict out of the interaction between the parties (in contrast, e.g., to ideas proposed by third parties) has several advantages. Such ideas are more likely to be responsive to the fundamental needs and fears of both parties; the parties are more likely to feel committed to the solutions they produce themselves; and the process of producing these ideas in itself contributes to building a new relationship between the parties, initially between the pronegotiation elements on the two sides and ultimately between the two societies as wholes. Let me turn then to the function of the workshop group in building relationships of both kinds.

The Group as a Coalition Across Conflict Lines

The workshop group can be conceived as a coalition across conflict lines—as part of a process of building a coalition between those elements on each side that are interested in a negotiated solution (Kelman, 1993a). This does not mean that workshop participants are all committed doves. Often, they are individuals who, out of pragmatic considerations, have concluded that a negotiated agreement is in the best interest of their own community. Workshops, then, can be seen as attempts to strengthen the hands of the pronegotiation elements on each side in their political struggle within their own communities and to increase the likelihood that the pronegotiation elements on the two sides will support and reinforce each other in pursuing their common interest in a negotiated solution.

Because the coalition formed by a workshop group (and by the entire array of joint efforts by the pronegotiation forces on the two sides) cuts across a very basic conflict line, it is almost by definition an uneasy coalition. It must function in the face of the powerful bonds that coalition members have to the very groups that the coalition tries to transcend. The coalition may well be perceived as threatening the national community that is so important to the identity, the long-term interests, and the political effectiveness of each coalition partner. As a result, the coalition work is complicated by participants' concern about their self-images as loyal members of their group; by their concern about their credibility at home and, hence, their long-term political effectiveness; by significant divergences in the perspectives of the two sets of coalition partners; and by the fact that even committed proponents of negotiation share the memories, concerns, fears, and sensitivities of their identity group.

Participants' bonds to their national communities create inevitable barriers to coalition work, which require systematic attention if problem-solving workshops are to achieve their goals. Thus, mutual distrust is an endemic condition that complicates coalition work. Even among individuals who have worked together for some time and have achieved a considerable level of working trust, old fears and suspicions that have deep historical roots are easily rearoused by events on the ground or by words and actions of a participant on the other side. Coalition work, therefore, requires a continuing process of mutual testing and reestablishment of working trust. A second impediment to coalition work is alienating language—the use of words or a manner of speaking that the other side finds irritating, patronizing, insulting, threatening, or otherwise oblivious to its sensitivities. One of the valuable outcomes of workshops is growing sensitivity to the meaning of particular words to the other side. Nevertheless, alienating language does crop up, both because participants speak from the perspectives and out of the experiences of their own communities and because the pragmatic terms in which peace is justified to one's domestic audiences (and perhaps to one's self) may appear dehumanizing or delegitimizing to the other side. Examples are the Israeli emphasis on the Palestinian "demographic threat" and the Palestinian emphasis on Israel's superior power as reasons for seeking a compromise. Finally, fluctuations in the political and psychological climate may affect one or the other party, creating a lack of synchronism in the readiness for coalition work between the two sides.

The uneasy quality of a coalition across conflict lines is an inevitable reality, insofar as coalition members are bona fide representatives of their national groups—as they must be if the coalition is to achieve its goal of promoting a negotiated agreement. This reality creates barriers to coalition work, and it is part of the task of the third party to help overcome them. But it is not only difficult to overcome these barriers, it may in fact be counterproductive to overcome them entirely. It is important for the coalition to remain uneasy in order to enhance the value of what participants learn in the course of workshops and of what they can achieve upon reentry into their home communities.

Experimental research by Rothbart and associates (Rothbart & John, 1985; Rothbart & Lewis, 1988) suggests that direct contact between members of conflicting groups may have a paradoxical effect on intergroup stereotypes. If it becomes apparent, in the course of direct interaction with representatives of the other group, that they do not fit one's stereotype of the group, there is a tendency to differentiate these particular individuals from their group: to perceive them as nonmembers. Since they are excluded from the category, the stereotype about the category itself can remain intact. This process of differentiating and excluding individual members of the other group from their category could well take place in workshops in which a high degree of trust develops between the parties. Therefore, it is essential for the participants to reconfirm their belongingness to their national categories—thus keeping the coalition uneasy—if they are to demonstrate the possibility of peace not just between exceptional individuals from the two sides but between the two enemy camps.

An even more important reason why a coalition across conflict lines must, of necessity, remain uneasy relates to what is often called the *reentry problem* (see, e.g.,Kelman, 1972; Walton, 1970). If a workshop group

> became overly cohesive, it would undermine the whole purpose of the enterprise: to have an impact on the political decisions within the two communities. Workshop participants who become closely identified with their counterparts on the other side may become alienated from their own co-nationals, lose credibility, and hence forfeit their political effectiveness and their ability to promote a new consensus within their own communities. One of the challenges for problem-solving workshops, therefore, is to create an atmosphere in which participants can begin to humanize and trust each other and to develop an effective collaborative relationship, without losing sight of their separate group identities and the conflict between their communities. (Kelman, 1992b, p. 82)

The Group as a Nucleus for a New Relationship

Our work is based on the proposition that in conflicts such as that between Palestinians and Israelis—conflicts about national identity and national existence between two peoples destined to live together in the same small space—conflict resolution must aim toward the ultimate establishment of a new cooperative and mutually enhancing relationship and must involve a process that paves the way to such a relationship. Nothing less will work in the long run, and, even in the short run, only a process embodying the principle of reciprocity that is at the center of a new relationship is likely to succeed. Perhaps the greatest strength of problem-solving workshops is their potential contribution to transforming the relationship between the conflicting parties.

Interaction in the workshop group both promotes and models a new relationship between the parties. It is based on the principles of equality and reciprocity. The participants are encouraged to penetrate each other's perspective and to gain an understanding of the other's needs, fears, and constraints. They try to shape solutions that are responsive to the fundamental concerns of both sides. They search for ways of providing mutual reassurance. Such ideas often emerge from acknowledgments that participants make to each other in the course of their interaction: acknowledgments of the other's humanity, national identity, view of history, authentic links to the land, legitimate grievances, and commitment to peace.

Out of these interactions, participants develop increasing degrees of empathy, of sensitivity and responsiveness to the other's concerns, and of working trust, which are essential ingredients of the new relationship to which conflict resolution efforts aspire. The working trust and responsiveness both develop out of the collaborative work in which the group is engaged and, in turn, help to enhance the effectiveness of that work. Thus, workshop participants can transmit to their respective communities not only ideas toward transformation of the relationship between the communities but also the results of their own experience: They can testify that a cooperative, mutually enhancing relationship is possible and can point to some of the conditions that promote such a relationship.

The joint working group on Israeli–Palestinian relations, which my colleague Nadim Rouhana and I are currently cochairing, is explicitly based on the conception of the group as the nucleus of a new relationship between the two societies. The main purpose of the working group is to focus on the peace-building processes that must follow successful peacemaking and to explore the nature of the long-term relationship envisaged in the aftermath of the final political agreement. At this point, as I mentioned earlier, we are addressing the difficult political issues—settlements, refugees, Jerusalem, Palestinian self-determination—that have been deferred to the final-status negotiations, in the light of the future relationship between the societies. That is, we try to assess different options for resolving these issues from the point of view of their congruence with a long-term relationship that is based on peaceful coexistence, cooperation, and mutual benefit.

Furthermore, we see the working group itself as a model and perhaps even as the seed of an institutional mechanism that a new relationship calls for. In our view, a mutually beneficial relationship between two units that are as closely linked and as interdependent as the Israeli and Palestinian communities requires the development of a civil society across the political borders. A useful institutional mechanism for such a civil society would be an unofficial joint forum for exploring issues in the relationship between the two communities within a problem-solving framework. It is not entirely unrealistic to hope that our current working group may evolve into or at least serve as a model for such an institution. This scenario thus provides an illustration of the way in which a group like our Israeli–Palestinian working group can serve not only as a means for promoting a new relationship between the parties but also as a model and manifestation of that new relationship.

REFERENCES

Alexander, F., & French, T. M. (1946). *Psychoanalytic therapy*. New York: Ronald Press.

Burton, J. W. (1969). *Conflict and communication: The use of controlled communication in international relations*. London: Macmillan.

Burton, J. W. (1979). *Deviance, terrorism and war: The process of solving unsolved social and political problems*. New York: St. Martin's Press.

Burton, J. W. (1984). *Global conflict: The domestic sources of international crisis*. Brighton, England: Wheatsheaf.

Frank, J. D., & Ascher, E. (1951). Corrective emotional experiences in group therapy. *American Journal of Psychiatry, 108*, 126–131.

Kelman, H. C. (1972). The problem-solving workshop in conflict resolution. In R. L. Merritt (Ed.), *Communication in international politics* (pp. 168–204). Urbana; University of Illinois Press.

Kelman, H. C. (1978). Israelis and Palestinians: Psychological prerequisites for mutual acceptance. *International Security, 3*, 162–186.

Kelman, H. C. (1979). An interactional approach to conflict resolution and its application to Israeli–Palestinian relations. *International Interactions, 6*, 99–122.

Kelman, H. C. (1986). Interactive problem solving: A social–psychological approach to conflict resolution. In W. Klassen (Ed.), *Dialogue toward interfaith understanding* (pp. 293–314). Tantur/Jerusalem: Ecumenical Institute for Theological Research.

Kelman, H. C. (1987). The political psychology of the Israeli–Palestinian conflict: How can we overcome the barriers to a negotiated solution? *Political Psychology, 8*, 347–363.

Kelman, H. C. (1988, Spring). The Palestinianization of the Arab–Israeli conflict. *The Jerusalem Quarterly, 46*, 3–15.

Kelman, H. C. (1991). Interactive problem solving: The uses and limits of a therapeutic model for the resolution of international conflicts. In V. D. Volkan, J. V. Montville, & D. A. Julius (Eds.), *The psychodynamics of international relationships, Volume II: Unofficial diplomacy at work* (pp. 145–160). Lexington, MA: Lexington Books.

Kelman, H. C. (1992a). Acknowledging the other's nationhood: How to create a momentum for the Israeli–Palestinian negotiations. *Journal of Palestine Studies, 22*(1), 18–38.

Kelman, H. C. (1992b). Informal mediation by the scholar/practitioner. In J. Bercovitch & J. Z. Rubin (Eds.), *Mediation in international relations: Multiple approaches to conflict management* (pp. 64–96). New York: St. Martin's Press.

Kelman, H.C. (1993a). Coalitions across conflict lines: The interplay of conflicts within and between the Israeli and Palestinian communities. In S. Worchel & J. Simpson (Eds.), *Conflict between people and groups* (pp. 236–258). Chicago: Nelson-Hall.

Kelman, H. C. (1993b). Foreword. In D. J. D. Sandole & H. van der Merwe (Eds.), *Conflict resolution theory and practice: Integration and application* (pp. ix–xii). Manchester, England: Manchester University Press.

Kelman, H. C. (1995). Contributions of an unofficial conflict resolution effort to the Israeli-Palestinian breakthrough. *Negotiation Journal, 11*, 19–27.

Kelman, H. C. (1996). Negotiation as interactive problem solving. *International Negotiations, 1*, 99–123.

Kelman, H. C., & Cohen, S. P. (1986). Resolution of international conflict: An interactional approach. In S. Worchel & W. G. Austin (Eds.), *Psychology of intergroup relations* (2nd ed., pp. 323–342). Chicago: Nelson Hall.

Rothbart, M., & John, O. P. (1985). Social categorization and behavioral episodes: A cognitive analysis of the effects of intergroup contact. *Journal of Social Issues, 41*(3), 81–104.

Rothbart, M., & Lewis, S. (1988). Inferring category attributes from exemplar attributes: Geometric shapes and social categories. *Journal of Personality and Social Psychology, 55*, 861–872.

Rouhana, N. N., & Kelman, H. C. (1994). Promoting joint thinking in international conflicts: An Israeli–Palestinian continuing workshop. *Journal of Social Issues, 50*(1), 157–178.

Walton, R. E. (1970). A problem-solving workshop on border conflicts in Eastern Africa. *Journal of Applied Behavioral Science, 6*, 453–489.

PSYCHOLOGY'S OWN PEACE CORPS

THE CLOSER WE GET TO A GLOBAL VILLAGE, THE GREATER THE THREAT OF ETHNOPOLITICAL WAR. WHAT THE WORLD NEEDS NOW IS A WHOLE NEW KIND OF PSYCHOLOGICAL SHOCK TROOP.

BY ANNIE MURPHY PAUL

Half a millennium after Columbus realized the world was round, his discovery is just now sinking in. That we're perched on a small piece of an enormous globe is a fact that only people living now have really *known*—known with the steadiness of pictures beamed to us from satellites, with the clarity of a voice on a cell phone, calling from the other side of the earth.

That awareness can be heady—and for some, unbearably frightening. The great irony of our time is that just as the horizons of globalization are opening wide, so many people are retreating to the dim, close caves of ethnic identity.

They have been "re-tribalized," in the phrase of Daniel Chirot, Ph.D., a sociologist at the University of Washington. He believes that the staggering size and unnerving fluidity of a globalized culture are causing some societies to run for cover, to seek safety and familiarity in the extended family of an ethnic group.

But that hunger for security can quickly turn ugly, as in Bosnia, in Rwanda, in other places where populations have drawn blood lines that bind them to some and separate them from others.

From a distance, these ethnopolitical conflicts seem to be one frantic, chaotic blur. But is there order to this apparent anarchy? Chirot believes that such conflicts have a logic of their own. He has identified five stages of social organization—from a peaceful, integrated society, to all-out civil war—and has described the conditions that

catapult a nation from one stage to the next. His theories could help explain how these conflicts begin—and how they might end.

IDENTITY RUN AMOK

Chirot looks first to history, noting that some of the fiercest ethnic conflicts have occurred in nations that were until recently under the sway of Soviet domination or European colonialism. The withdrawal of these foreign powers left persistent problems, as well as an often-frightening freedom, in its wake.

In some cases, such as the former Yugoslavia, one country split into hostile minority groups. In others, such as Armenia and Azerbaijan, long-standing national enmities re-emerged in the absence of a shared oppressor. "Not only have such passions not lessened, they are now played out on a much larger scale, and involve far more people than in the past," says Chirot.

Many of these repressive regimes imposed a uniform national identity on those they ruled. Russians told members of their republics that they were Soviets first, Latvians or Chechens second. European conquerors in Africa ignored tribal distinctions, seeing only skin color.

Now that these imperialists have packed their bags, their former subjects are asserting their distinctiveness—

Reprinted by permission of *Psychology Today,* July/August 1998, pp. 56-60. © 1998 by Sussex Publishers, Inc.

**THE FIVE STAGES
OF ETHNIC
CONFLICT**

1 Multi-ethnic societies without serious conflict.
Example: Switzerland.

2 Multi-ethnic societies with conflicts
that remain under control and far
short of war. Example: United States.

with a vengeance. The exaggeration and valorization of difference can reach absurd heights: though the language differences between Croats and Slovenes are slighter than those between Sicilians and Venetians in Italy, for example, the former Yugoslavs believe that they speak different tongues—and each group is convinced that theirs is far superior.

It's no surprise that these long-dominated peoples should choose ethnicity as the vehicle for their newly-liberated identities, says Chirot. Their former, often resented, personas were imposed from without, while ethnicity springs from our very genes.

But the emergence of distinct ethnic groups isn't enough to set off ethnic war, he says. That happens only when people feel that their ethnic group is competing with another one for limited resources—jobs, food, cultural clout. When people feel threatened by radical change, they seek safety in numbers, and any attack on the group is perceived as a personal affront.

Once people are looking through this lens, a crisis is all that is needed to inflame ethnic war. Sometimes the emergency is economic: Chirot observes that a severe recession in Germany in the 1930s propelled the Nazis into power. Fifty years later, economic hard times helped turn Yugoslavia into an ethnic battleground.

But Chirot also notes that other Eastern European countries had rocky economies during the same period, yet did not erupt in civil war. "Economics are a precipitating event, but not a long-run cause," he says. Financial distress simply touches a match to an already brittle political situation.

More often, the crisis is political, a shift in the balance of power between groups that makes both sides nervous. A study that attempted to tie outbreaks of violence in Northern Ireland to the ups and downs of its economy, for example, found no connection between the two. Rather, bloodshed invariably followed changes in the power relationship between Protestants and Catholics.

Ethnic conflict is most likely to occur, Chirot concludes, "when people believe that the other group is going to take power away from them, and that they'll be the long-term losers, in every way: culturally, politically, economically."

WARS WITHIN AND WITHOUT

As Chirot's investigation of ethnopolitical war moves from such historical and structural conditions into the realms of the mind, certainties are harder to capture.

How people think and feel about their ethnicity, about their leaders, about opposing groups, are questions that remain at large.

Psychology would seem to be a natural place to look for answers. But they are surprisingly scarce. Few psychologists have studied either the causes or consequences of ethnic war.

What psychology does have is experience tending to those wounded in the wars within families or within the individual psyche—and that expertise may be directly applicable to ethnic conflict. Knowing what aggravates or soothes tensions in marriage, for example, might prove useful in negotiating between warring factions. Understanding how we project our own fears and hatreds onto other individuals might help us see how that happens on a nationwide scale.

FROM FEAR TO ETERNITY

One of the most basic—and most vexing—questions psychology must answer is how ethnicity becomes such a crucial and closely-held part of people's identities. Ethnicity seems to carry much more weight than other broad groupings, like class or even religion.

A new line of thought in psychology may help explain the strength of ethnicity's grip. Terror management theory, as it's known, tries to understand how we deal with the awareness of our own mortality. It seems that when people are made to think about their own death—as they emphatically are when living in an ethnic war zone—they respond by cleaving more closely to some parts of their identity, especially ethnicity. That's because, unlike nationality or religion, ethnicity is passed on biologically to offspring, promising a kind of immortality.

A more unsettling mystery of ethnic conflicts is why, once people have embraced their own ethnic group, they so often feel moved to demean and dehumanize the members of other clans. From research on the relations between social groups, psychology offers some clues: excluding and disparaging others may be a way of consolidating one's identity, boosting self-esteem, and bonding more closely with one's own group. But how can these mild-sounding motives account for the slaughter of children in front of their mothers? For women raped and defiled so they will not be able to return to their families?

Perhaps the most puzzling and unpredictable phenomenon psychologists are called upon to explain is panic. Although a real crisis is often the catalyst for eth-

3 Societies where ethnic violence has broken out but has been resolved. Example: South Africa.

4 Societies with serious conflicts that have led to chronic warfare but not genocide. Example: Sri Lanka.

5 Genocidal ethnic conflict, including violent ethnic cleansing. Example: Yugoslavia.

nic war, that emergency may remain manageable—if it is not accompanied by irrational fear. "If the crisis doesn't provoke a sense of general panic, then reason may remain uppermost and moderates may prevail," says Chirot. "In South Africa, for example, the moderates on both sides seem to have won out."

But sometimes a frenzy of fear and dread will overtake a population, though there may seem to be slight evidence for alarm. The conviction on the part of the various ethnic groups in Yugolsavia that each was out to exterminate the other, for example, was founded on little more than overblown propaganda and outsized suspicions, observes Chirot. Indeed, psychological studies of lynch mobs, urban riots, and cult movements show that people in groups act in ways they never would on their own.

FOLLOW THE LEADER

They may also be urged on by a charismatic or commanding leader, like Mobutu Sese Seko of Zaire or Radovan Karadzic of Serbia. Here again, psychology can provide some insight. It has produced studies of relatively benign leaders—presidents, principals, CEOs—and psychohistories of more infamous ones like Hitler and Stalin. They may help us understand which qualities persuade people to identify with a leader and what motives drive the leader himself.

Though Chirot concedes that leaders are important, he insists that panic is first aroused in the rank and file. "Leaders can make a panic worse, but there has to be a predisposition to panic," he says. "There has to be something that has gone wrong in people's lives. There has to be a perception of threat."

Leaders can play on that perception, as Adolf Hitler did in his rise to power, or they can debunk it, as Franklin Roosevelt did when he told Americans that they had "nothing to fear but fear itself." More recently, Serbia's Slobodan Milosevic cynically capitalized on the fears of his people of a repeat of World War II, while members of India's government worked hard to dispel tensions between its ethnic factions. Psychology may be able to tell us why leaders go down one path rather than another, and why their supporters follow them there.

AIMING AT THE IRRATIONAL

These are the barest beginnings of a psychology of ethnic conflict, a slight scaffold upon which, it is hoped, a new discipline will be built. Construction will begin this summer at the first international conference on the subject to be held in Derry, Northern Ireland. Experts from sociology to history to political science will gather to discuss what psychology can do, in both theory and practice, to understand and to avert the rise of ethnic war.

For some psychologists, that will mean a trip back to the lab, where they will perform much-needed research on the roots of ethnic conflict. For others, it's back to school, to design an academic curriculum that will be given to a new generation of relief workers. The program, to be offered at the University of Pennsylvania, will train psychologists to work in the world's ethnic hot spots: a sort of psychological shock troops, a peace corps for the psyche.

"Psychologists have been taught how to help people after the event—for example, to treat post-traumatic stress syndrome," says Chirot. "But they haven't been trained in prevention." These shrinks on the brink will be alert to the earliest signs of ethnic conflict. "They'll be on the lookout for the exaggerations that form in people's minds, the polarizations that create a predisposition to accept the notion that 'it's us or them,' " says Chirot.

Psychology holds out hope for the resolution of ethnic conflict because it's a science of the subjective, a systematic approach to all that is irrational and unpredictable. If it can tame the beast of ethnic conflict, says Chirot, "it will be a great blessing for the world."

It would also be a boon for psychology. Hemmed in by managed care, battered by the inroads of biology, diluted by the popular press, psychology needs an opportunity to confirm its continuing relevance. It has here the chance to grapple with a great theme, to wrest life and light from the darkness of the human heart.

IQ and technical skills are important, but emotional intelligence is the sine qua non of leadership.

What Makes a Leader?

BY DANIEL GOLEMAN

Every businessperson knows a story about a highly intelligent, highly skilled executive who was promoted into a leadership position only to fail at the job. And they also know a story about someone with solid—but not extraordinary—intellectual abilities and technical skills who was promoted into a similar position and then soared.

Such anecdotes support the widespread belief that identifying individuals with the "right stuff" to be leaders is more art than science. After all, the personal styles of superb leaders vary: some leaders are subdued and analytical; others shout their manifestos from the mountaintops. And just as important, different situations call for different types of leadership. Most mergers need a sensitive negotiator at the helm, whereas many turnarounds require a more forceful authority.

I have found, however, that the most effective leaders are alike in one crucial way: they all have a high degree of what has come to be known as *emotional intelligence*. It's not that IQ and technical skills are irrelevant. They do matter, but mainly as "threshold capabilities"; that is, they are the entry-level requirements for executive positions. But my research, along with other recent studies, clearly shows that

Daniel Goleman is the author of Emotional Intelligence *(Bantam, 1995) and* Working with Emotional Intelligence *(Bantam, 1998). He is cochairman of the Consortium for Research on Emotional Intelligence in Organizations, which is based at Rutgers University's Graduate School of Applied and Professional Psychology in Piscataway, New Jersey. He can be reached at Goleman@javanet.com.*

emotional intelligence is the sine qua non of leadership. Without it, a person can have the best training in the world, an incisive, analytical mind, and an endless supply of smart ideas, but he still won't make a great leader.

In the course of the past year, my colleagues and I have focused on how emotional intelligence operates at work. We have examined the relationship between emotional intelligence and effective performance, especially in leaders. And we have observed how emotional intelligence shows itself on the job. How can you tell if someone has high emotional intelligence, for example, and how can you recognize it in yourself? In the following pages, we'll explore these questions, taking each of the components of emotional intelligence—self-awareness, self-regulation, motivation, empathy, and social skill—in turn.

Evaluating Emotional Intelligence

Most large companies today have employed trained psychologists to develop what are known as "competency models" to aid them in identifying, training, and promoting likely stars in the leadership firmament. The psychologists have also developed such models for lower-level positions. And in recent years, I have analyzed competency models from 188 companies, most of which were large and global and included the likes of Lucent Technologies, British Airways, and Credit Suisse.

In carrying out this work, my objective was to determine which personal capabilities drove outstanding performance within these organizations, and to what degree they did so. I grouped capabilities into three categories: purely technical skills like accounting and business planning; cognitive abilities like analytical reasoning; and competencies demonstrating emotional intelligence such as the ability to work with others and effectiveness in leading change.

To create some of the competency models, psychologists asked senior managers at the companies to identify the capabilities that typified the organization's most outstanding leaders. To create other models, the psychologists used objective criteria such as a division's profitability to differentiate the star performers at senior levels within their organizations from the average ones. Those individuals were then extensively interviewed and tested, and their capabilities were compared. This process resulted in the creation of lists of ingredients for highly effective leaders. The lists ranged in length from 7 to 15 items and included such ingredients as initiative and strategic vision.

When I analyzed all this data, I found dramatic results. To be sure, intellect was a driver of outstanding performance. Cognitive skills such as big-picture thinking and long-term vision were particularly important. But when I calculated the

Effective leaders are alike in one crucial way: they all have a high degree of emotional intelligence.

ratio of technical skills, IQ, and emotional intelligence as ingredients of excellent performance, emotional intelligence proved to be twice as important as the others for jobs at all levels.

Moreover, my analysis showed that emotional intelligence played an increasingly important role at the highest levels of the company, where differences in technical skills are of negligible importance. In other words, the higher the rank of a person considered to be a star performer, the more emotional intelligence capabilities showed up as the reason for his or her effectiveness. When I compared star performers with average ones in senior leadership positions, nearly 90% of the difference in their profiles was attributable to emotional intelligence factors rather than cognitive abilities.

Other researchers have confirmed that emotional intelligence not only distinguishes outstanding leaders but can also be linked to strong performance. The findings of the late David McClelland, the renowned researcher in human and organizational behavior, are a good example. In a 1996 study of a global food and beverage company, McClelland found that when senior managers had a critical mass of emotional intelligence capabilities, their divisions outperformed yearly earnings goals by 20%. Meanwhile, division leaders without that critical mass underperformed by almost the same amount. McClelland's findings, interestingly, held as true in the company's U.S. divisions as in its divisions in Asia and Europe.

In short, the numbers are beginning to tell us a persuasive story about the link between a company's success and the emotional intelligence of its leaders. And just as important, research is also demonstrating that people can, if they take the right approach, develop their emotional intelligence. (See "Can Emotional Intelligence Be Learned?")

Self-Awareness

Self-awareness is the first component of emotional intelligence—which makes sense when one con-

The Five Components of Emotional Intelligence at Work

	Definition	Hallmarks
Self-Awareness	the ability to recognize and understand your moods, emotions, and drives, as well as their effect on others	self-confidence realistic self-assessment self-deprecating sense of humor
Self-Regulation	the ability to control or redirect disruptive impulses and moods the propensity to suspend judgment—to think before acting	trustworthiness and integrity comfort with ambiguity openness to change
Motivation	a passion to work for reasons that go beyond money or status a propensity to pursue goals with energy and persistence	strong drive to achieve optimism, even in the face of failure organizational commitment
Empathy	the ability to understand the emotional makeup of other people skill in treating people according to their emotional reactions	expertise in building and retaining talent cross-cultural sensitivity service to clients and customers
Social Skill	proficiency in managing relationships and building networks an ability to find common ground and build rapport	effectiveness in leading change persuasiveness expertise in building and leading teams

siders that the Delphic oracle gave the advice to "know thyself" thousands of years ago. Self-awareness means having a deep understanding of one's emotions, strengths, weaknesses, needs, and drives. People with strong self-awareness are neither overly critical nor unrealistically hopeful. Rather, they are honest—with themselves and with others.

People who have a high degree of self-awareness recognize how their feelings affect them, other people, and their job performance. Thus a self-aware person who knows that tight deadlines bring out the worst in him plans his time carefully and gets his work done well in advance. Another person with high self-awareness will be able to work with a demanding client. She will understand the client's impact on her moods and the deeper reasons for her frustration. "Their trivial demands take us away from the real work that needs to be done," she might explain. And she will go one step further and turn her anger into something constructive.

Self-awareness extends to a person's understanding of his or her values and goals. Someone who is highly self-aware knows where he is headed and why; so, for example, he will be able to be firm in turning down a job offer that is tempting financially but does not fit with his principles or long-term goals. A person who lacks self-awareness is apt to make decisions that bring on inner turmoil by treading on buried values. "The money looked good so I signed on," someone might say two years into a job, "but the work means so little to me that I'm constantly bored." The decisions of self-aware people mesh with their values; consequently, they often find work to be energizing.

How can one recognize self-awareness? First and foremost, it shows itself as candor and an ability to assess oneself realistically. People with high self-awareness are able to speak accurately and openly—although not necessarily effusively or confessionally—about their emotions and the impact they have on their work. For instance, one manager I know of was skeptical about a new personal-shopper service that her company, a major department-store chain, was about to introduce. Without prompting from her team or her boss, she offered them an explanation: "It's hard for me to get behind the rollout of this service," she admitted, "because I really wanted to run the project, but I wasn't selected. Bear with me while I deal with that." The manager did indeed examine her feelings; a week later, she was supporting the project fully.

Such self-knowledge often shows itself in the hiring process. Ask a candidate to describe a time he got carried away by his feelings and did something he later regretted. Self-aware candidates will be frank in admitting to failure—and will often tell their tales with a smile. One of the hallmarks of self-awareness is a self-deprecating sense of humor.

Self-awareness can also be identified during performance reviews. Self-aware people know—and are comfortable talking about—their limitations and strengths, and they often demonstrate a thirst for constructive criticism. By contrast, people with low self-awareness interpret the message that they need to improve as a threat or a sign of failure.

Self-aware people can also be recognized by their self-confidence. They have a firm grasp of their capabilities and are less likely to set themselves up to fail by, for example, overstretching on assignments. They know, too, when to ask for help. And the risks they take on the job are calculated. They won't ask for a challenge that they know they can't handle alone. They'll play to their strengths.

Consider the actions of a mid-level employee who was invited to sit in on a strategy meeting with her company's top executives. Although she was the most junior person in the room, she did not sit there quietly, listening in awestruck or fearful silence. She knew she had a head for clear logic and the skill to present ideas persuasively, and she offered cogent suggestions about the company's strategy. At the same time, her self-awareness stopped her from wandering into territory where she knew she was weak.

Despite the value of having self-aware people in the workplace, my research indicates that senior executives don't often give self-awareness the credit it deserves when they look for potential leaders. Many executives mistake candor about feelings for "wimpiness" and fail to give due respect to employees who openly acknowledge their shortcomings. Such people are too readily dismissed as "not tough enough" to lead others.

In fact, the opposite is true. In the first place, people generally admire and respect candor. Further, leaders are constantly required to make judgment calls that require a candid assessment of capabilities—their own and those of others. Do we have the management expertise to acquire a competitor? Can we launch a new product within

Self-aware job candidates will be frank in admitting to failure—and will often tell their tales with a smile.

six months? People who assess themselves honestly—that is, self-aware people—are well suited to do the same for the organizations they run.

Self-Regulation

Biological impulses drive our emotions. We cannot do away with them—but we can do much to manage them. Self-regulation, which is like an ongoing inner conversation, is the component of emotional intelligence that frees us from being prisoners of our feelings. People engaged in such a conversation feel bad moods and emotional impulses just as everyone else does, but they find ways to control them and even to channel them in useful ways.

Imagine an executive who has just watched a team of his employees present a botched analysis to the company's board of directors. In the gloom that follows, the executive might find himself tempted to pound on the table in anger or kick over a chair. He could leap up and scream at the group. Or he might maintain a grim silence, glaring at everyone before stalking off.

But if he had a gift for self-regulation, he would choose a different approach. He would pick his words carefully, acknowledging the team's poor performance without rushing to any hasty judgment. He would then step back to consider the reasons for the failure. Are they personal—a lack of effort? Are there any mitigating factors? What was his role in the debacle? After considering these questions, he would call the team together, lay out the incident's consequences, and

Can Emotional Intelligence Be Learned?

For ages, people have debated if leaders are born or made. So too goes the debate about emotional intelligence. Are people born with certain levels of empathy, for example, or do they acquire empathy as a result of life's experiences? The answer is both. Scientific inquiry strongly suggests that there is a genetic component to emotional intelligence. Psychological and developmental research indicates that nurture plays a role as well. How much of each perhaps will never be known, but research and practice clearly demonstrate that emotional intelligence can be learned.

One thing is certain: emotional intelligence increases with age. There is an old-fashioned word for the phenomenon: maturity. Yet even with maturity, some people still need training to enhance their emotional intelligence. Unfortunately, far too many training programs that intend to build leadership skills—including emotional intelligence—are a waste of time and money. The problem is simple: they focus on the wrong part of the brain.

Emotional intelligence is born largely in the neurotransmitters of the brain's limbic system, which governs feelings, impulses, and drives. Research indicates that the limbic system learns best through motivation, extended practice, and feedback. Compare this with the kind of learning that goes on in the neocortex, which governs analytical and technical ability. The neocortex grasps concepts and logic. It is the part of the brain that figures out how to use a computer or make a sales call by reading a book. Not surprisingly—but mistakenly—it is also the part of the brain targeted by most training programs aimed at enhancing emotional intelligence. When such programs take, in effect, a neocortical approach, my research with the Consortium for Research on Emotional Intelligence in Organizations has shown they can even have a *negative* impact on people's job performance.

To enhance emotional intelligence, organizations must refocus their training to include the limbic system. They must help people break old behavioral habits and establish new ones. That not only takes much more time than conventional training programs, it also requires an individualized approach.

Imagine an executive who is thought to be low on empathy by her colleagues. Part of that deficit shows itself as an inability to listen; she interrupts people and doesn't pay close attention to what they're saying. To fix the problem, the executive needs to be motivated to change, and then she needs practice and feedback from others in the company. A colleague or coach could be tapped to let the executive know when she has been observed failing to listen. She would then have to replay the incident and give a better response; that is, demonstrate her ability to absorb what others are saying. And the executive could be directed to observe certain executives who listen well and to mimic their behavior.

With persistence and practice, such a process can lead to lasting results. I know one Wall Street executive who sought to improve his empathy—specifically his ability to read people's reactions and see their perspectives. Before beginning his quest, the executive's subordinates were terrified of working with him. People even went so far as to hide bad news from him. Naturally, he was shocked when finally confronted with these facts. He went home and told his family—but they only confirmed what he had heard at work. When their opinions on any given subject did not mesh with his, they, too, were frightened of him.

Enlisting the help of a coach, the executive went to work to heighten his empathy through practice and feedback. His first step was to take a vacation to a foreign country where he did not speak the language. While there, he monitored his reactions to the unfamiliar and his openness to people who were different from him. When he returned home, humbled by his week abroad, the executive asked his coach to shadow him for parts of the day, several times a week, in order to critique how he treated people with new or different perspectives. At the same time, he consciously used on-the-job interactions as opportunities to practice "hearing" ideas that differed from his. Finally, the executive had himself videotaped in meetings and asked those who worked for and with him to critique his ability to acknowledge and understand the feelings of others. It took several months, but the executive's emotional intelligence did ultimately rise, and the improvement was reflected in his overall performance on the job.

It's important to emphasize that building one's emotional intelligence cannot—will not—happen without sincere desire and concerted effort. A brief seminar won't help; nor can one buy a how-to manual. It is much harder to learn to empathize—to internalize empathy as a natural response to people—than it is to become adept at regression analysis. But it can be done. "Nothing great was ever achieved without enthusiasm," wrote Ralph Waldo Emerson. If your goal is to become a real leader, these words can serve as a guidepost in your efforts to develop high emotional intelligence.

---

offer his feelings about it. He would then present his analysis of the problem and a well-considered solution.

Why does self-regulation matter so much for leaders? First of all, people who are in control of their feelings and impulses—that is, people who are reasonable—are able to create an environment of trust and fairness. In such an environment, politics and infighting are sharply reduced and productivity is high. Talented people flock to the organization and aren't tempted to leave. And self-regulation has a trickle-down effect. No one wants to be known as a hothead when the boss is known for her calm approach. Fewer bad moods at the top mean fewer throughout the organization.

Second, self-regulation is important for competitive reasons. Everyone knows that business today is rife with ambiguity and change. Companies merge and break apart regularly. Technology transforms work at a dizzying pace. People who have mastered their emotions are able to roll with the changes. When a new change program is announced, they don't panic; instead, they are able to suspend judgment, seek out information, and listen to executives explain the new program. As the initiative moves forward, they are able to move with it.

Sometimes they even lead the way. Consider the case of a manager at a large manufacturing company. Like her colleagues, she had used a certain software program for five years. The program drove how she collected and reported data and how she thought about the company's strategy. One day, senior executives announced that a new program was to be installed that would radically change how information was gathered and assessed within the organization. While many people in the company complained bitterly about how disruptive the change would be, the manager mulled over the reasons for the new program and was convinced of its potential to improve performance. She eagerly attended training sessions—some of her colleagues refused to do so—and was eventually promoted to run several divisions, in part because she used the new technology so effectively.

I want to push the importance of self-regulation to leadership even further and make the case that it enhances integrity, which is not only a personal virtue but also an organizational strength. Many of the bad things that happen in companies are a function of impulsive behavior. People rarely plan to exaggerate profits, pad expense accounts, dip into the till, or abuse power for selfish ends. Instead, an opportunity presents itself, and people with low impulse control just say yes.

By contrast, consider the behavior of the senior executive at a large food company. The executive was scrupulously honest in his negotiations with local distributors. He would routinely lay out his cost structure in detail, thereby giving the distributors a realistic understanding of the company's pricing. This approach meant the executive couldn't always drive a hard bargain. Now, on occasion, he felt the urge to increase profits by withholding information about the company's costs. But he challenged that impulse—he saw that it made more sense in the long run to counteract it. His emotional self-regulation paid off in strong, lasting relationships with distributors that benefited the company more than any short-term financial gains would have.

The signs of emotional self-regulation, therefore, are not hard to miss: a propensity for reflection and thoughtfulness; comfort with ambiguity and change; and integrity—an ability to say no to impulsive urges.

Like self-awareness, self-regulation often does not get its due. People who can master their emotions are sometimes seen as cold fish—their considered responses are taken as a lack of passion.

People who have mastered their emotions are able to roll with the changes. They don't panic.

People with fiery temperaments are frequently thought of as "classic" leaders—their outbursts are considered hallmarks of charisma and power. But when such people make it to the top, their impulsiveness often works against them. In my research, extreme displays of negative emotion have never emerged as a driver of good leadership.

Motivation

If there is one trait that virtually all effective leaders have, it is motivation. They are driven to achieve beyond expectations—their own and everyone else's. The key word here is *achieve*. Plenty of people are motivated by external factors such as a big salary or the status that comes from having an impressive title or being part of a prestigious company. By contrast, those with leadership potential are motivated by a deeply embedded desire to achieve for the sake of achievement.

If you are looking for leaders, how can you identify people who are motivated by the drive to achieve rather than by external rewards? The first sign is a passion for the work itself—such people seek out creative challenges, love to learn, and take great pride in a job well done. They also display an unflagging energy to do things better. People with such energy often seem restless with the status quo. They are persistent with their questions about why things are done one way rather than another; they are eager to explore new approaches to their work.

A cosmetics company manager, for example, was frustrated that he had to wait two weeks to get sales results from people in the field. He finally tracked down an automated phone system that would beep each of his salespeople at 5 p.m. every day. An automated message then prompted them to punch in their numbers—how many calls and sales they had made that day. The system shortened the feedback time on sales results from weeks to hours.

That story illustrates two other common traits of people who are driven to achieve. They are forever raising the performance bar, and they like to keep score. Take the performance bar first. During performance reviews, people with high levels of motivation might ask to be "stretched"

The very word *empathy* seems unbusinesslike, out of place amid the tough realities of the marketplace.

by their superiors. Of course, an employee who combines self-awareness with internal motivation will recognize her limits—but she won't settle for objectives that seem too easy to fulfill.

And it follows naturally that people who are driven to do better also want a way of tracking progress—their own, their team's, and their company's. Whereas people with low achievement motivation are often fuzzy about results, those with high achievement motivation often keep score by tracking such hard measures as profitability or market share. I know of a money manager who starts and ends his day on the Internet, gauging the performance of his stock fund against four industry-set benchmarks.

Interestingly, people with high motivation remain optimistic even when the score is against them. In such cases, self-regulation combines with achievement motivation to overcome the frustration and depression that come after a setback or failure. Take the case of another portfolio manager at a large investment company. After several successful years, her fund tumbled for three consecutive quarters, leading three large institutional clients to shift their business elsewhere.

Some executives would have blamed the nosedive on circumstances outside their control; others might have seen the setback as evidence of personal failure. This portfolio manager, however, saw an opportunity to prove she could lead a turnaround. Two years later, when she was promoted to a very senior level in the company, she described the experience as "the best thing that ever happened to me; I learned so much from it."

Executives trying to recognize high levels of achievement motivation in their people can look for one last piece of evidence: commitment to the organization. When people love their job for the work itself, they often feel committed to the organizations that make that work possible. Committed employees are likely to stay with an organization even when they are pursued by headhunters waving money.

It's not difficult to understand how and why a motivation to achieve translates into strong leadership. If you set the performance bar high for yourself, you will do the same for the organization when you are in a position to do so. Likewise, a drive to surpass goals and an interest in keeping score can be contagious. Leaders with these traits can often build a team of managers around them with the same traits. And of course, optimism and organizational commitment are fundamental to leadership—just try to imagine running a company without them.

Empathy

Of all the dimensions of emotional intelligence, empathy is the most easily recognized. We have all felt the empathy of a sensitive teacher or friend; we have all been struck by its absence in an unfeeling coach or boss. But when it comes to business, we rarely hear people praised, let alone rewarded, for their empathy. The very word seems unbusinesslike, out of place amid the tough realities of the marketplace.

But empathy doesn't mean a kind of "I'm okay, you're okay" mushiness. For a leader, that is, it doesn't mean adopting other people's emotions as one's own and trying to please everybody. That would be a nightmare—it would make action impossible. Rather, empathy means thoughtfully considering employees' feelings—along with other factors—in the process of making intelligent decisions.

For an example of empathy in action, consider what happened when two giant brokerage companies merged, creating redundant jobs in all their divisions. One division manager called his people together and gave a gloomy speech that emphasized the number of people who would soon be fired. The manager of another division gave his people a different kind of speech. He was upfront about his own worry and confusion, and he promised to keep people informed and to treat everyone fairly.

The difference between these two managers was empathy. The first manager was too worried about his own fate to consider the feelings of his anxiety-stricken colleagues. The second knew intuitively what his people were feeling, and he acknowledged their fears with his words. Is it any surprise that the first manager saw his division sink as many demoralized people, especially the most talented, departed? By contrast, the second manager continued to be a strong leader, his best people stayed, and his division remained as productive as ever.

Empathy is particularly important today as a component of leadership for at least three reasons:

the increasing use of teams; the rapid pace of globalization; and the growing need to retain talent.

Consider the challenge of leading a team. As anyone who has ever been a part of one can attest, teams are cauldrons of bubbling emotions. They are often charged with reaching a consensus—hard enough with two people and much more difficult as the numbers increase. Even in groups with as few as four or five members, alliances form and clashing agendas get set. A team's leader must be able to sense and understand the viewpoints of everyone around the table.

That's exactly what a marketing manager at a large information technology company was able to do when she was appointed to lead a troubled team. The group was in turmoil, overloaded by work and missing deadlines. Tensions were high among the members. Tinkering with procedures was not enough to bring the group together and make it an effective part of the company.

So the manager took several steps. In a series of one-on-one sessions, she took the time to listen to everyone in the group—what was frustrating them, how they rated their colleagues, whether they felt they had been ignored. And then she directed the team in a way that brought it together: she encouraged people to speak more openly about their frustrations, and she helped people raise constructive complaints during meetings. In short, her empathy allowed her to understand her team's emotional makeup. The result was not just heightened collaboration among members but also added business, as the team was called on for help by a wider range of internal clients.

Globalization is another reason for the rising importance of empathy for business leaders. Cross-cultural dialogue can easily lead to miscues and misunderstandings. Empathy is an antidote. People who have it are attuned to subtleties in body language; they can hear the message beneath the words being spoken. Beyond that, they have a deep understanding of the existence and importance of cultural and ethnic differences.

Consider the case of an American consultant whose team had just pitched a project to a potential Japanese client. In its dealings with Americans, the team was accustomed to being bombarded with questions after such a proposal, but this time it was greeted with a long silence. Other members of the team, taking the silence as disapproval, were ready to pack and leave. The lead consultant gestured them to stop. Although he was not particularly familiar with Japanese culture, he read the client's face and posture and sensed not rejection but interest—even deep consideration. He was right: when the client finally spoke, it was to give the consulting firm the job.

Finally, empathy plays a key role in the retention of talent, particularly in today's information economy. Leaders have always needed empathy to develop and keep good people, but today the stakes are higher. When good people leave, they take the company's knowledge with them.

That's where coaching and mentoring come in. It has repeatedly been shown that coaching and mentoring pay off not just in better performance but also in increased job satisfaction and de-

Social skill is friendliness with a purpose: moving people in the direction you desire.

creased turnover. But what makes coaching and mentoring work best is the nature of the relationship. Outstanding coaches and mentors get inside the heads of the people they are helping. They sense how to give effective feedback. They know when to push for better performance and when to hold back. In the way they motivate their protégés, they demonstrate empathy in action.

In what is probably sounding like a refrain, let me repeat that empathy doesn't get much respect in business. People wonder how leaders can make hard decisions if they are "feeling" for all the people who will be affected. But leaders with empathy do more than sympathize with people around them: they use their knowledge to improve their companies in subtle but important ways.

Social Skill

The first three components of emotional intelligence are all self-management skills. The last two, empathy and social skill, concern a person's ability to manage relationships with others. As a component of emotional intelligence, social skill is not as simple as it sounds. It's not just a matter of friendliness, although people with high levels of social skill are rarely mean-spirited. Social skill, rather, is friendliness with a purpose: moving people in the direction you desire, whether that's agreement on a new marketing strategy or enthusiasm about a new product.

Socially skilled people tend to have a wide circle of acquaintances, and they have a knack for finding common ground with people of all kinds—a knack for building rapport. That doesn't mean they socialize continually; it means they work according to the assumption that nothing important gets done alone. Such people have a network in place when the time for action comes.

Social skill is the culmination of the other dimensions of emotional intelligence. People tend to be very effective at managing relationships when they can understand and control their own emotions and can empathize with the feelings of others. Even motiva-

Emotional intelligence can be learned. The process is not easy. It takes time and commitment.

tion contributes to social skill. Remember that people who are driven to achieve tend to be optimistic, even in the face of setbacks or failure. When people are upbeat, their "glow" is cast upon conversations and other social encounters. They are popular, and for good reason.

Because it is the outcome of the other dimensions of emotional intelligence, social skill is recognizable on the job in many ways that will by now sound familiar. Socially skilled people, for instance, are adept at managing teams—that's their empathy at work. Likewise, they are expert persuaders—a manifestation of self-awareness, self-regulation, and empathy combined. Given those skills, good persuaders know when to make an emotional plea, for instance, and when an appeal to reason will work better. And motivation, when publicly visible, makes such people excellent collaborators; their passion for the work spreads to others, and they are driven to find solutions.

But sometimes social skill shows itself in ways the other emotional intelligence components do not. For instance, socially skilled people may at times appear not to be working while at work. They seem to be idly schmoozing—chatting in the hallways with colleagues or joking around with people who are not even connected to their "real" jobs. Socially skilled people, however, don't think it makes sense to arbitrarily limit the scope of their relationships. They build bonds widely because they know that in these fluid times, they may need help someday from people they are just getting to know today.

For example, consider the case of an executive in the strategy department of a global computer manufacturer. By 1993, he was convinced that the company's future lay with the Internet. Over the course of the next year, he found kindred spirits and used his social skill to stitch together a virtual community that cut across levels, divisions, and nations. He then used this de facto team to put up a corporate Web site, among the first by a major company. And, on his own initiative, with no budget or formal status, he signed up the company to participate in an annual Internet industry convention. Calling on his allies and persuading various divisions to donate funds, he recruited more than 50 people from a dozen different units to represent the company at the convention.

Management took notice: within a year of the conference, the executive's team formed the basis for the company's first Internet division, and he was formally put in charge of it. To get there, the executive had ignored conventional boundaries, forging and maintaining connections with people in every corner of the organization.

Is social skill considered a key leadership capability in most companies? The answer is yes, especially when compared with the other components of emotional intelligence. People seem to know intuitively that leaders need to manage relationships effectively; no leader is an island. After all, the leader's task is to get work done through other people, and social skill makes that possible. A leader who cannot express her empathy may as well not have it at all. And a leader's motivation will be useless if he cannot communicate his passion to the organization. Social skill allows leaders to put their emotional intelligence to work.

It would be foolish to assert that good-old-fashioned IQ and technical ability are not important ingredients in strong leadership. But the recipe would not be complete without emotional intelligence. It was once thought that the components of emotional intelligence were "nice to have" in business leaders. But now we know that, for the sake of performance, these are ingredients that leaders "need to have."

It is fortunate, then, that emotional intelligence can be learned. The process is not easy. It takes time and, most of all, commitment. But the benefits that come from having a well-developed emotional intelligence, both for the individual and for the organization, make it worth the effort.

AE Article Review Form

We encourage you to photocopy and use this page as a tool to assess how the articles in **Annual Editions** expand on the information in your textbook. By reflecting on the articles you will gain enhanced text information. You can also access this useful form on a product's book support Web site at **http://www.dushkin.com/ online/.**

NAME: DATE:
_____

TITLE AND NUMBER OF ARTICLE:
_____

BRIEFLY STATE THE MAIN IDEA OF THIS ARTICLE:
_____

LIST THREE IMPORTANT FACTS THAT THE AUTHOR USES TO SUPPORT THE MAIN IDEA:

_____

WHAT INFORMATION OR IDEAS DISCUSSED IN THIS ARTICLE ARE ALSO DISCUSSED IN YOUR TEXTBOOK OR OTHER READINGS THAT YOU HAVE DONE? LIST THE TEXTBOOK CHAPTERS AND PAGE NUMBERS:

_____

LIST ANY EXAMPLES OF BIAS OR FAULTY REASONING THAT YOU FOUND IN THE ARTICLE:

_____

LIST ANY NEW TERMS/CONCEPTS THAT WERE DISCUSSED IN THE ARTICLE, AND WRITE A SHORT DEFINITION:

_____

ANNUAL EDITIONS revisions depend on two major opinion sources: one is our Advisory Board, listed in the front of this volume, which works with us in scanning the thousands of articles published in the public press each year; the other is you—the person actually using the book. Please help us and the users of the next edition by completing the prepaid article rating form on this page and returning it to us. Thank you for your help!

ANNUAL EDITIONS: Social Psychology 00/01

ARTICLE RATING FORM

Here is an opportunity for you to have direct input into the next revision of this volume. We would like you to rate each of the 45 articles listed below, using the following scale:

1. Excellent: should definitely be retained
2. Above average: should probably be retained
3. Below average: should probably be deleted
4. Poor: should definitely be deleted

Your ratings will play a vital part in the next revision. So please mail this prepaid form to us just as soon as you complete it. Thanks for your help!

We Want Your Advice

RATING — ARTICLE

1. The Nature of the Self
2. Race and the Schooling of Black Americans
3. The Science of Happiness
4. Making Sense of Self-Esteem
5. In Forecasting Their Emotions, Most People Flunk Out
6. Like Goes with Like: The Role of Representativeness in Erroneous and Pseudoscientific Beliefs
7. The Seed of Our Undoing
8. Something Out of Nothing: The Misperception and Misinterpretation of Random Data
9. Inferential Hopscotch: How People Draw Social Inferences from Behavior
10. Face It!
11. Motivational Approaches to Expectancy Confirmation
12. Culture, Idealogy, and Construal
13. Mindless Propaganda, Thoughtful Persuasion
14. How to Sell a Pseudoscience
15. A Social Psychological Perspective on the Role of Knowledge about AIDS in AIDS Prevention
16. The Heavy Burden of Black Conformity
17. Obedience in Retrospect
18. Reciprocation: The Old Give and Take . . . and Take
19. Suspect Confessions
20. Isolation Increases with Internet Use
21. Sad and Lonely in Cyberspace?
22. The Biology of Beauty

RATING — ARTICLE

23. Infidelity and the Science of Cheating
24. Marriage Styles: The Good, the Bad, and the Volatile
25. Where Bias Begins: The Truth about Stereotypes
26. Breaking the Prejudice Habit
27. Sex, Schemas, and Success: What's Keeping Women Back?
28. Is Feedback to Minorities Positively Biased?
29. Minorities' Performance Is Hampered by Stereotypes
30. Huck Finn vs. the 'Superpredators'
31. Gunslinging in America
32. Violence and Honor in the Southern United States
33. The American Way of Blame
34. Aggression and Self-Esteem
35. Low Self-Esteem Does Not Cause Aggression
36. Anatomy of a Violent Relationship
37. Volunteerism and Society's Response to the HIV Epidemic
38. Cities with Heart
39. Cause of Death: Uncertain(ty)
40. The Effects of "Mandatory Volunteerism" on Intentions to Volunteer
41. Collective Delusions: A Skeptic's Guide
42. Group Decision Fiascoes Continue: Space Shuttle *Challenger* and a Revised Groupthink Framework
43. Group Processes in the Resolution of International Conflicts: Experiences from the Israeli-Palestinian Case
44. Psychology's Own Peace Corps
45. What Makes a Leader?

(Continued on next page)

ANNUAL EDITIONS: SOCIAL PSYCHOLOGY 00/01

NO POSTAGE
NECESSARY
IF MAILED
IN THE
UNITED STATES

ABOUT YOU

Name   Date

Are you a teacher? ☐   A student? ☐
Your school's name

Department

Address   City   State   Zip

School telephone #

YOUR COMMENTS ARE IMPORTANT TO US!

Please fill in the following information:
For which course did you use this book?

Did you use a text with this *ANNUAL EDITION*?   ☐ yes   ☐ no
What was the title of the text?

What are your general reactions to the *Annual Editions* concept?

Have you read any particular articles recently that you think should be included in the next edition?

Are there any articles you feel should be replaced in the next edition? Why?

Are there any World Wide Web sites you feel should be included in the next edition? Please annotate.

May we contact you for editorial input?   ☐ yes   ☐ no
May we quote your comments?   ☐ yes   ☐ no